PERSONALITY THEORIES

McGRAW-HILL SERIES IN PSYCHOLOGY

Consulting Editors
Norman Garmezy
Lyle V. Jones

Adams Human Memory
Berkowitz Aggression: A Social Psychological Analysis
Berlyne Conflict, Arousal, and Curiosity
Blum Psychoanalytic Theories of Personality
Bock Multivariate Statistical Methods in Behavioral Research
Brown The Motivation of Behavior
Brown and Ghiselli Scientific Method in Psychology
Butcher MMPI: Research Developments and Clinical Applications
Campbell, Dunnette, Lawler, and Weick Managerial Behavior, Performance, and Effectiveness
Cofer Verbal Learning and Verbal Behavior
Crafts, Schneirla, Robinson, and Gilbert Recent Experiments in Psychology
Crites Vocational Psychology
D'Amato Experimental Psychology: Methodology, Psychophysics, and Learning
Dollard and Miller Personality and Psychotherapy
Edgington Statistical Inference: The Distribution-free Approach
Ellis Handbook of Mental Deficiency
Ferguson Statistical Analysis in Psychology and Education
Fodor, Bever, and Garrett The Psychology of Language: An Introduction to Psycholinguistics and Generative Grammar
Forgus Perception: The Basic Process in Cognitive Development
Franks Behavior Therapy: Appraisal and Status
Ghiselli Theory of Psychological Measurement
Ghiselli and Brown Personnel and Industrial Psychology
Gilmer Industrial and Organizational Psychology
Gray Psychology Applied to Human Affairs
Guilford Psychometric Methods
Guilford The Nature of Human Intelligence
Guilford and Fruchter Fundamental Statistics in Psychology and Education
Guilford and Hoepfner The Analysis of Intelligence
Guion Personnel Testing
Haire Psychology in Management
Hetherington and Parke Child Psychology: A Contemporary Viewpoint
Hirsch Behavior-Genetic Analysis
Hirsh The Measurement of Hearing
Hjelle and Ziegler Personality Theories: Basic Assumptions, Research, and Applications
Horowitz Elements of Statistics for Psychology and Education
Hulse, Deese, and Egeth The Psychology of Learning
Hurlock Adolescent Development
Hurlock Child Development

LARRY A. HJELLE
Associate Professor of Psychology
State University of New York
College at Brockport

DANIEL J. ZIEGLER
Professor and Chairman,
Department of Psychology
Villanova University

personality
THEORIES: BASIC ASSUMPTIONS, RESEARCH, AND APPLICATIONS

McGRAW-HILL BOOK COMPANY

New York
St. Louis
San Francisco
Auckland
Düsseldorf
Johannesburg
Kuala Lumpur
London
Mexico
Montreal
New Delhi
Panama
Paris
São Paulo
Singapore
Sydney
Tokyo
Toronto

Library of Congress Cataloging in Publication Data

Hjelle, Larry A
    Personality theories.

    Includes bibliographies and index.
      1. Personality. I. Ziegler, Daniel J., joint
author. II. Title. [DNLM: 1. Personality. 2. Psy-
chology—Biography. 3. Psychiatry—Biography. BF698
H677p]
BF698.H49 1976   155.2'092'2   75-6867
ISBN 0-07-029061-X

PERSONALITY THEORIES
Basic Assumptions, Research, and Applications

890FGRFGR79

This book was set in Times Roman by Black Dot, Inc.
The editors were Richard R. Wright and Barry Benjamin;
the cover was designed by Anne Canevari Green;
the production supervisor was Judi Frey.
Fairfield Graphics was printer and binder.

ACKNOWLEDGMENTS

We wish to express our gratitude to the following authors and/or publishers who have granted us permission to use and reproduce material from their books and journals. Full citations are provided elsewhere in this text.

Academic Press, Inc.
from Bonarius, J. Research in the personal construct theory of George A. Kelly: Role construct repertory test and basic theory. In B. Maher (ed.), *Progress in experimental personality research;* from Kelly, G. A brief introduction to personal construct theory. In D. Bannister (ed.), *Perspectives in personal construct theory.*

Aldine Publishing Company
from Kohut, H., and Seitz, P. Psychoanalytic theory of personality. Lundin R. Personality theory in behavioristic psychology. Shlien, J. Phenomenology and personality. In J. Wepman and R. Heine (eds.), *Concepts of personality.*

American Psychological Association
trom Allport, G. Traits revisited. *American Psychologist;* from Atthowe, J., and Krasner, L. Preliminary report on the application of contingent reinforcement procedures (token economy) on a "chronic" psychiatric ward. *Journal of Abnormal Psychology;* from Bronson, G. Identity diffusion in late adolescence. *Journal of Abnormal and Social Psychology;* from Dignan, M. Ego identity and maternal identification. *Journal of Personality and Social Psychology;* from McClain, E. Further validation of the Personal Orientation Inventory: Assessment of self-actualization of school counselors. *Journal of Consulting and Clinical Psychology;* from Medinnus, G., and Curtis, F. The relation between maternal self-acceptance and child acceptance. *Journal of Consulting Psychology.* Copyright by the American Psychological Association. Reprinted by permission.

British Journal of Social and Clinical Psychology
from Bannister, D., and Fransella, F. A grid test of schizophrenic thought disorder. *British Journal of Social and Clinical Psychology.*

Dialectia
from Murray, H. Some basic psychological assumptions and conceptions. *Dialectia.*

E. P. Dutton & Co., Inc.
from Evans, R. *B. F. Skinner: The man and his ideas.* Copyright © 1969 by Richard I. Evans. Reprinted by permission of the publishers, E. P. Dutton & Co., Inc.

Harcourt Brace Jovanovich, Inc.
from Allport, G. (ed.), *Letters from Jenny;* from Murphy, G. *Historical Introduction to modern psychology.*

Harper & Row, Publishers, Incorporated
from Evans, R. *Dialogue with Erik Erikson;* from Maslow, A. *Motivation and personality* (2d ed.).

The Hogarth Press, Ltd., and W. W. Norton & Company, Inc.
from Freud, S. (J. Strachey, trans. and ed.), *The standard edition of the complete psychological works of Sigmund Freud,* Vols. 20 and 23.

Holt, Rinehart and Winston, Inc.
from Allport, G. *Pattern and growth in personality;* from Kelly, G. Man's construction of his alternatives. In G. Lindzey (ed.), *Assessment of human motives.*

Houghton Mifflin Company

from Allport, G., Vernon, P., and Lindzey, G. *A Study of Values* (3d ed.); from Rogers, C. *Client-centered therapy: its current practice, implications, and theory.* Copyright © Houghton Mifflin Company, 1951. Used by permission of the publisher; from Rogers, C. *On becoming a person.* Copyright © Houghton Mifflin Company, 1961. Used by permission of the publisher.

The Journal of Humanistic Psychology

from Graham, W., and Balloun, J. An empirical test of Maslow's need hierarchy theory; Maslow, A. A. Theory of metamotivation: The biological rooting of the value-life; Rogers, C. My philosophy of interpersonal relationship and how it grew. *Journal of Humanistic Psychology.*

Gregory Kimble

from Kimble, G. Psychology as a science. *Scientific Monthly.*

Alfred A. Knopf, Inc.

from Kluckhohn, C., and Murray, H. Personality formation: The determinants. Murray, H. and Kluckhohn, C. Outline of a conception of personality. In C. Kluckhohn, H. Murray, and D. Schneider (eds.), *Personality in nature, society, and culture* (2d ed.); from Skinner, B. F. *Beyond freedom and dignity.*

Little, Brown and Company

from Coles, R. *Erik H. Erikson: The growth of his work.*

Liveright Publishing Corporation

from Freud, S. *A general introduction to psychoanalysis.*

Macmillan Publishing Co., Inc.

from Allport, G. Personality: Contemporary viewpoints (I). In D. Sills (ed.), *International encyclopedia of the social sciences,* Vol. 12; from Erikson, E. Life cycle. In D. Sills (ed.), *International encyclopedia of the social sciences,* Vol. 9; from Skinner, B. F. *Science and human behavior.*

McGraw-Hill Book Company

from Rogers, C. A. theory of therapy, personality, and interpersonal relationships, as developed in the client-centered framework. In S. Koch (ed.), *Psychology: A study of a science,* Vol. 3.

W. W. Norton & Company, Inc.

from Erikson, E. *Childhood and society,* 2d ed., Rev. By permission of W. W. Norton & Company, Inc. Copyright 1950, © 1963 by W. W. Norton & Company, Inc.; from Kelly, G. *The psychology of personal constructs.* By permission of W. W. Norton & Company, Inc. Copyright 1955 by George A. Kelly.

Oxford University Press, Inc.

from Murray, H. *Explorations in personality.* Copyright 1938 by Oxford University Press, Inc. Reprinted by permission.

Penguin Books, Inc.

from Bannister, D., and Fransella, F. *Inquiring man: The theory of personal constructs.* © D. Bannister and F. Fransella, 1971.

Prentice-Hall, Inc.

from Skinner, B. F. and Ferster, C. *Schedules of reinforcement.* © 1957. By permission of Prentice-Hall, Inc., Englewood Cliffs, New Jersey.

Psychology Today
from Evans, R. *Gordon Allport: A conversation.* April, 1971., Hall, M. *Conversation with Abraham H. Maslow,* July 1969. *Psychology Today* Magazine. Copyright © 1974 Ziff-Davis Publishing Company.

Random House, Inc.
from Maslow, A. Existential psychology—What's in it for us? In R. May (ed.), *Existential psychology.*

B. F. Skinner
from Skinner, B. F. Critique of psychoanalytic concepts and theories. *Scientific Monthly.*

Society For The Experimental Analysis of Behavior
from Ayllon, T., and Azrin, N. The measurement and reinforcement of behavior of psychotics. *Journal of the Experimental Analysis of Behavior.* Copyright 1965 by the Society for the Experimental Analysis of Behavior, Inc.

Springer Publishing Co., Inc.
from Sarnoff, I. *Testing Freudian concepts: An experimental social approach.*

Yale University Press
from Allport, G. *Becoming: Basic considerations for a psychology of personality.*

To Anjanette, Christian, Daniel,
Elizabeth, Jean, and Mark

CONTENTS

PREFACE

The central theme of this book is that all personality theories rest upon basic assumptions concerning human nature and that no personality theory can be fully or properly appreciated without reference to these assumptions. This theme, explicitly stated in Chapter 1 in terms of eight basic assumptions underlying personality theories, is carried through the book by means of a discussion in each theory chapter of the theorist's position on each of these dimensions.

In developing this approach to the study of personality, our intention is to provide the undergraduate student with a means of comparing and contrasting the different theories presented within a meaningful common framework and, it is hoped, to be able to use this framework to understand other theories of personality or human behavior that he or she may encounter in the future. Perhaps more importantly, we hope in this approach to stimulate students to see beyond the immediate details of a particular theory toward the basic philosophic and profoundly relevant implications of each theory for understanding themselves, those around them, and human behavior more generally.

Each theory chapter follows a specific format. First, a biographical sketch of the theorist is provided, reflecting our belief that a personality theory is better appreciated after one catches a glimpse of the nature of the individual who constructed it. Next comes the most lengthy section of each chapter, the detailed presentation of the personality theory itself. Various brief examples and illustrations are provided in this chapter section so that the student can more readily grasp the theoretical concepts described and see their practical significance in everyday life. Immediately following is a graphical representation and analysis of the theorist's basic assumptions concerning human nature, a representation which links the position of the theorist on our eight assumption dimensions with his theoretical concepts (presented in the preceding chapter section). In this fashion, students are able to see the intimate relationship between concepts of personality and the basic assumptions upon which they were founded. Then comes a discussion of empirical validation of the theory in question. In this section, our aims are to show the student how different personality theory concepts can be and have been empirically tested, to provide a brief overview of the amount and kind of research generated by a particular theory, and to present a few illustrative studies which at once reflect these aims and should be of interest to many undergraduate readers. Following this, in each chapter, is an application section which directly applies the theory or an aspect of it to some relevant dimension of human behavior. Our goal here is to indicate that, far from being meaningless academic abstractions from reality, personality theory concepts are alive and well and can be used to understand a wide range of human behavior. Last comes a summary of the chapter highlights, followed by a bibliography and brief list of suggested readings for the student who wishes to pursue the theory further.

Since we have chosen not to write an unusually lengthy volume, our approach to personality study dictates an in-depth focus upon a few theorists rather than a hasty look at many. Consistent with our central theme, we selected eight theorists for inclusion in this text, theorists who hold different basic assumptions about human nature, are clearly recognizable figures in the field, seem to represent or epitomize a particular tradition in personality theorizing, and whose total positions are likely to be of interest and relevance to today's undergraduate student. We believe that potential advantages accrue to students of personality who trace the positions of such diverse figures as Sigmund Freud, Eric Erikson, Henry Murray, B. F. Skinner, Gordon Allport, George Kelly, Abraham Maslow, and Carl Rogers through the basic assumptions underlying the theories of each, the theories themselves, illustrative attempts to empirically test their concepts, and direct application of their theories to aspects of human behavior. Specifically, we hope that such students will achieve a more meaningful and enduring understanding of personality theory than could typically be gained by means of a more cursory examination of more theorists, the distinctions between whom would tend rather quickly to become blurred and whose actual relevance to real human behavior would remain somewhat obscure in the student's mind. After examining the theorists mentioned above, we attempt, in the concluding chapter, to place our basic assumptions model in some perspective. Then we go out on what we hope is a sturdy limb to make some predictions about the future of personality theory and research.

In developing this book, we wish to acknowledge the invaluable assistance of Norman Garmezy who read the first drafts of all chapters, provided us with numerous constructive suggestions and criticisms, and was a significant source of encouragement from beginning to end. Second, sincere acknowledgment is also due to Burton Haggett for his early help to us in developing the idea for this book and in assisting us to crystallize its central theme. Finally, we express deep appreciation to our wives, Jean and Elizabeth, for their warm encouragement, helpful suggestions, constant emotional support, and sheer capacity to put up with their husbands' theoretical preoccupations throughout the writing of this book. Additional thanks are due them in that Jean Hjelle spent hours improving the style of our writing and Elizabeth Ziegler typed the bulk of the final manuscript.

Larry A. Hjelle
Daniel J. Ziegler

PERSONALITY THEORIES

The Nature of Personality Theory

Of all the problems that have confronted human beings since the beginnings of recorded history, perhaps the most significant has been the riddle of their own nature. Attempts to answer the question "What is man?" are countless; a great many avenues have been explored, with an enormous variety of concepts being employed along the way. Astrology, philosophy, and the life sciences are but a few of the many directions that the quest to understand human nature has taken. At this point in history, some of these avenues have proved to be dead ends, while others are just beginning to flourish. And today the problem is more pressing than ever, since most of the world's ills—for example, overpopulation, war, pollution, prejudice—are brought about by the behavior of people. So it may not be overstating the case to say that the quality of human life in the future, indeed our very survival, may well depend upon an increased understanding of human nature. Psychology is deeply committed to this undertaking.

Problem of Personality Psychology

Since 1879 there has been a recognizable science of psychology, one important part of which is directly concerned with the problem of understanding the human personality. *The fundamental problem, then, for the study of personality is to contribute significantly to our understanding of human beings from within the framework of the science of psychology.* Scientific psychology prefers relatively simple straightforward concepts that are open to empirical test. Psychologists also employ research methods that are as sound and precise as possible in testing these concepts. This orientation necessarily limits the kinds of concepts and methods that can legitimately be used in studying personality. However, most psychologists are convinced that these scientifically based concepts and methods will ultimately prove to be of most value in unraveling the complex nature of human behavior.

Theories of Personality

Little agreement presently exists concerning the type or content of personality concepts that psychology should employ. There is currently no one best way to understand human behavior in psychology. In fact, individuals in this field continue to develop different systems of internally consistent constellations of concepts called *theories of personality.* This book will describe some of these theories, examine their underlying assumptions, report illustrative research related to each theory, and provide concrete applications of each to relevant aspects of human behavior. There is much to be gained from the study of personality theories. Our subject matter is human nature; our goal is the understanding of what a person is.

If human behavior were fully understood, there would be no need for personality theories. Such theories actually represent elaborate speculations or hypotheses concerning why people behave as they do. They have both *descriptive* and *predictive* functions in psychology. A personality theory is *descriptive* in that it serves to organize human behavior systematically so as to render it intelligible. For example, without benefit of a theory, it would be very difficult to explain why little five-year-old Harry has a strong romantic attraction to his mother along with undue resentment toward his father. The problem would be compounded were we to discover that other small boys experience similar feelings. Armed with a theory that posits the universality of these emotions at a certain stage of personality development (along with a rationale for their emergence), we would be better able to understand Harry. We might not be correct, but at least we would be consistent in making sense of these feelings in children. A good personality theory, then, provides a meaningful framework within which human behavior can be consistently described and interpreted.

A theory should not only describe past and present events but also be able to predict future ones. The *predictive* function of a personality theory implies that its concepts are *testable.* To continue with the example, a theory should furnish a basis for predicting specific changes in little Harry's behavior as a function of parental treatment. What will happen if his mother actively encourages Harry's romantic overtures? What will happen if his father threatens him about these feelings? Not only should such general predictions be possible but, ideally, the concepts of a theory should be formulated to permit more rigorous and precise empirical testing. A good personality theory directly stimulates psychological research.

Personality theories, then, have distinct scientific functions in psychology. A crucially important point, however, is that all theories of human behavior are constructed by human beings. Personality theorists are people and, like the rest of us, they hold divergent views concerning the nature of man. Our contention is that personality theorists have different basic assumptions concerning human nature; their theories can be distinguished from one another on this basis. A theorist may recognize and make explicit his basic assumptions, fail to make them explicit, or simply incorporate them so fully into his thinking that he no longer recognizes that they are assumptions. In any case, his basic assumptions profoundly affect his personality theory. Suppose, for example, that a theorist basically believes that most of our actions result from reason and free choice. His personality conceptions are bound to be far different from those set forth by a theorist who believes that human behavior is largely determined by irrational, unconscious factors. To illustrate, Abraham Maslow (Chapter 8) took the former position. Believing in the potency of rationality and freedom in human behavior, Maslow focused on what he felt were the "higher" aspects of human nature, on what man could be, and he developed his personality theory concepts accordingly. On the other hand, Sigmund Freud (Chapter 2), assuming the prevalence of irrationality and determinism in human actions, evolved a theory replete with concepts reflecting the unconscious control of all behavior. Our point is simply that the foundations of a personality theory are rooted in the basic assumptions of the theorist; the implications of a theory for what humans are extend far beyond the present scope of psychology as a science.

THE MEANING OF "PERSONALITY"

Personality has many meanings. It is a reasonably distinct subfield of psychology that comprises both theory and research. However, even within psychology there is disagreement about the meaning of the term.

What Is Personality? Alternative Answers

The word "personality" in English is derived from the Latin *persona*. Originally, it denoted the masks worn by theatrical players in ancient Greek dramas; eventually, the term came to encompass the actor's role as well. Thus, the initial conception of personality was that of a superficial social image that an individual adopts in playing life roles—a "public personality." This view is consonant with that of the contemporary layman who equates personality with charm, popularity, physical attractiveness, and a host of other socially desirable characteristics. Such a conception is not widely held in scientific psychology.

A quick overview of the meaning of personality in psychology can be gained by briefly considering the views offered by a few recognized theorists in this field. For example, Carl Rogers (Chapter 9) views personality in terms of self, an organized, permanent, subjectively perceived entity which is at the very heart of all our experiences. Gordon Allport (Chapter 6) defines personality as what an individual really is, as an internal "something" that guides and directs all human activity. Still another conception is that of Freud, who described the structure of personality as composed of three elements—the id, ego, and superego.

These different conceptions clearly indicate that the meaning of personality in psychology extends far beyond the original "superficial social image" concept. It refers to something much more essential and enduring about a person. Beyond this basic point of agreement, definitions of personality have other features in common:

1 Most definitions depict personality as some kind of hypothetical internal structure or organization. Behavior, at least in part, is seen as being organized and integrated by personality.
2 Most definitions stress the need to understand the meaning of individual differences. Personality is what makes individuals unique; it is only through the study of personality that the relevant differences among persons can be made clear.

.   Aside from these common characteristics, personality definitions differ substantially. In fact, within psychology, *one's definition of personality depends upon one's theory of personality*. To understand what a theorist means by the term "personality," his theory must be examined in considerable detail.

Personality as a Field of Study

As any observant psychology student will note when flipping through a departmental catalog of course offerings, psychologists have managed to erect a huge variety of topical areas to teach, including the nature of exceptional children, neuropsychology, perception, and animal learning. These areas represent subfields of psychology—personality is one of these. What distinguishes personality from the other psychological domains is its attempt to *synthesize* and *integrate* the principles of these other areas. For example, in the psychology of perception, the basic structures and processes underlying how people perceive and interpret the world around them are studied. Perception, as a specialty area, has uncovered basic principles concerning its subject matter. The same is true for the other content areas of psychology, such as learning, motivation, and physiological psychology. But it is personality as a field of study that combines these principles in an effort to understand all of human behavior.

To be comprehensive, a personality theory must incorporate all the principles of general psychology. Further, the dynamic interrelationships among these principles must be taken into account. We need to know how perception relates to learning, how learning relates to motivation, and so on. Students of personality attempt to develop theoretical concepts that describe and explain these kinds of relationships. All the factors that influence or determine an individual's behavior and experience fall within the domain of the *personologist*—a term that has been used to designate personality theorists and/or researchers (Murray, 1938).

SOURCES OF INFLUENCE UPON PERSONALITY THEORY

Current conceptions of personality have been shaped by many events. To see personality theory in a meaningful perspective, it is necessary to examine some of the more important historical and contemporary influences upon it.

Historical Factors: The Past

As a part of the science of psychology, personality theory in some way has been touched by all the factors that have influenced psychology. Of the many historical forces that have coalesced to produce contemporary psychology, four appear to have been direct and major influences upon current personality theory—*European clinical medicine, psychometrics, behaviorism,* and *gestalt psychology.* After examining these historical factors, more contemporary sources of influence upon personality will be discussed.

European Clinical Medicine   Throughout history, medicine has always been intimately associated with concepts of the human personality. However, the clinical medicine of eighteenth- and nineteenth-century Europe (particularly France) had the most direct influence upon the structure of twentieth-century personality theory. The European clinical medicine of that time primarily dealt with the understanding, classification, and treatment of mental disorders. Based upon the then current mechanistic, physiological conceptions of mental activities, the noted French physician Philippe Pinel (1745–1826) was able to conceive of psychotic personality disorders in terms of brain dysfunction. This physicalistic conception of psychoses set in motion a scientifically based attempt to classify psychotic disorders, as epitomized in the work of the German physician Emil Kraepelin (1856–1926), as well as a widespread series of humanitarian reforms in the treatment of psychotics. The consistent important thread in these events for personality theory was that serious personality disorders could be conceptualized and classified in scientific terms. Yet, as Murphy notes:

Remarkably enough, there was throughout the nineteenth century very little recognition among physicians that normal psychology had anything to offer, and very little recognition among psychologists that mental disorder could teach them anything (1949, p. 128).

It is precisely within twentieth-century personality theory, particularly as it was initiated by Sigmund Freud, that such recognition came into being. Contemporary personality theory, rooted in today's clinical psychology and psychiatry, effectively unites the tradition of European clinical medicine with the history of psychology.

Another relevant aspect of the European clinical medicine of this period was the attempt to understand and treat neuroses. Throughout the eighteenth and nineteenth centuries, neuroses were treated largely by various techniques of suggestion (some skeptical psychologists believe that neuroses are still treated in this way). The term "suggestion" refers to the fact that a person's behavior can be altered by his or her uncritical acceptance of some notion or belief. Physicians, sometimes unknowingly, were able to alleviate neurotic symptoms simply by convincing the patient that their particular method would do so. Eventually, suggestion was recognized as the basis of *hypnosis,* and hypnotic suggestion became a means of treating certain kinds of neurotic disorders. The prominent French physician Jean-Martin Charcot (1825–1893), in theoretical disagreement with others in the field, developed his own unique interpretation of hypnosis as a phenomenon. Charcot succeeded in attracting many outstanding students from all over Europe to pursue the scientific and therapeutic study of hypnosis. One of these students was Sigmund Freud.

European clinical medicine, then, furnished the intellectual climate in which Freud was to develop his unique psychotherapeutic techniques and, ultimately, the first personality theory of major significance in the history of psychology. All of contemporary personality theory, in some way, has been affected by his views. European clinical medicine, because of its profound influence upon Freud, its scientific attempts to understand and classify personality disorders, and its therapeutic approaches to the treatment of disturbed persons, has left an indelible imprint upon modern personality theory.

Psychometrics   Psychometrics, or psychological measurement, has significantly helped to make a *science* of psychology. Before the advent of psychometrics, it was not possible, or even conceivable, to measure aspects of human psychological functioning, e.g., intelligence, aptitudes, interests, personality traits. Now, within certain limitations, such measurements can be made.

Contemporary psychometrics can be traced to the work of the German scientist and philosopher Gustav Fechner (1801–1887). Fechner conceived of the idea that there might be an observable and measurable relationship between an external stimulus and an internal sensation or, stated in broader terms, quantifiable relationships between the physical and mental worlds. On this historical foundation others subsequently built various psychometric approaches to measure these relationships. Moreover, statistical techniques were developed to analyze these relations mathematically. When psychological testing was introduced, the field of personality acquired the potential for quantification and measurement of its concepts. In brief, psychometrics made possible meaningful research in personality.

Consider a personologist who wishes to study the relationship between need for affiliation or friendship and a person's vocational interests. Without psychometric tools, he would have to be content with simply speculating that people with a high affiliation need are probably interested in occupations that permit close personal contact with others. But he could never know for sure. With current psychological measurement techniques, a personality researcher can quantify both need for affiliation and vocational interest as well as determine the mathematical degree of their relationship in the group studied. As will be seen in the research sections of succeeding chapters, personality theory concepts can now be empirically tested.

Behaviorism Behaviorism as a school of psychology was founded in 1913 by the American psychologist John B. Watson (1878–1958). It became an extraordinarily influential movement in American psychology and, although the days of psychology "schools" are distinctly over, its pervasive influences are still quite perceptible today. The historical roots of behaviorism are deep. A venerable procession of philosophers and scientists before Watson in one way or another proclaimed the virtues of an objective approach to the study of human beings based upon a mechanistic, materialistic view of their nature. However, it was the Russian physiologist Ivan Petrovich Pavlov (1849–1936) who was most influential in setting the stage for the focus of contemporary behavioristic approaches to personality.

Every student of psychology is familiar with Pavlov and his salivating dogs. His immensely important experimental work on conditioning progressively influenced Watson as the latter developed his views. In Watson's hands, Pavlovian conditioning became the key to an objective, scientific approach to the study of behavior. Watson's emphasis upon conditioning, within the behaviorist framework, was instrumental in stimulating enormous interest among American psychologists in the scientific study of *learning*. Learning became the central focus of interest for those of behaviorist persuasion and, in large part, it remains so today. Stimulated by such giants as Edwin Guthrie (1896–1959), Clark Hull (1884–1952), and Edward Tolman (1886–1959), all of whom developed their own elaborate theories of learning, behavioristically inclined psychologists of today continue to fill the psychological journals with studies designed to clarify, refine, and further enhance our understanding of the learning process. And more—this wealth of scientific investigation has furnished the basis for a group of innovative therapeutic techniques globally known as *behavior therapy.*

Contemporary behaviorists view the study of *personality* as a branch of the general field of learning (Lundin, 1963). As will be seen in Chapter 5, their imprint upon personality theory, therapy, and research has been great. Behaviorism has profoundly influenced personality because of its emphasis upon the centrality of learning in personality development, the necessity of rigorous scientific research in the personality field, and the relevance of animal investigations for understanding aspects of the human personality.

Gestalt Psychology   The German noun *gestalt* cannot precisely be translated into English. The closest approximations of its meaning are the words "form," "figure," "shape," "configuration," "structure." Gestalt psychology as a distinct school was founded in 1912 by the German psychologist Max Wertheimer (1880–1943). His ingenious and varied experiments upon the *holistic* nature of perception stimulated Kurt Koffka (1886–1941) and Wolfgang Kohler (1887–1967), two of his experimental subjects and colleagues, to develop and extend the principles of gestalt psychology to psychological spheres other than perception. For example, where the behaviorists discussed learning in terms of conditioning, the gestaltists conceived of learning in terms of insight; where the behaviorists investigated learned specific responses to simple stimuli, the gestaltists studied learned patterned responses to complex stimulus fields; where the behaviorists emphasized elements, the gestaltists stressed wholes.

Gestalt psychology, then, stresses the impossibility of understanding complex psychological processes by attempting to break them down into their component parts. The whole is greater than the sum of its parts. While this general idea is found in the writings of many philosophers and psychologists before Wertheimer's time, it was the gestalt psychologists who crystallized this notion and applied it to twentieth-century psychology. The gestalt influence in contemporary personality theory can best be seen in the various attempts to conceptualize and assess personality in a holistic manner. Whether or not they formally identify themselves as gestaltists, many psychologists view personality as an organized dynamic whole that cannot be reduced to the sum of its parts. Holistic conceptions of this type are an integral part of the theories of Gordon Allport (Chapter 6), Abraham Maslow (Chapter 8), and Carl Rogers (Chapter 9).

Contemporary Factors: What's Happening Now

While the shape of today's personality field has been determined by historical factors, new directions in personality will result from events occurring now. Any discipline that studies the behavior of people must, to remain viable, be responsive to emerging factors that have direct implications for understanding human nature. In a world of constant change, these factors are many indeed.

Within psychology, current advances in such diverse areas as *cross-cultural psychology, cognitive processes,* and *motivation* appear to be influencing both the present and foreseeable future of personality theory. Cross-cultural research has forced a reevaluation of the generalizability of psychological findings from one culture to another. What holds true for American college students may not apply to young people in the Trobriand Islands! Because of recent increased interest in the study of cognitive or thinking processes, human conceptual abilities are becoming a more salient aspect of personality theory. George Kelly's position (Chapter 7) presently reflects this cognitive emphasis. In the area of motivation, attention to the study of growth, fulfillment, and self-actualization has stimulated followers of theorists such as Maslow and Rogers to develop this view of human motivation as a legitimate part of personality.

Outside the boundaries of psychology, contemporary influences upon personality are even more varied. For example, traces of *existential philosophy,* with its emphasis upon the individual as a free, responsible, and changing organism, are unmistakably found in the thinking of major humanistic personality theorists (Frick, 1971). The factor of *social change* is forging new directions for personality theory and research, while *computer technology* (Loehlin, 1968) continues to open up new and exciting research possibilities. These are but a few of the diverse contemporary influences upon the personality field. Many forces, both within and outside of psychology, will continue to affect its development. This must be so because the subject is fundamentally concerned with *what human nature is.* There have been and there will continue to be important developments in many areas that are highly relevant to an understanding of the nature of human beings.

The different *basic assumptions* that personality theorists make concerning human nature will now be examined. These basic assumptions are of paramount significance in understanding and evaluating all personality theories; they will play an important part in the discussion of each theory presented in this book.

BASIC ASSUMPTIONS CONCERNING HUMAN NATURE

All thinking people entertain certain basic assumptions about human nature. Personality theorists are no exception to this principle. The suppositions that people make concerning the nature of human beings are, in all likelihood, rooted in their personal experiences. Such basic assumptions profoundly influence the way that individuals perceive one another, treat one another, and, in the case of personality theorists, construct theories about one another. The basic assumptions themselves may or may not be fully recognized by the individual, be he a personologist or not.

In this section each of the basic assumptions that one could hold regarding the nature of man will be made explicit. We are convinced that *all major theories of personality are built upon different positions on these basic assumptions and that no major personality theory can be fully or properly understood without reference to them.* The differences among theories of personality, to some extent, reflect more fundamental differences among theorists on these assumptions.

The basic assumptions concerning human nature are depicted on the polarities listed below:

1   Freedom . . . . Determinism
2   Rationality . . . . Irrationality
3   Holism . . . . Elementalism
4   Constitutionalism. . . . . Environmentalism
5   Subjectivity. . . . . Objectivity
6   Proactivity . . . . Reactivity
7   Homeostasis . . . . Heterostasis
8   Knowability . . . . Unknowability

The assumptions are portrayed here as relatively continuous, bipolar dimensions along which any personality theorist can place himself or be placed in terms of his basic position regarding that assumption. In other words, each assumption is depicted as a continuum with a pole, or extreme position, at its opposite ends; e.g., freedom is at one pole of the first continuous dimension above, while determinism is at the opposite pole or end. From a philosophic viewpoint, the issues inherent in these assumptions may be dichotomous rather than continuous; e.g., humans are either free *or* determined. However, among personologists, there are various differences in the extent to which a basic assumption is perceived as characteristic of humanity. For example, theorist A may see persons as less determined than does theorist B. Thus, it is desirable to conceptualize these assumptions as continuous so that important differences among theorists may be more readily apparent. A brief consideration of each basic assumption follows.

Freedom–Determinism

One of the most basic questions that individuals can ask about themselves is what degree of internal freedom, if any, they actually possess in directing and controlling their everyday behavior. To what extent is the subjective sense of freedom experienced by people in decision making valid? To what extent is their behavior actually determined by factors that are partially or totally outside the sphere of their conscious recognition? Philosophers and other thinking people have debated this issue for centuries. It is therefore not surprising to find that it is by no means a dead issue in modern psychology (Immergluck, 1964).

That major contemporary personality theorists differ sharply from one another on this basic assumption concerning human nature is quite clear. For example, Carl Rogers states that "man does not simply have the characteristics of a machine, he is not simply in the grip of unconscious motives, he is a person in the process of creating himself, a person who creates meaning in life, a person who embodies a dimension of subjective freedom (Shlien, 1963, p. 307)." By way of direct contrast, B. F. Skinner asserts that "Autonomous man is a device used to explain what we cannot explain in any other way. He has been constructed from our ignorance, and as our understanding increases, the very stuff of which he is composed vanishes (1971, p. 200)." At this point in history, neither of these positions is established as fact. Rather, they are *basic assumptions* made about the nature of man.

If a given personality theorist, based on his own personal experiences and a host of other influences upon his intellectual development, assumes that human beings are genuinely capable of free choice, his theory will thereby be profoundly affected. He will tend to formulate a personality theory in which people are seen as primarily responsible for their own actions and, at least to some extent, capable of transcending various environmental influences upon their behavior. In brief, he will see free choice as a quintessential part of what it means to be a human being. On the other hand, if a personologist is inclined toward determinism, his theory will depict human behavior as being controlled by definable factors. It then becomes incumbent upon the personologist to specify these factors, and much of his theory will involve this task. In point of fact, deterministically based personality theories differ markedly on the nature of these factors. For example, human behavior could be determined by unconscious motives, external reinforcements, early experiences, physiological processes, cultural influences—each one open to various interpretations. The major source of agreement among these types of personality theories, in this context, is that human behavior is determined.

The position, then, that a personality theorist assumes in the freedom–determinism dimension greatly influences the nature of his theory and the implications of his theory as to what man is. This is also true for the other basic assumption dimensions as well. *A personality theory reflects the pattern of positions that a theorist takes on the basic assumptions concerning human nature.*

Rationality–Irrationality

The basic issue underlying the rationality–irrationality dimension is the degree of potency and scope of man's reasoning powers in influencing his everyday behavior. Are humans primarily rational beings capable of directing their behavior through reasoning, or are they in fact principally directed by irrational forces? While no major personality theorist holds that people are "purely" rational or "purely" irrational, there are clear-cut differences among personologists on this basic assumption. For instance, George Kelly (1963) has employed the rational processes that people engage in as a model in constructing his entire theory of personality! Kelly sees man as "man the scientist," whose intellectual processes are of paramount significance in his overall behavior. In direct contrast to this view is Freud's psychoanalytic theory, a basic tenet of which is the essential unconsciousness of mental activities. Freud held that "it is our inflated self-esteem which refuses to acknowledge the possibility that we might not be undisputed master in the household of our own minds (Kohut & Seitz, 1963, p. 118)." Are we then the rational masters of our fate, the captains of our behavioral ships, or are we controlled by deep irrational forces whose very existence may not be fully known to us?

A personologist's position on this issue powerfully influences the nature and focus of his theory. As an example, if a theorist assumes that rationality is a particularly potent force in people, his personality theory would depict behavior as being largely governed by cognitive processes. Furthermore, it is quite likely that, at least to some degree, his theory would be concerned with the nature, variety, and development of cognitive processes in personality. If a personologist gravitated toward the opposite position, his theory would tend to portray behavior as motivated primarily by irrational forces of which the person is partially or totally unaware. Depending on the theory's content, the relationship between conscious, rational processes and perhaps unconscious, irrational processes might be depicted as analogous to an iceberg—with the conscious, rational processes above the ever slightly fluctuating waterline that separates them from the vast unrecognized depths below. The major focus of this theory would concentrate on the content of the "submerged" forces as well as their operations in human behavior. While both "rational-oriented" and "irrational-oriented" theorists may disagree among themselves regarding the nature of "rational" or "irrational" factors in personality, the differences among them on the basic assumption of rationality-irrationality are their most fundamental differences in this regard.

Holism–Elementalism

The *holistic* assumption is that human nature is such that behavior can be explained only by studying persons as totalities. Contrariwise, the *elementalistic* position assumes that human nature is such that behavior can be explained only by investigating each specific, fundamental aspect of it independently of the rest. The fundamental scientific issue here is the level and unit of analysis to be employed in studying individuals. Are persons best studied as totalities or can they be better understood by examining each of their characteristics separately? Disagreements about this research issue among personologists reflect their more fundamental differences on this basic assumption.

The holistic view assumes that persons can only be understood as total entities. To explain the elements, it is argued, does not account for the total configuration they form (the influence of gestalt psychology is evident here). Holists maintain that the more one fragments the organism, the more one is dealing with abstractions and not the living human being. As Shlien put it: "Half a piece of chalk is still a piece of chalk, only smaller; half a planarian worm is half of one worm, but still a worm in itself; half a man is not a man at all (1963, p. 305)." Those of the holist persuasion, then, attempt to describe and study personality as a totality.

By way of contrast, advocates of elementalism argue that a systematic understanding of human behavior can only be reached by means of a detailed analysis of its constituent parts. Elementalists believe that just as one does not question the underlying reality of cellular structures in the study of gross anatomy, one should not deny the critical importance of studying the specific factors underlying the overall behavior of people. In fact, elementalists have long asserted that propositions which are vague and untestable at a general behavioral level are testable at a more elemental one. In brief, it is argued that a true scientific approach to personality can only be founded upon specific, precise, and elementalistic concepts that are clearly open to empirical test. Elementalists in personality attempt to devise and research these types of concepts.

Constitutionalism–Environmentalism

Students in personality courses often raise a question such as this: "How much of what is called personality is inherited and how much is due to the environment?" This issue in one form or another has long plagued philosophers as well as psychologists. How much of the basic nature of individuals is fixed by bodily or constitutional factors and how much is a product of environmental influences? The issue is still with us today; it has a surreptitious way of creeping into the thinking of contemporary personality theorists so as to influence their concepts of human nature and, hence, their conceptions of personality structure.

Constitutionalism has a long history in psychology. As an illustration, the ancient Greek physician Hippocrates believed that an individual's temperament resulted from his or her unique balance of four fundamental bodily humors—blood, black bile, yellow bile, and phlegm. His twentieth-century counterparts (Kretschmer, 1936; Sheldon, 1944) have developed systematic theories relating constitution to temperament. An individual's physical makeup is also an important factor in certain of the major personality theories discussed in this text. For example, it is evident in Sigmund Freud's centrally important concept of the id, the inherited basic component of personality that is fixed in the constitution of the individual.

Environmentalism is also no newcomer to the thinking of psychologists. Watson's behavioristic emphasis upon the centrality of learning in personality is based upon the underlying assumption that environment is of paramount importance in shaping human behavior. In fact, the study of learning is seen as so important precisely because it is the psychological process through which the environment molds behavior. A long and distinguished list of contributors to psychology preceded that point of view; an equally distinguished group of psychologists followed and, in various ways, developed its implications. These implications for personality are most clearly seen in contemporary behavioristic learning theory (Chapter 5), although behaviorism has no monopoly on environmentalism in personality theory. Traces of environmentalism can be found in theories outside the behavioristic tradition.

What are some of the consequences of a personologist leaning toward one or the other side of the constitutionalism–environmentalism dimension? If a theorist is inclined toward constitutionalism, he will tend to see human nature more as a product of internal physical forces rather than external environmental agents; e.g., Jane and John are highly aggressive because they have strong ids or because aggression is fundamentally inherited. While he may acknowledge some environmental influences upon behavior, the concepts that he constructs to describe personality will reflect a constitutional presupposition. In contradistinction, the theorist who leans toward environmentalism will view human nature as much more subject to environmental whim; e.g., Jane and John are highly aggressive because of their past conditioning histories—in essence, their environments—made them that way. An environmentally inclined theorist's concepts will reflect this perspective and, in addition, he will be much concerned with the processes through which the environment presumably affects personality development, e.g., learning.

Finally, it must be recognized that many psychologists today adopt an *interactionist* position on this assumption. From this vantage point, human behavior is viewed as always resulting from the interaction of constitution with environment; e.g., a given constitutional factor operates differently under different environmental circumstances, an environmental influence differs in effect depending upon the constitution of the person on whom it is operating. However, for our purposes, constitution will be conceptually separated from environment so that the precise role of each in a theorist's thinking can be more clearly understood.

Subjectivity–Objectivity

Does man live in a highly personal, subjective world of experience that is the major influence upon his behavior? Or is his behavior influenced primarily, if not exclusively, by external, objective factors? This is the essence of the subjectivity–objectivity issue. Personologists differ markedly on this assumption; the differences are clearly reflected in their theories. In fact, a major difference on this assumption, perhaps above all others, seems to be at the philosophic root of the sharp cleavage between behaviorism and phenomenology in contemporary psychology. Some illustrations follow.

Carl Rogers, whose theory will represent the American phenomenological position in this book, has stated: "The inner world of the individual appears to have more significant influence upon his behavior than does the external environmental stimulus (1964, p. 124)." For Rogers (and for phenomenology), the individual's subjective world of experience is of paramount importance, and his observable behavior is forever unintelligible without reference to it. As is so often the case, B. F. Skinner is in direct opposition to Rogers. Skinner (1971), whose position will represent contemporary behaviorism in this text, has asserted: "The task of a scientific analysis is to explain how the behavior of a person as a physical system is related to the conditions under which the human species evolved and the conditions under which the individual lives (p. 14)"; "We can follow the path taken by physics and biology by turning directly to the relation between behavior and the environment and neglecting supposed mediating states of mind (p. 15)." For Skinner (and for part of contemporary behaviorism), man's behavior is largely the result of external, objective factors acting upon him—it is the lawful relationships between these factors and the organism's behavior with which the science of psychology should be exclusively concerned.

Consequently, a theory constructed by a personologist inclined toward subjectivity would tend to be mainly concerned with the nature of the individual's subjective experience. In fact, this kind of theorist might consider the scientific study of *human experience* as the most important part of psychology. Conversely, a personologist who tended toward objectivity would be likely to construct a theory primarily concerned with objective behavioral events and their lawful relationships to measurable factors in the external world. For such a theorist, psychology would truly be the science of *behavior,* and very little emphasis would be placed upon the individual's subjective experience as such.

Proactivity–Reactivity

The proactivity–reactivity issue is essentially concerned with "locus of causality" in explaining human behavior; i.e., where are the real causes of human actions to be found? Do people generate their own behavior internally or is their behavior simply a series of responses to outer stimuli? At the heart of the proactive view of human beings is the belief that the sources of all behavior reside within the person. Man *acts* rather than *reacts.* Personality theorists adopting a proactive view of human nature firmly believe that the causes of behavior are to be found within; persons beget their behavior internally. Abraham Maslow succinctly portrayed a proactive view of humanity when he stated that "man has his future within him, dynamically active at this present moment (1961, p. 59)." Personologists inclined toward proactivity formulate theoretical concepts that serve to explain how people generate their own behavior.

A reactive position, on the other hand, views behavior as fundamentally a reaction to stimulus input from the outside world. Persons do not internally cause their actions; they simply react to outside factors. The real causes of behavior are seen as completely external to the person. The reactive position is vividly described by Kimble as follows:

> For all practical purposes, it is possible to construct a science of psychology in which the organism is considered as empty. For my own part, I can conceive of a psychology based on stimulus and response events entirely, one in which the existence of the organism is a completely unimportant fact (1953, p. 158).

Reactive-oriented personologists, in their theories, tend to emphasize concepts concerning stimulus-response and/or behavior-environment relationships.

Homeostasis–Heterostasis

The homeostasis-heterostasis dimension is fundamentally concerned with human motivation. Are individuals motivated primarily or exclusively to reduce tensions and maintain an internal state of equilibrium *(homeostasis)?* Or is their basic motivation directed toward growth, stimulus seeking, and self-actualization *(heterostasis)?* Personologists who take different stands on this issue have diametrically opposed views on the motivational bases of human behavior. As Charlotte Buhler states: "One cannot simultaneously believe in the end goal of homeostasis and the end goal of a fulfilling self-realization (1971, p. 373)."

Some two decades ago, John Dollard and Neil Miller (1950) eloquently spoke for the homeostatic position. In their view, personality characteristics are acquired through learning, which always involves a relationship between the factors of drive (e.g., hunger) and reinforcement (e.g., food). Reinforcement, in Dollard and Miller's theory, always reduces the strength of the initial drive stimulus. Thus, people are what they are largely because they have acquired stable characteristics that reduce their various drives and maintain their internal states of equilibrium. Without a homeostatic motivational basis, personality development would be impossible.

At about the same time that Dollard and Miller were championing homeostasis, Abraham Maslow (1954) and Carl Rogers (1951) were developing a far different conception of human motivation. Such heterostatic theorists portray individuals as basically motivated by a continuing quest for growth and self-actualization. Man does not live by drive reduction alone. Instead of directing their behavior toward tension reduction, human beings, by nature, constantly seek new stimuli and challenging opportunities for self-fulfillment. Personality development occurs because of this basic motivational tendency.

A few logical derivatives of different positions on this basic assumption follow. Personality theories constructed by those of a homeostatic persuasion would be concerned with the nature and variety of man's basic drives or instincts, the various personality mechanisms individuals develop to reduce the tensions generated by same, and the processes by which these tension-reducing mechanisms are acquired. Conversely, personality theories developed by those of a heterostatic orientation would emphasize the integration of human motives under self-actualization, future-oriented strivings, and the various means by which persons seek growth and self-fulfillment.

Knowability–Unknowability

William James, the great psychologist and philosopher, has written: "Our science is a drop, our ignorance a sea (1956, p. 54)." Herein lies the essence of the knowability–unknowability issue regarding human nature. Ultimately, is man's nature fully knowable *in scientific terms* or is there something in it that transcends the potential of scientific understanding? It is clear that we do not now know all there is to know about human beings in psychology—the question posed here is whether we ever will!

Personality theorists differ sharply on this question. To some extent, their differences are related to their positions on the other basic assumptions. For example, a personologist inclined toward *determinism* and *objectivity* would view people as scientifically knowable; these two assumptions, in effect, place human behavior potentially within the traditional realm of scientific knowledge.

John B. Watson is a historical personification of the knowability side of this assumption dimension. According to Lundin (1963), Watson was absolutely convinced that, through systematic observation and experimentation, the principles underlying human behavior eventually could be discovered. Behavioristic psychologists since Watson's time have engaged in these processes of careful observation and experimentation and have thereby developed concepts applicable to personality. B. F. Skinner's contemporary behavioristic approach to personality, for example, clearly regards people as ultimately knowable in scientific terms. On the opposite pole of this dimension is the phenomenological theory of Carl Rogers. In his book *Client-centered Therapy,* Rogers (1951) argues that each individual lives in a continually changing world of subjective experience of which he is the center. He develops this notion by asserting that this personal world of experience is private and can only be known in any genuine or complete sense by the individual himself. In terms of the present issue, this view necessarily implies that persons are unknowable in scientific terms (given a science of psychology that is concerned with all people).

If a personologist believes that individuals are ultimately knowable in scientific terms, he will proceed to develop and test his theory with methodological rigor convinced that human nature will finally be comprehended through his approach. That this may not come to pass in his lifetime does not deter his efforts, since he believes that his work will significantly hasten the progress of psychology toward this ultimate objective. Conversely, should a theorist assume that individuals are unknowable in scientific terms, he would be more inclined to look beyond the ken of science in his quest to understand human beings. In fact, he may be tempted to incorporate traditionally "unscientific" concepts into his theory and/or to argue strongly for a redefinition of the science of psychology so that such concepts might be more acceptable to psychologists. In either case, his theory and methodology reflect the assumption that human nature is unknowable in terms of contemporary psychology.

Thoughtful examination of the eight basic assumptions discussed above indicates that there is some conceptual overlap among them. As one example, it is difficult to imagine a theorist who assumes *reactivity* without a corresponding commitment to *objectivity.* Part of the belief that human behavior is a reaction to external factors is the conviction that such outer, objective factors are that important in the first place. However, there is sufficient distinction among the eight assumptions to justify their conceptual separation. The opposite poles of the two overlapping assumptions we have used as examples, *proactivity* and *subjectivity,* serve to bear this out. Proactivity relates to a motivation question—do people generate their own behavior? Subjectivity refers to an experiential issue—what is the importance of an individual's subjective world of experience in his actions?

A major reason for treating these eight assumptions separately is that they permit relevant distinctions to be made among personality theorists. Certain assumptions are more salient than others in a given personality theory; the part that each assumption plays varies from theory to theory. If, for example, a personologist does not adopt a strong commitment to either pole of the subjectivity–objectivity dimension, this assumption would play a relatively unimportant part in his theory construction. Another theorist might lean markedly toward one of these two extremes—his thinking would then be dominated by his position on the subjectivity–objectivity issue. In succeeding chapters, the position of each theorist on each basic assumption will be made explicit so that the intimate relationship between assumptions and theory can be fully appreciated.

SUMMARY

Theories of personality represent organized attempts to contribute significantly to our understanding of human nature from within the province of psychology.

There is presently no general agreement within the field on a substantive definition of the term "personality." One's definition of personality depends upon one's theory of personality. The field of personality is distinguished within psychology by its attempt to synthesize and integrate important principles from all areas of psychology.

The emergence and development of the personality field is firmly rooted in the historical factors that have shaped modern psychology. Four major historical factors—European clinical medicine, psychometrics, behaviorism, and gestalt psychology—appear to have been particularly important influences upon personality theory as it exists today. Significant contemporary sources of influence upon this field can be found both within and outside of psychology.

Personality theories are founded upon certain basic assumptions concerning the nature of human beings. Differences among personality theorists on these assumptions constitute the principal basis for the differences among their respective personality theories. In this chapter, eight basic assumptions concerning human nature were specified and discussed—*freedom–determinism, rationality–irrationality, holism–elementalism, constitutionalism–environmentalism, subjectivity–objectivity, proactivity–reactivity, homeostasis–heterostasis,* and *knowability–unknowability.*

BIBLIOGRAPHY

Buhler, C. Basic theoretical concepts of humanistic psychology. *American Psychologist,* 1971, **26,** 378–386.

Dollard, J., & Miller, N. *Personality and psychotherapy.* New York: McGraw-Hill, 1950.

Frick, W. *Humanistic psychology: Interviews with Maslow, Murphy, and Rogers.* Columbus, Ohio: Merrill, 1971.

Immergluck, L. Determinism-freedom in contemporary psychology: An ancient problem revisited. *American Psychologist,* 1964, **19,** 270–281.

James, W. *The will to believe and other essays on popular philosophy.* New York: Dover, 1956 (Orig. publ. 1896).

Kelly, G. *A theory of personality.* New York: Norton, 1963.

Kimble, G. Psychology as a science. *Scientific Monthly,* 1953, **77,** 156–160.

Kohut, H., & Seitz, P. Psychoanalytic theory of personality. In J. Wepman & R. Heine (Eds.), *Concepts of personality.* Chicago: Aldine, 1963, 113–141.

Kretschmer, E. *Physique and character: An investigation of the nature of constitution and the theory of temperament* (Trans. by W. Spratt). New York: Harcourt, Brace & World, 1936.

Loehlin, J. *Computer models of personality.* New York: Random House, 1968.

Lundin, R. Personality theory in behavioristic psychology. In J. Wepman & R. Heine (Eds.), *Concepts of personality.* Chicago: Aldine, 1963, 257–290.

Maslow, A. *Motivation and personality.* New York: Harper, 1954.

Maslow, A. Existential psychology—What's in it for us? In R. May (Ed.), *Existential psychology.* New York: Random House, 1961, 52–60.

Murphy, G. *Historical introduction to modern psychology.* New York: Harcourt, Brace, & Co., 1949.

Murray, H. (and collaborators). *Explorations in personality.* New York: Oxford, 1938.

Rogers, C. *Client-centered therapy; its current practice, implications, and theory.* Boston: Houghton, 1951.

Rogers, C. Toward a science of the person. In T. Wann (Ed.), *Behaviorism and phenomenology: Contrasting bases for modern psychology.* Chicago: University of Chicago Press, 1964, 109–140.

Sheldon, W. Constitutional factors in personality. In J. McV. Hunt (Ed.), *Personality and the behavior disorders.* New York: Ronald, 1944, 526–549.

Shlien, J. Phenomenology and personality. In J. Wepman & R. Heine (Eds.), *Concepts of personality.* Chicago: Aldine, 1963, 291–330.

Skinner, B. F. *Beyond freedom and dignity.* New York: Knopf, 1971.

SUGGESTED READINGS

1 Bakan, D. *The duality of human existence.* Chicago: Rand McNally, 1966.

2 Chein, I. *The science of behavior and the image of man.* New York: Basic Books, 1972.

3 Hitt, W. Two models of man. *American Psychologist,* 1969, **24,** 651–658.

4 Madsen, K. Humanistic psychology and the philosophy of science. *Journal of Humanistic Psychology,* 1971, **11,** 1–10.

5 Rychlak, J. *A philosophy of science for personality theory.* Boston: Houghton Mifflin, 1968.

6 Wolman, B. Does psychology need its own philosophy of science? *American Psychologist,* 1971, **26,** 877–886.

Sigmund Freud *(Courtesy of The Bettman Archive).*

Sigmund Freud: A Psychoanalytic Theory of Personality

When psychology gained its independence from philosophy and became a science in the second half of the nineteenth century, its goal was to use a laboratory-based introspection to discover the basic elements of mental life. A thoroughly different approach to the study of human beings was developed almost single-handedly by Sigmund Freud, then a young Viennese physician. Rather than treating consciousness as the center of mental life, Freud likened the mind to an iceberg—only a small segment of which protruded above the surface of the water. In contrast to the then prevailing view of man as a rational being, he theorized that individuals are in a perpetual state of conflict motivated by a second, more comprehensive realm of mental functioning—unconscious sexual and aggressive urges. *unless Committed to God*

Freud is acknowledged as one of the intellectual giants in the history of modern thought. In forty years of active writing and clinical practice he developed (1) the first comprehensive personality theory; (2) a method for treating neurotic ills; and (3) an extensive body of clinical observations based on his therapeutic experience and self-analysis. In this chapter, Freud's personality theory and its underlying assumptions will be examined. Selected research stimulated by the theory as well as illustrative applications to everyday human behavior will also be discussed.

BIOGRAPHICAL SKETCH

Sigmund Freud was born May 6, 1856, at Freiberg, Moravia, an Austrian town now part of Czechoslovakia, but he lived for nearly eighty years in Vienna. He was the oldest of seven children, although his father had two sons by a former marriage and was a grandfather when Sigmund was born. Freud recalled that he often had childhood dreams of becoming a great Austrian general or minister of state, but, in the end, he selected medicine as the only feasible profession for an aspiring, impoverished Jew. He entered medical school at the University of Vienna in 1873 and received his M.D. degree in 1881. Shortly thereafter he accepted a position at the Institute of Cerebral Anatomy and did research comparing adult and fetal brains; he never intended to practice medicine. However, he soon resigned his post and entered private practice as a neurologist primarily because scientific work offered small financial gain and anti-Semitism within academe curtailed promotions. Freud's interest in the clinical aspects of neurology led him to specialize in the treatment of nervous conditions, which until then had lagged far behind other branches of medicine. As mentioned in the preceding chapter, he studied with Jean Charcot, a famous neurologist specializing in *hypnosis.* Although he later rejected hypnosis as a therapeutic technique, he was excited by Charcot's lectures and clinical demonstrations. During his brief stay at the famed Salpetriere hospital in Paris (1886–1887), Freud was transformed from a neurologist to a psychopathologist.

In 1886, Freud married Martha Bernays, a union that produced three daughters and three sons. One daughter, Anna Freud, later became a renowned child analyst. About this time, Freud also began to collaborate with Josef Breuer, a Viennese physician who had chanced upon *catharsis,* a procedure whereby the patient alleviates anxieties and symptoms by talking about them. Together, Freud and Breuer explored the beneficial effects of catharsis and in 1895 coauthored a book entitled *Studies in Hysteria.* Their friendship was short-lived, however, due to Breuer's strong disagreement with Freud concerning the role of sex in hysteria, a neurotic disorder. Freud's own convictions caused him to be dismissed from the Vienna Medical Society in 1896.

The years between 1890 and 1900 were lonely yet productive ones for Freud. He worked alone to develop the bedrock of psychoanalytic theory. These efforts culminated in what many consider to be his most outstanding work, *The Interpretation of Dreams* (1900). At first, this masterpiece was all but ignored by the psychiatric community and Freud received only $209 for his labors. From 1901 onward, however, his prestige grew to include the general populace as well as medical practitioners throughout the world. The following year a Psychoanalytic Society was founded, open only to a select group of his dedicated followers. Many of Freud's colleagues subsequently became famous psychoanalysts (including Ernest Jones, A. A. Brill, Sandor Ferenzci, Carl Jung, Alfred Adler, and Otto Rank). Later Adler, Jung, and Rank were to defect from Freud's ranks and develop their own rival schools of thought.

In 1909 a single incident propelled the psychoanalytic movement from relative isolation to international recognition. G. Stanley Hall invited Freud and Jung to present a series of lectures at Clark University, Worcester, Massachusetts. Freud later wrote:

> As I stepped on to the platform at Worcester to deliver my "Five Lectures on Psycho-Analysis" it seemed like the realization of some incredible day-dream: Psycho-analysis was no longer a product of delusion, it had become a valuable part of reality. It has not lost ground in America since our visit; it is extremely popular among the lay public and is recognized by a number of official psychiatrists as an important element in medical training (1935, p. 52).

World War I had a significant influence on Freud's life and theory. For one, his clinical work with German soldiers broadened his understanding of the variety and subtlety of psychopathology. The loss of practically all his life savings in 1919, the participation of two sons in the war, and soon thereafter the rise of anti-Semitism strongly affected Freud's conception of the social nature of man. In 1932 he was a persistent target of Hitler's terror policies (the Nazis in Berlin held numerous book burnings of his publications). It was only through the diplomatic efforts of influential citizens that he and certain members of his family were allowed to escape from the Nazis. From the middle 1920s, he suffered from an advancing cancer of the throat and jaw, but he obstinately refused all forms of drug therapy with the exception of a few aspirin. Freud died September 23, 1939, in London, a displaced Jewish expatriate. A three-volume biography written by his friend and colleague Ernest Jones, entitled *The Life and Work of Sigmund Freud* (1953, 1955, 1958), is recommended as a perceptive analysis of Freud's life.

LEVELS OF CONSCIOUSNESS: HOW PERSONALITY IS ORGANIZED

For a long time in the theoretical development of psychoanalysis, Freud employed a topographical model of personality organization. According to this model, psychic life can be represented by three levels of consciousness—the conscious, the preconscious, and the unconscious. Freud used this mental "map" of the mind to describe the degree to which mental events such as thoughts and fantasies vary in accessibility to awareness.

The *conscious* level includes everything that we are aware of at a given moment. Freud insisted that only a small part of mental life (thoughts, perceptions, feelings, memories) is contained in the realm of consciousness. Whatever the content of conscious experience may be for a given person at a given time, it is the result of a selective screening process largely regulated by external cues. Moreover, it is actually conscious only for a brief time and can be quickly submerged into preconscious or unconscious levels as the person's attention shifts to different cues.

The *preconscious* domain, sometimes called "available memory," encompasses all experiences that are not conscious at the moment but which can readily be summoned into awareness either spontaneously or with a minimum of effort. An example of preconscious material is a person's social security number—first he turns attention to it, next he is fully aware of it, and then it becomes available for such mental activities as planning and remembering. In Freud's view, the preconscious bridges the unconscious and conscious regions of the mind. For example, under the influence of certain therapeutic techniques, unconscious material may emerge into the preconscious and from there become conscious.

The deepest and major stratum of the human mind is the *unconscious.* Freud was not the first to focus attention on the importance of unconscious processes in understanding human actions; several philosophers during the 1700s and 1800s had suggested the influence of unconscious experience on behavior. Unlike his philosophical predecessors, however, Freud gave the concept of an unconscious life an empirical status. Specifically, he contended that the unconscious must not be conceived of as a hypothetical abstraction but as a reality which can be demonstrated and thus proved. Freud firmly believed that the really significant aspects of human behavior are shaped and directed by impulses and drives totally outside the realm of awareness. Not only are these forces unconscious, but there is great resistance within the individual to their ever becoming conscious. In contrast to preconscious modes of thought, unconscious ones are completely inadmissable to awareness, yet they largely determine the actions of people. However, unconscious material may be expressed in disguised or symbolized form, an observation Freud utilized in his work with disturbed persons. Psychoanalysis thus emphasizes the interpretation of fantasies and dreams as avenues for deeper understanding of the unconscious processes underlying behavior.

THE STRUCTURE OF PERSONALITY

The concept of unconscious mental processes was central to Freud's early description of personality organization. However, during the early 1920s he altered his conceptual model of mental life to include three structures—id, ego, and superego. This tripartite division of personality is known as the *structural model* of mental life, although Freud felt the divisions should be understood as hypothetical processes rather than as specific "structures" of personality. Freud insisted that these structures be considered as hypothetical constructs since the field of neuroanatomy was not sufficiently advanced to locate them

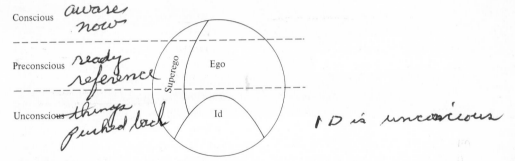

Figure 2-1 The relationship of the structural model of personality to levels of awareness. *(Adapted from Wolman, 1968.)*

within the central nervous system. The interrelationships between these personality structures and the levels of consciousness are diagramed in Figure 2-1. The figure shows that all of the id is unconscious, while both the ego and superego are composites of unconscious, preconscious, and conscious states of experience. The unconscious encompasses all three personality structures, although the major portion of it is made up of id impulses.

The Id

The word "id" comes from the Latin word for "it" and refers exclusively to the innate component of personality. The id is the mental agency containing everything inherited, present at birth, and fixed in the individual's constitution—especially instincts. It is raw, animalistic, unorganized, knows no laws, obeys no rules, and remains basic to the individual throughout life. Operating on a primitive basis, it is free from all inhibitions. The id, as the original personality system, expresses the primary principle of all human life—the immediate discharge of psychic energy produced by animal drives (especially sex and aggression) which, when pent up, create tension throughout the personality system. Immediate tension reduction is called the *pleasure princi- ple,* and the id obeys it, manifesting itself in an impulsive, irrational, and narcissistic (exaggeratedly self-loving) manner, regardless of the consequences of its actions for others or its own self-preservation. Furthermore, since the id does not recognize fear or anxiety, it takes no precautions in expressing its purpose—a fact which Freud felt may result in danger for the individual and/or society.

Freud considered the id as a mediator between the organism's somatic and mental processes. He described it as being "somewhere in direct contact with somatic processes, and takes over from them instinctual needs and gives them mental expression, but we cannot say in what substratum this contact is made (1915–1917, p. 104)." As such, it acts as a reservoir for all the instincts and derives its energy directly from bodily processes.

④

Freud identified two mechanisms the id employs to rid the personality of tension: *reflex actions* and *primary process*. In the former, the id responds automatically to sources of irritation, thereby promptly removing the tension which the irritant elicits. Examples of such inborn reflex mechanisms are sneezing, coughing, and blinking. On the other hand, primary process is a psychological phenomenon whereby the individual reduces tension by forming an internal image of an object previously associated with satisfaction of a basic drive. It is a prelogical, infantile form of human thought characterized by the inability to inhibit impulses and to discriminate between the real and the unreal, between the me and the non-me. For example, a hungry man experiences partial gratification of his hunger drive by forming a perceptual image of a savory steak or lobster tail. Freud held that the id does not distinguish between such a subjective mental image and the real object—the steak or lobster tail itself. Other examples of primary process thinking are found in dreams, the mental functioning of newborn infants, and the hallucinations of psychotics.

day-dreaming

The tragedy of behaving in accord with primary process is that the individual cannot differentiate between the actual object which will gratify a need and a mental image of the object·(e.g., between water and a mirage of water for a person stranded in the desert). Confusion of the two would eventually lead to death unless some external source of satisfaction were present. Thus, Freud believed that the most compelling task confronting the infant is to learn to delay gratification of primary needs. The capacity to postpone such gratification first emerges when infants learn that there is an external world apart from their own needs and desires. As this realization develops, the second structure of personality, the ego, appears.

The Ego

The ego is that part of the personality system that seeks to express and gratify the desires of the id in accordance with the restrictions of both outer reality and the superego. The ego acquires its structure and functions from the id, having evolved from it, and proceeds to borrow some of the id's energy for its own use in response to the demands of the environment. Ego thus assures the safety and self-preservation of the organism. In its battle for survival against both the external world and the instinctual demands of the id, ego must continuously differentiate between things in the mind and things in the outer world of reality. The hungry man in search of food, for example, must distinguish between a mental image of food and an actual perception of food if tension reduction is to occur. That is, he must learn to acquire and consume food before the tension can be reduced. This task is accomplished through adaptive strategies that enable the id to express its instinctual needs in accordance with the norms and ethics of the social world, a feat not always achieved. Such strategies require one to learn, think, reason, perceive, decide, memorize, and so on, which explains why ego functions are usually regarded as *cognitive capacities.*

⑤

In contrast to the id's pleasure-seeking nature, the ego obeys the *reality principle,* the aim of which is to preserve the organism's integrity by suspending instinctual gratification until either an appropriate object and/or environmental condition that will satisfy the need has been found. The reality principle enables the individual to inhibit, divert, or gradually release the id's energy within the bounds of social restrictions and the individual's conscience. For instance, expression of the sexual drive is delayed until an appropriate "object" and environmental circumstances are available. Thus, when the object and conditions are ideal, the pleasure principle is satisfied. Unlike the id, the ego distinguishes between fact and fiction, tolerates moderate amounts of tension, changes as a function of new experience, and develops cognitive-perceptual skills. The purpose of the cognitive-perceptual skills, or what Freud termed *secondary process,* is to establish suitable courses of action to satisfy instinctual needs without endangering the safety of the individual and/or others. The ego, then, is the "executive" of personality and the seat of intellect. One of the main goals of psychoanalytic therapy is to free some of the ego's energy so that it can generate higher levels of problem solving.

The Superego

In order for a person to function constructively in society, he or she must acquire a system of values, norms, ethics, and attitudes which are reasonably compatible with that society. These are acquired via the process of "socialization," and in terms of the structural model of psychoanalysis are developed through the formation of a superego. The superego is the last major system of personality to be developed and represents an internalized version of society's norms and standards of behavior. In Freud's view, the human organism is not born with a superego; rather, children must incorporate it through interactions with parents, teachers, and other "formative" figures. As the moral-ethical arm of personality, the superego results from the child's prolonged dependence upon parents. It makes its formal appearance when the child is said to know right from wrong, good from bad, moral from immoral. Initially, the superego reflects only parental expectations of what is good and right. The child's every effort is expended to match these expectations so as to avoid conflict and punishment. However, as his social world begins to broaden (via school, church, peer groups), his superego expands to incorporate whatever behavior these groups also deem appropriate. The superego may be considered as an individualized reflection of society's "collective conscience," although the child may distort his perceptions of the real values of society.

Freud divided the superego into two subsystems—the *conscience* and the *ego-ideal*. Conscience is concerned with things that parents say are "naughty" behavior and for which the child is reprimanded. It includes man's capacity for punitive self-evaluation, moral prohibitions, and guilt feelings as he fails to live up to what he believes is ideal. The ego-ideal is derived from whatever the parents approve and reward. It leads the individual to set up goals and aspirations which, if achieved, create a sense of self-esteem and pride. For example, the child who is rewarded for scholarly efforts will feel proud whenever he or she shows academic accomplishment.

The superego is said to be fully developed when self-control replaces parental control. However, this principle of self-control is not served by the reality principle. The superego, while attempting to control id impulses, also tries to persuade the ego that perfectionistic goals are better than realistic ones.

INSTINCT: WHAT MOTIVATES HUMAN BEHAVIOR

Psychoanalytic theory is based on the notion that persons are complex energy systems. Limited by nineteenth-century conceptions of physics and physiology, Freud was taught that human behavior is activated by a unitary kind of energy in accordance with the *law of conservation of energy* (i.e., energy may be converted from one state to another, but it is all the same energy). Freud accepted this principle of nature, translated it into psychological terms, and theorized that the source of psychic energy derives from neurophysiological states of excitation. He further postulated that each individual has a limited amount of such energy available for mental activity, and that the goal of all human behavior was the reduction of tension created by the unpleasant accumulation of energy over time. For example, if most of your energy is presently being expended to recognize the words on this page, then little is left over for other types of mental activity like daydreaming or viewing a TV program. Similarly, the reason you are reading these words is to reduce tension associated with an exam scheduled for next week.

Freud thus depicted human motivation as based entirely upon energy aroused by the body's tissue needs. He believed that the total amount of psychic energy deriving from tissue needs is invested in mental activities designed to reduce the excitation created by the need. In Freudian theory, mental representations of these bodily excitations reflected in the form of wishes are termed *instincts*. An instinct, then, refers to an innate bodily state of excitation that seeks expression and tension release. Freud maintained that all human activity is determined by the instincts; their influence on behavior can be devious and disguised as well as direct. Human beings behave because instinctual tension impels them to behave, their actions serving to reduce this tension.

A Matter of Life and Death

Although there may be an indeterminate number, Freud recognized the existence of two basic groups of human instincts—*life* and *death* instincts. The former group includes all the forces which serve to maintain vital life processes and assure propagation of the species. Because of the significance attributed to them in the psychic organization of individuals, the *sex instincts* were singled out by Freud as being the most salient of the life instincts for the development of personality. The energy force underlying the sexual instincts is called *libido* or "libidinal energy," a term which came to refer to the energy of the life instincts in general. Libido is that portion of the psychic energy which seeks its gratification from purely sexual activities.

A second category, the death instincts (also know as Thanatos), underlies all the manifestations of cruelty, aggression, suicide, and murder. Unlike the libidinal energy of the life instincts, no name was assigned to the energy system of the death instincts. However, Freud considered them to be biologically rooted and equally as important as the life instincts in determining the individual's behavior. Furthermore, he saw an empirical basis for the death instinct in the principle of *entropy*, i.e., a thermodynamic law which states that any energy system seeks a state of balance or equilibrium. Quoting Schopenhauer, Freud dramatically claimed that "The goal of all life is death (1920, p. 38)." What he intended to convey is that there exists in all living organisms a compulsion to reestablish the inanimate state out of which they were formed. That is, Freud believed that every person has an unconscious wish to die.

What Are Instincts Really Like?

This is part of the mental state of fallen man

Freud distinguished four characteristics of an instinct—source, aim, object, and impetus. The *source* of the instinct is the bodily condition or need from which it arises. The sources of life instincts are clearly embedded in neurophysiology (e.g., hunger or thirst). In the case of death instincts, the sources were not as clearly defined by Freud in physiological terms. The *aim* of an instinct is always to abolish or reduce the excitation deriving from its need. If the aim is achieved, the person then experiences a momentary state of blissfulness. Although there are numerous ways of attaining the aim of an instinct, there is a consistent tendency to maintain the state of excitation at minimal level.

The *object* refers to any person or thing in the environment or within the individual's own body that provides for the satisfaction (i.e., the aim) of an instinct. The activities leading to instinctual pleasure are not necessarily fixed. In fact, the object may be susceptible to change throughout the course of the individual's life. In addition to flexibility in the choice of objects, individuals are capable of delaying expression of instinctual energy for prolonged periods of time. Practically every behavioral process in psychoanalytic theory can be described in terms of (1) the attachment or investment of energy in an object *(cathexis)* or (2) an obstacle preventing gratification of an instinct *(anticathexis)*. Object cathexis is exemplified by emotional attachments (i.e., energy being invested) to other people, one's work, and one's ideals, whereas anticathexis is represented by external or internal barriers preventing immediate reduction of instinctual drives. Thus, the interplay between instinct expression and its inhibition, between cathexis and anticathexis, forms the bulwark of the psychoanalytic motivational system.

Finally, the *impetus* of an instinct refers to the amount of energy or force generated by its underlying need. It may be estimated indirectly by observing the number and kinds of obstacles the individual will overcome in seeking a specific goal.

The key to understanding the dynamics of instinctual energy and its expression via object-choices is the concept of *displacement*. This concept

represents the shift in behavioral activity by which energy is discharged and
tension reduction attained. Displacement occurs when, for some reason, the
original object-choice of an instinct cannot be reached. In such instances, the
instinct can displace and thus express its energy by focusing upon some
object-choice other than the original one. Freud claimed that a wide range of
social-psychological phenomena could be understood in terms of displacement
of the two primary instincts, sex and aggression. For instance, the socialization
of the child may be explained, in part, as a result of the sequential displacement
of the sexual drive from one object to another in relation to the demands
imposed by parents and society. Similarly, racial prejudice and wars can be
attributed to the displacement of the aggression drive. Freud even suggested
that the entire fabric of modern civilization is a product of inhibited sources of
libidinal and aggressive energy. Unable to obtain direct and immediate gratification, human beings have learned to displace their instinctual energy onto
persons, things, and activities other than those permitting direct tension
release. Thus, elaborate religious, political, economic, and other institutional
structures result.

HUMAN DEVELOPMENT VIEWED PSYCHOSEXUALLY

The psychoanalytic theory of development is based on two premises. The first,
the *genetic* approach, emphasizes that adult personality is shaped by various
types of early childhood experiences. The second is that a certain amount of
sexual energy (libido) is present at birth and thereafter progresses through a
series of *psychosexual* stages that are rooted in the instinctual processes of the
organism.

Freud theorized that there are four universal stages of psychosexual
development which are decisive for the formation of personality—*oral, anal,
phallic,* and *genital.* A period of *latency,* normally occuring between the ages of
six or seven and the onset of puberty, was included by Freud in the overall
scheme of development, but, strictly speaking, it is not a stage. The first three
stages of development extend from birth to five years of age and are called
pregenital stages, since the genital zones of the body have not yet attained a
dominant role in personality formation. The fourth stage coincides with the
attainment of puberty. The names of these stages are based on the region of the
body whose stimulation allows for the discharge of sexual energy.

Each stage is earmarked by a *primary erogenous* zone, a region of the body
surface where the inner and outer skin join that is a focus of sexual excitement.
For instance, the lips are more sensitive to stimulation than is the calf of the leg
or the back of the hand. Freud suggested that the more protruding the mucous
membranes, the more susceptible they are to sensual gratification. The
following are considered as erogenous zones: the ears, eyes, mouth (lips), the
male and female sex organs, the breasts, and the anal aperture.

The term "psychosexual" emphasizes that the major factor underlying
human development is the sexual instinct as it moves through the erogenous

zones during the early developmental years. According to the theory, at any particular point in the developmental sequence some region of the body seeks objects or activities to produce pleasurable tension. Psychosexual development is a biologically determined sequence, invariant in its order of unfolding and characteristic of all persons regardless of their cultural heritage. The individual's social experiences at each stage supposedly leave some permanent residue in the form of attitudes, traits, and values acquired at that stage.

The logic of this formulation was explained by Freud in terms of two factors—*frustration* and *overindulgence.* In the case of frustration, the child's psychosexual needs (e.g., sucking, biting, or chewing) are thwarted by the mothering one and thus fail to be optimally gratified. In overindulgence, the parents provide little or no challenge for the child to master internal functions (e.g., control over elimination activity) and thus instigate feelings of dependence and incompetence. In either the frustrated or overindulged child, Freud felt that the outcome would be an overinvestment of libido which, depending upon its intensity, would then become manifest in adulthood via residual behaviors (traits, values, attitudes) associated with the psychosexual stage at which these experiences occurred.

A related concept in psychoanalytic theory is that of *regression* (reverting to an earlier stage of psychosexual development). Regression is actually a special case of what Freud called *fixation* (remaining at an early psychosexual stage). Regression and fixation are seen as complementary by Freudians; the probability of regression depends mainly upon the strength of fixation (Fenichel, 1945). Fixations reveal inadequately resolved problems in the developmental stage during which they occur. For example, an eight-year-old boy who persists in sucking his thumb is exhibiting an oral fixation; energy is invested in an activity appropriate to an earlier stage of development. The weaker the resolution of psychosexual conflicts, the more vulnerable the individual is to the forces of regression under conditions of emotional or physical stress. Each individual's personality structure is thus characterized in terms of the stage of psychosexuality he has reached or at which he has become fixated. A variety of *character types,* soon to be discussed, are correlated with each of the psychosexual stages of development.

The Oral Stage

The *oral* stage extends throughout the first year of life. Infants are totally reliant upon others for survival; dependence is their only way of obtaining instinctual gratification. The mouth is obviously the body structure most frequently associated with reduction of biological drives at this time. Infants are nourished—satisfy their hunger drive—through sucking; at the same time, manipulation of the mouth is pleasurable. Therefore, the oral cavity—including the lips, tongue, and associated structures—becomes their basic focus of activity and interest. It is their prime contact with the social and physical environment, capturing most of their sexual energy. In fact, Freud believed that the mouth remains an important erogenous zone throughout life. Even in adulthood there are vestiges of oral behavior in the forms of gum chewing, nail biting, smoking, kissing, and overeating—all of which Freudians cite as evidence of the attachment of libido to the oral zone.

Pleasure and sexuality are closely related in Freud's theory of development. In this context, sexuality refers to a state of excitation which, for the infant, is connected with the intake of food. Accordingly, the first pleasure-producing objects are the mother's nipples or the bottle, and the first region of the body that experiences the pleasure of tension reduction is the mouth. Sucking and swallowing thus become the prototype of every later sexual gratification. A central task of the infant during this oral-dependent period is to establish general attitudes (rudimentary to be sure) of dependence, independence, trust, and reliance in regard to other people. Since the infant is initially unable to distinguish between his own body and the mother's breast (source of nourishment), the gratification of hunger and the expression of affection are confused during sucking. This confusion accounts for the infant's *egocentrism*. In time, the mother's breast loses value as a love object and is replaced by a part of the infant's own body. The infant sucks his thumb or tongue in order to lessen the tension created by a lack of continuous maternal care.

The oral stage ends when the infant is weaned. It is a central premise of psychoanalytic theory that all infants experience some difficulty in giving up the mother's breast (or the bottle) and its accompanying pleasure. The greater such difficulty becomes, that is, the greater the amount of libido concentrated at the oral stage, the less will be available for dealing with conflicts at subsequent stages.

Freud postulated that the infant who is given either excessive or insufficient amounts of stimulation is likely to become an *oral-passive* personality in adulthood. This is the person who has an optimistic view of the world, who has established trusting dependent relationships with others, and who has come to expect that others will "mother him." His psychological adjustment is characterized by gullibility, passivity, and immaturity.

During the latter half of the first year of life, a second phase of orality commences—the *oral-aggressive* or *oral-sadistic* phase. When the infant acquires teeth, biting and chewing become important means of expressing frustration caused by the mother's absence or by delay of gratification. The infant comes to seek oral satisfaction via aggressive acts such as spitting. Fixation at the oral-sadistic stage is reflected in adults who are argumentative, pessimistic, "bitingly" sarcastic, and often cynical about everything surrounding them. People of this personality type also tend to exploit and dominate others as long as their own needs exist.

The Anal Stage

During the second and third years of life, the focus of libidinal energy shifts from the mouth to the anal region. Young children derive considerable pleasure

Feces

from both the retention and expulsion of feces and gradually learn to enhance this pleasure by delaying bowel movements (i.e., allowing minor pressure to be exerted against the lower intestine and anal sphincter). Although bowel and bladder control are fundamentally the consequence of neuromuscular maturation, Freud was convinced that the way in which parents carry out toilet training has specific effects on later personality development. With the onset of toilet training the child must learn to distinguish between the demands of the id (pleasure from immediate defecation) and the social restraints imposed by parents (self-control over excretory needs). In fact, Freud claimed that all later forms of self-control and mastery have their origin in the anal stage.

Freud identified two types of parental strategies for dealing with the inevitable frustrations of toilet training. If the mother is harsh and repressive, children may withhold their feces and become constipated. If this tendency to "hold back" becomes excessive and generalizes to other modes of behavior, the child will become an *anal-retentive* personality. Adults supposedly manifest strong anal-retentive fixations in character traits of obstinacy, stinginess, orderliness, punctuality, and extreme cleanliness or extreme messiness. This is also the prototype for a variety of "expulsive" traits such as the inability to make fine distinctions or to tolerate confusion and ambiguity.

Alternatively, if the mother pleads with her child to have regular bowel movements and showers him with praise when he does, the child will develop an *anal-aggressive* character structure. A person fixated at this level would show traits of cruelty, destructiveness, disorderliness, and hostility. With respect to adult love relationships, such a person would tend to perceive others primarily as objects to be possessed.

The Phallic Stage

At about age four, the child's libidinal interests once again shift to a new erogenous zone of the body, the sex organs. During this phallic stage of psychosexual development, children can be observed examining their genitalia, masturbating, and expressing interest in matters pertaining to birth and sex. Although their notions of adult sexuality are usually inaccurate, vague, and poorly formulated, Freud believed that most children understand sexual relations more clearly than parents may suspect. They might have witnessed their parents having intercourse, or perhaps they have fantasized the "primal scene" based on parental remarks or the comments of other children. Freud also felt that most children view sexual intercourse as the father's aggressive act against the mother.

The dominant conflict of the phallic stage is what Freud termed the *Oedipus complex* (called the *Electra complex* in girls). Freud modeled his description of this complex afer *Oedipus Rex,* the Greek tragedy by Sophocles, in which Oedipus, king of Thebes, unknowingly murdered his father and married his mother. When Oedipus realized his sin, he punished himself by tearing out his eyes. Although Freud recognized that the story of *Oedipus Rex* was a Greek myth, he also saw this tragedy as a symbolic description of one of man's greatest psychological conflicts. In effect, the myth represents every child's unconscious desire to possess the opposite-sexed parent and simultaneously dispose of the same-sexed parent. The typical male child does not, of course, actually kill his father nor does he have sexual intercourse with his mother—but Freudians believe that he does have the unconscious wish to do both.

The development and resolution of the Oedipus conflict is somewhat different for boys and girls. The boy's initial love object is the mother or surrogate mother. She has been a prominent source of gratification for him since birth. He wants to possess his mother—to express his feelings toward her as older people he has observed express sexual feelings. He may, for example, try to seduce his mother by proudly showing her his penis. This act is one of the little boy aspiring to his father's role, since the father is perceived as a competitor who prevents him from fulfilling his wish for genital gratification. Hence, the father becomes the chief rival or enemy of his son. The boy is dimly aware of his inferiority in comparison to his father (whose penis is larger); he realizes that the father is not likely to tolerate or accept his son's romantic affections for the mother. The ensuing rivalry results in the boy's fear that his father will hurt him—more specifically, he may earnestly believe that his father will cut off his penis! The boy's fear of retaliation from his father, called *castration anxiety*, forces the boy to renounce his wish to have incestuous relations with his mother.

Somewhere between five and seven years of age, the Oedipus conflict is normally resolved as the boy *represses* (puts out of awareness) his sexual desire for the mother and begins to *identify* with his father (incorporate his father's characteristics). The process of father identification, called *identification with the aggressor*, provides the boy with a conglomerate set of values, morals, attitudes, and sex-related behaviors—all of which delineate for him what it means to be a male. Freud further believed that by identifying with the father, the boy can vicariously keep the mother as a love object, since he now possesses the attributes valued by the mother vis-à-vis the father. But even more important than these aspects of Oedipal resolution, at least in terms of societal norms, is the fact that the boy internalizes his parents' prohibitions and standards of good conduct. It is this specific quality of identification that Freud felt led to the child's development of a superego (i.e., the superego is heir to the resolution of the Oedipus conflict).

The feminine version of the boy's Oedipus complex in Freudian theory is the *Electra complex*. Like the boy, the girl's first object of love is the mother. However, as she moves into the phallic stage she discovers that, unlike her father or brother, she lacks a penis. As soon as the girl makes this anatomical discovery, she wishes she had one. In the language of Freud, the girl develops *penis envy* which, in a certain sense, is the psychological counterpart of castration anxiety in the boy. (Little wonder why Freud is anathema to advocates of women's liberation!) Thereafter, the girl becomes openly hostile toward her mother, blaming the mother for depriving her of a penis, or holding the mother responsible for taking the penis away from her as punishment for some misdeed. In some instances, Freud suggested that the girl may also devalue her own femininity because of her "defective" condition. Simultaneously, the girl wishes to possess her father, since he has the enviable organ. Believing that she is unable to acquire a penis, the girl seeks other sources of sexual pleasure as penis substitutes. Sexual gratification is focused in the clitoris and, for girls aged five to seven, clitoral masturbation is sometimes accompanied by masculine fantasies in which the girl's clitoris becomes a penis.

Most experts agree that Freud's explanation of the Electra conflict resolution is obscure. One reason suggested is that mothers do not have the same apparent power in the family as fathers and therefore are not as threatening. Another is that since she originally does not have a penis, the girl cannot develop the same intensity of fear as the boy regarding mutilation as retribution for an incestuous desire. For the latter reason, Freud theorized that girls develop a less compulsive sense of morality in adulthood. However one wishes to interpret this matter, Freud suggested that both the girl's resentment toward the mother and illicit feelings for the father are normally repressed; she comes to accept a feminine-receptive sexual identity. Later, some women desire to have as their firstborn a baby boy, a phenomenon which Freudians interpret as an expression of penis substitution—women's liberation to the contrary!

Adult males fixated at the phallic stage are usually brash, vain, boastful, and ambitious. Phallic types strive to be successful (success symbolizes winning out over the opposite-sexed parent) and attempt at all times to assert their masculinity and virility. In the case of women, Freud noted that phallic fixation results in traits of flirtatiousness, seductiveness, and promiscuity, although the individual may appear naive and innocent in sexual relationships. Unresolved Oedipal problems were also considered by Freud as the primary source of subsequent neurotic patterns, especially those pertaining to impotency and frigidity.

The Latency Period

Between the ages of six or seven and the onset of adolescence, the child passes through a period of comparative sexual quiescence. During the *latency* period, the libido is *sublimated;* i.e., it is channeled into nonsexual activities such as intellectual interests, athletics, and peer relationships. The decline in sexual interest was regarded by Freud as a purely physiological phenomenon. Latency thus does not qualify as a stage of psychosexual development since no new erogenous zones emerge and the sexual instincts are presumed dormant. Freud devoted only minor attention to the developmental processes occurring during latency, a strange fact when one considers that it occupies a chronological span of the child's life equally as long as that of the combined preceding stages. It seems to be an intermission for the theorist as much as it is for the child.

The Genital Stage

With the onset of puberty there is a resurgence of sexual and aggressive impulses coupled with an increased awareness of and interest in the opposite sex. The initial phase of the *genital* stage (a period extending from adolescence until death) is brought about by biochemical and physiological changes in the organism. The genital organs mature, and the endocrine system secretes hormones that result in secondary sex characteristics (e.g., beards in males; breast development in females). These changes have the combined effect of increasing the adolescent's state of excitability and sexual activity.

From a Freudian perspective, all individuals go through a "homosexual" period in early adolescence. The new outburst of sexual energy is directed toward a person of the same sex (e.g., teachers, neighbors, peers) in much the same way that characterized the resolution of the Oedipal conflict. Although overt homosexual behavior is by no means a universal experience of this period, Freud believed that young adolescents prefer the company of their same-sex peers. Gradually, however, the object of libidinal energy shifts to a member of the opposite sex, and courting begins. The "crushes" of early adolescence normally lead to the selection of a marriage partner and the raising of a family.

The genital character epitomizes the ideal type of personality in psychoanalytic theory. This is the person who, having developed mature and responsible social-sexual relationships, experiences satisfaction through heterosexual love. While Freud opposed sexual license, he did condone greater sexual freedom than Viennese bourgeois society permitted. To discharge libido through sexual intercourse makes the physiological control of genital impulses possible; it stems the damming up of instinctual energies and thus culminates in a genuine concern for one's fellow man, free from any residue of guilt or conflict.

Freud believed that in order for people to attain the ideal genital character, they must relinquish the passivity of early childhood days when love, security, physical comfort—indeed all gratifications—were freely given and nothing was expected in return. They must learn to work, postpone gratification, become responsible, and above all, assume a more active role in dealing with life's problems.

THE NATURE OF ANXIETY

Freud's original inquiry into the phenomenon of anxiety was motivated by his interest in explaining neurotic symptoms and treating people suffering from them. This interest at first led him to propose that anxiety is a consequence of inadequately discharged libidinal energy. He further theorized that the state of increased tension resulting from blocked libido and undischarged excitation was converted into and manifested by anxiety neuroses. However, as he acquired additional insight while treating neurotics, Freud discovered the inadequacy of this interpretation of anxiety. Accordingly, he eventually proposed that anxiety is an ego function which alerts individuals to sources of impending danger so that they can react in an adaptive way (Freud, 1926).

Where Anxiety Originates

According to this later conception, the first source of human anxiety lies in the neonate's inability to master internal and external excitations. Since infants cannot control their new world, a diffuse sense of impending peril overwhelms them. This situation creates a traumatic condition known as *primary anxiety,* the essence of which is exemplified by the birth process.

Other psychoanalytic theorists have suggested that the "birth trauma" is the source of all subsequent feelings of anxiety. Otto Rank (1929) believed that the trauma of birth forms a reservoir of anxiety, portions of which are expended throughout life. Biological separation from the mother was seen by Rank as the most critical aspect of this trauma. Freud, in contrast, accepted the psychic shock attributed to mother-infant separation as only one source of anxiety. He modified Rank's theory by asserting that the birth process is the prototype rather than the original source of human anxiety. He felt that the birth process leaves no indelible imprint upon the infant's psyche. Thus, in Freud's view, the experience of biological separation from the mother acquires a traumatic quality so that later separations (e.g., being left alone, being left in the dark, or discovering a stranger in the place of one's mother) produce strong anxiety reactions. Such a feeling of distress and helplessness is apparent in the birth trauma, in weaning, and later on in castration anxiety—all of these experiences lead to increased tension and apprehension.

Types of Anxiety or How Many Ways People Feel Anxious

We all have a need to be connected or plugged in to a power

Based on the sources of threat to the ego (the outside environment, the id, and the superego), psychoanalytic theory identifies three types of anxiety.

Realistic Anxiety   The emotional response to threat and/or perception of real dangers in the external environment (e.g., poisonous snakes, wild animals, natural disasters, final examinations) is called realistic or objective anxiety. It is essentially synonymous with fear and may have a debilitating effect on the individual's ability to cope effectively with the source of danger. Realistic anxiety abates as the source of threat subsides and, furthermore, helps to ensure self-preservation.

Neurotic Anxiety   An emotional response to the threat that id impulses will become conscious is called neurotic anxiety. It is caused by the fear that the ego will be unable to control the id instincts. The small child quickly learns that active discharge of his libidinal or destructive urges will be met by threats of retaliation from parents or other social agents. For this reason, neurotic anxiety is initially experienced as realistic anxiety, since punishment did originally derive from an external force. *Ego defenses* (to be explained shortly) are thus deployed to hold down the child's id impulses, and they surface only in the form of general apprehension. It is only when the instinctual impulses of the id threaten to break through the ego controls that neurotic anxiety occurs.

Moral Anxiety   When the ego is threatened by punishment from the superego, the ensuing emotional response is called moral anxiety. It occurs whenever the id strives toward active expression of immoral thoughts or acts and the superego responds with feelings of shame, guilt, and self-condemnation. Moral anxiety derives from an objective fear of parental punishment for doing or thinking something that violates the perfectionistic dictates of the superego. Hence, it directs behavior into activities that are acceptable to the individual's conscience. The subsequent development of the superego leads to *social anxiety,* which is evident in concerns over exclusion from peer-group membership because of unacceptable attitudes or actions. Freud further believed that anxiety originating from within the superego is ultimately extended to fear of death and the anticipation in an afterlife of punishment for one's transgressions.

Ego Defense Mechanisms

The major psychodynamic functions of anxiety are to help the individual avoid conscious recognition of unacceptable instinctual impulses and to allow impulse gratification only indirectly. *Ego defense mechanisms* help to carry out these functions as well as to protect the person from overwhelming anxiety. Freud defined an ego defense mechanism as a strategy used by the individual to defend against open expression of id impulses and opposing superego pressures. He suggested that the ego reacts to the threatened breakthrough of id impulses in either of two ways: (1) by blocking the impulse from expression in conscious behavior, or (2) by distorting it to such a degree that the original intensity is markedly reduced or deflected.

All defense mechanisms share two common features: (1) they operate at an unconscious level and are therefore self-deceptive and (2) they distort one's perception of reality, so as to make anxiety less threatening to the individual. Freud believed that persons rarely rely upon a single defense to protect themselves from anxiety; it is more common for people to use several mechanisms of this type. Some examples of ego defense mechanisms follow.

Sublimation   According to Freud, *sublimation* is an ego defense that enables the individual adaptively to divert impulses so that they may be expressed via socially approved thoughts or actions. Sublimation is considered as the only healthy, constructive strategy against objectionable impulses since it allows the ego to change the aim or object (or both) of impulses without inhibiting their expression. For example, if during development masturbation becomes too anxiety-provoking to the young boy, he may sublimate his impulses into a socially approved substitute activity, such as football, swimming, or other sporting endeavor. Or the person with a great deal of unrecognized hostility may become a butcher so that he can spend an unconscious lifetime symbolically cutting up the people he hates.

Freud claimed that the sublimation of sexual instincts served as the prime instigator for great advances in Western culture and knowledge. As he said:

> The sublimation of the sexual motive is an especially conspicuous feature of cultural evolution; sublimation alone makes it possible for the zealous scientific, artistic, and ideological activities which play so important a part in our civilized lives (Cohen, 1969, p. 34).

Repression Freud regarded *repression* as the primary ego defense, not only because it serves as a basis for more elaborate mechanisms of defense but also because it involves the most direct approach in avoiding anxiety. Sometimes described as selective forgetting, repression completely obstructs the expression of unconscious sexual and aggressive impulses so that they cannot be admitted to awareness, at least as long as they remain objectionable to the person. Hence, no tension reduction is permitted. As a result of repression, individuals are neither aware of their own anxiety-provoking conflicts nor do they remember emotionally traumatic past events. For example, a person who has suffered a terrifying personal failure may through repression become unable to recount the experience.

The relief from anxiety provided by repression is not without cost. Freud theorized that repressed impulses remain active in the unconscious and require continuous psychic energy to prevent their emergence into consciousness. This persistent drain on the ego's resources may seriously limit the amount of energy available for more constructive, self-enhancing, and creative behavior. However, the constant striving of repressed impulses for overt expression may find momentary gratification through dreams, jokes, slips of the tongue, and other manifestations of what Freud called the "psychopathology of everyday life."

Projection As a defense mechanism, *projection* ranks next to repression in terms of theoretical importance. It refers to the process of unconsciously attributing one's own unacceptable impulses, attitudes, and behaviors to other people or to the environment. Projection thus enables us to blame someone or something else for our own shortcomings. The golf player who muffs a shot and looks critically at his club is engaging in a primitive projection. On a different level, the young woman who is unaware of her own sexual strivings but sees everyone she dates as attempting to seduce her is also projecting. Finally, there is the classic example of the student who inadequately prepares for an examination and then attributes his or her failing grade to an unfair test, the cheating of others, or a professor who failed to explain the points at issue. Projection has also been used as an explanation of social prejudice and scapegoating, since ethnic and racial stereotypes provide a convenient target for the attribution of one's own negative personal characteristics.

Displacement   In *displacement,* when viewed specifically as a defense mechanism as opposed to the more general meaning of the term described earlier in this chapter, the expression of an instinctual impulse is redirected from a more threatening person or object to a less threatening one. The student angered by his professor instead swears at his roommate. Or the child scolded by her parents proceeds to hit her little sister, kick her dog, or smash her toys. Displacement is also observed in an adult's hypersensitivity to minor annoyances; e.g., the husband who is criticized by an overdemanding employer reacts with violent rage to the slightest provocation by his wife or children. He fails to recognize that, as objects of his hostility, they are simply substitutes for the boss. A less common form of displacement is *turning against the self,* whereby hostile impulses toward others are redirected to oneself, producing feelings of depression and self-depreciation.

Rationalization   Another important way in which the ego attempts to cope with frustration and anxiety is to distort reality and thus protect self-esteem. *Rationalization* refers to "fallacious reasoning" in that it misrepresents irrational behavior in order to make it appear rational. One's mistakes, poor judgments, and failures can be explained away through the magic of rationalization. One frequently employed type, known as "sour grapes," is based on one of Aesop's fables about a fox who couldn't reach the grapes he desired and thus concluded that they were sour anyway. People rationalize in the same way, as in the example of the student who is refused a date by the "campus queen" and consoles himself by concluding that she wasn't very attractive anyway.

Reaction Formation   Sometimes the ego can control or defend against the expression of a forbidden impulse by consciously expressing its opposite. This is known as *reaction formation.* As a defensive process it operates in two steps: first, the unacceptable impulse is repressed; next, the opposite is expressed on a conscious level. Reaction formation is especially evident in socially acceptable behavior that is compulsive, exaggerated, and rigid. For instance, a woman threatened by her own unconscious sexual desires becomes a crusader to disallow pornographic movies in her town. She may also actively picket particular movie houses or write to production companies about the degrading state of films today.

This brief description of the major ego defense mechanisms concludes our discussion of Freud's central theoretical concepts. Let us now turn to the basic assumptions concerning the nature of man that underlie psychoanalytic theory.

FREUD'S BASIC ASSUMPTIONS CONCERNING HUMAN NATURE

The unifying theme of this book is that all personality theorists hold certain basic assumptions concerning human nature. Furthermore, such assumptions, while neither directly provable or unprovable, help delineate the essential differences and similarities among the various theories. Now that the core concepts of psychoanalytic theory have been discussed, Freud's position on the eight assumptions presented in Chapter 1 can be examined. His position on the respective dimensions (depicted in Figure 2-2) are as follows.

1 Freedom–Determinism Freud was a strict biological determinist. He assumed that all human events (actions, thoughts, feelings, aspirations) are lawful and determined by powerful instinctual forces, notably sex and aggression. Thus, human beings are seen as essentially mechanistic; they are governed by the same natural laws that apply to the behavior of other organisms. If this were not so, a rigorous science of man could not exist.

In such a theoretical system, there is no room for concepts such as free will, choice, personal responsibility, volition, spontaneity, and self-determination (i.e., people do not have free choice). Freud clearly recognized the individual's overpowering illusion of freedom, yet he insisted that persons are incapable of actually "choosing" between alternative courses of action. Freudian man is determined by unconscious forces of which he can never be fully aware. The clearest examples of determinism noted by Freud include misplacing personal possessions, forgetting familiar names and addresses, and so-called "slips" of the tongue and pen. He interpreted such occurrences as revealing something of the person's unconscious mental processes.

Freedom ✓————————✓ Determinism *no free will*
Rationality ✓———————✓ Irrationality
Holism ———✓————————— Elementalism
Constitutionalism ———✓——————✓ Environmentalism
Subjectivity ————✓——✓——— Objectivity
Proactivity ————✓————✓—— Reactivity
Homeostasis —✓————✓———— Heterostasis
Knowability ✓———✓————————— Unknowability

Figure 2-2 Freud's position on the eight basic assumptions concerning human nature. (The check marks indicate the degree to which the theorist favors one of the two bipolar extremes.)

2 Rationality–Irrationality In Freud's view, people are basically irrational. They are motivated by irrational, almost uncontrollable instincts which are largely outside the sphere of conscious awareness. While a degree of rationality exists within the ego, this part of personality is ultimately subservient to the demands of the id. The only real glimmer of rationality that Freud detected in humanity resided in his conception of psychoanalytic therapy as a vehicle for systematic personality growth. Insight into unconscious motivation via psychoanalysis would pave the road for mastery and control over oneself. His credo—*where id was, there ego shall be*—reflects his optimism that the forces of reason can bring primitive and irrational drives somewhat under conscious control. In spite of his conviction that a higher degree of rationality could be attained through psychoanalysis, Freud's theory of personality is firmly anchored to the importance of irrational elements in human behavior.

3 Holism–Elementalism Freud leaned toward a holistic view of persons believing that they must be studied as totalities in order to be understood. Central to his theory is the portrayal of the individual in terms of id-ego-superego interactions and interdependencies. The person's behavior cannot be fully grasped without reference to the dynamic interplay of these three molar structures of mental life. Furthermore, while Freud believed that these structures might ultimately be reduced to a more elementalistic level of analysis (probably biological or neurological), he never attempted this task himself. Finally, Freud relied almost exclusively upon the clinical method in developing his theory, a method which stresses the unity of personality.

4 Constitutionalism–Environmentalism Several of Freud's early concepts (e.g., psychic energy, instincts, pleasure principle) were derived from neuroanatomy and neurophysiology (Weinstein, 1968). Psychoanalytic theory never substantially altered its course from this beginning and, on the whole, Freud must be regarded as having adopted a constitutional position concerning human nature. As has been seen, the all-powerful id is the inherited, constitutional basis of personality structure and development. In addition, he conceived of psychosexual development as an invariant, biologically determined sequence characteristic of all persons regardless of their cultural heritage. What human beings are, then, is very much a result of innate biological hereditary factors.

Conversely, Freud strongly emphasized the importance of the person's early environmental history for understanding behavior. He stressed that parental influence during early childhood years had profound, irreversible effects upon subsequent personality growth. Moreover, the ego evolves only to meet environmental demands with which the id cannot deal, while the superego is exclusively a product of the social world. The net importance of environmental factors, however, is secondary to biologically rooted instincts in psychoanalytic theory.

5 Subjectivity–Objectivity   Freud saw persons as living in a subjective world of feelings, emotions, perceptions, and meanings. While he recognized the "private world" of an individual as an important part of personality, Freud also considered it as a guide to something else—objective conditions like traumas and repressions, and universal human drives. Thus, psychoanalytic theory claims that a person's uniqueness is partly determined by external realities, e.g., parental attitudes and behavior, sibling relationships, social norms. Once the individual is exposed to these objective conditions, however, they persist experientially to form the permanent world of unique, subjective meanings within which he or she resides. Thus, while Freud leans somewhat toward subjectivity, this assumption does not occupy an important role in his theory.

6 Proactivity–Reactivity   Concerning the question of the locus of causality in explaining human behavior, B. F. Skinner (1954) pointed out that Freud's theoretical account of man's actions followed a traditional pattern of looking *inside* the person for the causes of behavior. Consequently, in this sense only, Freud must be construed as assuming a proactive view of human nature. As will become evident in subsequent chapters, however, Freud's proactivity takes a form markedly different from that adopted by humanistic or phenomenological theorists.

The essence of Freud's proactive position is clearly reflected in his concept of motivation—the locus of causality for all human behavior is found in the energy flowing from the id and its instincts. People do not consciously generate their own behavior; rather, the sexual and aggressive instincts generate the psychic energy which underlies the variety and multiplicity of human actions. Freudian man, then, is not proactive in the full sense of the term. He is reactive to the extent that all instincts have external objects that operate as environmental stimuli to elicit behavior. For example, sex "objects" in the environment call forth the activity of the sexual instinct, thus suggesting shades of reactivity within the theory. Weighing all factors, Freud's position on this assumption seems best described as a moderate inclination toward proactivity.

7 Homeostasis–Heterostasis   Freud believed that all human behavior was regulated by the tendency to reduce excitations created by unpleasant bodily tensions. The id instincts constantly demand expression—people behave to reduce the tensions generated by the instinctual energy source. This view clearly reflects a homeostatic position. In Freud's system, a man is basically an "instinct satisfier" who never seeks out conditions which would upset homeostatic balance.

8 Knowability–Unknowability   There are many indications that Freud was committed to the belief that human nature is ultimately knowable in scientific terms. For example, he insisted that people obey the same laws of nature as do any other living organisms. Likewise, he viewed human beings as biologically determined organisms whose deepest motivations can be uncovered by the "scientifically based" techniques of psychoanalysis. To be sure, Freud never considered psychoanalysis as a complete theory of personality (Nuttin, 1956). However, he was convinced that psychoanalysis definitely had and would continue to shed substantial light upon the true nature of humans. It is likely that Freud's training in natural science, coupled with his personal rejection of the validity of mysticism, religion, and other nonscientific belief systems, fostered his conviction that science holds the key to the enigma of man.

Thus we conclude our assessment of Freud's position on the eight basic assumptions regarding human nature. Let us now consider some illustrative empirical studies stimulated by the theory.

EMPIRICAL VALIDATION OF
PSYCHOANALYTIC CONCEPTS

Having studied Freud, students inevitably ask "What scientific evidence is there to support psychoanalytic theory?" Insofar as a theory is regarded as an empirically valid conceptualization of the phenomenon it presumes to explain, it is only natural to expect the scientific testing of hypotheses derived from that theory. In the years that followed his death, personologists all but totally ignored the objective and systematic verification of Freud's concepts. A quick overview of the history of psychoanalysis as a method of therapy explains in good part why this was so. In Freud's time psychoanalysts generally were not interested in the use of research methods for investigating the theory. This antiresearch attitude was further fostered by the fact that experimental psychology, still in its infancy, had little to offer. Even today, despite their formal training in the natural sciences, some practicing analysts disparage the use of research techniques (Hilgard, 1968). Many believe that the only method appropriate to verify psychoanalytic hypotheses is the clinical interview—that is, the verbalizations of patients undergoing intensive, long-term therapy. Thus, the primary source of evidence for determining the "truthfulness" of psychoanalytic theory until recently has been the systematic accumulation of patients' reconstructed life histories. Most analysts consider the patient's reported experiences as highly relevant confirmations of the theory.

Although clinical observations and case histories have served as the main methods for developing and testing psychoanalytic formulations (indeed, the approach relied upon most by Freud himself), there are several deficiencies associated with their use. Foremost is the fact that despite all efforts to remain objective in the therapeutic setting, the analyst is not a truly impartial observer. Nor does clinical observation adequately meet the experimentalist's demands for objectivity. Another methodological shortcoming derives from the professional training of most analysts. Such training, which necessarily includes a self-analysis plus intensive supervision by a seasoned training analyst during the initial stages of practice, commonly results in an unusually strong philosophical and personal commitment to the assumptions of Freudian theory. This commitment predisposes analysts selectively to bias their interpretations of the patient's disturbance and its causation. Complicating the validity of clinical observations even further is the patient's own bias. Patients often know what is proper and improper to report during therapy sessions—hence, they may subtly seek approval by producing experiential material which conforms to the analyst's expectations. Collectively, these deficiencies are potent sources for the "self-fulfilling prophecy" concerning the validity of Freud's observations. Given such limitations, it is understandable why most psychologists refuse to consider case reports of therapeutic effectiveness as sufficient evidence for Freud's conceptions of personality.

The major pitfall confronting the personologist interested in testing Freudian theory is that there is no known way of replicating clinical observations and findings in a controlled experiment. A second major stumbling block in determining the validity of psychoanalysis is the lack of operational definitions of theoretical concepts; i.e., the concepts are often defined in a way that eludes precise measurement. This does not mean that psychoanalysis is an invalid theory. Rather, it means that, at present, there are no commonly agreed upon methods and procedures by which the theory can be objectively evaluated. Finally, psychoanalytic theory has a "postdictive" character. In other words, it more adequately explains past events than predicts future ones.

Conversely, under certain conditions psychoanalytic concepts can be empirically tested. Sarnoff explains how this might be achieved:

> Since Freudian theory contains a multitude of concepts, the first step in any contribution toward its experimental evaluation requires a researcher to choose a particular concept for focal study. Then, the chosen concept must be clarified in linguistic terms that define its particular psychological properties explicitly and precisely. Finally, the semantically defined concept must be theoretically related to a behavioral or experiential phenomenon by stating how and under what conditions the postulated relationship may be observed to obtain (1971, p. 29).

Where, then, can one look for valid evidence pertaining to psychoanalytic theory? With some justification, personologists debunk most animal studies on the grounds of their artificiality and oversimplification of conceptually complicated processes. Basically, the search for adequate evidence has taken the direction of developing experimental analogs (i.e., simulating theoretical concepts in a laboratory context) of psychoanalytic constructs. No attempt is made here to cover exhaustively all the studies pertaining to Freudian theory. Instead, the focus is on illustrative and representative research currently being done. Accordingly, three studies characteristic of the kinds of ongoing investigations of major psychoanalytic concepts will be examined: studies of (1) repression, (2) dreams, and (3) humor.

Repression in a Laboratory   Repression is a key concept for most psychoanalysts and there has been more experimental research on it than perhaps any other single concept in Freudian theory (Mischel, 1971; Sarason, 1972). One aspect of repression has to do with the notion that forgetting occurs as a function of unpleasant associations. Glucksberg and King (1967) demonstrated by way of a laboratory analog of repression that there is a strong tendency to forget events identified with unpleasant associations. These investigators hypothesized that if a given word is associated with an unpleasant event (e.g., electric shock), the saying or thinking of an associated word will evoke fear. Translating this hypothesis into testable terms, Glucksberg and King predicted that the pairing of electric shocks with specific words would cause differential forgetting of previously learned words.

The stimulus materials used in this experiment consisted of a paired-associate list, the first word (A) being a nonsense syllable and the second (B) being an English word. A chained word (C) was assumed to form a link between the English word in the paired-associate list and a second list of English words (D). For example, if the A-B pair were DAX-memory, then the B-C association was memory-mind, and the C-D association, mind-brain. The association between A and D was thus made by way of B-C and C-D verbal links.

Initially, sixteen male undergraduates learned the A-B paired-associate list (ten paired associates) by the method of anticipation. Learning of this list continued until each subject correctly anticipated all pairs for one perfect trial. Then, electrodes were placed on the subject's fingers. Words in the second list (D) were then projected on a screen, with three of the words being accompanied by an electric shock. Subjects were instructed to press a key-operated buzzer whenever one of the shock words appeared. The presentation of words in the second list continued until each subject had correctly anticipated shock for three consecutive trials. Thereafter, subjects were given a single relearning trial of the A-B list of words. The chained words (C) were never presented since they were assumed to occur as implicit associative responses linking the B words with the D words. The measure of "motivated forgetting" was based on the percentage of shock-associated B words forgotten relative to the percentage of control B words (nonassociated shock words) forgotten during relearning. Glucksberg and King found that significantly more of the shock-associated B words were forgotten than were control B words (29.2 percent of the shock-associated A-B pairs as compared with 6.3 percent of the A-B control words). It was found that no subject was better able to recall the shocked words (D) of the second list than he was able to recall the control, nonshocked words. This experiment demonstrates that the pairing of electric shocks with associates of memory items significantly interferes with the subsequent recall of such memory items; i.e., memory items which are associated with an unpleasant event are more readily forgotten (repressed) than are affectively neutral memory items.

   Finally, as intriguing as this study is from an experimental perspective, it is only fair to note that Freud himself would have probably regarded it as "typically American" and a long way from his clinical concept of repression. Nonetheless, such empirical investigations of Freudian concepts must continue to be undertaken if psychoanalysis is to gain genuine scientific respectability.

   Castration Anxiety and Penis Envy in Dreams   Hall and Van de Castle (1965) have reported a study based on Freud's dream theory. Since dreams are characterized as "the royal road to the unconscious," they reasoned that manifestations of the castration complex would be detectable in dreams. Specifically, it was hypothesized that "Male dreamers will report more dreams expressive of castration anxiety than they will dreams involving castration wishes and penis envy while the pattern will be reversed for females, i.e., they will report more dreams containing expressions of castration wishes and penis envy than they will dreams containing castration anxiety (p. 21)."

   This hypothesis was tested by instructing male and female undergraduates to maintain a record of their nocturnal dreams as part of a class project. A scoring manual was developed by the investigators in which specific criteria for castration anxiety, castration wish, and penis envy were set forth. The criteria for scoring castration anxiety dreams involved such themes as actual or threatened loss, removal, or injury to a specific part of the body, inability or difficulty in using the penis, the changing of a man into a woman, and actual or threatened injury to or loss of an object or animal belonging to the dreamer. The criteria for castration wish were the same except that they do not occur to the dreamer but to another person in his dreams. Finally, the system for scoring penis envy included the changing of a woman into a man, envy or admiration for a man's physical characteristics, and the acquisition of objects that have male characteristics. Insofar as scoring dream content for such themes is partly based on subjective interpretation, the researchers had to demonstrate adequate agreement among scorers. Hall and Van de Castle reported interjudge agreement scores higher than 87 percent on each of the three variables considered here. Consistent with Freudian theory, their results indicated that men evidenced significantly more dreams about castration anxiety than did women, and women reported significantly more dreams expressive of castration wish and penis envy than did men. These findings were interpreted as supporting the theoretical validity of the castration complex.

   Why We Laugh   Laughter and humor have always been recognized as a salient feature of human experience. Perhaps the most influential theory of humor to date is that proposed by Freud in *Jokes and Their Relation to the Unconscious* (1905). Briefly stated, Freud theorized that normally inhibited sexual or aggressive impulses are vicariously released through socially sanctioned jokes. Pent-up instinctual energies find expression in the form of laughter. He also believed that pleasure gained from humor depends upon a sudden reduction of inner tension or anxiety. The anxiety arises from intra-psychic conflict concerning the direct expression of an unacceptable wish or impulse activated by the content of most sexual and aggressive types of humor.

If, as Freud postulated, humor depends on relief from a state of anticipated discomfort due to heightened emotional arousal, then the following hypothesis should hold: "the greater the subject's arousal prior to relief, the greater should be the judged humor (Shurcliff, 1968, p. 360)." In a cleverly designed experiment, Shurcliff tested the validity of this hypothesis. Procedurally, he established three levels of anxiety (the index of arousal) by giving separate groups of male students different instructions and directions concerning a laboratory task. The groups were designated as low, moderate, and high anxiety, respectively. Subjects in each group were brought to the laboratory individually and informed that they were to take part in an experiment concerned with their reaction to small animals. During the first phase of the experiment three carrying cages, the first two containing white rats, were made clearly visible to the subject. The third cage was deliberately placed behind the other two in such a way that the subject could not see into it prior to opening the cage door. At this point, the description of and instructions for the experimental task were systematically varied for the different groups. Subjects in the *low* anxiety condition were told that their task was simply to pick up the rat in the third cage and hold him for five seconds. The experimenter then said, "These rats are bred to be docile and easy to handle, and I don't think you will have any trouble with this task (p. 361)." Subjects in the *moderate* anxiety condition were shown two slides which ostensibly contained blood samples from the rats in the two visible cages and were told that their task was to obtain a blood sample from the rat in the third cage and place it on a fresh slide. Specific directions for this procedure were then given, including the use of a hypodermic needle, and it was explained to the subject that the task was easier than it looked. Finally, subjects in the *high* anxiety condition were told that their task was to obtain a blood sample from the third rat, but they were also shown plastic bottles which supposedly contained blood from the first two rats and warned that the procedure of extracting blood was extremely dangerous because the rat might bite them.

Following the task instructions, subjects in each condition reached into the third cage and, with considerable astonishment and relief, discovered a toy rat! They were then given a questionnaire in which they rated the humor of the event that had just occurred as well as the amount of anxiety they had felt prior to discovering the toy rat (a check on the fact that the three groups did represent different levels of experimentally induced anxiety). Shurcliff's results are in strong agreement with the relief theory of humor appreciation. Specifically, it was found that the greater the subjects' anxiety prior to holding the third "rat," the more humorous they judged the event to be.

Taken collectively, the three experiments described here illustrate how psychoanalytic concepts might be subjected to empirical test. They also reveal something of the breadth of research interest in Freud's concepts. However, careful analysis of these kinds of investigations indicates that many do not serve as direct, unequivocal tests of the particular theoretical concept in question. Freud's theory is extremely difficult to verify. As we see it, the major scientific question for psychoanalytic theory is whether its concepts can be translated into operational procedures which allow for unequivocal test or whether it eventually will yield to another theory that is equally comprehensive and functionally significant but more amenable to systematic research investigation and verification.

APPLICATION: PSYCHOANALYTIC THERAPY

Psychoanalytic theory has been applied to the understanding of virtually every area of human behavior. Such diverse fields as anthropology, art, criminology, education, philosophy, sociology, and religion have felt its impact. Without exaggeration, there is no other theory in modern-day psychology that is as manifold in its range of concrete applications as psychoanalysis. To be sure, psychoanalysis has not escaped bitter criticism from contemporary personologists. For example, many believe that in Freud's theory there is an overemphasis upon the negative, pathological side of human life accompanied by a deemphasis upon the positive, healthy, self-actualizing aspects of human existence. However, even those who reject Freud's theory acknowledge his many contributions to the solution of human problems. It is to one of these, perhaps the most significant and far-reaching application of psychoanalytic theory to date, that we now turn.

Freudian Techniques: What Happens in Psychoanalysis

Consideration of psychotherapy seems appropriate since Freud's clinical experience with neurotic patients was the basis for his theoretical system. In fact, Freud adamantly insisted that his concepts could only be properly evaluated by psychoanalytic patients or psychoanalytic therapists:

> The teachings of psychoanalysis are based on an incalculable number of observations and experiences, and no one who has not repeated those observations upon himself and upon others is in a position to arrive at an independent judgment of it (1964, p. ix).

Today there are a substantial number of psychoanalysts (the professional membership of the American Psychoanalytic Association alone numbers about 1,300 at present) who practice therapy strictly in accordance with Freud's theoretical views and methods of treatment. In addition, there are many other mental health workers who are distinctly psychoanalytically oriented in their professional activities. To see what a Freudian therapist actually does, consider the following example:

A young man, 18 years of age, is referred to the psychoanalyst by his family physician. It seems that, for the past year, the young man has experienced a variety of symptoms such as headaches, dizziness, heart palpitations, waking up in the middle of the night with extreme anxiety—all of these pervaded by a constant, periodically overwhelming fear of death. Basically, he thinks that he has a brain tumor and is going to die. Yet, in spite of numerous medical tests and examinations, no physical basis for his symptoms can be found. The physician finally concludes that the "symptoms" of the young man (let's call him Albert) are probably psychologically based.

Albert arrives at the analyst's office, located two blocks away from his home, accompanied by his parents. He describes his problems and depicts his relationships with his parents as "rosy," although he feels that his father is "a little on the strict side" (He doesn't let Albert go out on week nights, makes him come in by 11 P.M. on Saturday nights, and successfully broke off Albert's relationship with a girl one year ago because he thought Albert was getting "too close" to her). But Albert displays no conscious resentment about any of this, instead describing the events in an unemotional, matter-of-fact fashion.

In the eyes of a Freudian psychotherapist, Albert's symptoms are seen as determined, rooted in early childhood experience, and motivated by unconscious factors. Collectively, these factors prevent Albert from using his own resources to change his feelings and behavior. However, Dr. F. (as we shall cleverly call our therapist) believes that through psychoanalysis Albert can be led to understand the causes of his intense fear of death and related symptoms, thereby making it possible for him to overcome them. Essentially, Dr. F.'s task in psychoanalysis is to get Albert to face his problems, master them, and then conduct his life with greater conscious awareness of his real motives (i.e., strengthen his ego). Freud believed that psychoanalysis was unrivaled as a vehicle for constructive personality change. Toward this end, Albert would be expected to see Dr. F. almost daily for a period of several years. Successful analysis requires a great deal of time, effort, and expense. Briefly, in Freudian theory, it takes a long time for the patient to become the way that he is; consequently, it will take a long time for him to change. Discussed below are illustrative techniques used in psychoanalysis, applicable to Albert's problem or any other problem area faced by orthodox practicing analysts.

Free Association The therapeutic situation is arranged in order to maximize free association. In this procedure, Albert would be instructed to relax, either in a chair or on the classic couch, and report everything that comes into his consciousness, regardless of how irrelevant, absurd, or obscene it may seem. Dr. F. would urge Albert to relinquish all conscious reflection, follow his spontaneous thoughts and feelings, and impart *everything,* no matter how apparently trivial. As the basic rule agreed upon by those undergoing psychoanalysis, free association is predicated on the assumption that one association leads to another that is deeper in the unconscious. Associations verbalized by the patient are interpreted as disguised expressions of repressed thoughts and feelings.

In line with Freud's deterministic position, then, the patient's "free associations" are not really free at all. Like his other behavior, Albert's cognitive and affective associations are determined by unconscious processes. Because of repression and unconscious motivation, Albert is unaware of the underlying meaning of what he is saying. By employing free association, Dr. F. believes that Albert's relaxed state will permit repressed material to emerge gradually, thus releasing more psychic energy for adaptive use. Dr. F. should also be in a better position to understand the nature of Albert's unconscious conflicts and their presumed causes. Perhaps, for example, Albert's free associations will lead him to recollect his earlier feelings of intense resentment toward his father (the Oedipal theme) and corresponding childhood wishes that his father would die.

Interpretation of Resistance   During the initial stage of psychoanalysis Freud discovered that the patient is usually unable or quite reluctant to recall repressed feelings and ideas. The patient *resists*. Thus, despite the fact that Albert consciously desires to change his feelings and end his suffering, he unconsciously resists Dr. F.'s efforts to help him eliminate his old, unsatisfactory behavior patterns. It is Dr. F.'s task to make Albert aware of his resistance maneuvers; it is necessary to deal with them successfully if therapeutic progress is to occur.

Resistance is a means of keeping the unconscious conflict intact, thereby impeding any attempts to probe into the real sources of personality problems. Resistance reveals itself in many ways. It may cause the patient to be late for therapy sessions, "forget" them, or simply find excuses for not coming. It is also evidenced when the patient is temporarily unable to free associate; e.g., "I remember one day when I was a little kid and my mother and I were planning to go out shopping together. My father came home and, instead, the two of them went out leaving me behind with a neighbor. I felt . . . (pause) . . . For some reason, my mind is suddenly a complete blank right now." The ultimate form of resistance, of course, is for the patient to discontinue therapy prematurely. Skillful interpretation of the reasons for resistance is one method Dr. F. would employ to help Albert bring repressed conflicts into the open and rid himself of unconscious defenses.

Dream Analysis   Another prominent technique for uncovering repressed material from the unconscious is that of dream analysis. Freud considered dreams as a direct avenue to the unconscious, since he viewed their contents as determined by repressed wishes. Dreams are thus understood and interpreted as essentially symbolic wish fulfillments whose contents partially reflect early childhood experiences (Freud, 1953). By means of rather elaborate techniques of dream interpretation involving analysis of the disguised meaning of dream

symbols, psychoanalysts believe that they can enhance the patient's understanding of the causes of his symptoms and motivational conflicts.

For example, Albert may report a dream in which his father is departing
(death symbol) on a train while Albert remains on the platform holding hands
with his mother and former girlfriend, while feeling at once glad and intensely
guilty. If the psychotherapeutic moment is right, Dr. F. might help Albert to see
that this dream reflects his long repressed Oedipal-related wish for his father's
death, reactivated last year by the father's severing of Albert's love relationship with his girlfriend. Thus, through dream analysis and interpretation, Albert
may begin to gain greater insight into the real conflict underlying his present
symptoms.

Analysis of Transference   Earlier in the chapter, displacement was
identified as a defense mechanism in which an unconscious impulse is
discharged upon some person or object other than the one toward which it was
initially directed. When it occurs in psychotherapy, this phenomenon is termed
transference. More precisely, transference occurs whenever patients displace
to the analyst feelings of love or hate which they had previously attached to a
significant person (often a parent). Freud believed that transference reflected
the patient's need to find a love object in order that repressed love feelings
might be expressed. The analyst serves as a substitute love object in such a
setting. Transference may reveal itself in direct verbal communication, free
association, or the content of dreams. As an example, Albert might be showing
signs of tranference if he said something like the following: "Dr. F., why the
hell did you decide to take a two week vacation with your damned beloved wife
just when we were starting to get somewhere in analysis?" On a deeper level,
Albert is emotionally reacting to Dr. F. as he formerly felt toward his father in
childhood (the Oedipal theme again).

Insofar as the phenomenon of transference operates unconsciously, the
patient is totally unaware of its functional importance. Not interpreting the
transference immediately, the therapist encourages its development until the
patient has established what Freud called a *transference neurosis.* In essence,
this is a "miniature neurosis" that serves to enhance the analyst's insight into
the patients' deep, characteristic ways of perceiving, feeling, and reacting to
significant figures in their early lives. According to Freud, as patients become
gradually aware of the true meaning of their transference relationship with the
analyst, they gain insight into their past experiences and feelings, relating these
more fully to their ongoing difficulties. Orthodox psychoanalysts regard
analysis of transference as absolutely vital to the therapeutic process—
successful outcomes depend utterly upon it.

In Albert's case, Dr. F.'s interpretation of the transference relationship
may reveal that he both loved and hated his father a great deal. Deeply
resenting his father's relationship with his mother, Albert strongly wished his
father dead. But also loving his father, Albert felt extremely guilty and thus

deeply repressed this wish. However, revitalized by his father's severing of the relationship between Albert and his new "love object" (former girlfriend), this old feeling charged into consciousness in the distorted form of a fear of his own death. Thus, Albert's own overwhelming death fear—his central symptom— may be interpreted psychoanalytically as a symbolic wish for his father's death (perhaps an unconscious dread that he will kill his father) accompanied by an overriding guilt resulting in unconscious self-punishment for this wish. Albert's intense death fear and accompanying symptoms nicely accomplish this self-punishment objective. Other elements, such as a possible relationship between castration anxiety and fear of death, could also probably be worked into this kind of interpretation of Albert's symptoms. And the therapist, of course, employs all the previous techniques (not only analysis of transference) in arriving at the final interpretation.

Emotional Reeducation Encouraging patients to convert their newly-discovered insights into everyday living is called *emotional reeducation.* In different ways, each of the previous therapeutic techniques is designed to help patients achieve greater insight into the causes of their behavior. However, this insight alone, while necessary in psychoanalytic therapy, is not a sufficient condition for behavioral change. Urged by the analyst, patients must eventually apply their self-understanding to their day-to-day existence; they must learn to think, perceive, feel, and behave differently. Otherwise, psychoanalysis is nothing more than an emotionally draining exercise of excessive duration and expense.

Emotional reeducation is primarily employed during the final phases of therapy since the insights upon which it depends must necessarily be acquired first. Thus, Dr. F., having led Albert progressively toward a deeper understanding of the origins of his fear of death and accompanying symptoms, would help him to explore concrete ways of restructuring his feelings and behavior. Based on his newly acquired self-understanding, Albert would be encouraged to get rid of his childhood "hangups," begin to relate to his father as he is now, function more autonomously in relation to his parents, and develop more mature love relationships. In time, Albert should be able to accomplish these objectives with Dr. F.'s help. A good deal of this emotional reeducation would stem from therapeutic discussions of Albert's present life situation in light of his now well-understood past emotional history. When Albert makes substantial progress in these realms on his own, therapy is terminated by mutual agreement.

Each of the procedures discussed above is illustrative of "classical" psychoanalysis as it is practiced today, variations of which are dealt with in detail elsewhere (King, 1965; Wolman, 1968). Albert's case exemplifies the emphasis on the Oedipal complex and the importance Freud placed upon early experience in subsequent neurotic behavior.

Psychoanalysts and other contemporary therapists have introduced many treatment variations and innovations, not the least of which is the practical matter of how long therapy should continue (Harper, 1959). Psychoanalytic therapy can be an extremely lengthy ordeal, often involving one hour per day, five days per week, and extending over a period of one to five years or even longer! Thus, it is a very expensive form of therapy which is often limited to the affluent. However, the major goal of analysis is to produce basic changes in an individual's personality structure. Increased insight, personal integration, social effectiveness, and psychological maturity are the objectives. Obviously, such goals cannot be accomplished quickly or easily. Regardless of the ultimate judgment that history will pass on its actual therapeutic benefits, psychoanalysis stands as a significant pioneering effort in the continuing attempt to alleviate human misery.

SUMMARY

The psychoanalytic theory of personality was discussed in terms of theory, basic assumptions, research, and applications. Sigmund Freud, the founder of psychoanalysis, based his theory almost entirely on extensive clinical observation of neurotic patients as well as self-analysis.

Freud proposed three levels of consciousness—the conscious, preconscious, and unconscious—to describe the degree to which mental events vary in accessibility to awareness. The most significant mental events take place in the unconscious.

In Freudian theory, human psychological makeup is comprised of three structural components—id, ego, and superego. The id, representing the instinctual core of the person, is irrational, impulsive, and obedient to the pleasure principle. Reflex actions and primary process are used by the id in obtaining gratification of instinctual urges. The ego represents the rational component of personality and is governed by the reality principle. Its task, through secondary process, is to provide the individual with a suitable plan of action in order to satisfy the demands of the id within the restrictions of the social world and the individual's conscience. The superego, the final structure developed, represents the moral branch of personality. It has two subsystems, the conscience and the ego-ideal.

Freud's motivational theory is based on the concept of instinct, defined as an innate state of excitation which seeks tension release. An instinct has four essential properties: (1) source, (2) aim, (3) object, and (4) impetus.

Freud's account of psychosexual development is based on the premise that sexuality begins at birth and progresses thereafter through a biologically defined set of erogenous zones until adulthood is reached. Freud conceived of personality development as proceeding through the following stages: oral, anal, phallic, and genital.

Freud recognized three types of anxiety: reality, neurotic, and moral. He proposed that anxiety serves as a warning signal to the ego of impending danger from instinctual impulses. In response, the ego employs a number of defense mechanisms, including sublimation, repression, projection, displacement, rationalization, and reaction formation.

Freud's theory is founded upon certain basic assumptions concerning human nature. Psychoanalytic theory reflects (1) a strong commitment to the assumptions of determinism, irrationality, homeostasis, and knowability; (2) a moderate commitment to the assumptions of holism, constitutionalism, and proactivity; and (3) a slight commitment to the assumption of subjectivity.

A number of Freudian concepts have yet to be submitted to rigorous empirical assessment by psychologists. However, illustrative studies related to repression, castration complex in dreams, and humor suggest that certain psychoanalytic constructs are amenable to scientific inquiry.

Applications of psychoanalytic concepts to everyday life are numerous. One of the most significant of these, psychoanalytic therapy, uses well-developed methods such as free association, interpretation of resistance, dream analysis, and analysis of transference to probe the person's unconscious with the aim of making possible a deeper understanding of self. These newly acquired self-insights are then converted into the person's everyday life through the method of emotional reeducation.

BIBLIOGRAPHY

Breuer, J., & Freud, S. (1895). *Studies in hysteria* (Trans. A. Brill). New York: Nervous and Mental Diseases Publishing Company, 1936.

Cohen, J. *Personality dynamics: Eyewitness series in psychology.* Chicago: Rand McNally, 1969.

Fenichel, O. *The psychoanalytic theory of neurosis.* New York: Norton, 1945.

Freud, S. (1900). The interpretation of dreams. In J. Strachey (Trans. and Ed.), *The standard edition of the complete psychological works of Sigmund Freud,* Vols. 4 and 5. London: Hogarth Press, 1953.

Freud, S. (1905). Jokes and their relation to the unconscious. *Standard edition,* Vol. 8, 1960.

Freud, S. (1915–1917). *A general introduction of psychoanalysis.* New York: Doubleday, 1943.

Freud, S. (1926). Inhibitions, symptoms, and anxiety. *Standard edition,* Vol. 20, 1959.

Freud, S. (1935). An autobiographical study. *Standard edition,* Vol. 20, 1959.

Freud, S. (1940). An outline of psychoanalysis. *Standard edition,* Vol. 23, 1964.

Glucksberg, S., & King, L. Motivated forgetting mediated by implicit verbal chaining: A laboratory analog of repression. *Science,* Oct. 27, 1967, 517–519.

Hall, C., & Van de Castle, R. An empirical investigation of the castration complex in dreams. *Journal of Personality,* 1965, **33**, 20–29.

Harper, R. *Psychoanalysis and psychotherapy: 36 systems.* Englewood Cliffs, N.J.: Prentice-Hall, 1959.

Hilgard, E. Psychoanalysis: Experimental studies. In D. Sills (Ed.), *International encyclopedia of the social sciences,* Vol. 13. New York: Macmillan and the Free Press, 1968, pp. 37–45.

Jones, E. *The life and work of Sigmund Freud:* Vol. I (1856–1900); *The formative years and the great discoveries,* 1953; Vol. II (1901–1919); *Years of Maturity,* 1955; Vol. III (1919–1939); *The last phase,* 1957. New York: Basic Books.

King, P. Psychoanalytic adaptations. In B. Stefflre (Ed.), *Theories of counseling.* New York: McGraw-Hill, 1965.

Mischel, W. *Introduction to personality.* New York: Holt, Rinehart and Winston, 1971.

Nuttin, J. Human motivation and Freud's theory of energy discharge. *Canadian Journal of Psychology,* 1956, **10,** 167–178.

Rank, O. *The trauma of birth.* New York: Harcourt, Brace, and Co., 1929.

Sarason, I. *Personality: An objective approach* (2d ed.). New York: Wiley, 1972.

Sarnoff, I. *Testing Freudian concepts: An experimental social approach.* New York: Springer, 1971.

Shurcliff, A. Judged humor, arousal, and the relief theory. *Journal of Personality and Social Psychology,* 1968, **8,** 360–363.

Skinner, B. F. Critique of psychoanalytic concepts and theories. *The Scientific Monthly,* 1954, **79,** 300–305.

Weinstein, E. Symbolic neurology and psychoanalysis. In J. Marmor (Ed.), *Modern psychoanalysis: New directions and perspectives.* New York: Basic Books, 1968, pp. 225–250.

Wolman, B. *The unconscious mind: The meaning of Freudian psychology.* Englewood Cliffs, N.J.: Prentice-Hall, 1968.

SUGGESTED READINGS

1 Kline, P. *Fact and fantasy in Freudian theory.* London: Methuen, 1972.
2 McGuire, W. (Ed.). *The Freud/Jung letters.* Princeton, N.J.: Princeton University Press, 1974.
3 Murphy, G. *Psychological thought from Pythagoras to Freud: An informal introduction.* New York: Harcourt, Brace & World, 1968.
4 Smirnoff, V. *The scope of child analysis.* New York: International Universities Press, 1971.
5 Van de Castle, R. *The psychology of dreaming.* New York: General Learning Corporation, 1971.
6 Wiseman, R., & Reyer, J. Hypnotically induced dreams using the Rorschach inkblots as stimuli: A test of Freud's theory of dreams. *Journal of Personality and Social Psychology,* 1973, **27**, 329–336.

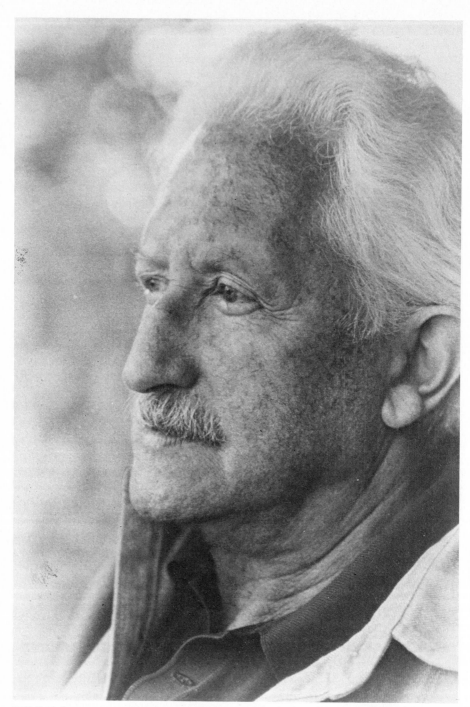

Erik H. Erikson

Erik Erikson:
A Psychosocial Theory
of Personality

η ον

Erik Erikson's theory has been selected for presentation here because (1) it is representative of the *ego psychology* approach to personality; (2) it emphasizes the importance of developmental change throughout the life cycle; and (3) it explicitly illustrates the effort to combine clinical insight with social and historical forces in explaining personality organization. In his "Eight Ages of Man," Erikson has provided the student of human behavior with fresh and genuine advances in understanding major psychological problems confronting modern man.

BIOGRAPHICAL SKETCH

Erik Erikson was born of Danish parents in Frankfurt, Germany, in 1902. Not long after his birth his father died, his mother remarried Dr. Theodor Homburger, a pediatrician who had cured her son of a childhood disease. Later, in signing his first psychoanalytic articles, Erikson used his stepfather's surname as his own, although he chose to be known by his original name when he became a naturalized American citizen in 1939. Unlike any other personologist discussed in this text, Erikson did not pursue formal education beyond high school. He attended a "humanistic gymnasium" in Karlsruhe, Germany, and, although he was not a good student, he did excel in the subjects of ancient history and art. Shortly after graduation, spurning his stepfather's urgings that he become a physician, Erikson left home to travel across central Europe. A year later, he enrolled in art school and for a brief period accepted the fact that even an aspiring artist could learn something in an educational setting. However, he soon became restless again and set out for Munich to study at the famous art school there, the Dunst-Akademie. Two years later, Erikson moved to Florence, Italy, although for a period he wandered aimlessly throughout Italy, spending endless time soaking up sunshine and visiting art galleries. Fortunately, however, he came to realize that "such narcissism obviously could be a young person's downfall unless he found an overweening idea and the stamina to work for it (Erikson, 1970b, pp. 743–744)."

In 1927, at the age of twenty-five, Erikson ended his occupational "moratorium" when he accepted an unexpected invitation from Peter Blos, a high school classmate, to join him and Dorothy Burlingham as teachers at a small American day nursery in Vienna. The school, known as the Kinderseminar, had been established by Anna Freud for children whose parents were learning to become psychoanalysts. Some of Erikson's young students were in analysis themselves, and eventually their teacher—Herr Erik, as he was affectionately called—joined them.

Erikson's introduction to the study of psychoanalysis began at a mountain spa near Vienna. There, as a tutor, he first came to know the Freud family and was subsequently selected as an acceptable candidate for training at the Vienna Psychoanalytic Institute. From 1927 to 1933, Erikson continued his training in psychoanalysis under the guidance of Anna Freud and August Aichhorn. This constituted his only formal academic training aside from a certificate he acquired from the Maria Montessori Teachers Association in Vienna. Today, requirements are far more stringent for students wishing to prepare for professional careers in the field of mental health.

In 1929, Erikson married Joan Serson, an American teacher and dancer who was then also a member of the experimental school led by Anna Freud. In 1933, the Erikson family (including two sons) went to Copenhagen, where Erikson attempted to regain his Danish citizenship and to help establish a psychoanalytic training center in that country. When this proved impractical, the family emigrated to the United States and settled in Boston where a psychoanalytic society had been founded the year before. Erikson's timely arrival in this country afforded him the distinction of being the first child-analyst in the New England area. For the next two years he practiced in Boston and, for one year, held a clinical and academic appointment as Research Fellow in Psychology in the Department of Neuropsychiatry of the Harvard Medical School. He also enrolled at Harvard as a candidate for the Ph.D. in psychology, although he withdrew from the program a few months later.

During the years 1936 to 1939, Erikson had an appointment with the

Department of Psychiatry in the Institute of Human Relations and the Yale University School of Medicine, which allowed him complete freedom to pursue whatever research he desired. During this period he also became interested in cultural anthropology and, in 1938, undertook a field trip to the Pine Ridge Reservation in South Dakota to observe how members of the Sioux Indians raised their children.

In 1939, Erikson moved to California where he resumed his analytic work with children as well as furthering his interest in anthropology and history. By 1942, he was a professor of psychology at the University of California at Berkeley. At the same institution, he participated in the famous longitudinal *Child Guidance Study* under the direction of Jean MacFarlane. What followed was an intense period of close clinical observations and reflections as Erikson prepared to establish—through books—his professional identity as a psychoanalyst. His professorship at Berkeley tragically ended, however, when he refused to sign a loyalty oath. He was later reinstated as politically reliable but chose to resign because others were fired for the same "crime." He published his first book, *Childhood and Society,* in 1950 (revised and reissued in 1963), and this work soon won him recognition as a leading spokesman of ego psychology in this country.

In 1951, Erikson joined a group of mental health professionals at the Austen Riggs Center in Stockbridge, Massachusetts, a private residential treatment center for disturbed young people. He also maintained part-time teaching appointments at the Western Psychiatric Institute in Pittsburgh, the University of Pittsburgh, and the Massachusetts Institute of Technology. For the next decade, his writings and research extended the theory of psychosocial development he had originally proposed in *Childhood and Society.*

In the summer of 1960, following a year at the Center for Advanced Studies of the Behavioral Sciences at Palo Alto, California, Erikson rejoined Harvard University as lecturer and professor of Human Development. Erikson says he reentered academia "in order to learn how to teach my whole conception of the life cycle—including identity crisis—to people normatively very much in it (1970b, p. 749)." Although he is now retired, he continues to devote much time and energy to the application of his scheme of the human life cycle to the study of historical persons and American children, predominantly minority groups. His brilliant psychobiographical study of the origins of militant nonviolence, *Gandhi's Truth* (1969), won him a Pulitzer Prize and the National Book Award in philosophy and religion. Moreover, he has published three other important books: *Young Man Luther, A Study in Psychoanalysis and History* (1958), *Insight and Responsibility* (1964a) and *Identity: Youth and Crisis* (1968a), as well as editing another, *Youth: Change and Challenge* (1963b). Robert Coles, a Harvard psychiatrist and student of Erikson, recently acknowledged his mentor's accomplishments as a theoretician and practitioner of psychoanalysis in a volume entitled: *Erik H. Erikson: The Growth of His Work* (1970).

EGO PSYCHOLOGY: PSYCHOANALYSIS COMES OF AGE

Erikson's major theoretical formulations are exclusively concerned with growth of the ego. Although he has persistently maintained that his own contributions to the understanding of human development are nothing more than a systematic extension of Freud's conceptions of psychosexual development in light of current social, anthropological, and biological data, Erikson does represent a decisive departure from Freudian theory in four essential ways (Maier, 1965). To begin with, Erikson's work completes a shift in emphasis from the id to the ego which Freud only partially acknowleged during the final years of his work. That is to say, Erikson emphasizes the ego rather than the id as the basis of human behavior and functioning. He regards the ego as an autonomous structure of personality (i.e., some portion of ego functioning is not determined by the attempt to avoid conflict between the id and the demands of society) which follows a course of social-adaptive development that parallels the id and the instincts. This conception of human nature, called *ego psychology,* constitutes a radical change from earlier psychoanalytic thought in that it depicts persons as much more rational and logical in making decisions and solving problems. Second, Erikson has introduced a new perspective concerning the individual's relationship to parents and the historical matrix in which the family is located. Whereas Freud concerned himself with the influence of parents on the child's emerging personality, Erikson stresses the psychohistorical setting in which the child's ego is molded. He relies on case studies of people living in different cultures to show how the ego's development is inextricably bound up with the changing nature of social institutions and value systems.

Third, Erikson's theory of ego development encompasses the entire life span of the individual (i.e., from infancy to adolescence and eventually to maturity and old age). In contrast, Freud limited himself to the effects of early childhood experiences and devoted no attention to development beyond the genital stage. Closer inspection makes it evident, however, that some degree of correspondence does exist between the two theorists with respect to the first five stages of life.

Finally, Freud and Erikson differ on the nature and resolution of psychosexual conflicts. Freud's ambition was to unravel the existence and operation of unconscious mental life and explain how early trauma may bring about psychopathology in adulthood. Conversely, Erikson's mission is to draw attention to the human capacity to triumph over the psychosocial hazards of living. Thus, his theory focuses on *ego qualities* that emerge at various developmental periods. Perhaps this distinction is the key to understanding Erikson's own conception of personality organization and development. Freud's fatalistic warning that man is doomed to social extinction if left to his instinctual strivings is countered by Erikson's optimistic premise that every personal and social crisis furnishes challenges that are conducive to growth and mastery over the world. To know how a person has mastered each of a series of significant life problems and how the inadequate mastery of early problems incapacitates him in dealing with later problems is, for Erikson, the only avenue to understanding a person's life. Erikson thus emphasizes the creative and adaptive powers of the individual and, in agreement with humanists, views persons as potentially good.

Insofar as major theoretical differences between Erikson and Freud have been stressed, it would be only reasonable to note that there are also substantive areas of similarity. For example, both theorists consider the stages of personality as being predetermined and invariant in order of their appearance. Erikson also acknowledges the biological and sexual foundations for all later motivational and personal dispositions and is committed to Freud's structural model (id, ego, superego) of personality. Despite these overlapping areas of agreement, many personologists see Erikson's theoretical efforts as constituting a totally different perspective vis à vis the human life cycle.

THE EPIGENETIC PRINCIPLE AND MAN'S EIGHT AGES

Central to Erikson's theory of ego development is the assumption that the development of the person is marked by a series of stages that are universal to humanity. The process whereby these stages evolve is governed by the *epigenetic principle* of maturation. By this Erikson means:

> (1) that the human personality in principle develops according to steps predetermined in the growing person's readiness to be driven toward, to be aware of, and to interact with, a widening social radius; and (2) that society, in principle, tends to be so constituted as to meet and invite this succession of potentialities for interaction and attempts to safeguard and to encourage the proper rate and the proper sequence of their enfolding (1963a, p. 270).

In *Childhood and Society* (1963a), Erikson outlined a sequence of eight separate stages of psychosocial ego development, colloquially, "the eight stages of man." He postulates that these stages are the result of the epigenetic unfolding of a "ground plan" of personality that is genetically transmitted. An epigenetic (*epi* means "upon" and *genetic* means "emergence") conception of development mirrors the notion that each stage in the life cycle has an optimal time (i.e., critical period) in which it is dominant and hence emerges, and that when all of the stages have matured according to plan, a fully functioning personality comes into existence. Furthermore, Erikson hypothesizes that each psychosocial stage is accompanied by a *crisis,* that is, a critical turning point in the individual's life that arises from physiological maturation and social demands made upon the person at that stage. The different components of personality are determined by the manner in which each of these crises is resolved. Conflict is a vital and integral part of Erikson's theory, because

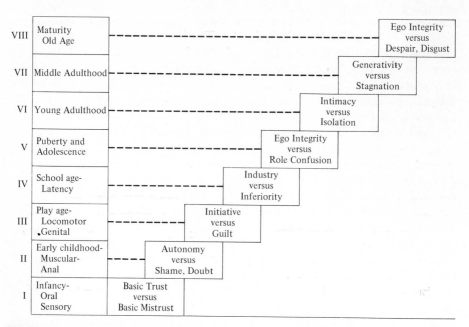

Figure 3-1 Erikson's epigenetic chart of the eight stages of psychosocial development. (*Adapted from* Childhood and Society, *by Erik H. Erikson 1963a, p. 273.*)

growth and an expanding interpersonal radius are associated with increased vulnerability of the ego functions at each stage. At the same time, he notes that crisis connotes "not a threat of catastrophe but a turning point and, therefore, the ontogenetic source of generational strength and maladjustment (1968b, p. 286)." *forward to another stage*

Each psychosocial crisis, when viewed as a dimensional attribute, includes both a positive and a negative component. If the conflict is handled in a primarily satisfactory manner (i.e., the person has a history of ego achievements), the positive component (e.g., basic trust, autonomy) is to a larger degree absorbed into the emerging ego and further healthy development is assured. Conversely, if the conflict persists or is primarily resolved in an unsatisfactory fashion, the developing ego is damaged and the negative component (e.g., mistrust, shame, and doubt) is to a larger degree incorporated into the ego. While the various theoretically defined conflicts emerge in developmental sequence, this does not mean that earlier achievements and failures are necessarily permanent. Ego qualities attained at each stage are not impervious to new inner conflicts or to changing conditions (Erikson, 1964a). The major point, however, is that the person must adequately resolve each crisis in order to progress to the next stage of development in an adaptive and healthy fashion. *otherwise the next stage will be affected*

Erikson's reliance on the epigenetic principle of maturation may be clearly seen from his chart of the psychosocial crises of the life cycle (see Figure 3-1).

This chart presents the eight developmental stages in terms of a staircase hierarchy, arranged in chronological order. The diagonal boxes include both the positive and the negative components for each successive stage. Consistent with the principle of epigenesis, each stage builds upon the resolution and integration of the previous psychosocial conflicts. Erikson proposes, however, that all the conflicts are present in some form from the beginning of postnatal life. For each crisis period, Erikson has delineated the conditions under which relative psychosocial health and corresponding ill health are likely to occur. Let us now consider the eight stages.

I Infancy: Basic Trust versus Mistrust—Hope

The first psychosocial stage corresponds to Freud's oral stage and extends through approximately the first year of life. For Erikson, a general sense of trust is the cornerstone of a healthy personality, while others regard this same characteristic as "confidence." A child with a basic sense of "inner certainty" sees the social world as a safe, stable place and people as nurturant and reliable. This sense of certainty is only partially conscious during infancy.

Erikson suggests that the degree to which infants are able to acquire a sense of trust in other people and in the world depends upon the qualitative nature of maternal care that they receive. It is the mother who controls both gratification and security:

> Mothers, I think, create a sense of trust in their children by that kind of administration which in its quality combines sensitive care of the baby's individual needs and a firm sense of personal trustworthiness within the trusted framework of their culture's life style. This forms the basis in the child for a sense of being "all right," of being oneself, and of becoming what other people trust one will become. . . . Parents must not only have certain ways of guiding by prohibition and permission; they must also be able to represent to the child a deep, an almost somatic conviction that there is a meaning to what they are doing (Erikson, 1963a, p. 249).

In addition, Erikson stresses the fact that infants must trust not only the external world but the internal world as well; they must learn to trust themselves and, in particular, the capacity of their organs to cope effectively with biological urges. Such behavior is shown when the infant can tolerate the mother's absence without suffering undue anxiety.

The question of what evokes life's first major psychological crisis for the child has been carefully considered by Erikson. He attributes the crisis to a quality of maternal care which is unreliable, inadequate, and rejecting, thus fostering a psychosocial attitude of fear, suspicion, and apprehension in the infant toward the world in general and people in particular that will manifest its ill effects in later stages of personality development. Furthermore, Erikson feels that a sense of mistrust may be augmented when the mother turns from the baby as the primary focus of her attention to other pursuits that she had given up during pregnancy and the early postnatal life of the child (e.g., resuming a career or becoming pregnant again). Finally, parents who display divergent patterns of child care, who lack self-confidence in their role as parents, and who have value systems conflicting with the dominant life-style of the culture may create an atmosphere of ambiguity for the child, resulting in feelings of distrust. The behavioral consequences of a seriously defective development of basic trust, according to Erikson, are acute depression in infants and paranoia in adults. He observes that such individuals, when they enter into a psychotherapeutic relationship, must first be reassured that they can trust the therapist and then trust themselves and finally come to trust the world.

A basic premise of psychosocial theory is that the crisis of trust versus mistrust (as is true for all subsequent stages) is not permanently resolved during the first year or two of life. Consistent with the epigenetic principle, trust versus mistrust will reappear at each successive stage of development, although it is focal during infancy. However, adequate resolution of the crisis of trust does have major consequences for the future development of the infant's personality. The establishment of self-trust and trust in mother enables infants to tolerate the frustrations that they will inevitably experience during subsequent stages of development.

Erikson notes that the emergence of healthy growth in the infant does not result exclusively from a sense of trust but rather from a favorable ratio of trust over mistrust. It is as important to learn what not to trust as to learn what to trust. The ability to anticipate danger and discomfort are just as essential for mastery of the enviroment and effective living; thus, basic trust should not be viewed in terms of an achievement scale. In animals, Erikson contends, there is almost an instinctive readiness to acquire this psychosocial ability; but in humans it must be learned. Moreover, he suggests that mothers in different cultures and classes will teach trust and mistrust in different ways, thus acknowledging the impact of cultural variation. Yet the attainment of a sense of trust is universal in substance—namely, that one can trust the social world in the form of one's mother, that she will come back and feed one the right thing at the right time.

The psychosocial strength gained from successful resolution of the trust-versus-mistrust conflict is termed *hope* by Erikson. Trust, in other words, becomes the infant's capacity for hope, which, in turn, is the foundation of the adult's faith in some form of institutionalized religion. Hope as the first psychosocial strength also serves to maintain the individual's belief in the meaning and trustworthiness of a common cultural world. Conversely, Erikson emphasizes that when religious institutions fail to provide tangible significance for the individual, these institutions may become irrelevant, outmoded, and possibly even be replaced by other more significant sources of faith and conviction in the future (e.g., commitment to scientific and artistic endeavors, and social action programs).

STOP

II Early Childhood: Autonomy versus Shame and Doubt—Will Power

Acquisition of a sense of basic trust sets the stage for the attainment of a sense of autonomy. This period coincides with Freud's anal stage and roughly spans the second and third years of life. According to Erikson, the child has a choice of social modes during this period to keep or let go.

Muscular maturation sets the stage for an ambivalent set of social modalities—holding on and letting go. To hold on can become *either* a destructive retaining or restraining *or* a pattern of care—to have and to hold. To let go, too, can turn either into an inimical letting loose, or into a relaxed "letting be." This stage, therefore, becomes decisive for the ratio of goodwill and willfulness. A sense of self-control without loss of self-esteem is the ontogenetic source of confidence in free will; a sense of overcontrol and loss of self-control can give rise to a lasting propensity for doubt and shame (Erikson, 1968b).

Prior to this stage, children are almost totally dependent on adults who care for them; their behavior is largely governed by external forces. However, as they rapidly gain neuromuscular maturation, verbalization, and social discrimination, they begin to explore and interact with their environments more independently. In particular, they feel pride in their newly discovered locomotor skills and want to do everything themselves (e.g., dressing and feeding themselves). There is a tremendous desire to explore, choose, and manipulate coupled with an attitude toward parents of "let me do it" and "I am what I will."

In Erikson's view, satisfactorily meeting the psychosocial crisis of this stage depends primarily on the parents' willingness to gradually allow children freedom to control those activities that affect their lives. At the same time, Erikson stresses that parents must maintain reasonable but firm limits in those areas of children's lives that are either potentially or actually harmful to themselves or destructive to others. Autonomy does not mean giving the child unrestricted freedom; rather, it means that parents must maintain "degrees of freedom" over the child's growing ability to exercise choice.

Erikson perceives the child's experience of shame as something akin to rage turned upon himself because he has not been allowed to exercise his autonomy. Shame may come about if the parents are impatient and insist on doing for children what they are capable of doing themselves or, conversely, if parents expect of children what they are not capable of doing themselves. To be sure, every parent has occasionally pushed his or her child beyond the limits of appropriate expectation. It is only when parents are persistently overprotective or insensitive that children acquire a dominant sense of shame with respect to others and a dominant sense of doubt about their own effectiveness in controlling the world and themselves. Rather than feeling self-confident about their ability to cope effectively with the environment, such children are conscious of being scrutinized (disapprovingly) or of being considered essentially helpless. They are uncertain of their "will power" and of those who would dominate or exploit it. The result is a psychosocial attitude of self-doubt, ineptitude, and powerlessness.

Since each psychosocial stage builds upon the ones preceding it, the attainment of a stable sense of autonomy adds substantially to the child's sense of trust. This interdependence of trust and autonomy may sometimes have the effect of impairing future psychosocial growth. Children for example, who have acquired a "shaky" amount of trust may, during the state of autonomy, become hesitant, fearful, and insecure about asserting themselves; hence, they continue to seek help and encourage others to do things for them. As adults, Erikson finds that such individuals are likely to manifest obsessive-compulsive behavior (to ensure control) or paranoid apprehension of secret persecutors.

The institutional counterpart of autonomy is "law and order." Despite the current emotional connotation of these terms, Erikson believes that parents must convey a deep and abiding commitment to the goals of establishing a sense of justice and respect for the rights and privileges of others if their children are to be properly prepared for acceptance of a limited autonomy in adulthood. In Erikson's words:

> Willpower is the unbroken determination to exercise free choice as well as self-restraint in spite of the unavoidable experience of shame, doubt, and a certain rage over being controlled by others. Good will is rooted in the judiciousness of parents guided by their respect for the spirit of the law (1968b, p. 288).

III Play Age: Initiative versus Guilt—Purpose

Initiative versus guilt is the final psychosocial conflict experienced by the preschool child during what Erikson calls the "play age." It occurs during the developmental period Freud designates as the phallic stage and extends from about age four to entry into formal school. Now is when the child's social world challenges him or her to be active, to master new tasks and skills, and to win approval by being productive. Children also begin to assume additional responsibility for themselves and for that which comprises their world (their bodies, toys, pets, and, occasionally, younger siblings). They become interested in the work of others, in trying out new things, and in assuming the responsibilities available in the society around them. The facility for language and locomotor skills makes possible associations with peers and older children beyond their immediate home environments, thus allowing participation in a variety of social games. This is the age when children begin to feel that they are counted as persons and that life has a purpose for them. "I am what I will be" becomes the child's dominant sense of identity during the play age. To quote Erikson:

Initiative adds to autonomy the quality of undertaking, planning, and "attacking" a task for the sake of being on the move, where before self-will, more often than not, inspired acts of defiance or, at any rate, protested independence (1963a, p. 155).

Whether children will leave this stage with their sense of initiative favorably outbalancing their sense of guilt depends largely upon how parents react to their self-initiated activities. Children who are encouraged to undertake their own activities have their sense of initiative reinforced. The development of initiative is further facilitated when parents acknowledge their children's curiosity and do not ridicule or inhibit fantasy activity. As Erikson notes, successful development in this stage leads to a "goal-directedness" in the child's behavior:

The child begins to envisage goals for which his locomotion and cognition have prepared him. The child also begins to think of being big and to identify with people whose work or whose personality he can understand and appreciate. "Purpose" involves this whole complex of elements. For example, when the child plays, it's not just a matter of practicing his will or practicing his ability to manipulate. He begins to have projects, as it were (Evans, 1967, p. 25).

In psychosocial theory, the sense of guilt in children is due to parents who are unwilling to allow them the opportunity of completing tasks on their own. A sense of guilt is also fostered by parents who employ excessive amounts of punishment (verbal or physical) in response to the child's urge to love and be - loved by the opposite-sexed parent. Erikson endorses the Freudian conception of the sexual nature of the developmental crisis involved (i.e., sex-role identification and the Oedipus complex), although his own conception is decidedly more social in scope. In any event, the child who is immobilized by guilt experiences feelings of resignation and unworthiness. Such children are fearful of asserting themselves, hang on the fringes of groups, and rely unduly on adults. They lack the purpose or courage to establish and pursue tangible goals. Erikson also suggests that a persistent sense of guilt may eventuate in a variety of adult forms of psychopathology including generalized passivity, sexual impotence, and psychopathic acting out.

Finally, the degree of initiative acquired in this phase of the child's life is related by Erikson to the economic system of the community. He states that the child's future potential to work productively and achieve self-sufficiency within the context of his or her society's economic system depends markedly upon the ability to master this psychosocial crisis.

IV School Age: Industry versus Inferiority—Competency

The fourth psychosocial period occurs from about six to eleven years of age ("school age"). This is the period classical psychoanalysis describes as latency.

Here for the first time the child is expected to learn the rudimentary skills of the culture via formal education (i.e., reading, writing, cooperating with others in structured activities). This period of life is associated with the child's increased capability of deductive reasoning, self-discipline, and relating with peers according to prescribed rules. For example, it is not until this age that children can participate in "take-turn" games that demand compliance to elaborately structured rules. The child's love for the parent of the opposite sex and rivalry with the same sexed parent are typically sublimated and expressed by an intense desire to learn and to be productive.

In primitive cultures, Erikson notes, the education of children is uncomplicated and socially pragmatic. The facility to handle utensils, tools, weapons, and other objects is directly related to the child's future role as an adult. Conversely, in cultures where there is a written language, children are first educated in the tools of literacy which, in time, enable them to master the complex skills demanded by various occupations and activities. In effect, although the kind of instruction offered children will vary with the culture, children do become sensitized to the technological ethos of their culture and their identity with it.

According to Erikson, children develop a sense of industry when they begin to comprehend the technology of their culture through attending school. The term "industry" characterizes the major developmental theme of this period because children are now preoccupied with the manner in which things are made and operate. Such interest is reinforced and facilitated by the people in their neighborhoods and schools who introduce them to the "technological elements" of the social world by teaching and working with them. The child's ego identity is now "I am what I learn."

The danger of this stage lies in the potential development of a sense of inferiority or incompetency. For example, if children doubt their skill or status among their peers, they may be discouraged from pursuing further learning (attitudes toward teachers and learning are established during this period). A sense of inferiority may also develop if children discover that their sex, race, religion, or—socioeconomic status—rather than their own skill and motivation—is what determines their worth as persons.

As noted above, the child's feeling of competency and industry is, at least in literate cultures, largely affected by his or her educational achievement. Erikson perceives a possible negative value resulting from this limited definition of success. To be specific, if children accept scholastic accomplishment or work as the only standard by which to judge their self-worth, they may become mere slaves to their culture's work force and to its established role hierarchy (Karl Marx described such persons as submitting to "craft-idiocy"). Therefore, a genuine sense of industry involves more than simply one's educational achievements and occupational aspirations. For Erikson, industry includes a feeling of being interpersonally competent—the confidence that one can exert positive influence on the social world in quest of meaningful individual and social goals. The psychosocial strength of competency thus underlies the basis for participation in the social-economic-political order.

V Adolescence: Ego Identity versus Role Confusion—Fidelity

Adolescence, the focus of the fifth stage in Erikson's chart of the life cycle, is regarded as highly significant in the individual's psychosocial development. No longer a child but not yet an adult (roughly the ages twelve or thirteen to about twenty in our society), the adolescent is confronted with various social demands and role changes that are essential for meeting the challenges of adulthood. In fact, Erikson's theoretical interest in adolescence and the problems accompanying it have led him to present a more elaborate analysis of this phase than of any other stage of development.

Erikson theorizes that the new psychosocial dimension which appears during adolescence has a sense of ego identity at the positive end and a sense of role confusion at the negative end. The crisis confronting adolescents is to consolidate all the knowledge they have gained about themselves (as sons or daughters, students, athletes, musicians, choirboys, Girl Scouts, etc.) and integrate these various self-images into a personal identity that shows aware-ness of a past and of a future that follows logically from it. Erikson stresses the psychosocial nature of ego identity, with the focus not on conflicts between psychic structures but rather on a conflict within the ego itself, namely, of identity versus role confusion. Emphasis is placed on the ego and the way it is affected by society, particularly peer groups. Ego identity can therefore be defined as follows:

> The growing and developing youths, faced with this physiological revolution within them, are now primarily concerned with attempts at consolidating their social roles. They are sometimes morbidly, often curiously, preoccupied with what they appear to be in the eyes of others as compared with what they feel they are and with the question of how to connect the earlier cultivated roles and skills with the ideal prototypes of the day. . . . The integration now taking place in the form of ego identity is more than the sum of the childhood identifications. It is the inner capital accrued from all those experiences of each successive stage, when successful identifications led to a successful alignment of the individual's basic drives with his endowment and his opportunities. The sense of ego identity, then, is the accrued confidence that one's ability to maintain inner sameness and continuity (one's ego in the psychological sense) is matched by the sameness and continuity of one's meaning for others (Erikson, 1963a, p. 261).

Erikson's definition reveals three elements involved in the formation of an identity. First, individuals must perceive themselves as having "inner sameness and continuity"; i.e., they must, over time, experience themselves as essentially the same persons they have been. Second, the persons in one's social milieu must also perceive a "sameness and continuity" in the individual. This means that adolescents need confidence that the inner unity that they have developed earlier will be recognized in others' perceptions of them. Insofar as adolescents may be uncertain about their self-concepts and social images, feelings of doubt, confusion, and apathy may counteract their emerging sense of identity. And finally, individuals must have "accrued confidence" in the correspondence between the internal and external lines of continuity. Their self-perceptions must be validated by appropriate feedback from their interpersonal experiences.

Socially and emotionally, the maturation of the adolescent encompasses several other dimensions as well. Adolescents are capable of developing many new ways of appraising and evaluating the world and their relationship to it. They can conceive of ideal families, religions, philosophies, and societies which, in turn, they can compare and contrast with the imperfect persons and institutions of their own limited experience. To quote Erikson: "The adolescent mind becomes an ideological mind in search of an inspiring unification of ideas (1968b, p. 290)." Thus, a "diffusion of ideals" results from the failure to find enduring values in one's culture, religion, or ideology. The person who suffers from identity diffusion has neither reevaluated past beliefs nor achieved a resolution that leaves him free to act.

Finally, an appropriate adult sex role is essential for the development of a sense of personal identity. Erikson indicates that where adequate feminine and masculine identifications take place, the personality develops a healthy and harmonious blend of sexually defined qualities. Failure to achieve an appropriate sexual identity frequently results in "bisexual diffusion," thus weakening the identity structure. Where sex identity is unclear, overall ego identity will inevitably be affected.

Erikson claims that the foundation for a successful adolescence and the attainment of an integrated identity originates in early childhood. Above and beyond what adolescents bring with them from childhood, however, the development of a sense of personal identity is significantly affected by the social groups with which they identify. Erikson has stressed, for example, how overidentification with popular heroes (movie stars, superathletes, revolutionary leaders) or counterculture groups (hippies, "acidheads," delinquents) cuts off a "budding identity" from its milieu, thus stifling the ego and restricting emergent identity. Likewise, ego identity may be harder for certain groups of people to attain than for others. For instance, it may be considerably more difficult for a young woman to arrive at a firm sense of identity in a society where she is accorded second-class citizenship status. In Erikson's view, the women's liberation movement has attracted many supporters for the very reason that society, until recently, has frustrated their efforts to attain a positive identity (i.e., society has been unwilling to assimilate women into new social and occupational roles). Minority group members are also beset by difficulties in establishing a firm and coherent sense of identity (Erikson, 1964b).

Erikson has also considered the adolescent's vulnerability to the stresses of rapid social, political, and technological change as a factor which may jeopardize the development of identity. Such change, exacerbated by the information explosion, contributes to a nebulous sense of uncertainty and discontinuity. It also threatens to break down many traditional and cherished values which young people have learned and experienced as children. The gap between generations reflects at least some of this generalized dissatisfaction with the values of society, perhaps best illustrated by the recent turmoil on college campuses throughout the country. The truths of one generation become the myths of the next. Accordingly, Erikson interprets much of the social action movement of youth as an attempt to establish some continuity between past, present, and future—a search for identity.

The failure of the young person to develop a personal identity, because of either unfortunate childhood experiences or present social circumstances, results in what Erikson has called the "identity crisis." The crisis of identity (role confusion) most often is characterized by an inability to select a career or pursue further education. Many adolescents who are in the throes of this age-specific conflict experience a profound sense of futility, personal disorganization, and aimlessness. They feel inadequate, depersonalized, alienated, and sometimes even seek "negative identity," an identity which is opposite to the one prescribed for them by their parents and peers. Some delinquent behavior is interpreted by Erikson in this way. However, the failure to establish adequate personal identity does not necessarily doom the adolescent to a life of perpetual defeat. Perhaps more than any other personologist treated in this text, Erikson has emphasized that life is constant change. Resolving problems at one stage of life is no guarantee against the reappearance of these problems at later stages—or against the discovery of new solutions to them. Ego identity is a lifelong struggle.

Fidelity emerges from adequate resolution of the ego-identity—role-confusion crisis. As used by Erikson, it refers to the adolescent's "ability to sustain loyalties freely pledged in spite of the inevitable contradictions of value systems (1968b, p. 290)." As the cornerstone of identity, fidelity represents the young person's capacity to perceive and to abide by the social mores, ethics, and ideologies of society. Erikson contends that a lack of faith in some ideological system may result in widespread confusion and disrespect for those who govern the systems of social rule.

VI Young Adulthood: Intimacy versus Isolation—Love

Stage six in the life cycle earmarks the formal beginning of adult life. This is roughly the period when the person becomes involved in courtship, marriage, and early family life; it extends from late adolescence until early adulthood (twenty to twenty-four years). During this time, young adults usually orient themselves toward enriching vocations and "settling down." Erikson maintains, as did Freud, that it is only now that the person is genuinely ready for social as well as sexual intimacy with another person. Prior to this time, much of the person's sexual behavior was motivated by the search for ego identity. In contrast, the previous attainment of a sense of personal identity and the involvement in productive work that marks this period gives rise to a new interpersonal dimension of intimacy at the one extreme and isolation at the other.

Erikson's use of the term "intimacy" is multidimensional in meaning and scope. He has in mind the sense of intimacy most of us share with a spouse, friends, brothers and sisters, and parents or other relatives. However, he also speaks of intimacy with oneself, that is, the ability to "fuse your identity with somebody else's without fear that you're going to lose something yourself (Evans, 1967, p. 48)." It is this aspect of intimacy (i.e., merging one's own identity with that of another person) which Erikson sees as essential for the successful establishment of a meaningful marriage. Likewise, he contends that a true sense of intimacy cannot be attained unless the person has already achieved a consolidated personal identity. In other words, to be really intimate with another person or oneself, the person must have already developed a firm sense of who and what he or she is. By contrast, adolescent "falling in love" may be nothing more than an attempt to explore one's own identity through the use of another person. This line of reasoning is quite consistent with the fact that marriages of the young (aged sixteen to nineteen) are not as stable (in terms of divorce statistics) as marriages of those in their twenties. Erikson explains this phenomenon as stemming largely from the fact that many people, especially women, marry someone in order to find their own identity in and through that person. In Erikson's view, it is not possible to attain intimacy by seeking for one's identity in this fashion.

Erikson's description of one who is capable of intimacy closely resembles Freud's definition of the healthy person, namely one who has the ability to love and to work. Although Erikson does not feel that this formula can be improved upon, it is intriguing to consider the question of whether (in Erikson's scheme) a celibate is capable of developing a sense of intimacy. The answer is yes, since Erikson believes that intimacy involves more than just sexuality; it may also include the deep relationship between friends or, in the broader sense, a commitment to one's fellow human beings.

The chief danger of this psychosocial stage is self-absorption or the avoidance of interpersonal relationships which commit one to intimacy and social involvement. The inability to enter into comfortable and intimate personal relationships leads to feelings of social emptiness and isolation. Such people may seek interpersonal encounters which are purely formal (employer-employee) and superficial (bridge clubs). They insulate themselves against any type of real involvement because they are threatened by the demands of intimacy. Self-absorbed persons are also likely to have attitudes of futility and alienation regarding their vocations. Finally, Erikson believes that social conditions (e.g., difficulty in achieving intimacy in an urbanized, mobile, impersonal, technological society) may hinder the establishment of a sense of intimacy. In cases of extreme isolation, he cites examples of "character disorders" or psychopathic personality types who manipulate and exploit others without feeling remorse. These are the young adults whose inability to share their identities with others makes it impossible for them to enter into intense and long-term relationships.

Healthy resolution of the intimacy versus isolation crisis produces the psychosocial strength of *love*. In addition to its romantic and erotic qualities, Erikson regards love as the ability to commit oneself to others and abide by such commitments, even though they may require self-denial and compromise. This type of love is expressed when the person shows an attitude of care, respect, and responsibility toward another.

VII Middle Adulthood: Generativity versus Stagnation—Care

Stage seven in the Eriksonian scheme corresponds to the middle years of life (twenty-five to sixty-five years) and encompasses what Erikson describes as either generativity or stagnation. Generativity occurs when a person begins to show concern not only for the welfare of the next generation but also for the nature of the society in which that generation will live and work. He contends that each adult must either accept or reject the challenge of assuming responsibility for the continuation and betterment of whatever is instrumental to the maintenance and enhancement of the culture. This conviction is based on Erikson's belief that evolutionary development has "made man the teaching and instituting as well as the learning animal (1968b, p. 291)." Generativity, then, represents the older generation's concern in establishing and guiding those who will replace them. It is best exemplified by the sense of personal fulfillment associated with the production, rearing, and subsequent achievements of one's offspring. However, generativity resides not only in parents but also in those who contribute to the betterment of young people. The creative and productive elements of generativity are personified in everything that is passed on from one generation to the next, e.g., technological products, ideas, books, and works of art. An ultimate concern for the welfare of humanity embodies the developmental theme of this second phase of adulthood. As Erikson puts it, the new generation depends on the adults and the adults depend on the young (1968b).

From the psychosocial crisis of generativity emerges the strength of *care*. As Erikson sees it, care stems from the feeling that something or someone matters; it is the psychological opposite of apathy. Those who fail to establish a sense of generativity slip into a state of self-absorption in which their personal needs and comforts are of dominant concern. These are the persons who don't care for anyone or anything except that which nourishes their self-indulgence.

Lacking generativity, such persons cease to function as productive members of society, live only to satisfy their needs, and are interpersonally impoverished. This is commonly known as the "crisis of middle age"—the person has a sense of hopelessness and tends to feel that life is meaningless.

VIII   Maturity: Ego Integrity versus Despair—Wisdom

The final stage in the epigenetic chart marks the period when individuals reflect upon their nearly complete efforts and achievements. In practically all cultures this period signals the onset of old age, a time often beset with numerous demands: adjustments to deterioration of physical strength and health, to retirement and reduced income, to the death of spouse and close friends, and the need to establish new affiliations with one's age group. During this period, there is also a definite shift in a person's attention from future to past life.

According to Erikson, this final phase of adulthood is not so much marked by the appearance of a new psychosocial crisis but rather by the summation, integration, and evaluation of all the preceding stages of ego development:

> Only in him who in some way has taken care of things and people and who has adapted himself to the triumphs and disappointments adherent to being, the originator of others or the generator of products and ideas—only in him may gradually ripen the fruit of these seven stages—I know no better word for it than ego integrity (Erikson, 1963a, p. 268).

The sense of ego integrity thus arises from the individual's ability to glance back on his or her life in full perspective (including marriage, children or grandchildren, job, accomplishments, hobbies, social relationships) and humbly but assuredly affirm "I am satisfied." Death is no longer feared, since such persons see their own existence as continuing through either their offspring or creative accomplishments. Erikson also believes that only in old age does true maturity and a practical sense of the "wisdom of the ages" come into being, provided that the person is so "gifted." At the same time, he notes that "the wisdom of old age remains aware of the relativity of all knowledge acquired in one lifetime in one historical period. Wisdom is a detached and yet active concern with life in the face of death (1968b, pp. 291–292)."

At the other extreme are the individuals who regard their lives as a series of unfulfilled opportunities and missed directions. Now, in the sunset years, they realize that it is far too late to start over again. The lack or loss of ego integration in such a person is earmarked by a hidden dread of death, a feeling of irrevocable failure, and an incessant preoccupation with what "might have been." Alternately, Erikson observes that there are two prevailing moods in the embittered and disgusted old person—regret that life cannot be lived over again and rejection of one's shortcomings and deficiencies by projecting them onto the outside world. At times, Erikson is poetic in his description of despair in the old person:

> . . . fate is not accepted as the frame of life, death not as its finite boundary. Despair indicates that time is too short for alternate roads to integrity: this is why the old try to "doctor" their memories (1968b, p. 291).

In cases of severe psychopathology, Erikson suggests that bitterness and remorse may lead the old person to become senile, depressed, hypochondriacal, and intensely spiteful and paranoid. Fear of being placed in an institution is common among such individuals.

Now that we have concluded a description of the eight stages of ego development, reflection upon what they offer in the way of new perspectives is in order. First, Erikson has formulated a theory in which the roles of society and of persons themselves are accorded equal emphasis with respect to the development and organization of personality. This perspective, in turn, has enabled those in the helping professions to look upon the problems of adults as—at least to some extent—failures to adequately resolve genuine adult personality crises, rather than to see them merely as residual effects of early childhood frustrations and conflicts. Second, Erikson has been sensitive to the age of adolescence, a period largely ignored by Freud, regarding this period as pivotal in the formation of the person's psychological and social well-being. Finally, Erikson has stimulated a sense of optimism by demonstrating that each stage of psychosocial growth has the potential for both strength and weakness, so that failure at one stage of development does not necessarily indicate doom at a later stage. Let us now consider Erikson's position concerning the eight basic assumptions of man's nature.

ERIKSON'S BASIC ASSUMPTIONS CONCERNING HUMAN NATURE

Robert Coles, in a biographical account of Erikson's work, observed that "When a man builds on another man's work, as Erikson has on Freud's, he does not always have to repeat his predecessor's every single tenet or assumption (1970, p.xx)." Erikson's assumptions about man do in fact differ from those of Freud. His positions on the basic assumptions concerning human nature, discussed below, are depicted in Figure 3-2.

Freedom	_ _ _ _ _ _ _ _ ✓ _ _ _	Determinism
Rationality	_ _ ✓ _ _ _ _ _ _ _ _	Irrationality
Holism	✓ _ _ _ _ _ _ _ _ _ _	Elementalism .
Constitutionalism	_ _ _ _ _ _ _ _ ✓ _	Environmentalism
Subjectivity	_ _ _ _ _ _ _ ✓ _ _ _	Objectivity
Proactivity	_ _ ✓ _ _ _ _ _ _ _ _	Reactivity
Homeostasis	_ _ _ _ _ _ _ _ ✓ _ _	Heterostasis
Knowability	_ _ _ ✓ _ _ _ _ _ _ _	Unknowability

Figure 3-2 Erikson's position on the eight basic assumptions concerning human nature.

1 Freedom–Determinism   In Erikson's view, human behavior is primarily determined. Biological maturation interacting with the individual's expanding social radius produces a rich–complexity of behavioral determinants. Parental treatment, school experiences, peer groups, and differential cultural opportunities all play a powerful role in charting the course of one's life. In fact, the outcomes of the first four stages of psychosocial development are practically fixed by these types of environmental forces, whereas resolutions of the crises associated with the remaining four stages are less dependent upon such external factors. Erikson believes that each person, especially during the latter four developmental stages, has some capacity to resolve earlier and present crises. Thus, there is some acknowledgment of freedom in Erikson's theory; individuals, to this extent, are held responsible for their successes and failures.

Although he accepts the id as the biological foundation of personality, Erikson's less than complete commitment to determinism is reflected in his theoretical preoccupation with ego development. Erikson regards the ego as an autonomous personality structure that is particularly prone to alteration from adolescence onward. Unlike Freud, he does not believe that personality is utterly fixed by experiences in childhood. The choices of adults, however, are always restricted by the ever-present effects of childhood experiences. For example, it is difficult to achieve intimacy in young adulthood without a previously developed sense of basic trust. When Erikson's total theory is placed on the freedom–determinism scale, determinism is accorded more weight.

2 Rationality–Irrationality   The mixture of rationality and irrationality in Eriksonian man appears to contain considerably more of the former. Erikson's primary theoretical concern, the psychosocial development of the autonomous ego, reveals his abiding commitment to the importance of rationality, since reasoning processes are such an integral part of ego functioning. Such processes are most evident in the individual's attempts to resolve the latter four psychosocial crises in Erikson's theory.

Along with other "ego psychologists" in the psychoanalytic movement, Erikson feels that such an emphasis upon rationality was lacking in Freud's account of human behavior. His theory thus represents an important effort to extend the Freudian view of man. However, as Erikson has often noted, he is clearly within the orthodox psychoanalytic tradition and, as such, accepts Freud's basic theoretical concepts: e.g., the biological and sexual foundations of personality, the structural model (id, ego, superego). Within the psychoanalytic framework, Erikson helped to move the emphasis toward ego and rationality. Erikson invests people with a much larger measure of rationality than did Freud.

3 Holism–Elementalism   Erikson's strong commitment to a holistic conception of persons is clearly evident in the essence of his theory, the eight stages of man. To be understood, human beings must be viewed as developing totalities. Individuals are depicted as moving through eight broad stages of psychosocial development; while doing so, they are attempting to resolve crises of the most profound nature—e.g., ego identity, ego integrity—and always within the matrix of highly complex individual, cultural, and historical forces.

Consider, for example, the holistic theme underlying just the two concepts of ego identity (adolescence) and ego integrity (maturity and old age). In the former, persons are seen as expending many years in discovering who they are and developing a stable sense of continuity between past and future. Specific elements of adolescent behavior can only be fully understood when interpreted within the total gestalt of the ego-identity versus role-confusion crisis. During the period of maturity and old age, the person attempts to grasp his or her life as a totality, to see meaning in it, and to view it in perspective. Old-age-related behaviors are understood within the holistic framework of the ego-integrity versus despair crisis. In Erikson's epigenetic conception, then, an individual's personality can be understood only with reference to his or her entire life cycle as it is lived within the context of complex and interacting environmental forces.

4 Constitutionalism–Environmentalism Erikson's tendency toward environmentalism is revealed in his strong emphasis upon parental, cultural, and historical factors in personality development. The individual must be understood in the context of these environmental influences. The degree to which persons resolve their early psychosocial crises is largely determined by parental treatment; child-rearing practices, in turn, are significantly influenced by cultural and historical factors. Resolution of subsequent psychosocial crises is a function of the individual's interaction with cultural opportunities. Erikson's environmentalism, then, is quite broad in scope. However, his environmentalist commitment is somewhat less than entire since he accepts Freud's emphasis upon the biological, instinctual basis of personality.

5 Subjectivity–Objectivity The major theoretical concepts employed by Erikson in describing psychosocial growth—e.g., trust, mistrust, hope, etc.—refer to significant subjective experiential states. Furthermore, each individual's capacity to deal with a given psychosocial crisis depends considerably upon his or her unique resolutions of former crises. However, the crises themselves are evoked by biological maturation interacting with an expanding social world. Biological maturation is not unique to an individual, and such maturation is seen by Erikson as constantly interacting with objective, external factors (e.g., parental treatment). In this sense, psychosocial stages and crises are objectively determined, strongly suggesting that Erikson leans somewhat toward the assumption of objectivity.

6 Proactivity–Reactivity From largely reactive developmental beginnings, Eriksonian man becomes progressively more proactive over time, with the unfolding of each successive psychosocial stage. In fact, successful resolution of the first four crises (hope, will power, purpose, competence) is a prelude to proactive functioning in subsequent life stages. During these earlier periods, however, the biological maturation level of persons limits the part that they can play in generating their own behavior.

By way of contrast, Erikson's descriptions of the stages from adolescence to old age clearly convey the idea that people are capable of internally generating their behavior. Concepts such as the search for an adequate sense of ego identity, intimacy, generativity, and ego integrity are best understood from a proactive frame of reference. In Erikson's scheme, then, individuals are primarily proactive for most of their lives. Throughout the life stages, however, the course of human development is seen largely in terms of reactions to biological, social, and historical realities; in this broad sense, there is some acknowledgment of reactivity in Erikson's view of human nature.

7 Homeostasis–Heterostasis In Erikson's theory, human beings are depicted as constantly challenged by psychosocial crises, each of which is potentially conducive to growth and mastery over the world. As persons successfully resolve one crisis, they move on to the next. There is an unmistakable sense of forward movement in Erikson's portrayal of human development that clearly suggests a heterostatic view of motivation at its base. It is man's nature that he must grow and attempt to meet the different challenges of each developmental stage.

A further suggestion of Erikson's heterostatic commitment is the fact that successful resolution of each psychosocial crisis allows the person more opportunity for growth and self-fulfillment. Consider, for example, that the entire adult stage (approximately forty years of life) is described in terms of generativity versus stagnation. The use of such concepts reflects the intimate relationship between personal growth and healthy development in Erikson's system. However, Erikson's tendency toward heterostasis is tempered by his acceptance of the biological-instinctual basis of personality proposed by Freud. Eriksonian man seeks to grow—but only within the constraints imposed by the instinctual roots of his development.

8 Knowability–Unknowability While Erikson has adopted several traditional psychoanalytic concepts of personality, he has also developed new ones by resorting to various clinical, anthropological, and psychohistorical research strategies. Some commitment to the ultimate knowability of human nature is suggested by his significant effort to develop a comprehensive account of the human life cycle. However, Erikson's reliance upon multidisciplinary approaches outside of "hard core" science coupled with his lack of a single, rigorous scientific means of researching personality suggests a less than complete commitment to man's knowability through science. When compared with Freud, Erikson seems less convinced of the all-importance of science for understanding human nature.

Erikson, then, has not repeated his predecessor's every single assumption.

It is again worth noting that the uniqueness of Erikson's theory, like that of each major personality theorist, depends markedly upon his unique set of assumptions concerning the nature of human beings. Let us now turn to some illustrative research that has been engendered by Erikson's theory.

EMPIRICAL VALIDATION OF PSYCHOSOCIAL CONCEPTS

Although Erikson's theory has gained prominence in both clinical and academic settings, research efforts toward testing it have been sparse. In part, the paucity of systematic research bearing on Erikson's position may reflect the fact that he has yet to outline his conception of how psychosocial constructs should be examined within an empirical framework. Erikson admits that his own conceptions of personality may not be directly amenable to experimental verification: "Maybe my formulations of a series of interlocking stages, based as it is on clinical and developmental observations, does not lend itself easily to . . . empirical validation (1972, personal communication)." Furthermore, he does not believe that a theorist has the exclusive responsibility of showing the experimental personologist how to study theoretical concepts.

Occasionally, one will come across a study which attempts to explain a set of findings by reference to the conceptual perspective of psychosocial theory. Such post hoc interpretation, however, adds little to the goal of ascertaining the empirical validity of Erikson's descriptions of the eight ages of man. Another difficulty stems from the fact that psychosocial theory represents a strong developmental orientation (Ciaccio, 1971). This has tended to minimize the personologist's interest in evaluating several of the psychosocial stages since a developmental perspective is considered inadequate by some investigators with respect to the goal of understanding adult behavior.

In a more positive vein, certain concepts of psychosocial theory are quite amenable to rigorous investigation. For instance, Erikson has established the criteria for psychosocial health and ill health for each crisis period in terms of well-defined behavioral characteristics. Such well-formulated descriptions constitute a definite advantage over psychoanalytic theories which attempt to reconstruct the individual's previous life history, since they allow for the direct study of the resolution of earlier crisis periods through currently manifested behaviors and attitudes. The theory also seems to lend itself to empirical test inasmuch as it deals with the social dimensions of development as opposed to theories which focus on the intrapsychic nature of personality. Hypothetical internal factors are often more difficult to study than observable social behavior. Finally, Erikson has achieved an orderly sequential account of the relevant psychosocial phenomena of personal development, whereas other theorists often lack this longitudinal synthesis of developmental problems. Until carefully planned studies are brought to fruition, however, the empirical status and developmental implications of Erikson's theory remain obscure.

In this section, discussion of research illustrations of psychosocial theory will be confined to the period of ego identity versus role confusion. Our selection of the three representative studies reported below reflects the fact that the majority of studies published to date, sparse in number as they are, deal almost exclusively with this phase of Erikson's comprehensive account of human development.

Research on Ego Identity versus Role Confusion

As has been noted, Erikson (1968a) devotes more theoretical attention to the period of adolescence than any other psychosocial stage in his epigenetic conception of the life cycle. His main thesis is that adolescence is a period during which individuals are deeply involved in a process of self-definition, a process frequently accompanied by increased tension and anxiety. Accordingly, reappraisal of personal assets, social goals, and interpersonal ideals defines the central task confronting the adolescent.

In one of the first studies in this area, Bronson (1959) attempted to demonstrate empirical support for the existence of four personal characteristics presumably associated with a sense of role confusion. Specifically, he hypothesized that persons with a firm sense of identity as contrasted with those in a state of identity diffusion will (1) be more certain about the relationship between their past and present notions of themselves, (2) have a lower degree of internal tension and anxiety, (3) be more certain about the existence of their dominant personal characteristics, and (4) be more stable over time in their feelings about themselves. Bronson reasoned that significant positive intercorrelations among these four individual characteristics would empirically substantiate Erikson's clinical descriptions of the fifth stage of man.

To test these hypotheses, Bronson had forty-six upper-division college students (the majority of whom were females between nineteen and twenty-two years of age) serve as subjects. He felt that there would be sufficient variation in degree of identity diffusion within this age group so as to permit the clear emergence of the hypothesized relationships. The first two characteristics (continuity with the past and degree of tension or anxiety) were assessed on the basis of ratings of the behavior of eighteen randomly selected subjects during a twenty-minute semistructured interview conducted by the same interviewer. The interview probed such areas as subject's self-evaluation, aspirations and ideals, relations with other people, and childhood, peer, and parent relationships. The interviews were tape-recorded and later submitted to three clinically experienced psychologists for rating, the average of their ratings on a six-point scale being used as measures on these two characteristics. The judges were instructed to rate continuity with the past in terms of whether or not the subject's "conscious evaluation of himself seems to have evolved as an integrated expression of past experiences (Bronson, 1959, p. 415)." Degree of tension or anxiety was rated in terms of the amount of anxiety implicit in the interview material, the judges being told: "This refers not only to manifestations of subjectively experienced anxiety but to the over-all level of tension or conflict inferred to be present in the personality structure of the individual

(Bronson, 1959, p. 415)." High ratings on these measures represented judgments of low "continuity with the past" and high "degree of anxiety," respectively.

In order to assess the final two characteristics (certainty of dominant personal attributes and temporal stability of self-conceptions), subjects were directed to complete an adaptation of the semantic differential. The semantic differential provides ratings of the meaning of concepts (e.g., persons, events, and objects). The rater is given a stimulus word like "teacher," "Vietnam," or "football" and is instructed to rate the word on a series of seven-point, bipolar adjective scales. The bipolar adjectives, such as "weak-strong" or "hot-cold," define the end point of each scale. In Bronson's study, the task consisted of having all forty-six subjects give self-descriptions on a series of five-point scales for a set of fifteen concepts representative of a broad range of salient characteristics of self-conception. Included were such concepts as forcefulness, kindness, rebellion, bitterness, sympathy, competence, and cooperativeness. Four weeks later, the subjects rated the same characteristics again in order that the stability or fluctuation implicit in the fourth hypothesis could be examined.

The results, computed in the form of product-moment correlations among the four measures, are presented in Table 3-1.

Table 3-1   Correlations among Measures Relating to Aspects of Identity Diffusion*

	1	2	3	4
	Continuity with past	Freedom from anxiety	Certainty of self-conception	Temporal stability of self-rating
1 Continuity with the past (interview rating)	—			
2 Freedom from anxiety (interview rating)	.59‡	—		
3 Certainty of self-conception (semantic differential measure)	.71‡	.47†	—	
4 Temporal stability of self-rating (semantic differential measure)	.53†	.47†	.54‡	—

Source: Bronson, 1959.
*Note: $N = 18$ for the correlations involving the interview measures; $N = 46$ for the remaining value.
†$p < .05$, two-tailed test.
‡$p < .01$, two-tailed test.

As can be seen from Table 3-1, all relationships are statistically significant in the expected directions. Hence, Bronson's study, consistent with Erikson's theory, demonstrates that those adolescents who are judged on the basis of interview material as having a stable foundation for their currently held self-conceptions (measure 1) also tend to be more free of anxiety (measure 2), show greater certainty about the dominant characteristics of self (measure 3), and tend to be more consistent in their feelings about themselves through time (measure 4). In a word, these adolescents manifest a sense of ego identity. The opposite characteristics would describe subjects high in identity diffusion. Taken collectively, results reported by Bronson indicate that Erikson's concept of identity crisis is a measurable parameter of personality development.

In describing the various elements of ego-identity development, Erikson has explained how either weak identification or over-identification with the same-sexed parent may be detrimental to the young person's psychosocial adjustment. Dignan (1965) predicted that, for females, "ego identity is weak with poor maternal identification, strong with good maternal identification, and poor again with over-identification which borders on the pathological (pp. 477–378)." In this study, 182 college freshman and sophomore female students and their mothers served as subjects. Two test instruments were developed to provide indices of ego identity and maternal identification, respectively. The first instrument, labeled "The Ego-Identity Scale" by Dignan, consisted of fifty true-false statements constructed on the basis of the writings of Erikson and others who have critically examined and developed the construct of ego identity. This scale tapped seven different areas relevant to a sense of ego identity: (1) sense of self, (2) uniqueness, (3) self-acceptance, (4) role expectations, (5) stability, (6) goal-directedness, and (7) interpersonal relations. Two sample items of this scale are: "I know I'm not perfect but I prefer to be as I am" (self-acceptance) and "People seldom mistake me for another girl" (uniqueness). The measure of maternal identification, based on a semantic differential instrument, consisted of having both the students and their mothers rate ten concepts (e.g., myself, father, mother) on a series of nine bipolar adjective scales (e.g., happy-sad; rugged-delicate; hot-cold). In a single testing session, all students completed the ego-identity scale and rated the ten concepts according to standard instructions (i.e., self-evaluation). During this session the students also rated the same semantic differential concepts as they believed their mothers would do it. Mothers of the subjects received, completed, and returned the semantic differential instrument by mail. Two measures of maternal identification, assumed similarity and real similarity, were derived from the semantic differential ratings. Assumed similarity was determined by comparing the degree to which the student rated her mother as being similar to herself, whereas real similarity was based upon the degree of actual similarity between the student's self-ratings and the mother's self-ratings.

The results of this study are presented in Figure 3-3. The hypothesis that

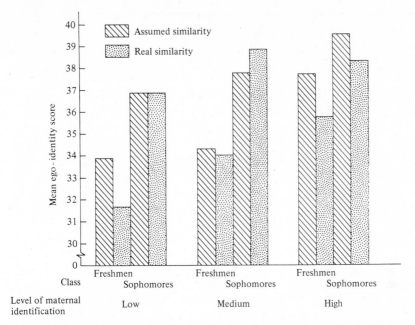

Figure 3-3 Mean ego-identity scores as a function of three levels and two measures of maternal identification and two levels of class standing. Note: —*N* = 20 for ego-identity scores based on assumed similarity; *N* = 15 for ego-identity scores based on real similarity. *(Adapted from Dignan, 1965.)*

ego identity would be positively related to maternal identification was statistically supported when analyzed in terms of the assumed similarity measure. A similar trend was found by Dignan for ego-identity scores and real similarity, although the relationship failed to reach statistical significance. Accordingly, Dignan concluded: "These findings suggest that identity formation is more closely related to the girl's subjective experience of mother-daughter similarity than to any objective likeness of thought between them (p. 482)."

In a unique study, Waterman, Beubel, and Waterman (1970) provided additional evidence for the empirical adequacy of Erikson's concept of "identity crisis." Basing their study on the epigenetic principle, these investigators reasoned that the degree of success in resolving the identity crisis should be positively correlated with levels of the previously developed ego components: basic trust, autonomy, initiative, and industry. In the first part of the study, an interview technique devised by Marcia (1966) was used to assess level of ego identity. The interviews, taped and scored independently by at least two judges, included questions pertaining to the subject's occupational choice and the nature and content of his political belief system. The questions elicited information concerning the presence or absence of a crisis in each of these areas, in addition to determining the subject's degree of commitment to his ideas. Ninety-two male freshmen at a private college served as subjects.

Rotter's (1966) "Internal-External Locus of Control" scale was used to measure the subjects' degree of autonomy. This scale indicates the extent to which an individual believes that events are under his control (i.e., internality) as opposed to the belief that events are determined by factors such as fate, chance, powerful others, and the complexity of the social world (i.e., externality). As a measure of basic trust, subjects completed Rotter's (1967) "Interpersonal Trust" scale, a measure of the extent to which others can be relied upon. It was predicted that subjects with high developmental levels of ego identity would have higher scores on the "Internal-External Control" scale (greater internality) and show a greater degree of interpersonal trust than subjects with developmentally lower ego-identity statuses. Based on interview protocols, subjects were assigned to high, mixed, or low identity levels, depending on their judged level of ego-identity development. As hypothesized, subjects high on ego identity showed the greatest degree of internal control (autonomy), while subjects low on ego identity were the least internal. However, no support was found for the predicted relationship between level of ego identity and degree of basic trust. In the second part of their study, Waterman et al. tested the same relationships derived from the epigenetic principle, except that this time measures of psychosocial development specifically constructed within an Eriksonian framework were used. Eighty-seven male college students were administered a series of self-report scales constructed to measure both successful and unsuccessful resolutions of the first five psychosocial stages. It was predicted that scores on the ego-identity scale would be positively correlated with scores for basic trust, autonomy, initiative, and industry. Consistent with Erikson's theory, all correlations were significant in the expected direction (r's ranged between +.43 for identity-basic trust and +.24 for identity-industry). Collectively, the findings reported by Waterman et al. support the Eriksonian hypothesis that successful coping with the identity crisis is related to positive outcomes of the previous psychosocial crises.

Although Erikson's psychosocial stages are clearly delineated, his theorizing has hardly provoked much research. The studies described above represent an attempt at empirical analysis and should prove helpful in encouraging personologists to conduct more rigorous research on psychosocial theory.

APPLICATION: ADOLESCENCE IN AMERICA OR "WHO AM I?"

Erikson has applied his theoretical views to such fascinating and diverse topics as children's play behaviors (1937), childhood in American Indian tribes (1945), juvenile delinquency (1957), identity problems of black youth (1964b), dissent in contemporary youth (1970a), and various historical personages such as Luther (1958), Hitler (1963a), Gandhi (1969), and Jefferson (1974). In particular, he has stressed various social-emotional experiences influencing adolescent personality development in American society. More than any other personologist, Erikson is credited with elaborating the concept of "ego identity" and establishing a place for it in current studies of the adolescent personality.

There is no dearth of published material on adolescence today. Young persons who want to know why they think, feel, or do what they do can find a wide variety of "answers" offered in numerous books, newspaper articles, magazines, and TV discussion programs. Along with other professionals, psychologists have contributed to this burgeoning wealth of information by proposing theories and concepts that highlight specific dimensions of adolescent experience and also illuminate the general psychological significance of this life stage. Examples range from G. Stanley Hall's historical biogenetic view of the "storm and stress" aspects, through Otto Rank's emphasis on the need for independence, to the cultural relativism proposed by the anthropologists Margaret Mead and Ruth Benedict (Muuss, 1962). Erikson, however, seems to identify, capture, and articulate an essential element that all others have missed.

From Erikson's viewpoint, the fundamental question confronting the adolescent is "Who am I?" More abstractly, the young person must develop a sense of personal identity, of stable selfhood, so that experienced past and anticipated future are meaningfully connected. In a rigidly patterned culture (e.g., Chinese) with many prescribed social roles, such identity problems are minimized since there are relatively few options available. By comparison, American society offers a much wider latitude of potential life-styles to its young people—consequently, American adolescents are more vulnerable to identity problems precisely because they have more options. According to Erikson's perspective, it is the democratic system in America that poses special problems in this regard since democracy requires "self-made identities." In American society, then, young people bear considerable individual responsibility for defining who and what they are.

When democracy is coupled with the technological sophistication of our social world, identity crises are further intensified. Our technology demands an extended period of formal education—in primitive cultures, one can become a witch doctor by heredity alone; in America, it takes years of study to become a psychiatrist or clinical psychologist. Such prolonged education, often involving financial dependence upon parents during college years, markedly extends adolescence. Further, considering the exceedingly rapid social change in which basic values and norms are continually questioned (Toffler, 1970), the young person's identity problems become immeasurably more complicated. American adolescents have not only more time to search for their identities but also more alternatives from which to select.

Five major areas of contemporary American adolescent behavior that can be interpreted, at least in part, as manifestations of the identity crisis are discussed below. They are (1) the problem of vocational choice, (2) conflict with parents, (3) peer-group membership, (4) love relationships, and (5) drug usage.

1 The Problem of Vocational Choice   Erikson believes that the inability to settle on an occupational identity is a source of great concern to many young people. Simply stated, the adolescent must define who he or she *is* before a decision on what he or she wishes to become is possible. Since different life-styles accompany different occupations in our society, selecting a vocation is, in reality, selecting a whole way of life. To make a wise choice, people must have an accurate view of themselves as well as a reasonably good estimate of where they might best "fit" in the occupational world. In the final analysis, an individual's vocational choice may well represent a definition and expression of the kind of person that he or she wishes to become (Ziegler, 1973).

Adolescent vocational indecision, then, often reflects a more fundamental indecisiveness about personal identity. This is especially true for young women who, because of their biological potential for bearing children, are faced with the choice of wife and mother roles versus other career goals (or some combination of the two). Some women who opt for the former may eventually believe they have no ego identity apart from their marital role. Because traditional society has dictated passive acceptance of "feminine" values and aspirations, it is the adolescent women of the activist 1970s who experience significant vocational conflicts in the struggle for identity achievement. By the same token, males are subjected to intense pressures to select an occupational career and are more susceptible to the potential disruptive effects of competing for lucrative jobs. A sense of integrity and personal worth often hangs in the balance.

2 Conflict with Parents   One need not study personality theory to know that parents often resist or try to curtail independence in their adolescents. A typical example would be the case of the sixteen-year-old whose father vetoes his Saturday evening request for the family car (both knowing that the car will be in the garage anyway at that time). In this situation, the adolescent may feel or say "Look, damn it, I'm no longer the kid whose diapers you used to change and whose nose you used to wipe—I'm a *person* in my own right and I expect to be treated as such!"

Underlying many superficially different conflicts of this type is the adolescents' feeling that their parents simply do not recognize their individuality. Thus, they will often counteract (i.e., test the limits of their freedom) to prove they are psychologically separate entities. Some rebellion against parental authority and values is often essential if a deeper sense of individuality and self-confidence is to develop. To this end, adolescents must often define and express their ego identity *against* parental standards and expectations, suggesting that some degree of parent-adolescent conflict is inevitable. The outcomes of such conflicts will vary. However, if the adolescent can find a satisfactory path toward an independent identity, then it is likely that serious problems will be avoided. From an Eriksonian perspective, it seems that parents must relinquish their control voluntarily if young persons are to move toward full realization of their unique potentials.

3 Peer-Group Membership Rejecting parents as models in establishing their identity, adolescents often seek in their peers an alternative source of support as they reorganize their conception of themselves. In our culture, peer-group bonds are particularly strong during this period; they often affect the adolescent's values and attitudes more than parents, schools, religious institutions, or any other social influence. Such groups help to reassure individuals at a time when they are undergoing dramatic internal changes. By communicating their own feelings as well as sharing vicariously in the experiences of peers, adolescents are able to cope with otherwise confusing and sometimes frightening situations.

Erikson (1963a) has noted that the cliquishness and uniformity of dress and gestures so often observed in adolescent peer groups are really defenses against identity confusion. If young persons are uncertain about who they are, dressing and acting like their friends provides some sense of internal stability and security. Moreover, wearing apparel, hairstyles, and music serve to symbolize their separateness from parents and the associated adult world. Membership in a peer group also provides for exposure to new and different ideologies—e.g., political, social, economic, and religious. Erikson believes that the appeal that various ideologies and alternative life-styles have for adolescent groups is largely based upon the identity search. In part, they are searching for new personal values to replace childhood rules. Furthermore, learning to believe in and act upon a new set of social values coupled with experimentation and possible rejection of old ideologies can significantly assist the adolescent's emerging sense of identity.

4 Love Relationships Erikson argues that through love relationships adolescents often are able to clarify some of their identity confusion:

> To a considerable extent adolescent love is an attempt to arrive at a definition of one's identity by projecting one's diffuse ego image on another and by seeing it thus reflected and gradually clarified. This is why so much of young love is conversation (1963a, p. 262).

Thus, depending upon the reactions they receive, adolescents may be able to resolve some of their uncertainties. Intimate, understanding love relationships also permit the young person self-expressions that otherwise have no social outlet. Hopes, dreams, aspirations, and ideals can be explored along with disappointments, fears, guilts, and disillusionments. At the same time, such relationships enable young people to learn how to conduct themselves in new situations, explore their sexual conceptions of themselves, experiment with overt sex to some degree, and thus prepare for later, riskier exposures of self in more involved heterosexual activities. Individuals must, according to Erikson, know who they are and who they want to become before they can enter into permanent relationships involving adult responsibilities (e.g., marriage).

5 Drug Usage   The fantastic range of known drugs today makes it clear that there are no simple explanations of the factors which lead to their use or abuse by adolescents. The immediate and long-term effects of opium, morphine, heroin, barbituates, cocaine, amphetamines, hallucinogens, and marijuana vary so immensely as to make a search for just one underlying cause pointless. Two drugs, however—marijuana and LSD (d-lysergic acid diethylamide)—have received widespread attention because of their relatively common use by American adolescents. One Gallup Poll (1971), for example, reported that 42 percent of college students admitted to using marijuana, while 14 percent had tried LSD. It is doubtful that any substantial number continue to use the latter (Reese, 1970). Likewise, it is estimated that 65 percent of those who experiment with marijuana stop after one to ten tries while only 10 percent continue on to habitual use (Yolles, 1969).

The types of motives which initiate and sustain drug usage among young people range from such things as curiosity, thrill seeking, peer pressure, escape from emotional and social stress, and rebellion against authority to more philosophical motives such as desire for self-knowledge, self-improvement, creativeness, spiritual enlightenment, or expansion of consciousness (Coleman, 1972). When these motives are considered in terms of Erikson's theory, a case can be built for their relation to an underlying sense of identity confusion. Young people who do not know who they are might find drug-related experiences attractive in exploring the outer boundaries of selfhood; they may think that they can find a dimension of themselves which evades them in the "straight" world.

Using drugs may also temporarily relieve the emotional stresses accompanying the identity crisis. Beset by vocational indecision, parental conflict, and fragile love relationships, young persons may see drugs as a way of momentarily stepping outside of themselves. Marijuana, in particular, functions like alcohol (also a drug) in this respect. Moreover, when adolescents are surrounded by a drug-using peer group so crucial to their identity search, it is easy to understand how they could be "pressured" toward drugs, especially if their peer group status is contingent on use of them. A person with an established sense of ego identity could resist such pressure—the Eriksonian adolescent would probably find it quite difficult not to conform.

It would be erroneous to assume that all facets of adolescent behavior can be explained in terms of Erikson's identity concept. Nonetheless, the concept of "identity crisis" furnishes an excellent theoretical perspective from which to view the diversity of psychological problems displayed during this period of life. By attempting to identify the critical mainstreams running through psychosocial development, Erikson has made a rich and valuable contribution to personological theory.

SUMMARY

Erik Erikson's psychosocial theory, developed within a psychoanalytic framework, emphasizes the importance of ego psychology, developmental change throughout the life cycle, and understanding personality against the background of social and historical forces. In contrast to Freud, Erikson regards the ego as an autonomous personality structure; his theory focuses on ego qualities that emerge at various developmental periods.

Erikson asserts that ego development proceeds through a series of universal stages. In his epigenetic conception of human development, each stage in the life cycle has an optimal time to emerge. The sequential unfolding of these life stages is a function of the individual's biological maturation interacting with his expanding social radius.

In Erikson's view, eight psychosocial stages characterize the human life cycle. Each is marked by a particular kind of crisis or turning point in the person's life. The eight stages, depicted in terms of the essential psychosocial conflicts associated with each, are as follows: (1) basic trust versus mistrust, (2) autonomy versus shame and doubt, (3) initiative versus guilt, (4) industry versus inferiority, (5) ego identity versus role confusion, (6) intimacy versus isolation, (7) generativity versus stagnation, and (8) ego integrity versus despair. The individual's personality is determined by the resolutions of these conflicts.

Erikson's theory is rooted in his basic assumptions concerning human nature. His psychosocial theory reflects (1) a strong commitment to the assumptions of holism and environmentalism and (2) a moderate commitment to the assumptions of determinism, rationality, objectivity, proactivity, heterostasis, and knowability.

Erikson's theory has thus far generated very little research. Illustrative studies on ego identity versus role confusion reported in this chapter represent beginning efforts to empirically test Erikson's theoretical concepts.

Application of Erikson's theory to an understanding of the adolescent period in American society was discussed in the concluding section of this chapter. Diverse areas of contemporary adolescent behavior—the problem of vocational choice, conflict with parents, peer-group membership, love relationships, and drug usage—were interpreted as partial reflections of the identity crisis.

BIBLIOGRAPHY

Bronson, G. Identity diffusion in late adolescence. *Journal of Abnormal and Social Psychology,* 1959, **59,** 414–417.

Ciaccio, N. A test of Erikson's theory of ego epigenesis. *Developmental Psychology,* 1971, **4,** 306–311.

Coleman, J. *Abnormal psychology and modern life.* Glenview, Ill.: Scott, Foresman, 1972.

Coles, R. *Erik H. Erikson: The growth of his work,* Boston: Little, Brown, 1970.

Dignan, M. Ego identity and maternal identification. *Journal of Personality and Social Psychology,* 1965, **1,** 476–483.

Erikson, E. Configurations in play—Clinical notes. *Psychoanalytic Quarterly,* 1937, **6,** 139–214.

Erikson, E. Childhood and tradition in two American Indian tribes. In *The psychoanalytic study of the child.* Vol. I. New York: International Universities Press, 1945, pp. 319–350.

Erikson, E. Growth and crises of the healthy personality: VI. Identity versus self-diffusion In M. Senn (Ed.), *Symposium on the healthy personality. II: Problems of infancy and childhood.* New York: Josiah Macy, Jr. Foundation, 1950, pp. 134–140.

Erikson, E. *Young man Luther: A study in psychoanalysis and history.* New York: Norton, 1958.

Erikson, E. *Childhood and society.* New York: Norton, 1963a (2d ed.).

Erikson, E. (Ed.), *Youth: Change and challenge.* New York: Norton, 1963b.

Erikson, E. *Insight and responsibility.* New York: Norton, 1964a.

Erikson, E. Memorandum on identity and Negro youth. *Journal of Social Issues,* 1964b, **xx,** 29–42.

Erikson, E. *Identity: Youth and crisis.* New York: Norton, 1968a.

Erikson, E. Life cycle. *International Encyclopedia of the Social Sciences.* New York: Crowell Collier and Macmillan, 1968b, **9,** 286–292.

Erikson, E. *Gandhi's truth.* New York: Norton, 1969.

Erikson, E. Reflections on the dissent of contemporary youth. *Daedalus,* 1970a, **99,** 154–176.

Erikson, E. Autobiographic notes on the identity crisis. *Daedalus,* 1970b, **99,** 730–759.

Erikson, E. *Dimensions of a new identity: The 1973 Jefferson lectures in the humanities.* New York: Norton, 1974.

Erikson, E., & Erikson, K. Confirmation of the delinquent. *Chicago Review,* 1957, **10,** 15–23.

Evans, R. *Dialogue with Erik Erikson.* New York: Harper and Row, 1967.

Gallup, G. Drugs on campus. *Newsweek,* Jan. 25, 1971, 52.

Maier, H. *Three theories of child development: The contributions of Erik H. Erikson, Jean Piaget, and Robert R. Sears, and their applications.* New York: Harper and Row, 1965.

Marcia, J. Development and validation of ego-identity status. *Journal of Personality and Social Psychology.* 1966, **3,** 551–558.

Muuss, R. *Theories of adolescence.* New York: Random House, 1962.

Reese, J. Marijuana: Is it time for a change in our laws? *Newsweek,* Sept. 7, 1970, 20–22, 27–32.

Rotter, J. Generalized expectancies for internal versus external control of reinforcement. *Psychological Monographs*, 1966, **80** (1, Whole no. 609).

Rotter, J. A new scale for the measurement of interpersonal trust. *Journal of Personality*, 1967, **35**, 651–655.

Toffler, A. *Future shock*. New York: Random House, 1970.

Waterman, C., Buebel, M., & Waterman, A. Relationship between resolution of the identity crisis and outcomes of previous psychosocial crises. *Proceedings of the Annual Convention of the APA*, 1970, **5**, 467–468.

Yolles, S. Pop drugs: The high as a way of life. *Time,* Sept. 26, 1969, 74.

Ziegler, D. Distinctive self and occupational member concepts in different occupational preference groups. *Journal of Vocational Behavior,* 1973, **3**, 53–60.

SUGGESTED READINGS

1 Breger, L. *From instinct to identity: The development of personality.* Englewood Cliffs, N.J.: Prentice-Hall, 1974.

2 Loevinger, J. The meaning and measurement of ego development. *American Psychologist,* 1966, **21**, 195–206.

3 Loevinger, J., & Wessler, R. *Measuring ego development.* Vol. 1. San Francisco: Jossey-Bass, 1970.

4 Newman, B., & Newman, P. *Development through life: A psychosocial approach.* Homewood, Ill.: Dorsey, 1975.

5 Orlofsky, J., Marcia, J., & Lesser, I. Ego identity status and the intimacy versus isolation crisis of young adulthood. *Journal of Personality and Social Psychology,* 1973, **27**, 211–219.

6 Toder, N., & Marcia, J. Ego identity status and response to conformity pressure in college women. *Journal of Personality and Social Psychology,* 1973, **26**, 287–294.

Henry A. Murray (*Public Relations Department, News Office, Harvard University*)

Henry Murray: A Need Theory of Personality

Many students are first drawn to the study of psychology by the question "What makes people tick?" Psychology may explain why people behave as they do, what drives them, and what is "underneath" their behavior. These are really questions of *motivation* and, to that extent, are in some way answered by all personality theorists. But some theorists are more closely identified than others with motivation as a dynamic, energizing, and directing force within persons. Henry Murray is clearly one of these. Having evolved a *need theory* of personality into a personological system over several decades, Murray qualifies as one who has addressed himself pointedly to the question of the internal motivational forces that guide and direct human activities.

BIOGRAPHICAL SKETCH

Henry Alexander Murray was born in New York City in 1893. He obtained his B.A. in history from Harvard in 1915 where he attended one psychology lecture which bored him, so he walked out. In 1919, Murray received his medical degree from Columbia College of Physicians and Surgeons. The following year he secured an M.A. in biology from Columbia and then returned to Harvard where he divided his time between research and an instructorship in physiology. After this came two years of surgical internship at the Presbyterian Hospital in New York City, following which he was appointed assistant and then associate member of the Rockefeller Institute for Medical Research where he conducted embryological research. In 1924–1925, he took a year's leave of absence to study biology and biochemistry at Trinity College, Cambridge, England. He was awarded a Ph.D. in physiological chemistry from Cambridge University in 1927.

It was during his year abroad that Murray first became interested in medical psychology. Murray credits his attraction toward a professional psychology career to a period of analytic work, including a brief personal analysis, with Carl Jung in Zurich. In later years, reflecting upon his personal conversations with Jung, he wrote:

> We talked for hours, sailing down the lake and smoking before the hearth of his Faustian retreat. "The great floodgates of the wonder-world swung open," and I saw things that my philosophy had never dreamt of. Within a month a score of bi-horned problems were resolved, and I went off decided on depth psychology. I had experienced the unconscious, something not to be drawn out of books (Murray, 1940, p. 153).

Swept away with enthusiasm for psychoanalysis, Murray returned to the Rockefeller Institute as an associate for one year, in addition to studying at various New York psychiatric clinics. In 1927, he accepted an invitation from Morton Prince to return to Harvard University, this time to teach psychology and to be assistant director of the newly founded Harvard Psychological Clinic. Murray assumed leadership of the clinic in 1928 and was appointed assistant professor of abnormal psychology, followed by promotion to associate professorship in 1937. During the period from 1928 to the onset of World War II, Murray collaborated on research in personology that proved to be both creative and fruitful. This work culminated in the publication of *Explorations in Personality* (1938), still a classic in the field. Under his stimulating guidance, psychoanalytic theory was submitted to vigorous empirical investigation. He was also one of the charter members of the Boston Psychoanalytic Institute, where in 1935 he completed training under Franz Alexander and Hans Sachs (two members of Freud's inner circle) which enabled him to practice psychoanalysis part-time.

Murray left Harvard in 1943 to become a major and then a lieutenant colonel in the Army Medical Corps. He was assigned to the Office of Strategic Services to develop screening and selection methods for OSS personnel who were about to embark upon espionage missions in the European theater. His wartime research, which took him to Britain, France, and China, resulted in the publication of *Assessment of Men* (1948), a compilation of the work in which he and his coworkers successfully applied ingenious psychological techniques in selecting OSS personnel. At the war's end, Murray was awarded the Army's Legion of Merit for his services.

In addition to his other pursuits, Murray has made a lifelong commitment to the study of literature. Since 1925, he has studied the life and literary works of Herman Melville, and in 1949 he published an edition of Melville's *Pierre,* to which he added a lengthy discussion of the psychology of creative writing. The next year he rejoined the Harvard faculty as professor of clinical psychology in the newly formed Department of Social Relations.

Aside from his theoretical conceptions of personality, perhaps Murray's best-known achievement is the development (with Christiana Morgan) of the Thematic Apperception Test, a projective assessment device still widely used. He also conducted research on fear, humor, dreams, religion, and myth making. In September 1961, he received the American Psychological Association's Distinguished Scientific Contribution Award for his theoretical and practical contributions to the understanding of the complexity of human behavior. He was awarded the Gold Medal Award of the American Psychological Foundation in 1969. After thirty-six years of teaching and research, Murray retired from the Harvard faculty in 1962, having been named professor emeritus of clinical psychology. This theorist's foremost professional aim has been the development of a comprehensive personological system for the representation and explanation of the unfolding series of events constituting an individual's life history. His accomplishments in this domain of theory and practice were celebrated in a volume of essays (*The Study of Lives: Essays on Personality in Honor of Henry A. Murray*) written by admiring colleagues and edited by one of his former students, Robert W. White, which was presented to him on his seventieth birthday.

WHAT IS PERSONALITY?

Murray provided several answers to this question in his various writings. Certain of Murray's definitions of personality are so intricately couched in his total theory as to be virtually impossible to understand apart from it. Other definitions, such as the following, are more immediately comprehensible:

> Personality may be biologically defined as the governing organ, or superordinate institution of the body. As such, it is located in the brain. No brain, no personality (Murray, 1951a, p. 267).

Murray's various definitions of personality all stress that it is a hypothetical entity, rather than something of real physical substance. Personality is not the brain itself, but the hypothetical structure of the mind. As a fairly gross example, if a person's head were opened for inspection, his personality could not be "seen." If, however, his brain was then removed from his head, he would immediately be rendered "personality-less." Personality, while itself hypothetical, is completely and utterly dependent on brain processes in Murray's system.

Rooting personality in brain processes carries with it some definite theoretical implications. For instance, one always "has" a personality since one always has a brain, And, for Murray, personality represents a process of development from birth to death (Murray, 1968). Further, since brain processes largely integrate, organize, and regulate the rest of the individual's physical functioning, it follows that personality would do about the same thing in the behavioral domain. More specifically, Murray believes that personality integrates and directs the person's behavior. It is what accounts for the recurring, stabilizing elements in behavior that help individuals to adapt to their environment. Stated another way, personality is what makes you today basically the same kind of person that you were yesterday. Same brain, same personality.

To highlight the intimate relationship between brain and personality, Murray (1938) coined the term *regnancy.* The physiological and neurological brain activities underlying personality functioning are termed *regnant processes.* In Murray's scheme, all personality variables can ultimately be reduced to their regnant-process underpinnings. By way of illustration, take a well-known personality variable such as "need for achievement." People differ noticeably on this variable. For example, one college student with a high need for achievement would drive hard to get her A's and raise her grade point average as high as possible. Another student with a low achievement need would predictably be less motivated to do so. While Murray recognizes that this and other needs could be measured without reference to the brain (see the "Application" section of this chapter), he strongly argues that all such psychological variables were founded in regnant processes. Although some personality variables can be measured on a purely *psychological* level (e.g., by personality tests), they cannot be fully accounted for without reference to the brain. Murray's concept of personality, then, is intimately tied to brain processes.

NEED THEORY   *Caulen*

Reading the works of Henry Murray is truly a mind-boggling experience not only because of the numerous theoretical concepts that he proposes but also because of the detailed classifications of these concepts that he develops. Rather than give passing notice to many of these varied and sundry ideas, valuable though they are, primary attention here is devoted to the three central theoretical concepts that seem most accurately to reflect Murray's unique view of human beings: *need, press,* and *thema.*

Need: What Drives People

The very title of this chapter indicates that *need* is central in Murray's theorizing. Murray is recognized as a major personality theorist primarily because of his extensive efforts to demonstrate the pervasive effects of needs on human actions. Which raises the logical question "What is a need?" Consistent with his conception of personality, Murray (1938) defined "need" as a construct which stands for a force in the brain region, a force either internally or externally instigated which organizes other psychological processes.

For example, need for achievement (labeled "nAchievement" and probably the most widely studied of all needs in Murray's system) is a *construct,* meaning a convenient fiction or hypothetical concept. It does not exist in the sense that one can see, feel, smell, or taste it (no personality theory concept does). However, nAchievement is an extremely useful abstraction for purposes of describing and explaining what may underlie and direct a person's activities. Second, nAchievement represents a force in the brain region. While the state of present day science does not allow precise delineation of the physiochemical nature of such a force, Murray conceived it to be activated from either within or without. College students with high nAchievement, for example, could either seek out situations in which they could achieve or simply be confronted by outside events that would instigate their achievement motivation; e.g., a professor suggests that the student consider preparing his or her term project for submission to a professional journal for publication. Third, nAchievement, like all Murray's needs, also serves to organize various psychological processes, such as *perception.* The high nAchievement student *perceives* a final examination as an opportunity to achieve; a low nAchievement person would perceive it in other terms, e.g., a threat, waste of time, game, etc. Needs, then, organize the way people perceive, think, feel, and act.

How Many Needs Are There?   Growing out of an elaborate series of investigations at the Harvard Psychological Clinic back in the 1930s, Murray proposed a list of twelve "viscerogenic" (physiological) needs and twenty-eight "psychogenic" (nonphysical) needs as the basis for human behavior. Examples from the long list of psychogenic needs, those which occupy a major place in Murray's theory, are presented in Table 4-1. Word changes have been made to avoid some of the unique and not readily understandable terms coined by Murray. Note that all needs in Murray's theory are always preceded by the lower case "n," as in "nDominance."

One of the major tasks confronting any personality theory is to explain how people fundamentally differ from one another. Murray's answer lies in the realm of needs, since his need listing does not imply that all people experience all needs to the same degree. In his system, some people may never experience certain needs in their lifetime while the actions of other persons are dominated by these same needs. Some individuals may be attracted to a particular need or set of needs and express the remaining needs only infrequently. Then, too, other people may experience the entire range of needs within a relatively brief time period in their lives. As an intellectual exercise, the reader is invited to reexamine the exemplar needs presented in Table 4-1 and simply assess how important each is in his or her own behavior. Then take a few other persons

---

Table 4-1   Illustrative List of Murray's Psychogenic Needs

Need	Definition or behavioral example
1 nAchievement	To accomplish something difficult. To master, manipulate, or organize physical objects, human beings, or ideas as rapidly and independently as possible. To overcome obstacles and attain a high standard. To excel oneself. To rival and surpass others.
2 nDominance	To control one's human environment. To influence or direct the behavior of others by suggestion, persuasion, or command. To convince others of the correctness of one's opinion.
3 nExhibition	To make an impression. To be seen and heard. To excite, fascinate, entertain, shock, or amuse others. To attract attention by mannerisms, gestures, or emphatic speech. To monopolize the conversation.
4 nInfavoidance	To avoid humiliation. To quit embarrassing situations which may lead to belittlement. To refrain from action because of fear of failure. To associate with inferiors. To conceal a disfigurement.
5 nNurturance	To give sympathy, and gratify the needs of a helpless person. To assist a person in danger. To feed, help, support, console, protect, comfort, and heal.
6 nOrder	To put things in order. To achieve cleanliness, arrangement, organization, balance, neatness, tidiness, and precision.
7 nSuccorance	To have one's needs gratified by the sympathetic aid of an allied object. To be supported, sustained, protected, advised, guided, and indulged. To exaggerate an injury. To remain close to a devoted protector. To always have a supporter.

Source: Adapted from Murray, 1938, pp. 152–266.

---

whom you know reasonably well and carry out the same assessment. While this exercise is admittedly less than scientific in terms of personality measurement, it should intuitively reveal how Murray's need theory can be used to account for individual differences.

When Is a Need Present?   Given that needs are hypothetical constructs rather than directly observable phenomena, how does the personologist know when a particular need is operative in behavior? On what basis is behavior attributed to a need for achievement, dominance, exhibition, etc.? To grapple with this important theoretical question, Murray (1938) proposed *five criteria by which needs can be recognized.* First is the consequence or end result of the mode of behavior involved. To illustrate, let's carry through with the example of college students with high nAchievement. They consistently get their A on the final, turn in the best term papers, or do the highest quality class projects. The second criterion is the kind or pattern of behavior involved. These students thoroughly prepare for examinations, work hard in the library or lab, and forgo activities directly conflicting with their scholastic achievement, e.g., drinking or carousing immediately before finals.

The selective perception of and response to a group of circumscribed stimulus objects constitutes Murray's third criterion. High nAchievement students pay particular attention to important aspects of lectures, books, or other assigned readings that will help them master the subject matter and do well in each course. Fourth is the expression of a characteristic emotion or feeling: e.g., "I want to do well," "I need to do well," "I want an A in this course so much I can taste it!" Finally, Murray's fifth criterion is the manifestation of satisfaction associated with the attainment of a certain effect or the manifestation of dissatisfaction associated with the failure to attain a certain effect. Attaining their A should result in "Wow!" (or a more contemporary equivalent verbal expression), accompanied by a feeling of satisfaction. Depending on the colorfulness of the student's vocabulary, failure to attain the much wanted grade may result in phrases often discussed in comic books and other pornography free publications disguised by the terms "Blank!" or "Blankety blank blank!", expressing deep disappointment and dissatisfaction. The same five criteria, of course, can be applied with equal cogency to any of the needs on Murray's lengthy list.

Kinds of Needs   Murray devoted a great deal of time and energy to developing a variety of schemes for classifying types of needs. While his complete need taxonomy is too exhaustive to present here, it may prove useful to examine a few of the distinctions Murray made. One illustration has already been mentioned—viscerogenic and psychogenic needs. In Murray's system, *viscerogenic* needs stem from the tissue requirements of the person. Reflecting the universal biological requirements for human life, this category includes needs for food, water, air, and other such necessary, life sustaining activities. *Psychogenic* needs derive from viscerogenic needs and would include among them the needs depicted in Table 4-1. Interestingly, Murray argued that some psychogenic needs may become extremely influential and even assume priority over viscerogenic needs in certain situations. Examples might be the high nAchievement business executive who neglects his health to earn $10 million a year, or the high nNurturance altruist who risks his own life to save another's.

A second illustration of Murray's need classifications, proactive and reactive, is based on the origin of the need. *Proactive* needs are aroused by some change of state occurring within the person. Common experience suggests that the need for food falls in this category. By contrast, *reactive* needs are evoked by environmental stimuli. They are often instigated by situations that are unsought, unexpected, and dissatisfying, e.g., the need to avoid extreme temperatures. As with any other classification system, however, some needs can be perceived as falling in both categories. The need for sex is a good example; sometimes nSex appears to be a function of the time interval since the last sexual outlet (proactive), while at other times it seems to rise directly in response to environmental "sex objects" (reactive).

Overt and covert needs constitute another of Murray's categories. *Overt* needs are allowed free expression by society. For example, in American society one can freely express nAchievement, nAffiliation, or nOrder. On the other hand, *covert* needs are not permitted open expression by the culture. Instead, they remain partly or completely unconscious and find their outlets primarily in dreams, fantasies, projections, and neurotic symptoms. Depending on social norms, nAggression, nSex, and nSuccorance could easily fall in this category. Interestingly, the implication here is that overt needs in one society may be covert in another. Anthropological findings seem to bear this out in that need based behaviors vary widely from culture to culture.

A final illustration of Murray's need categories is that of effect versus modal. An *effect* need is linked with some direct or specific goal state. A student enrolled in a personality theory course, for example, usually is motivated toward some identifiable goal (e.g., passing the course, fulfilling a requirement for graduation). The need or needs involved (e.g., achievement) are directed toward some tangible result. *Modal* needs, by contrast, are those in which experienced satisfaction is present to some degree throughout the activity rather than being linked only to its end result (Murray, 1951a). An illustration would be playing or listening to music. Or, getting back to our student, he or she may actually come to *enjoy* learning about personality theory in the process of completing the course! Murray describes this as the *sheer pleasure function*— the need to attain a high degree of excellence or perfection of performance. In Murray's system, then, how one satisfies a need is just as important as that one satisfies it.

How Needs Interact   There is constant dynamic interplay among needs in Murray's theory. Persons are by no means static entities in this system; the world within is characterized by continuous cooperation and conflict among forces. Again, however, the principles elaborated by Murray to describe the organization and interplay of needs are simply too numerous to catalog here. A few samples of these principles follow.

The principle of *prepotency* serves as a good beginning example. In Murray's view, needs are arranged in a hierarchy of prepotency or urgency. Murray (1951a) describes prepotent needs as those which come to the fore with the greatest urgency if they are not satisfied. The need to avoid physical danger, for example, is more compelling (i.e., has greater prepotency) than nNurturance. A man does not go to the assistance of another if a person holding a gun to his head commands otherwise. Consequently, needs are ordered in terms of their relative importance in assuring the person's survival—the order being determined less by the person than by the nature of the need itself.

The principle of *fusion* is a second illustration. Whenever a single course of action satisfies two or more needs simultaneously, there is a fusion of needs. For instance, a person might satisfy both nAffiliation and nNurturance through a single activity, e.g., joining a social sorority or doing volunteer hospital work.

Fusion, then, does not mean that the two needs become identical. Rather, they complement one another in that they both are expressed in the same behavior.

Subsidiation is another of Murray's principles governing need interaction. Basically, the principle states that certain needs are satisfied only through the fulfillment of other less demanding needs. In brief, a subsidiary need serves to gratify another need. As an illustration, consider the student who consistently displays admiration and conformity toward a professor (a deference need). Through the subsidiary nDeference, the student may really be attempting to gratify his more hidden nAchievement, i.e., get his A. Of course, all students who respond to professors in this way are not so motivated; some professors are actually worthy of admiration!

A fourth and final illustration of Murray's interaction principles is *conflict*. Needs may often be in conflict with one another and thus produce tension. Murray believes that much of human misery and most neurotic behavior are direct results of such inner conflict. Consider, for example, the plight of the young person with strong needs for autonomy and independence who also wants to get married. The various needs that push the person toward marriage are in direct conflict with needs to come and go as one pleases. Obviously, tension and a great deal of uncertainty can result. One hopes that this young person may be able to resolve the conflict by finding in a marital partner the kind of individual who will allow great autonomy in the relationship. Unfortunately, all need conflicts do not lend themselves to such ready resolution.

Careful thought about the latter three principles will reveal that true needs cannot be readily inferred by casually observing behavior. Human actions may result from two or more needs (fusion), one need operating in the service of another (subsidiation), or a compromise or lack thereof among incompatible needs (conflict). While needs motivate behavior, it is not always easy to determine what needs are motivating what behavior. In Murray's system, you truly "can't tell a book by its cover!" Murray did, however, propose a novel and highly useful means of assessing needs, the Thematic Apperception Test, which will be taken up in a subsequent section of this chapter.

Press: The Person's Environment

Needs are always gratified or thwarted in some environmental context. Thus, to be comprehensive, Murray's theory must describe aspects of the outer world that aid or impede need satisfaction. His concept of *press* (the plural is also press) fulfills this requirement. Specifically, Murray describes press as follows:

> The press of an object is what it can do to the subject or for the subject—the power it has to affect the well-being of the subject in one way or another (1938, p. 121).

As an example, take aggression press (called pAggression in Murray's system). When people find themselves in an environment surrounded by others who assault, criticize, or belittle them, pAggression is present. Such press can do a great deal to the person in terms of blocking need satisfactions. Very few needs can be gratified in such an environment. Yet for masochistic, guilt-ridden, and self-punishing people, this type of press may actually work for them in terms of need satisfaction. They like it. In Murray's theory, press in the form of persons or objects may either facilitate or block an individual's efforts to gratify his or her needs.

Varieties of Press   Murray draws an important distinction between alpha and beta press in his system. *Alpha press* represents persons, objects, or events as they actually exist in reality. For example, alpha pAggression reflects the fact that there actually are people out there in one's environment harboring and acting upon their hostile feelings toward oneself. *Beta press,* on the other hand, represents the environment as *perceived* and *experienced* by the individual. Beta pAggression, then, means that the person sees hostility in those around him. According to Murray, it is the beta aspect of press which exerts the greater influence on behavior since that is what is felt, interpreted, and responded to by the person.

In well-balanced individuals, there is good correspondence between alpha and beta press. What you see is what you get! By contrast, serious discrepancy between the two types of press can result in *delusional* thinking. The paranoid patient, for example, experiences a high degree of beta pAggression without there really being corresponding alpha pAggression. Thus, he manifests a delusion of persecution, thinking that people are actively plotting against him when in fact they are not.

Aside from these two basic aspects of press, Murray (1938) developed several lists of specific press terms which he believes are significant sources of influence on a person's life. Again, Murray was consistently thorough and detailed here; Table 4-2 presents a few illustrations from his exhaustive listings. As in pAggression, each specific variety of press is preceded by a lower case "p" in his system.

Table 4-2   Common Forms of Press

	Press	Definition or behavioral example
1	pAffiliation	Companions who are friendly
2	pAggression	Others who assault, criticize, or belittle one
3	pRejection	Being refused membership in a club or organization
4	pCounteraction	Being attacked either verbally or physically
5	pDominance	Persons or obstacles which restrain or prohibit one
6	pLack	Living in a state of poverty
7	pRecognition	Competing for awards and honors

Katherine

Need-Press Relationships The person is a dynamic moving force in Murray's theory. Needs are constantly interacting with press to mold behavior. Thus, people's actions can never be fully understood by reference to their need states alone. Nor can we explain their behavior simply as a product of their environment alone. Both needs and press, and particularly the relationships between the two, must be taken into account in attempting to understand a person.

For illustration purposes, let's consider the seven sample forms of press listed in Table 4-2 and see how they might interact with just one need. Specifically, take the case of a young business executive with very high nAchievement. He drives himself hard, works hard, and is completely willing to "play the game" in order to get ahead. In fact, his nAchievement is so high that everything else in his life is secondary to it; our young man sees everything in terms of his goal to reach the top.

Of the kinds of press depicted in Table 4-2, pAffiliation and pRecognition probably would greatly facilitate the satisfaction of this expression of nAchievement. Having companions around who are friendly (pAffiliation) could conceivably help one get ahead, especially if they are bosses! An environment which presses him to compete for awards and honors (pRecognition) could hardly be more ideal for a high nAchievement person of this type, e.g., annual award for personally generating the highest sales volume. On the other hand, pAggression, pRejection, pCounteraction, and pDominance would appear to work against gratifying his nAchievement. Office companions who assault, criticize, or belittle him (pAggression), attack him verbally or physically—perhaps for outselling them—(pCounteraction), or restrain and prohibit his efforts (pDominance) certainly do not facilitate his climb up the ladder of success. Moreover, being refused membership in the club or organization (pRejection) necessary to rise in a particular field could seriously frustrate his achievement strivings.

The precise impact of pLack seems more open to alternative interpretations in this case. For example, living in a state of poverty could block nAchievement if the person must work at another job during the evening to make ends meet. In this situation, he might be forced to forgo the chance to attend night classes that he may need to further his career. When viewed developmentally, however, pLack could be seen as facilitating this type of nAchievement. There are many instances in which having lived in poverty as a child strongly prompts the individual to drive for high achievement later in life. Basically, he has made up his mind early to achieve later so that he will never be forced to live in poverty again.

More generally, then, needs interact with press to produce behavior. The above example is restricted to only one need in possible relation with seven forms of press. When the great variety of needs interacting with the numerous press forms is imagined, the truly dynamic picture of individuals that Murray portrayed is strikingly revealed. In his theory, human behavior is indeed complex, produced by many interacting forces, and subject to both internal and external pressures.

Thema: The Interaction

Thema is Murray's theoretical concept that formally links need to press. It essentially refers to the interaction between press and need resulting in a particular behavioral episode. As an illustration, let us suppose that a high school student who earns a final grade of A in his math course is subjected to pAggression. Specifically, another student in the course publicly and with obvious hostile intent makes fun of him and calls him derogatory names, e.g., "brown-noser." Such pAggression may instigate nAggression on our A student, thus prompting him to punch the name-caller in the mouth ("behavioral episode"). Murray's term "thema" refers to these kinds of press-need interactions resulting in specific behavioral episodes. As such, the concept represents a more comprehensive unit of analysis for personality study than either need or press alone.

In the above "behavioral episode" example of a thema in action, one form of press instigated one need on one occasion. But all human behavior is not so simple. For instance, the student involved may not react this way to all forms of pAggression but only that which emanates from a few of his fellow classmates. Further, all people do not characteristically respond to pAggression in this fashion. Some withdraw from it, others try to overlook it, and still others may even accept it to alleviate their guilt. Theoretically, then, Murray required a more elaborate concept than thema to represent complex, ongoing person-environment interactions. His term "serial thema" largely accomplishes this purpose.

A *serial thema* reflects more than one need-press interaction. Specifically, it represents some combination of the simple themas underlying the person's behavior. Suppose, for example, that our fist-swinging high schooler *always* reacted to pAggression in this way. Murray's serial thema concept could then be employed here to reflect the fact that, for this student, various forms of pAggression always instigate nAggression, which in turn is characteristically expressed physically, e.g., fighting. In brief, we have here a characteristic way in which the person interacts with aspects of his environment, based on the underlying serial thema.

Conceivably, the student may not consistently handle pAggression in this manner. When pressed by male peers, he may punch—but he might respond to parental or teacher pAggression with deference. Nonetheless, these different situations represent simple themas which can be combined to form a serial thema, the central core of which is various reactions to aggression press. Serial themas, then, represent the more complex, varied, and ongoing need-press relationships underlying behavior.

Unity-Thema: The Key to Uniqueness   Each person is, in a profound sense, like no other. Many personologists acknowledge this fact, and some formally attempt to account for it. While Murray recognized that individual uniqueness was the product of many interacting factors, he singled out one as the essential key to an individual's uniqueness. He termed this key the *unity-thema* (Murray, 1938).

In Murray's theory, the unity-thema refers to the person's basic and individual pattern of need-press relationships. Viewed as a kind of underlying reaction system, it is largely an unconscious force originating in early childhood experience. Murray believed that, with intense study, it is possible to identify a person's unity-thema which, in effect, renders him or her different from other people. Once identified, the unity-thema allows one to make sense of the person's various behaviors which otherwise would seem inconsistent and unintelligible.

In essence, the unity thema constitutes the *psychological core* of the individual. It provides the fundamental continuity in personality over time. For example, while there are many things that might have changed within John Doe over the past ten years, Murray would argue that he is still fundamentally the same person that he was then. And in spite of future changes, he basically will continue to be that same person ten years from now. Why? Because there is a unique constellation of dominant needs inextricably linked to certain kinds of press to which he was exposed in early life. This fundamental set of need-press relationships is fixed and goes on to become the pervasive and dominant force in an individual's personality. Without it there would be no meaning or coherence to his behavior. In this sense, Murray's unity-thema is the closest his system comes to defining the psychological essence of a person. Since it is constituted of need-press patterns particular to a given individual, the unity-thema stands as the "key to the uniqueness" of personality.

HOW PERSONALITY DEVELOPS

Murray focused much theoretical attention on the development of personality. While the various concepts that he employed in this respect are too numerous to catalog here, suffice it to say that, in one sense, Murray regarded the history of the personality as *being* the personality (Murray & Kluckhohn, 1953). What a person is today directly reflects his or her past history. And more—Murray argued that personality can never be understood outside a time dimension. It is not enough to describe what needs are interacting with what press at what time. To be understood, persons must be viewed as constantly developing entities against the background of both their past history and future goals. To understand who an individual is, one must understand where he has been and where he intends to go as a person.

Proceeding: Behavior in Time

Murray divided the individual's past history into temporal units of subject-subject or subject-object interactions which he termed *proceedings.* His developmental view of personality, perhaps most fundamentally expressed in this theoretical concept, was that a sample of behavior must be observed through a sufficient period of time in order to be properly studied. Instantaneous records, such as a photograph taken during the expression of a particular emotion, are abstractions from reality and, in this sense, distort it (Murray, 1951b). A photograph cannot tell us what led up to the event, which needs are associated with the emotional expression, or what the person did afterwards. Behavior, to be understood, must be analyzed in terms of a time dimension.

Murray distinguished two types of proceedings—internal and external. An *internal proceeding* involves some segment of time during which individuals are absorbed in their private world of feelings, images, and ideas. Examples would be daydreaming, interpreting the symbolic meaning of a movie, solving a math problem, or figuring out Henry Murray's theory. By contrast, an *external proceeding* involves a stretch of time during which the person is actively engaged in dealing with the environment in terms of observable motor and/or verbal behavior. Playing tennis, registering for a course, participating in a class discussion, and going to lunch with friends are illustrations. While internal proceedings have only a scarcely appreciable behavioral aspect, then, external proceedings are marked by their overt or observable behavioral character (Murray, 1968). Although he placed equal emphasis on both for understanding personality, Murray felt that the latter could more readily be studied by personologists because of their greater direct "observability." In particular, he believed that *interpersonal* or *dyadic* proceedings were very fruitful for personality study, e.g., the interaction between parent and child, sister and brother, wife and husband, teacher and student. In basic theoretical terms, such proceedings allow for the observation of the behavioral aspects of a person's need-press relationships in a time dimension.

Space does not permit consideration of Murray's additional developmental units for behavioral analysis. The basic point here is simply that personality, to be properly understood, must be seen in a time dimension in Murray's system. This idea inevitably leads to a broader quesion—what are the developmental forces that determine the formation of personality?

Personality Formation

In describing how personality is formed, Murray employed four sets of determinants—constitutional, group membership, role, and situational (Murray and Kluckhohn, 1953).

1 Constitutional Determinants   The person's total physical makeup at any given time is what Murray means by constitutional determinants of personality. Included in this category would be such factors as the individual's age, sex, body type, skin pigmentation, physical strength, disabilities, and conformity of physique to the culturally fashionable type. But these constitutional forces do not act in a vacuum. Rather, in Murray's system, they are differentially important according to the person's environment.

As an illustration, consider the male in our culture who is and always has been thin, fragile, and physically weak. By themselves, these constitutional factors play little or no part in Murray's scheme of personality development. But placed in a social context, they can assume great importance. For example, this male will never successfully play football and have the opportunity to develop whatever aspects of personality that he might if he were able to participate in this sport. Because of his physique, he will never make the high school team, much less run against the defensive line of the Minnesota Vikings! Further, assuming that he attends a high school in which Joe Namath types are most popular with females, our hypothetical male could experience pRejection on these grounds alone. Thus, he may be led to develop his personality, or satisfy his needs, in other ways, e.g., strive for high grades. While constitutional factors are part of personality determination, then, their precise effects upon the person are a function of their constant interactions with the environment.

2 Group Membership Determinants The social groups to which an individual belongs or aspires to belong also contribute to molding personality in Murray's system. Among these determinants are such groupings as familial, ethnic, religious, racial, political, regional, and socioeconomic ones. Belonging to any one or more of these groups affects personality primarily because membership carries with it exposure to a particular social environment and value system. Thus, certain needs will be both developed differently and expressed differently depending upon these external variables.

An example requiring little elaboration would be the potential differences in personality development between a white, suburban, middle-class child and a black, urban-ghetto, poor child just as a function of the differences in their social environments and accompanying value systems alone. On a broader cultural level, most middle-class citizens of the United States, regardless of their regional, occupational, and religious differences, have developed certain motivational structures and behavior patterns which distinguish them somewhat from Norwegians, Italians, Chinese, or any other cultural group. The individual's culture and the groups within it are accorded special significance by Murray in determining personality development.

3 Role Determinants Role determinants of personality are viewed by Murray as a special subclass of group membership determinants but are treated separately here because they are so potent in differentiating individuals within a group. The culture prescribes how roles necessary to group life are to be performed, and the personality formation of individuals becomes intimately bound up with the roles ascribed to them (e.g., sex) as well as those which they select (e.g., occupation).

As an illustration, consider the classic female sex role in our culture. Many little girls, solely because they are females, are taught in various ways to be subservient to males, not to manifest nAchievement in certain directions, and to acquire those characteristics designed to make them the "good" wives and mothers of the future. The female sex role, then, fosters certain directions of personality development while seriously curtailing others. Needs compatible with this role are allowed free expression by society—e.g., nSuccorance—while the expression of needs incompatible with it are frowned upon—e.g., nDominance (particularly over chauvinistic males!). To some extent, all other roles perform about the same kind of personality-formation function in Murray's theory.

4 Situational Determinants This group of personality determinants is made up of the day-to-day experiences of the individual, which for the most part are capricious and unpredictable. Situational determinants may include things that have happened a thousand times as well as those that happen only once—provided they are not uniform for a whole group (Murray and Kluckhohn, 1953). Accordingly, this is an omnibus category of factors shaping personality, including such diverse elements as interpersonal contacts of brief duration, family constellations (e.g., the oldest born in a five-child family), friendships with particular individuals, and divorced parents.

What seems of particular interest here is that random occurrences which happen only once may set in motion a whole chain of subsequent events that may profoundly affect personality development. Consider, for example, the random or "chancy" way that a person may first meet his or her marital partner. The initial event does not, of course, immediately and directly change personality. But it may initiate what will become a deep, involved, and extraordinarily intimate relationship that will decisively affect subsequent personality formation. These types of determinants, unique to a particular individual's life situation, may play an extremely important part in molding the kind of person he or she will become.

MURRAY'S BASIC ASSUMPTIONS CONCERNING HUMAN NATURE

Although Murray's need theory has been heavily influenced by the psychoanalytic tradition, there are distinct elements of humanism in his thinking (Maddi and Costa, 1972). This blend of psychoanalysis and humanism makes for an interesting profile of basic assumptions (graphically portrayed in Figure 4-1).

1 Freedom–Determinism Even though Murray (1962) believes that human beings possess a small margin of freedom in making decisions, for the most part he endorses a deterministic point of view. Murray's behavioral determinants include both the person (needs) and the environment (press). He advocates a kind of biosocial determinism in which internal changes or external stimuli evoke an existing need. This need, brought on by the perceived external force, then instigates behavior to satisfy it. Thus, individuals are pushed by

Freedom   ___ ___ ___ ___ ___ ___ ___ ___ ✓ ___ Determinism
Rationality   ✓✓ ___ ___ ___ ___ ___ ___ ___ ___ ___ Irrationality
Holism   ___ ___ ✓ ___ ___ ___ ___ ___ ___ ___ Elementalism
Constitutionalism ___ ___ ___ ___ ___ ✓ ___ ✓ ___ ___ Environmentalism
Subjectivity   ___ ___ ___ ✓ ___ ___ ✓ ___ ___ ___ Objectivity
Proactivity   ___ ___ ___ ✓ ___ ___ ✓ ___ ___ ___ Reactivity
Homeostasis   ___ ✓ ___ ___ ___ ___ ___ ___ ___ ___ Heterostasis
Knowability   ___ ___ ___ ___ ___ ✓ ___ ___ ___ ___ Unknowability

Figure 4-1   Murray's position on the eight basic assumptions concerning human nature.

needs and pulled by press, with the primary goal being the satisfaction of needs.

Take nExhibition as an example. Suppose that a young man, because of his past learning experiences, has developed a high need for exhibition. Put him in a situation that he perceives as calling for exhibition—e.g., a fraternity party—and he will try mightily to be exciting, entertaining, amusing, shocking, or, more generally, to exhibit himself psychologically to others. For Murray, this person has some flexibility (freedom) in deciding how he might "exhibit" in this situation, but that he will strive to exhibit is entirely outside his voluntary control. It is the interaction between need and press that determines a person's behavior in any given situation.

It will also be recalled that Murray has always stressed the physiological processes which underlie behavior (concept of regnancy). He considers the brain as the locus of the personality—the place where it's at. The implication is that brain processes ultimately determine behavior. Only a staunch determinist could hold such a position.

2 Rationality–Irrationality   Although he recognizes traces of irrationality in human behavior, Murray invests people with a large measure of rationality. The irrational side of life is seen most vividly when a person engages in inconsistent or self-defeating behavior; for instance, when a student refuses to study for final exams, a motorist speeds through a red light in heavy traffic, a patient ignores a physician's advice, and an adolescent takes drugs with known dangerous side effects. The usual consequence of such actions is "Why did I do that—that's not like me." Despite such instances of apparent irrationality, Murray is convinced that rationality more often characterizes human activities. Human beings think, anticipate, plan, and pursue long-range goals.

Murray's strong stand on rationality is best seen in his *serial* conception of human behavior. In an aspect of his complex theory not previously covered here, Murray clearly asserted that the adult person is quite capable of (1) organizing a set of subgoals leading to an important future goal (*serial program*); (2) employing creative strategies to avoid or minimize need-press demands that may conflict with long-range goals (*schedules*); and (3) establishing long-term plans and their priorities (*ordination*). Organisms that can consciously direct their behavior over time in such an ordered fashion must be highly rational.

Because people differ in terms of needs, press, and especially prior learning experiences, one person may not be as rational as another in conducting his life. A culturally deprived person, for example, may have relatively less opportunity than an affluent person to learn to make long-term plans or even to understand why such plans are necessary. Thus, he or she probably will be less able to make logical decisions affecting his or her life-style. Nonetheless, Murray maintains that the adult's functioning is characteristically rational, being governed by long-term objectives, plans of action, and philosophies of life.

3 Holism–Elementalism Early in his theorizing, Murray set forth as his goal the complete understanding of the whole person: "Personality is a temporal whole and to understand a part of it one must have a sense, though vague, of the totality (Murray, 1938, p. 4)." This insistence upon the wholeness of the individual, of course, is a common orientation among humanistic personologists. His various definitions of personality, stressing the interrelatedness of dynamically organized brain and psychological processes, also imply a holistic emphasis. Conversely, Murray recognizes the importance of avoiding the vagueness of holistic concepts insofar as they encourage "those lazy white elephants of the mind—huge, catchall, global concepts signifying nothing (Murray, 1959, p. 19)." This view makes Murray critical of personality explanations which do not include some reference to personality's component parts.

Murray's theory constitutes a rich and highly detailed attempt to bridge the gap between holism and elementalism. In so doing, he construes personality in a hierarchical way, including both general and specific "components." For example, the "unity-thema" concept is quite broad while "need" is much more narrow. For Murray, then, it is impossible to understand the wholeness of personality without at least some reference to its specific parts, suggesting that his commitment to holism is less than extreme.

4 Constitutionalism–Environmentalism Murray assumes that behavior cannot be understood unless the dynamic interaction between persons and their environments is taken into account. In this scheme, constitution and environment are given equal emphasis. Murray's early training in medicine, biology, and physiological chemistry made him appreciate the importance of constitutional factors underlying behavior. His central theoretical concept of *need,* rooted in brain processes, clearly reflects this orientation. Further, all psychological events depend on organized brain processes in Murray's system—"No brain, no personality."

On the environmental side of the coin are Murray's four determinants of personality. Of these—constitutional, group membership, role, and situational—three deal with external influences. For one who has been strongly indoctrinated in Freudian theory, Murray assigns a significant role to sociocultural factors: "A person is an emergent entity *of* and *in* a certain physical, social and cultural milieu (Murray and Kluckhohn, 1953, p. 6)." Thus, persons cannot be properly understood apart from their surroundings—constitutional and environmental forces combine to produce behavior.

5 Subjectivity–Objectivity *no more objective* Murray seems moderately committed to subjectivity, as indicated by the following statement: "The need to describe and explain varieties of inner experience decided the original, and, I predict, will establish the final orientation of psychology (Murray, 1938, p. 470)." Murray's theory includes several important concepts for understanding man's subjective experience, e.g., needs, unity-thema. Even environmental influences are seen from a subjective perspective—beta press, representing the person's unique interpretation of external forces, exerts a great influence upon his or her behavior. What is in objective reality (alpha press) is important in Murray's system, but what is privately experienced and interpreted as well as subjectively felt is the dominant factor in accounting for human behavior.

Be that as it may, Murray falls short of making a fetish of subjectivity. His major theoretical concern is with motivation rather than subjective experience per se. For Murray, needs cut across people and, more generally, behavior can be described adequately without relying unduly upon individual subjectivity. External, objective factors (e.g., sociocultural determinants), while always subject to individual interpretation, are nevertheless prominent in his scheme. All things considered, however, Murray appears to believe that subjective factors are more potent (though just a bit more) determinants of behavior than are external, objective variables.

6 Proactivity–Reactivity *yes more react* In line with his humanistic leanings, Murray is moderately committed to a proactive view of human nature. He feels that people are capable of generating (self-initiating) their own behavior, particularly as it relates to future goals and aspirations. The fact that the human being is more of a "proactor"—an active agent in dealing with the environment—than a "reactor"—simply responding when stimulated—is what in Murray's judgment helps to make human beings uniquely different from lower organisms. An animal's behavior is largely governed by external forces over which it has no control and by the necessity of promptly reacting to biological need states. Conversely, there is an "inner-directedness" to human behavior that goes far beyond the demands of the immediate social-physical environment. This is best understood in terms of the individual's pursuit of life goals (schedules and serial programs) which provide a sense of purpose and self-enhancement. Persons are thus somewhat future-oriented in Murray's system.

However, Murray does recognize the existence of both proactive and reactive needs. Acknowledgment of reactive needs clearly suggests that no individual is entirely free of immediate reality demands—all persons must respond to physiological and environmental pressures if they are to survive. Furthermore, Murray's need-press account of behavior, stressing the instigating effects of press upon need, logically requires a reactive view of human nature. Hence, Murray's commitment to proactivity is less than complete.

7 Homeostasis–Heterostasis Murray strongly favors a homeostatic conception of human behavior. He argues that needs lead to tension which, in turn, leads to tension reduction. It is Murray's belief that reducing need tension comes closest to an "all-embracing" principle of personality. This simple need-reduction model, however, applies only to negative needs in Murray's theory, e.g., need to avoid aversive stimuli. As for positive need systems, Murray insists that a tensionless state itself is not satisfying, as Freud assumed, but rather that the process of reducing tension creates satisfaction. We are satisfied to the degree that we are able to reduce the tensions which we experience. For example, the hungrier people are, the more likely they will be to enjoy their favorite dinner. In fact, some people deliberately work up an appetite so that they can increase the bliss of eating. Thus, Murray's homeostatic view of motivation is not limited to simple tension reduction but is expanded to include the *generation of tension* as well. Individuals first generate the tensions of positive need systems so that they can subsequently enjoy the process of reducing them. This "generation of tension—reduction of tension" formula represents an ongoing motivational pattern as opposed to an end state, a way of life rather than a final goal (Murray and Kluckhohn, 1953). It is the nature of human beings to constantly generate and reduce various need-related tensions. Murray's view of motivation, while a significant variation on the homeostatic theme, nonetheless reveals the assumption of homeostasis at its base.

8 Knowability–Unknowability An important key to understanding Murray's position on this assumption is found in the statement: "Every man is in certain respects, a. like all other men, b. like some other men, c. like no other man (Kluckhohn and Murray, 1953, p. 53)." Murray regards the scientific disciplines of anthropology, biology, and psychology as potentially able to discover most if not all that there is to know about people in categories a and b. To this important extent, he supports the knowability side of the continuum.

However, in category c, individual uniqueness, Murray considers the potential contributions of psychology to be much more limited. Why? Murray's answer is that since individuals are unique, there will always be a subjective, idiosyncratic element in each person that will elude scientific explanation, given a science of psychology concerned with all people. In other words, scientific concepts cannot encompass all aspects of human personality, since it is a practical impossibility for science to study the idiosyncracies of every individual in the human race, even if the appropriate scientific methods were available to do so. Murray quotes Aristotle in this regard: "It is the part of an educated man to seek exactness in each class of subjects only so far as the nature of the subject admits (1954, p. 453)."

The nature of Murray's subject, man, admits only a partial degree of exactness (knowability) through scientific methods. This is especially true when the personologist strives to explain why every person is in certain respects like no other person. Despite his efforts to develop a science of persons, then, Murray is a humanist who appears doubtful about the capacity of science to establish meaningful laws of individual behavior. When his position is viewed in total, Murray is not markedly inclined to either pole of the knowability–unknowability assumption.

To here

EMPIRICAL VALIDATION OF NEED THEORY CONCEPTS

mark

What evidence is there to support Murray's personological system? In attempting to answer this question, one must distinguish between research which is an outgrowth of Murray's conceptions of personality and research aimed at determining his theory's empirical validity. Despite his enormous influence on personality assessment, there is an alarming absence of studies designed to test specific predictions derived from his theoretical formulations. Thus, at present, there is little basis on which to evaluate the empirical validity of Murray's concepts directly.

This assessment does not imply that he has failed to stimulate interest among personologists concerning certain variables outlined in his theory. There is, for instance, a voluminous literature on nAchievement (McClelland, 1961, 1965). But this research cannot be regarded as indicative of the empirical existence of his list of needs. Most of this research treats nAchievement simply as an avenue for investigating theoretical variables outside the domain of Murray's system.

Murray's professional life has been one of deep commitment to the scientific study of personality. He has conducted studies examining the effects of fear on personality judgments (Murray, 1933) and clairvoyance phenomena in dreams (Murray and Wheeler, 1936), and he has made a psychological interpretation of Melville's novel *Moby Dick* (1951b). Fascinating as they are to read, such reports do not clarify the empirical adequacy of his position. Murray would undoubtedly agree. Nonetheless, his pioneering efforts to develop a comprehensive and detailed science of persons has inspired many psychologists to devise new and effective procedures for understanding human behavior.

Why hasn't Murray's theory attracted others to evaluate its empirical status? Perhaps the most commonly cited reason is that his concepts are limited to elaborate descriptions, rather than explanations, of human behavior. His rich taxonomy of needs is seen by many personologists as a bewildering array of overlapping classifications largely devoid of theoretical utility (Maddi, 1963). Furthermore, it has been noted (Hall and Lindzey, 1970) that Murray has offered no explicitly stated psychological assumptions linked to his concepts, rendering no testable consequences based on the theory. In brief, his various theoretical concepts need to be made more coherent and explicit before they can be properly tested. While these kinds of criticisms may be leveled against any personality theorist, they do constitute a partial explanation of why Murray's position has failed to capture research attention.

Murray's Approach to Research

Murray has always insisted that predicting human behavior is an impossible task, an attitude clearly compatible with his theoretical emphasis on the complexity and uniqueness of the individual. Nonetheless, he keeps at it. Based on his humanistic respect for individuality, he has approached human behavior from an *idiographic* perspective. Thus, Murray believes that a scientific appraisal of human personality must be based on intensive, multifaceted studies of persons as individuals as opposed to searching for common tendencies in groups of people. In fact, he deplores any assessment of behavior in which the results reflect group differences, statistical averages, or summary relationships between specific measures of personality. Murray contends that this latter approach, *nomothetic* in nature, fails to account for the complex subtleties of individuals and their relationships with others.

At the same time, he argues that the future development of a coherent science of persons can evolve if the tested methods of experimental specialists are integrated with those of personologists into what he calls a "multiform assessment program" (Murray, 1963). Toward this end, he has proposed two rules which would govern the activities of personological investigators. First, all investigators would use the same limited population of subjects. The advantage of this procedure in Murray's judgment is that investigators would have at their disposal not only the results of other experiments but also the massive accumulation of data obtained via the assessment process in general. This recommended strategy would be something akin to a central information file from which competent investigators would select or contribute relevant data. The second rule (possessing even greater potential significance for personality researchers) would require two series of meetings of experimental-ists and personologists: one series to formulate the personality profile of each subject, and another series to establish plausible explanations of the individual differences observed in each experiment taken as a unit. The goal of this second meeting would be to explain, within a reasonable degree of accuracy, the individual's behavior in everyday life. Additionally, Murray has argued that the *ecological validity* of psychological experiments (i.e., their generalizability to nonlaboratory contexts) would be greatly enhanced if experimental settings could more closely approach the individual's real world. While these are lofty ideals for any investigator, they serve as guiding principles for Murray's own research efforts.

What Are Harvard Men Really Like? Murray's principal contribution to personality research resulted from an exhaustive study of fifty college males conducted under his auspices as director of the Harvard Psychological Clinic. These young men were extensively studied for several months by a staff of experienced investigators representing various disciplines and theoretical perspectives. The techniques employed in this longitudinal study included projective and objective personality tests, behavioral observations and ratings, in-depth interviews, and a variety of experimental procedures. They were really put through the mill. Below is a partial listing of methods used in this multiform clinical assessment program:

   1 Autobiographical Sketch (family and personal history, school and college experiences, sexual development, future goals, self-appraisal).
   2 Present Dilemmas (discussion of personal problems and solutions for them).
   3 Predictions and Sentiments Test (measurement of the similarity between one's prediction of economic, political, social, scientific, etc., events and one's hopes regarding such events).
   4 Musical Reverie Test (report of thought processes elicited by phonograph music).
   5 Abilities Test (self-report measures of such abilities as mechanical, social, artistic, and theory-creative).
   6 Memory for Failures Test (recall of failure and successes in solving jigsaw puzzles).

After gaining a comprehensive picture of the student's personality using these and other procedures, the interdisciplinary team would study each student and then share their information and observations in a case conference setting, or "diagnostic council." Rigorous debate followed by a majority vote would then be used as the basis for developing a synthesized account of each student's personality. Presently this approach to personality assessment would be regarded as unscientific, but personology then was in its infancy and Murray was exploring alternatives. By the same token, it would be erroneous to think that Murray's complicated theory can be verified merely by studying the needs of a group of fifty Harvard undergraduate men. Harvard students do not necessarily reflect the rest of the world. In other words, unless the observations upon which Murray's theory rests are representative of the general population, its validity is likely to be restricted if not totally suspect.

Debbie Bell

Assessment of Needs   Another indication of Murray's pervasive influence on personality research is the extent to which some of his techniques for assessing needs remain in active use today. The Thematic Apperception Test (TAT), developed by Murray and a coworker, is one of the most widely used psychological tests in contemporary clinical psychology. However, the TAT is actually a method of personality assessment rather than an integral part of Murray's theory. Further discussion of the TAT may be found in the "Application" section of this chapter.

Murray's conception of needs has also provided the rationale for the development of several personality inventories. The most notable have been Stern's (1958) Activities Index and the Edwards (1953) Personal Preference Schedule (EPPS). Both of these clinically useful tests were constructed on the basis of Murray's descriptions of psychogenic needs. In particular, the EPPS is regarded as a reliable and valid measure of certain of Murray's needs (Maddi, 1972). This inventory provides a profile of fifteen different variables (e.g., need for endurance, autonomy, change) drawn from Murray's hypothesized list of needs.

Finally, three of the psychogenic needs enumerated by Murray have provoked considerable attention. They are nAchievement, nAffiliation, and nPower. The quantity of research and theorizing on these variables is overwhelming and documents Murray's influence on personological investigators. Additionally, a theory of achievement motivation (Atkinson, 1957; McClelland, Atkinson, Clark, and Lowell, 1953) has been developed on the basis of Murray's descriptive account of the achievement need and his construction of the TAT. Conversely, Murray himself would consider all this research and theorizing as a poor substitute for comprehensive studies that attempt to establish a coherent formulation of each individual's personality. It is quite conceivable that this goal can be realized if psychologists can learn to deal with the full range of human behavior. Murray is one example of a small number of theorists who have challenged this frontier.

APPLICATION: THE THEMATIC APPERCEPTION TEST   *Brewer*

The Thematic Apperception Test or TAT was developed by Morgan and Murray (1935) as one method of exploring unconscious thoughts and fantasies. It is currently one of the most popular *projective techniques* (the meaning of this term will be clear shortly) used by clinical psychologists and is second only to the Rorschach Inkblot test in terms of the amount of research it has stimulated (Buros, 1972). Its primary areas of application are clinical diagnosis and motivational research.

The TAT consists of a set of thirty black-and-white pictures (some fairly realistic and some quite symbolic) and one blank card. Most of the pictures have one or several people in them who are engaged in some ambiguous action. For example, one picture depicts a young man standing with downcast head buried in his arm, with the figure of a seminude woman lying in bed behind him. A second picture depicts the huddled form of a boy on the floor against a couch with his head bowed on his right arm. On the floor beside him is a revolver (Murray, 1943). Somewhat different sets of pictures are available for children, adolescents, and minority groups. The task of subjects is to make up as dramatic or interesting a story as they can for each picture. In the story they are to tell what has led up to the scene depicted on the card, what is happening at the moment, and then to state what the outcome will be. In short, the story should have a past, present, and future. They also are instructed to describe what the characters in their stories are thinking and feeling. Their imagination is taxed to the limit if they are shown the blank card, since they must first imagine a picture on it and then construct a related story! Typically, twenty cards are administered one at a time to a subject in two separate testing sessions, and he or she is allotted an average of five minutes per story. The examiner usually records each story verbatim, occasionally requesting the subject to clarify or expand some portion of the narrative.

The assumptions underlying projective techniques (e.g., Rorschach, TAT) reflect the influences of psychoanalytic theory, specifically projection. The review of Freudian theory (Chapter 2) described projection as a defense mechanism whereby individuals unconsciously attribute their own thoughts, needs, or characteristics to other persons or objects in their environment. Although this is the sense in which "projection" has been commonly used, it is not precisely what Murray meant by the term in the projective test situation. The TAT is a storytelling test, in a sense a game of "make-believe," a situational task in which subjects are encouraged to give free rein to their imagination and to say whatever comes into their mind. Thus, Murray stresses that in projective testing we are dealing with *imaginative* projection rather than with Freudian projection per se. The thoughts or feelings which the subject gives are not necessarily negative or totally foreign to his personality. Rather, they are all those expressions he has relating to a specific card.

It is assumed that imaginative projection is maximal if the stimulus material is ambiguous—the more unstructured something is, the more likely subjects are to reveal something of themselves in interpreting it. The TAT deliberately furnishes subjects with a series of unstructured stimuli (pictures) that they are expected to "structure" ("What is going on here?"). How they interpret these stimuli largely depends on aspects of their personality—i.e., their individual readiness to perceive in a certain way (their apperception). The idea is that because there is no established meaning, any meaning that the subject gives his story must come from him and should therefore reveal something about his innermost feelings and desires. In short, it is assumed that the stories subjects tell reflect their own dominant needs, emotions, and conflicts; without being aware of the process, they identify with the principal characters in the pictures and thereby reveal themselves.

As might be expected, scoring and interpretation of the TAT requires considerable skill and training. Even though a few quantitative scoring systems exist, in actual practice many clinicians invent their own systems of analysis. This is because there are no right or wrong answers to the TAT cards. Murray (1943) recommends that the subject's responses be studied to determine if there are predominant *themes* repeated throughout many of the stories. This method of TAT interpretation, primarily content-oriented and qualitative in nature, is comparable to the psychoanalyst's interpretation of a patient's associations. That is, the interpreter looks for major motivations (or needs), conflicts, and strategies used to resolve conflicts and satisfy needs.

In Murray's system, the content of TAT stories is analyzed into two parts: (1) the force or forces emanating from the "hero" and (2) the force or forces emanating from the environment. The hero is the character with whom the subject has identified himself or herself—the character whose point of view is adopted and whose motives and feelings are most intimately portrayed. Murray also suggests that the examiner direct attention to the hero's outstanding traits—e.g., intelligence, leadership, dominance. Once the hero or heroes have been identified, the examiner analyzes the forces (needs) within the hero and the environmental forces (press) acting upon him or her. In other words, TAT stories are interpreted in terms of needs such as those for achievement, aggression, and sex—and of press—such as physical danger and rejection by loved ones. The interaction of hero need and environmental press together with the outcome of a single story constitutes a *simple thema. Complex themas* (interlocked simple themas forming a sequence) are inferred from common themes that permeate several stories. Murray's need-press approach to TAT interpretation is thus concerned with questions such as these: Do subjects act on the environment or are they controlled by it? Are they active or passive? Do they overcome obstacles in the path of achievement or does the environment block them? Do others help or hinder them? Do they respond to frustration with aggression or withdrawal? Are they dominant or submissive?

According to Murray, careful TAT interpretation can answer these kinds of questions. However, TAT stories are never to be understood as literal translations of the subject's behavior in everyday life. Murray (1943) distinguished two levels of functioning in this regard: *first-level functioning*—physical and verbal behavior (actual overt needs) and *second-level functioning*—ideas, plans, fantasies, and dreams about behavior. TAT content belongs in the latter category. Moreover, it is primarily a symbolic rather than a literal representation of this level of functioning. Thus, TAT stories represent working hypotheses for the interpreter rather than proved facts; they require verification by other methods. The psychologist's interpretations of TAT stories, which provide a window to the subject's private world of experience, also rely heavily upon a knowledge of personality theory as well as a highly developed sense of clinical intuition. Translation of these interpretations to actual subject behavior, even under the best of circumstances, is exceptionally difficult and hazardous.

A greater appreciation of the psychological significance of TAT stories can be gained by way of illustration. Below are excerpts from a story told by a male college student in response to a TAT card depicting a young boy contemplating a violin which rests on a table in front of him:

> This is a boy seated in his room gazing at the violin . . . (pause) His parents bought it for him and want him to learn to play it well . . . they *expect* this of him. They are *always* expecting something of him. He is looking at the thing and he doesn't want to play it . . . besides, it's a nice day, the window is open, and he hears his friends playing outside. He *resents* his parents for making him do this. (pause) It's hard to see what he's going to do. Maybe he'll try to play it for awhile, but if he still hates it, he may check out by way of the window (laughs)—it's on the first floor.

This student gave a number of other stories with a similar theme. The heroes consistently felt "pressed" by the expectations of significant others in the environment, especially by parents and teachers. The heroes also felt a great need to escape their difficult life situations; yet the outcomes of many stories were difficult for the student to articulate, e.g., "It's hard to see what he's going to do." As counseling progressed, he began to understand how deeply pressured by his parents he felt. The student felt that his parents expected him to attend college and do quite well, and he experienced their high expectations as both anxiety-provoking and overly constricting. Furthermore, he indicated a strong desire to escape his situation in two ways: by leaving college and by having occasional suicidal impulses (e.g., "but if he still hates it, he may check out by way of the window . . ."). While the feeling of being "pushed" was very evident in this case, lesser intensities of the same kind of feeling are experienced by many psychologically healthy college students.

In sharp contrast are excerpts from a story constructed by another male college student in response to the same TAT card:

> The boy in this picture often daydreams about his future accomplishments—he's doing so now. He's using the violin to stimulate his thinking. The kid is day-dreaming about the time when he'll become a world-famous violinist—another Isaac Stern. He diligently goes to his room every day to practice with this idea in mind. He's always felt that he could accomplish something worthwhile—becoming a great violinist is what he has decided to do. It's hard to stop a person like this. As far as the ending of this story goes, I think he'll make it. The boy will continue to practice until he achieves his ambition.

This student, a subject in a pilot study of certain TAT variables, presented other stories with similar achievement themes. Heroes consistently had high aspiration; they worked at something important with energy and persistence in striving to reach their objectives in life. They were seen as ambitious, persuasive, and creative. Environmental obstacles were either not present (as in this story) or rather easily overcome by the hero. The subject in this case had an excellent scholastic record. He was bright, purposeful, and self-confident. He knew who he was and where he wanted to go. At the time he was tested, he was applying to outstanding law schools with a view toward becoming a lawyer and then eventually entering politics.

The striking differences between the two students' responses above reflect significant personality differences. Murray's theoretical concepts of need, press, thema, and individual uniqueness thus come alive in TAT stories. In the hands of a skilled examiner, such stories are gateways to an understanding of the operation of Murray's hypothesized personality dynamics in any given individual. Although the TAT is far from perfect as a psychometric tool and is certainly not a magic key that will automatically unlock the doors to the unconscious, it has proved to be a productive and flexible method which has added significantly to our understanding of human motivation.

SUMMARY

Murray portrays personality as the hypothetical integrating agent within individuals that serves to organize and stabilize their behavior over time. In this scheme, all psychological events are functionally dependent upon underlying brain processes; without a brain, there would be no personality.

Murray's central theoretical concept, need, represents a force in the brain region which organizes psychological processes and behavior. There are various means of classifying needs in Murray's theory, such as viscerogenic-psychogenic, proactive-reactive, overt-covert, and effect-modal. Further, needs are organized and interrelated according to such principles as pre-potency, fusion, subsidiation, and conflict.

Needs constantly interact with environmental forces (press) to produce behavior. Different need-press combinations that characterize a person's behavior are called themas. Moreover, each person's uniqueness resides in the basic underlying pattern of his individual need-press relationships: the unity-thema.

Murray maintains that personality is deeply embedded in a time dimension. To represent behavioral continuity over time, he employs concepts such as "proceeding" (a temporal unit of either subject-subject or subject-object interaction). Murray also believes that as personality develops, it is powerfully influenced by four major groups of determinants: constitutional, group membership, role, and situational.

Murray's basic assumptions concerning human nature reflect an interesting blend of psychoanalytic and humanistic elements in his thinking. Need theory is based upon (1) a strong commitment to the assumptions of determinism, rationality, and homeostasis; (2) a moderate commitment to the assumptions of holism, subjectivity, and proactivity; and (3) a "middle of the road" position on the constitutionalism–environmentalism and knowability–unknowability assumptions.

While Murray has had enormous influence on personality assessment, there is an absence of empirical studies directly designed to test aspects of his theory. Murray's own idiographic approach to personality research, the multiform clinical assessment program, was described in this chapter.

One major application of need theory is the Thematic Apperception Test. The TAT is currently among the most widely used projective techniques in clinical diagnosis and motivational research.

BIBLIOGRAPHY

Atkinson, J. Motivational determinants of risk-taking behavior. *Psychological Review,* 1957, **64,** 359–372.

Buros, O. (Ed.). *The seventh mental measurements yearbook.* Highland Park, N.J.: Gryphon Press, 1972.

Edwards, A. *Edwards personal preference schedule.* New York: Psychological Corporation, 1953.

Hall, C., & Lindzey, G. *Theories of personality* (2d ed.). New York: Wiley, 1970.

Kluckhohn, C., & Murray, H. Personality formation: The determinants. In C. Kluckhohn, H. Murray, & D. Schneider (Eds.), *Personality in nature, society, and culture* (2d ed.). New York: Knopf, 1953, pp. 53–67.

Maddi, S. Humanistic psychology: Allport and Murray. In J. Wepman & R. Heine (Eds.), *Concepts of personality.* Chicago: Aldine, 1963, pp. 162–205.

Maddi, S. *Personality theories: A comparative analysis* (2d ed.). Homewood, Ill.: Dorsey, 1972.

Maddi, S., & Costa, P. *Humanism in personology: Allport, Maslow, and Murray.* Chicago: Aldine Atherton, 1972.

McClelland, D., Atkinson, J., Clark, R., & Lowell, E. *The achievement motive.* New York: Appleton-Century-Crofts, 1953.

McClelland, D. *The achieving society.* Princeton: Van Nostrand, 1961.

McClelland, D. N achievement and entrepreneurship: A longitudinal study. *Journal of Personality and Social Psychology,* 1965, **1,** 389–392.

Morgan, C., & Murray, H. A method for investigating fantasies: The Thematic Apperception Test. *Archives of Neurology and Psychiatry,* 1935, **34,** 289–306.

Murray, H. The effect of fear upon estimates of the maliciousness of other personalities. *Journal of Social Psychology,* 1933, **4,** 310–329.

Murray, H., & Wheeler, D. A note on the possible clairvoyance of dreams. *Journal of Psychology,* 1936, **3,** 309–313.

Murray, H. *Explorations in personality: A clinical and experimental study of fifty men of college age.* New York: Oxford University Press, 1938.

Murray, H. What should psychologists do about psychoanalysis? *Journal of Abnormal and Social Psychology,* 1940, **35,** 150–175.

Murray, H. *Thematic Apperception Test manual.* Cambridge, Mass.: Harvard University Press, 1943.

Murray, H. Introduction. In H. Melville, *Pierre, or the ambiguities.* New York: Farrar Straus, 1949, pp. xiii–ciii.

Murray, H. Some basic psychological assumptions and conceptions. *Dialectica,* 1951a, **5,** 266–292.

Murray, H. In nomine diaboli. *New England Quarterly,* 1951b, **24,** 435–452.

Murray, H., & Kluckhohn, C. Outline of a conception of personality. In C. Kluckhohn, H. Murray, & D. Schneider (Eds.), *Personality in nature, society, and culture* (2d ed.). New York: Knopf, 1953, pp. 3–49.

Murray, H. Toward a classification of interaction. In T. Parsons & E. Shils (Eds.), *Toward a general theory of action.* Cambridge: Harvard University Press, 1954, pp. 434–464.

Murray, H. Preparations for the scaffold of a comprehensive system. In S. Koch (Ed.), *Psychology: A study of a science,* Vol. 3. New York: McGraw-Hill, 1959, pp. 7–54.

Murray, H. The personality and career of Satan. *Journal of Social Issues,* 1962, **28,** 36–54.

Murray, H. Studies of stressful interpersonal disputations. *American Psychologist,* 1963, **18,** 28–36.

Murray, H. Personality: II. Contemporary viewpoints, components of an evolving personological system. In D. Sills (Ed.), *International encyclopedia of the social sciences.* New York: Macmillan and Free Press, 1968, Vol. 12, pp. 5–13.

Office of Strategic Services Assessment Staff. *Assessment of Men.* New York: Rinehart, 1948.

Stern, G. *Preliminary manual: Activities index–college characteristics index.* Syracuse, N.Y.: Syracuse University Psychological Research Center, 1958.

White, R. (Ed.). *The study of lives: Essays on personality in honor of Henry A. Murray.* New York: Atherton, 1963.

SUGGESTED READINGS

1 Dailey, C. *Assessment of lives.* San Francisco: Jossey-Bass, 1971.
2 Hall, M. A conversation with Henry A. Murray. *Psychology Today,* 1968, **4,** 56–63.
3 Megargee, I., & Parker, G. An exploration of the equivalence of Murrayan needs as assessed by the Adjective Check List, the TAT and Edwards' Personal Preference Schedule. *Journal of Clinical Psychology,* 1968, **24,** 47–51.
4 Murray, H. American icarus. In A. Burton & R. Harris (Eds.), *Clinical studies of personality.* New York: Harper Torchbooks, 1966, Vol. II., pp. 615–641.
5 Murray, H. *Encounter with psychology.* San Francisco: Jossey-Bass, 1969.
6 White, R. *Lives in progress: A study of the natural growth of personality* (2d ed.). New York: Holt, Rinehart & Winston, 1966.

B. F. Skinner (*Photo by Jill Krementz*)

B. F. Skinner:
A Behavioristic-Learning
Theory of Personality

Much of human behavior is either learned or modified by learning. Through learning we acquire knowledge, language, attitudes, values, manual skills, fears, personality traits, and self-insight. Therefore the discovery of the laws of learning can justifiably be viewed as one of the key avenues toward understanding man's activities. One of the most prolific of all psychologists who have devoted themselves to the goal of explaining, predicting, and controlling human behavior is B. F. Skinner. Building on the work of Pavlov and Watson, Skinner has become the leading present-day exponent of a behavioristic-learning approach to psychology. His efforts, based on the premise that nearly all behavior is directly governed by environmental contingencies of reinforcement, have provided the basis for a science of behavior unparalleled in the history of modern thought. In the eyes of many, Skinner is the most influential psychologist of our time.

BIOGRAPHICAL SKETCH

Burrhus Frederic Skinner was born March 20, 1904, in Susquehanna, Pennsylvania, a railroad town a few miles south of the New York State border. He recalls his early years as occurring in a stable environment where learning was esteemed, discipline prevailed, and rewards were given when deserved:

> I was never physically punished by my father (a lawyer) and only once by my mother. She washed my mouth out with soap and water because I had used a bad word. My father never missed an opportunity, however, to inform me of the punishments which were waiting if I turned out to have a criminal mind. He once took me through the county jail, and on a summer vacation I was taken to a lecture with colored slides describing life in Sing Sing. As a result I am afraid of the police and buy too many tickets to their annual dance (Skinner, 1967, pp. 390–391).

During his childhood years, Skinner was mechanically inclined, evidenced by his building roller-skate scooters, steerable wagons, rafts, and similar gadgets. Likewise, he had a special interest in exploring his environs:

> I roamed the hills for miles around. . . . With another boy I built a shack in the hills alongside a creek, and I learned to swim in the pool with a poisonous watersnake. Four other boys and I once went three hundred miles down the Susquehanna River in a fleet of three canoes (1967, p. 388).

In high school, he earned money by lettering advertising show cards, played in a jazz band, and with three other boys organized an orchestra that performed two nights a week in a local movie theater.

Skinner received his B.A. degree in English literature in 1926 from Presbyterian-founded Hamilton College, a small liberal arts school. As an undergraduate, he did not take any psychology courses. Following graduation he pursued writing as a career for two years, at one point living in Greenwich Village as a bohemian. An encouraging letter from Robert Frost, who had appraised three of his short stories, was a high point of his literary life. Since by his own admission he had nothing important to say, he enrolled in the Harvard graduate psychology program in 1928. Although his interest in literature has never been abandoned, Skinner explains his change in careers as follows: "A writer might portray human behavior accurately, but he did not therefore understand it. I was to remain interested in human behavior, but the literary method had failed me; I would turn to the scientific (1967, p. 395)." During his student years at Harvard (M.A. degree in 1930; Ph.D. degree in 1931) he studied animal behavior, thereby developing several of his principles of scientific methodology. Although he did not follow in the footsteps of any particular faculty member, he did take course work under E. G. Boring, Carroll Pratt, and Henry A. Murray. His life-style as a Harvard graduate student was Spartan:

> I would rise at six, study until breakfast, go to classes, laboratories, and libraries with no more than fifteen minutes unscheduled during the day, study until exactly nine o'clock at night and go to bed. I saw no movies or plays, seldom went to concerts, had scarcely any dates, and read nothing but psychology and physiology (1967, p. 398).

From 1931 to 1936, he continued to work at Harvard, the first two years supported by a National Research Council Fellowship and the last three as a Junior Fellow in the prestigious Harvard Society of Fellows.

Skinner began his teaching career at the University of Minnesota in 1936, remaining there until 1945. This was a period of remarkable productivity and established Skinner as one of the leading behaviorists in the United States. During the years 1942–1943, he conducted war research sponsored by General Mills, Inc., and was a Guggenheim Fellow in 1944–1945. In the fall of 1945 he was appointed chairman of the psychology department at Indiana University, a position he held until 1947, when he rejoined Harvard as William James Lecturer. The following year Skinner was promoted to Professor of Psychology at Harvard and in 1958 he became Edgar Pierce Professor of Psychology.

Dr. Skinner is a member of a great number of professional and honorary societies. He was awarded the Warren Medal by the Society of Experimental Psychologists in 1942, an honorary Sc.D. by Hamilton College in 1951, and the American Psychological Association (APA) Distinguished Scientific Contribution Award in 1958. He is one of a handful of psychologists who have received the President's Medal of Science and is a 1971 recipient of the APA's Gold Medal Award with the following citation: "To B. F. Skinner—pioneer in psychological research, leader in theory, master in technology, who has revolutionized the study of behavior in our time (*American Psychologist*, 1972, January, p. 72)." Responding to his many accolades, Skinner says: "Many notes in my files comment on the fact that I have been depressed or frightened by so-called honors. I forego honors which would take time away from my work or unduly reinforce specific aspects of it (1967, p. 408)."

The volume of work that Skinner has published is gigantic—*The Behavior of Organisms* (1938); *Walden Two* (1948a, requiring only seven weeks to write); *Science and Human Behavior* (1953); *Verbal Behavior* (1957a); *Schedules of Reinforcement* (1957b, with C. B. Ferster); *Cumulative Record* (1961); *The Technology of Teaching* (1968); *Contingencies of Reinforcement* (1969); *Beyond Freedom and Dignity* (1971); and *About Behaviorism* (1974). Perhaps best known among college students is Skinner's *Walden Two,* a novel depicting the creation of an experimental community based on the control of behavior through psychological principles of reinforcement. Twin Oaks, a functioning commune in rural Virginia, is currently implementing social life proposed by Skinner in this book. In addition, *A Festschrift for B. F. Skinner,* edited by Dews (1970)—a collection of edited papers—was presented to Skinner on his sixty-fifth birthday. His autobiography appears in Volume 5 of the *History of Psychology in Autobiography* (1967, pp. 385–413).

Skinner's dominant area of interest is the experimental analysis of behavior. He has worked primarily with infrahuman organisms, usually rats or pigeons, but has in recent years applied the principles of operant conditioning to the study of adult psychotics and autistic children, an analysis of human language, and the design of teaching machines. In addition to the widely known "Skinner box," a device used to study the operant behavior of animals, he has designed a temperature-controlled crib in which he raised one of his two daughters. Most recently he has developed a number of instructional machines to facilitate learning from kindergarten through college. His contributions to psychology have been both varied and immense.

SKINNER'S APPROACH TO PSYCHOLOGY

Most personological theorists share two perspectives: (1) a commitment to the study of persistent differences among people and (2) a reliance on hypothetical constructs to account for the variety and complexity of human behavior. These perspectives constitute the mainstream, if not the essence, of virtually all theorizing about personality to date. Throughout most of his career, Skinner questioned whether abstract theories are necessary or desirable or whether they should be abandoned in favor of an approach based solely on observed relationships between behavior and its consequences (1950). He insisted that psychology, particularly the field of learning, is not sufficiently advanced to justify efforts devoted to grand-scale, formalized theory building. Second, he also contended that there is no need for theory-directed research since it provides "explanations of observed facts which appeal to events taking place in different terms and measured, if at all, in different dimensions (Skinner, 1961, p. 39)." Finally, Skinner suggested that theories of human behavior often give psychologists a false sense of security about the state of knowledge, when in fact they do not comprehend the relationships between ongoing behavior and its environmental antecedents.

In light of Skinner's apparent antitheoretical position, it is questionable whether he should be included in a volume concerned with personality theories. Fortunately, Skinner now admits to being a psychological theorist, thus justifying our presentation of his system as illustrative of a behavioristic-learning approach to the study of personality. In a recent interview he noted:

> I defined theory as an effort to explain behavior in terms of something going on in another universe, such as the mind or the nervous system. Theories of that sort I do not believe are essential or helpful. Besides, they are dangerous; they cause all kinds of trouble. But I look forward to an overall theory of human behavior which will bring together a lot of facts and express them in a more general way. That kind of theory I would be very much interested in promoting, and I consider myself to be a theoretician (Evans, 1968, p. 88).

Furthermore, he has asserted that whether some experimental psychologists approve or not, experimental psychology is inevitably committed to the task of constructing a theory of behavior (Skinner, 1969). While Skinner's view of such a theory is far different from that of most personologists, it nonetheless is essential to the scientific understanding of human behavior.

Out With Autonomous Man!

Skinner passionately repudiates all explanations of behavior based on the presumed existence of an inner metaphysical man (a little man or *homunculus*), the self, the unconscious, or any other hypothetical entity referring to events which "lie under the skin." Such mentalistic and intrapsychic mechanisms, he notes, originated in primitive animism but persist because there is ignorance of the environmental conditions governing behavior:

> Autonomous man serves to explain only the things we are not yet able to explain in other ways. His existence depends upon our ignorance, and he naturally loses status as we come to know more about behavior. . . . We do not need to try to discover what personalities, states of mind, feelings, traits of character, plans, purposes, intentions, or the other prerequisites of autonomous man really are in order to get on with a scientific analysis of behavior (Skinner, 1971, pp. 12–13).

Skinner's objection to the use of such hypothetical constructs or inner causes is not that they are inappropriate phenomena for psychologists to study but rather that they are shrouded in terminology that makes objective definitions and empirical tests impossible. In the history of science, he observes, it has usually been necessary to completely abandon such conceptions rather than modify them to a form which permits empirical study. To explain why a competent student flunks out of college, we might easily say "because he had a strong fear of failure," "because he lacked motivation," or "because he cut classes due to an unconscious fear of success." Such hypotheses about the student's dismissal from college may sound like explanations, but Skinner warns that they explain nothing unless the motives involved are explicitly defined and unless the antecedents of flunking out are established.

Thus, if a so-called mentalistic (unobservable) concept is invoked to explain behavior, it must be translatable into terms relevant to the experimental operations involved in investigation and measurement. To settle for less would be to resort to the very armchair philosophizing that Skinner so vehemently deplores. One could start with what can be observed (i.e., the incident of flunking out) and then determine whether additional explanations augment the understanding of the behavior in question. If a competent student flunks out of college, is it not more illuminating to examine what environmental variables preceded that behavior than to propose as its cause some mental entity that cannot be objectively identified? For instance, did dormitory noise disrupt his sleep so that he could not study effectively? Did he work forty hours per week and thus lack the time to study? Or did he play on the varsity basketball team whose schedule forced him to miss numerous classes and exams? These questions clearly reveal that Skinner places responsibility for the individual's actions on environmental circumstances rather than the autonomous man within.

Skinner also believes that the mental or intentional explanation of events brings curiosity to an end. He says:

> We can see the effect in casual discourse. If we ask someone, "Why did you go to the theatre?" and he says, "Because I felt like going," we are apt to take his reply as a kind of explanation. It would be much more to the point to know what has happened when he has gone to the theatre in the past, what he heard or read about the play he went to see, and what other things in his past or present environments might have induced him to go (as opposed to doing something else), but we accept "I feel like going" as a sort of summary of all this and are not likely to ask for details (1971, p. 10).

In Skinnerian psychology, then, no attempt is made to ask questions or to infer processes about the individual's inner state. It is considered irrelevant for a scientific explanation of behavior. To avoid the notion that describing is explaining, Skinner contends that the human organism is an unopened box (an "empty organism"), and hence that all variables (motives, drives, conflicts, attitudes, emotions, etc.) which mediate the inputs and outputs of behavior should be discarded from the domain of psychological inquiry. These organismic variables add nothing to our understanding of human activity and only serve to delay the development of a scientific study of behavior. According to Skinner, adequate explanations can be accomplished without recourse to any constructs other than those accounting for the functional relationships between various stimulus conditions (tangible characteristics of the environment affecting the individual) and behavioral responses overtly emitted by the individual.

Down With Physiological-Genetic Explanations!

Unlike many contemporary psychologists, Skinner does not believe that the ultimate answers to the questions of psychology will be found in the laboratory of the physiologist. This disregard for physiological-genetic conceptions of behavior is based largely on the conviction that they do not facilitate behavioral control. Skinner explains his aversion to "physiologizing" by noting:

> Even when it can be shown that some aspect of behavior is due to season of birth, gross body type, or genetic constitution, the fact is of limited use. It may help us in predicting behavior, but is of little value in an experimental analysis or in practical control because such a condition cannot be manipulated after the individual has been conceived (1957b, p. 371).

Thus, Skinner does not oppose recognition of the biological-genetic elements of behavior but rather ignores them because they are not (at least currently) amenable to modification through manipulation.

What Behavioral Science Should Be

In his approach to the study of people, Skinner assumes that all behavior is lawfully determined, predictable, and able to be brought under environmental control. To understand behavior is to control it, and vice versa. He is unalterably opposed to any admission of free will or any other "volitional," uncaused event. Human beings, in his system, are machines—highly complicated ones, but machines nonetheless. While he is by no means the first psychologist to propose a mechanistic approach to the study of behavior (Watson advocated throwing out mentalistic concepts in the 1920s), his formulation is exceptional in that he carries the idea to its logical conclusion. To Skinner, the science of human behavior is basically no different from any other data-oriented natural science; thus, its goals are the same—prediction and control of the phenomena studied (behavior in this case).

Additionally, Skinner argues that since all science advances from the simple to the complex, it is logical to study infrahumans prior to studying humans. The former enables the psychologist to discover more easily the basic processes and principles of behavior. Among other advantages, the researcher is able to exert more precise control over the conditions influencing an animal's environment and to collect data over longer periods of time. There is, of course, a serious question as to how much of the findings uncovered by studying one species (e.g., rats) are truly applicable to another species (e.g., humans). Skinner, however, advocates the use of lower species as experimental subjects because he believes there is ample evidence showing definite relationship between principles of behavior established at that level and their application to human functioning. To illustrate, the recent development of teaching machines and programmed learning are direct products of Skinner's work in the animal laboratory. *Man has the same abilities as a rat*

Unlike most current psychological research, Skinner's work stresses a thorough analysis of a single organism's behavior. Skinner believes that the study of a single organism is appropriate because laws governing such organisms are identical to the laws which govern all organisms. Thus, while the behavior of individual rats, pigeons, or people may vary, the basic scientific laws controlling that behavior do not. By studying *one* rat, *one* pigeon, or *one* person, Skinner argues that such basic laws can be uncovered.

This orientation, often referred to as the *single-subject experimental design*, does not require the traditional statistical techniques (i.e., inferential) that most students learn in their psychological training. Instead of seeking to make statistical predictions about the behavior of the nonexistent average individual, Skinner strongly argues that psychological science should attempt

Perfect environnement

to predict and determine experimentally the influence of one or more controlled variables upon a specified component of an individual organism's behavior in a controlled environment. This approach requires a nonstatistical strategy which yields laws relevant to real individual behavior. This, says Skinner, is what psychology as a behavioral science should have as its aim. Skinnerian psychology might be summarized by a statement Skinner (1956) quotes from Pavlov: "Control your conditions and you will see order." *are had this*

In keeping with his behavioristic approach, Skinner advocates a *functional analysis* of the behaving organism. In such an analysis the psychologist strives to establish exact, real, and specifiable relationships between the organism's observable behavior (responses) and the environmental conditions (stimuli) that control or determine it. The variables employed must be external, visible, and defined in quantitative terms. It is the cause-and-effect relationships emerging from a functional analysis which become the laws of behavioral science. The practical goal is to be able to manipulate the environmental (independent) variables from which predictions are made and then to measure the resulting changes in behavior (dependent variable). Thus, one can work within the boundaries of a natural science and yet discover laws relevant to the behavior of individual organisms.

Perfect environnement in 'The Garden of Eden but was not satisfied.'

OPERANT BEHAVIOR

In formulating a system of behavior, Skinner (1938) distinguishes two types of behavioral responses: respondent and operant. In its simplest terms, *respondent behavior* (also known as classical or Pavlovian conditioning) refers to a specific kind of response which is elicited by a known stimulus, the latter always preceding the former in time. Familiar respondents include pupillary constriction or dilation to changes in light stimulation, knee jerk to a hammer tapped on the patellar tendon, shivering to cold, and salivation to food. In each of these examples, the relationship between the stimulus (light stimulation, hammer, etc.) in involuntary and spontaneous—it always occurs. In fact, the same stimulus elicits the same response from all organisms of the same species. Thus, respondent behavior usually entails *reflexes* involving the autonomic nervous system. However, respondent behavior may also be learned. For example, a person who perspires profusely and has "butterflies in his stomach" prior to delivering an important speech is manifesting respondent behavior.

In the early 1900s Ivan Pavlov, the famous Russian physiologist and Nobel Prize winner, first discovered, while studying the physiology of digestion, that respondent behavior can be conditioned. He observed that meat powder placed in the mouth of a hungry dog always evokes salivation. In this case, salivation is an unlearned response or, as Pavlov called it, an *unconditioned response* (UCR). It is elicited by the meat powder which, in this instance, is termed the *unconditioned stimulus* (UCS). Pavlov's great discovery was that if a previously neutral stimulus is repeatedly paired with the unconditioned stimulus, eventually the neutral stimulus acquires the capacity to elicit the unconditioned response when it is presented alone *without* the unconditioned stimulus. For example, if a bell is rung each time immediately before the meat powder reaches his mouth, gradually the dog will begin to salivate upon hearing the bell, even if the meat powder is no longer presented. The new response, salivation to the bell sound, is termed a *conditioned response* (CR), while the previously neutral eliciting stimulus, the bell, is known as the *conditioned stimulus* (CS). If, on subsequent trials, meat powder is regularly omitted, the magnitude of the salivary response gradually diminishes until it ceases to occur when the conditioned stimulus (bell) is presented. This process, known as *extinction* of the conditioned response, demonstrates that reinforcement (meat powder) is essential for both the acquisition and maintenance of respondent learning.

A well-known experiment conducted by Watson and Raynor (1920) illustrates the phenomenon of human classical conditioning. These investigators conditioned an emotional fear response in Albert, an eleven-month-old child. Prior to the experiment it was determined that Albert showed no fear reactions to a number of stimuli—loss of support; burning newspapers; masks with and without hair; and several animals including a rabbit, cat, dog, monkey, and white rat. Likewise, he had never been seen in a state of fear or rage. Watson and Raynor's procedure was to present a tame white rat (conditioned stimulus) together with a loud noise (unconditioned stimulus) produced by striking a steel bar with a hammer. After the rat and the frightening sound were paired seven times, a strong fear response (CR), crying and falling over, was elicited when the rat alone was presented. Subsequent tests indicated that Albert had generalized his fear reactions to a wide range of stimuli including a rabbit, dog, fur coat, and even a Santa Claus mask. Tragic though this case may seem, it does reveal how similar fears (of strangers, dentists, and doctors) may be acquired via the process of classical conditioning.

Although Skinner has incorporated many of the principles of Pavlovian conditioning into his system, he does not believe that the major portion of human behavior is composed of simple reflexes or conditioned responses. According to Skinner (1953), most human social behavior falls into a second class, that of behavior "freely" emitted by an organism. Because this type of behavior implies an active organism that "operates" upon its environment, controlling the environment and being controlled by it, Skinner labeled the responses *operants.* Operant behavior (produced by instrumental or operant conditioning) is determined by the events that follow the response. That is, a behavior is followed by a consequence and the nature of the consequence modifies the organism's tendency to repeat the behavior in the future. For instance, riding a bicycle, playing the piano, throwing a ball, and writing one's name are considered operant response patterns or operants since they are controlled by the consequences which follow their respective performances. They are "voluntary," learned responses for which an identifiable stimulus does

Figure 5-1 This is a photograph of a Skinner box, widely used in studying operant learning in the rat and other animals. *(Photo courtesy of Ralph Gerbrands Co., Arlington, Mass.)*

not exist. If the outcomes or consequences following the response are favorable to the person, then the likelihood of the operant being emitted again in the future is thereby increased. When this happens, the consequence is said to be *reinforcing* and the operant response which has been affected by the reinforcement (in the sense that it is more likely to occur) has been conditioned. The strength of a positive reinforcing stimulus is thus defined in terms of its effects on the subsequent frequency of the response which immediately preceded it.

Alternatively, if the outcomes of responses are unfavorable or nonreinforcing, then the likelihood of the operant occurring again is decreased. For example, you will soon stop smiling at a person whose consistent response to your smile is a scowl. In other words, operant behavior may be controlled by another class of consequences called negative reinforcers or *aversive stimuli*. By definition, these stimuli weaken the behavior that produces them and strengthen the behavior that removes them. If the person consistently scowls, you will eventually try to avoid him altogether.

In order to study operant behavior in the laboratory, Skinner devised a deceptively simple type of procedure called the free *operant method*. In this procedure, a semistarved rat is placed in an experimental chamber (commonly referred to as the Skinner box—see Figure 5-1) which is empty except for a lever and a food dish at one end of it. (Isolation is required in order to minimize the effects of outside, extraneous influences.) At first, the rat will normally exhibit a variety of operants: walking, sniffing, scratching, grooming, and urinating. Such responses are not elicited by any recognizable stimulus; they are just "freely" emitted. Eventually, in the course of its exploratory activity, the rat will strike the lever, causing a pellet of food to be automatically delivered to the dish. Because the response of lever pressing has an initially low probability of occurrence, it must be considered as purely accidental in regard to feeding; that is, we cannot predict when the rat will press the lever, nor can we make him do it. However, by depriving the rat of food, say, for twenty-four hours, we can ensure that the lever-pressing response will eventually have a high probability of occurrence in this particular situation. This is done through a method called *magazine training,* whereby the experimenter delivers a food pellet each time the rat presses the lever. It can then be observed that the rat spends more time in the vicinity of the lever and the feeding dish until, in due course, it is pressing the lever at an ever-increasing rate. Lever pressing thus quickly becomes the rat's most dominant and frequent response under conditions of food deprivation. In the operant conditioning situation, then, the rat's behavior is instrumental (i.e., operates upon the environment) in producing the reinforcement (food). If nonreinforced trials now occur, that is, if food fails to appear consistently following the lever-pressing response, the rat eventually stops pressing and undergoes *experimental extinction.*

Now that we have covered the nature of operant conditioning, it may be helpful to consider an example of it encountered in almost any family with young children—the operant conditioning of crying behavior. Whenever young children are in obvious pain, they cry, and the parents' immediate reaction is to express attention and other positive reinforcements. Since attention is reinforcing for the child, the crying response naturally becomes conditioned. However, crying may occur even when pain is absent. Most parents believe that they can discriminate between crying due to pain and crying evoked by the desire for attention. Yet many parents persist in reinforcing the latter!

Is it possible for parents to eliminate conditioned crying behavior or is the child destined to be a "crybaby" the rest of his life? A case study reported by Williams (1959) illustrates how conditioned crying was extinguished in a twenty-one-month-old child. Due to serious illness during the first eighteen months of life, the child had received considerable attention from his concerned parents. In fact, because of his screaming and crying when put to bed, the parents or an aunt, who lived with the family, stayed in his bedroom until he went to sleep. These bedside vigils usually took from $1^1/2$ to 2 hours. By remaining in the room until he fell asleep, the parents were undoubtedly providing positive reinforcement for the maintenance of the child's crying behavior. He had his parents under perfect control. To extinguish this objectionable behavior, the parents were instructed to leave the child awake in the bedroom by himself and to ignore any subsequent crying. Within a period of seven nights, the crying behavior had virtually disappeared. By the tenth night, the child even smiled as his parents left the room and could be heard making happy sounds as he fell asleep. A week later, however, the child immediately began screaming when his aunt put him to bed and left the room. She returned to the room and remained there until the child went to sleep. This one instance of reinforcement was sufficient to necessitate going through the entire extinction process a second time. By the ninth night the child's crying was finally extinguished and Williams reported that no remission occurred within a two-year period.

Sueton

How to Quantify Operant Behavior

In Skinner's view, functional laws of behavior are best developed by focusing on factors which increase or decrease the probability of a response occurring over time rather than establishing which specific stimuli instigate a response. Thus, Skinner contends that the most useful and significant source of psychological data is the organism's *rate of responding* (i.e., the number of responses emitted in a given unit of time). As an easily identifiable measure of operant conditioning, it yields an orderly account of the individual organism's behavior as it occurs. Referring to a previous example, every time the rat presses the lever, a pen is activated by an electric timer making a mark on a constantly moving paper tape recording the response. This automated device, called a *cumulative recorder,* provides students of operant behavior with a *cumulative response record* of the organism's response rate. In addition to recording responses automatically, the apparatus enables the investigator to examine how variables, such as the kind and amount of reinforcement or punishment, affect operant behavior over extended periods of time. Skinner's method of obtaining data affords the psychologist a powerful means of controlling behavior.

Schedules of Reinforcement

The essence of operant conditioning relies on the fact that, all other things being equal, reinforced behavior tends to be repeated, whereas behavior that is nonreinforced or punished tends not to be repeated or is extinguished. Hence, the concept of reinforcement occupies a key role in Skinner's theory.

The rate at which operant behavior is acquired and maintained is a function of the schedule of reinforcements employed. A *schedule of reinforcement* is, in brief, a rule stating the contingencies under which reinforcements will be delivered. The simplest and most obvious contingency rule would be to reinforce the organism every time it emits the correct or desired response. This schedule, utilized by Skinner in his early research, is termed *continuous reinforcement* and is commonly used at the outset of all operant conditioning when the organism is learning to acquire the correct response. In most everyday-life situations, however, this is neither the most feasible nor economical way to maintain the desired response, since reinforcement of behavior does not usually occur on a uniform or regular basis. Most human social behavior is reinforced only intermittently. A baby cries many times before it elicits the mother's attention. A young man proposes matrimony many times before his proposal is honored. A scientist tries many approaches before arriving at a correct solution to a difficult problem. In each of these instances, a number of unreinforced responses occurs before one of them is reinforced.

Skinner (1956) humorously relates that he initially discovered the possibility of using intermittent reinforcement schedules as the solution to a practical problem. He had automated his experimental apparatus so that each bar press released one pellet of rat food from a magazine (a kind of storage container). Skinner himself manufactured his own food pellets through a laborious and painstaking process. At one point in his research the pellet supply was near depletion and more time was needed to replenish it. The easiest solution was to reduce the number of reinforcements. Skinner adds: "There were two results: (a) my supply of pellets lasted almost indefinitely, and (b) each rat stabilized at a fairly constant rate of responding (1956, p. 226)." Impressed by this regularity, Skinner and his coworkers embarked on a series of investigations of various intermittent reinforcement schedules.

In Skinner's system, many different reinforcement schedules are possible, but they all can be categorized according to two basic dimensions: (1) the individual is reinforced only after a fixed or irregular *time interval* has elapsed since the previous reinforcement (called *interval* reinforcement schedules) and (2) the individual is reinforced only after a fixed or irregular *number of responses* have been made since the previous reinforcement (called *ratio* reinforcement schedules). In terms of these two dimensions, the following four basic schedules of reinforcement are most extensively studied by students of operant conditioning.

A *fixed-ratio* (FR) schedule is one in which the reinforcement is given only after the organism has emitted a predetermined or "fixed" number of responses. To illustrate, a rat may be rewarded after every third lever-pressing response, every fifth response, every tenth response, or on whatever schedule is desired, with the intervening responses never being rewarded. The ratio designates the number of unreinforced to reinforced responses (e.g., if the FR is 8:1, the rat emits seven unreinforced responses and is reinforced on the eighth). FR reinforcement generates extremely high operant levels since the more the organism responds, the more reinforcement he receives. This schedule is fairly common and exercises considerable control over behavior. For many jobs, employees are paid partly or even exclusively according to the number of units they produce or sell. In industry, this payment system is known as piecework. FR schedules may also control the behavior of professors when they are required to publish a specified number of research articles per year in order to receive salary increases, promotions, lighter teaching loads, and sabbatical leaves. In academia this reinforcement system is known as "publish or perish."

When reinforcement is supplied only after an established or "fixed" period of time has elapsed since the previous reinforcement, without regard to the response rate of the organism, it is referred to as a *fixed-interval* (FI) schedule. For example, a rat that is rewarded every two minutes, even if it presses the lever only once during this interval, is on a FI-2 schedule. Although there are very few instances in everyday life where behavior is maintained on a "pure" FI schedule, there are some situations that approximate it. FI schedules are operative in paying salaries for work done by the day, week, or month. Similarly, giving a child a weekly allowance constitutes an FI form of reinforcement. At one time pediatricians recommended that infants be fed on an FI schedule (e.g., every four hours). Universities typically operate in terms of an FI time schedule. Examinations are administered on a regular basis and reports of academic progress are issued at designated time intervals.

Judy

Skinner has noted that an FI reinforcement schedule is characterized by a pattern in which the rate of responding gradually increases with time and then sharply accelerates near the end of the interval. This particular pattern of responding, called a *fixed-interval scallop,* occurs because the time for reinforcement is approaching. Consider, for example, the student who loafs through the semester and then suddenly accelerates his work as deadlines for term papers and final exams approach. Interestingly, FI schedules also yield low rates of responding immediately after the reinforcement has been obtained, a phenomenon called *postreinforcement pause.* This is evidenced by the student who experiences difficulty in studying after a midterm exam since a long interval will elapse before the next reinforcement occurs. He literally pauses his studying.

When the number of responses required for reinforcement is varied randomly around some designated average value, the organism is said to be on a *variable-ratio* (VR) schedule. In a VR-20 schedule, for instance, a rat is rewarded for every twentieth lever-pressing response on the average, but sometimes the sixth response is reinforced, sometimes the thirty-first, and so on. The VR schedule produces an extremely high and constant response rate inasmuch as the organism does not know precisely when the next reinforcement will be forthcoming. Perhaps the most dramatic illustration of the operation of this schedule at the human level is gambling behavior. Consider the actions of a person operating a slot machine or one-armed bandit. These devices are constructed so that reinforcement (i.e., money) is distributed according to the number of times the person pays to pull the handle. However, the payoffs are unpredictable, irregular, and rarely yield a return surpassing what the gambler invests. This explains why owners of gambling casinos receive more reinforcement than do their patrons.

Another commonplace example of behavior on a VR schedule is the door-to-door salesperson who quickly learns that the more she knocks on doors, the more she earns. Perhaps she makes twenty house calls but does not sell even one subscription. Then she takes large-volume orders from two homemakers in succession, providing her with sufficient incentive to ensure that her responding will not extinguish. It should not be surprising that many salespeople adopt the attitude "If at first you don't succeed, try, try again." Persistence brings reward. Extinction of behavior acquired on a VR reinforcement schedule is extremely slow. Thus, a gambler compulsively feeds coins into a machine, even though his returns are slim, in the conviction that next time he will "hit the jackpot." Such persistence is typical of the behavior generated by VR reinforcement schedules.

Finally, when reinforcements are contingent on some stated time interval but the intervals between reinforcements are irregular and cannot be anticipated, the organism is said to be on a *variable-interval* (VI) schedule. Although reinforcement in this condition is a function of time alone, the organism must make an appropriate response after the interval is over in order to receive reinforcement again. Thus, a rat performing on a VI five-minute schedule might be rewarded for lever pressing after eight minutes, two minutes, six minutes, and four minutes. The averages of these four intervals is five minutes. It is generally true that response rates under VI schedules are a direct function of the interval length employed, with short intervals generating high rates and long intervals generating low rates. However, VI reinforcement also tends to establish steady response rates and is slow to extinguish because the organism cannot precisely anticipate when the next reinforcement will come.

Illustrations of true VI schedules are not common in our culture, although several variations can be observed. A parent, for example, may praise a child's behavior on a rather random time basis, thus assuring that the child will continue to behave appropriately during nonreinforced intervals. The child has no way of knowing when the next reinforcement will occur. Professors who give "pop quizzes" are also depending upon a VI schedule. Students can be expected to maintain a relatively stable rate of studying under these conditions.

Superstitious Behavior: Conditioning by Chance *aliashe*

As we have seen, the frequency of occurrence of an operant response depends on whether that response is followed by positive or negative reinforcement; if followed by negative reinforcement, the response will be decreased (weakened); if followed by positive reinforcement, the response will be increased (strengthened). Thus, operant conditioning is mediated by a *causal-temporal* relation between the organism's behavior and the consequences which it produces—i.e., the organism operates upon its environment to generate consequences. Often, however, the association between a response and the outcome which follows its expression is accidental. For example, a gambler shouts "Come on baby" while throwing dice, and a winning roll occurs. Or a tennis player insists that she use a particular racquet while competing in a major tournament, and she goes on to win all her matches. In both cases an adventitious connection between the two events may result in the person's behaving in the future as though the connection were causal. Closer inspection reveals that the behavior-reinforcement contingency is merely coincidental. This type of conditioning, in which there is an apparent (but nonfunctional or chance) relationship between response and reinforcement, Skinner (1948b) calls *superstitious behavior*.

It is unlikely that saying "Come on baby" or using a particular tennis racquet will consistently be followed by a favorable outcome on every occasion that they occur but, as previously noted, the intermittent reinforcement of operant responses leads to the acquisition and maintenance of very stable behavior patterns. Thus, superstitious behavior abounds in any setting where chance reinforcements are likely. Athletes seem especially susceptible to the ritualistic effects of this phenomenon. Baseball players often perform unique hat ceremonies before they position themselves in the batter's box; bowlers sometimes twist in indescribable gyrations as their balls travel down the alley; and golfers adopt unaccountable stances while attempting to putt. Such idiosyncratic actions become the embarrassing trademarks of many outstanding athletes simply because they were formerly connected with fortuitous reinforcement.

Superstitious behavior, according to Skinner, is not necessarily the result of the individual's own conditioning history. Much of it is handed down from one generation to the next in the form of folklore, myth, and, in certain primitive cultures, magic. In our own culture, for instance, many people believe that walking under a ladder, seeing a black cat across their path, breaking a mirror, or making a decision on Friday the thirteenth bring "bad luck." While many such persons have never directly experienced bad fortune under these conditions, the ideas persist as superstition since they have been transmitted and occasionally reinforced through the social context of their culture.

Successive Approximation: How to Get the Mountain to Come to Mohammed

Skinner's first attempts at operant conditioning were directed to responses normally emitted at moderate or high frequency—e.g., pigeons' key pecking and rats' bar pressing. However, it soon became evident that the standard procedure for operant conditioning (i.e., the experimenter waits until the animal makes the correct response before it is reinforced) was ill suited for vast numbers of complex operant responses whose probability of spontaneous occurrences was near zero. In the realm of human behavior, for example, it is doubtful that the general strategy of operant conditioning would be successful in establishing verbal behavior in autistic children. In order to alleviate this problem, Skinner devised a procedure by which experimenters could efficiently and rapidly accelerate the time required to condition almost any behavior within the repertoire and capabilities of the organism. This procedure is referred to as the *method of successive approximation* or *shaping.*

As is often the case in science, Skinner's discovery that behavior could be rapidly conditioned by reinforcing a series of successive approximations occurred accidentally. He and a group of colleagues were working on a wartime project and, in one of their lighter moments, they decided to teach a pigeon to bowl. Skinner relates the following story:

> The pigeon was to send a wooden ball down a miniature alley toward a set of toy pins by swiping the ball with a sharp sideward movement of the beak. To condition the response, we put the ball on the floor of an experimental box and prepared to operate the food magazine as soon as the first swipe occurred. But nothing happened. Though we had all the time in the world, we grew tired of waiting. We

decided to reinforce any response which had the slightest resemblance to a swipe—perhaps at first, merely the behavior of looking at the ball—and then to select responses which more closely approximated the final form. The result amazed us. In a few minutes, the ball was caroming off the walls of the box as if the pigeon had been a champion squash player (1961, p. 138).

Thus, the technique of shaping consists of reinforcing progressively closer approximations of the operant behavior the experimenter wishes to condition. To revert to an earlier example, if a hungry rat is placed in a Skinner box, eventually it presses the bar, and sooner or later it learns that pressing the bar brings a pellet of food. By utilizing the method of successive approximations, the psychologist could markedly shorten the time required to condition this response. The first reinforced response might be any movement that orients the rat toward the end of the box where the lever is mounted. Next, the rat must approach the area of the lever before it is reinforced. Reinforcement is then reserved only for responses that bring the animal into contact with the lever. Finally, only the correct response, actual bar pressing, is reinforced. Thereafter, every bar press is rewarded and bar pressing grows in frequency. This step-by-step process—whereby one response is reinforced and then replaced by another which more closely resembles the desired behavior—greatly increases the range of possible operants which can be brought under the psychologist's control.

The shaping technique has also been applied to several different kinds of human operant responses. Isaacs, Thomas, and Goldiamond (1960) have reported an especially dramatic demonstration of the effectiveness of this method. These investigators, all therapists, wanted to reinstate verbal behavior in a hospitalized catatonic schizophrenic patient who had been mute for nineteen years. Shaping occurred accidentally when one of the therapists dropped a package of gum while searching for some cigarettes in his pocket. He noted that this incident caused the patient's eyes to move in the direction of the gum. Thus, he had a simple response from which to start shaping the desired behavior. For the first two weeks the therapist and patient met privately, during which time the therapist held up a stick of gum and waited until the patient noticed. When this response occurred, the patient was given the gum. This was followed by two weeks in which the therapist held the gum as before but demanded that the patient's lips move before giving it to him. By the end of four weeks, presentation of the gum as reinforcement readily elicited eye and lip movements, and a vocalization "resembling a croak." Thereafter followed two more weeks of shaping in which the therapist required the patient to say "gum, gum" in order to receive the reward. At the end of six weeks the patient was able to spontaneously say "gum please." Subsequently, the patient responded to questions regarding his age and name in group therapy sessions. Aside from the therapeutic benefits this patient derived from having some of his verbal behavior reinstated, the reader should note that shaping plays a crucial role in the way children acquire speech. Beginning with rather crude forms of babbling in infancy, the child's verbal behavior is gradually shaped until it comes to resemble the language of adults. The reader is referred to Skinner's *Verbal Behavior* (1957) for a more detailed behavioral analysis of the development of language.

Conditioned Reinforcers *Couleen*

Like almost all contemporary learning theorists, Skinner recognizes two types of reinforcement—primary and secondary. A *primary* reinforcement (also referred to as *unconditioned* reinforcement) is any event or object which possesses inherent reinforcing properties. Thus, it does not require prior association with other reinforcements in order to satisfy physiological needs and drives. Specifically, food for a hungry person and water for a thirsty one are primary reinforcers. Their reward value to the organism is independent of learning. A *secondary* or *conditioned* reinforcement, on the other hand, is any event or object which acquires its reinforcing qualities through close association with a primary reinforcement in the past conditioning history of the organism.

A slight alteration in the standard operant conditioning procedure demonstrates how a neutral stimulus can acquire reinforcing powers for other behavior. When a rat is trained to bar-press in a Skinner box, a tone comes on momentarily (as the animal makes the response), followed by a pellet of food. In this case, the tone acts as a *discriminative stimulus*—i.e., the animal learns to respond only in the presence of the tone since it signals the arrival of the food reward. After the animal has acquired this specific operant response, extinction is begun so that when it bar-presses neither the food nor the tone appears. In time the rat ceases to bar-press altogether. Next, the tone is presented whenever the animal engages in bar pressing, but the food pellet is withheld. Despite the absence of the primary reinforcer, the animal learns that bar pressing elicits the tone so it continues to respond persistently, thereby overcoming the extinction phase of the experiment. In other words, the stabilized rate of bar pressing reflects the fact that the tone is now functioning as a conditioned reinforcing agent. The exact rate of responding depends on the strength of the tone as a conditioned reinforcer (i.e., the number of times the tone was associated with the primary reinforcer, food, during the acquisition phase of conditioning). Skinner has demonstrated that practically any neutral stimulus may become reinforcing in its own right if it is connected with other stimuli that have primary reinforcing properties. Hence, the phenomenon of conditioned reinforcement greatly increases the range of possible operant conditioning, particularly in reference to human social behavior. Stated otherwise, if everything we learned had to be contingent upon primary reinforcement, the occasions for learning would be very restricted and the complex variety of human activity would not exist.

A significant feature of conditioned reinforcement is its propensity to become generalized when paired with more than one primary reinforcement.

Money is an especially conspicuous example. It is obvious that money cannot nourish any of our primary drives. Yet, through the establishment of a cultural exchange system, money is a powerful and robust agent for obtaining a host of basic gratifications—e.g., food, clothing, housing, medical aid, and sex. Other kinds of generalized conditioned reinforcers suggested by Skinner (1953) include *attention, approval, affection,* and *submission of others.* These so-called social reinforcers (because they involve the behavior of other people) often act in subtle and intricate ways but are essential to the maintenance of our behavior in a variety of situations. Attention is a simple case. The incident of a child who gains attention by feigning an illness or misbehaving is familiar. Children often are noisy, ask ridiculous questions, interrupt adult conversations, show off, tease younger siblings, and wet their beds as means of attracting attention. The attention of an attractive other—parent, teacher, loved one—is an especially effective generalized reinforcer which may promote strong attention-getting behavior.

A still stronger generalized reinforcer is approval. For example, many people spend a great deal of time preening themselves before a mirror, hoping to elicit an approving glance from their spouses or dates. Both women's and men's fashions are subject to approval and remain in vogue only as long as social approval is forthcoming. High school students compete for the varsity team in athletics or participate in extracurricular events (drama, debate, school newspaper) in order to procure approval from their parents, peers, teachers, and neighbors. Good grades in college are positively reinforcing because they have been followed in the past by parental praise and approval. As powerful conditioned reinforcers, satisfactory grades also foster studying behavior and the pursuit of higher academic goals. Finally, many simple verbal responses enhance a sense of self-approval and esteem—for example, "That's right," "Good going," or "Excellent job."

Skinner (1953) has pointed out that conditioned reinforcers are extremely potent in the control of human behavior. He has also noted that since each person is subjected to a unique history of conditioning, it is improbable that all people will be governed by the same reinforcers. For example, some people are strongly reinforced by entrepreneurial success; others are more readily rewarded by affectionate responses; and still others derive reinforcement from athletic, academic, or musical accomplishments. The possible variations in behavior maintained by conditioned reinforcers are endless. Accordingly, the understanding of human conditioned reinforcers is far more complex than the comprehension of a food-deprived rat bar pressing for the reinforcing properties of a tone.

Controlling Behavior Through Aversive Stimuli

We have stressed how operant responses are acquired and maintained through the presentation of stimuli (food, money, affection, grades) that are regularly associated with positive reinforcement. In Skinner's view, however, a great deal of human behavior is controlled by the use of *aversive stimuli*—that is, painful, unpleasant, obnoxious, or anxiety-arousing consequences associated with certain responses made by the individual. Two commonly employed methods of aversive control are *punishment* and *negative reinforcement*. Since these terms are often used synonymously to describe the conceptual properties and behavior effects of aversive control, Skinner has offered the following distinction:

> You can distinguish between punishment, which is making an aversive event contingent upon a response, and negative reinforcement, in which the elimination or removal of an aversive stimulus, conditioned or unconditioned, is reinforcing (Evans, 1968, p. 33).

Thus, punishment refers to any aversive stimulus or event whose presentation follows and depends upon the occurrence of some operant response. Skinner notes that it is a prevalent method of behavioral control in most cultural groups. Some simple examples are these: if children misbehave, they are spanked or scolded; if students cheat on an exam, they are dismissed from the course or school; if adults are caught stealing, they are fined or imprisoned. Instead of strengthening the response it follows, punishment decreases, at least temporarily, the probability that the response will occur again. The intended purpose of punishment is thus to induce people not to behave in given ways.

Unlike punishment, negative reinforcement generates and maintains operant behavior which allows the organism to terminate, escape, or avoid an aversive stimulus whenever it is administered. Any behavior that prevents an aversive state of affairs tends to increase in frequency and is said to be negatively reinforced. *Escape* behavior is such a case. An animal will tend to repeat whatever behavior he is performing (e.g., pressing a lever, moving to the other side of a cage) if it is associated with cessation of painful electric shock. Likewise, a person who escapes from a hot sun by moving indoors is more likely to move indoors when the sun is again hot. It should be noted that escaping from an aversive stimulus is not the same as avoiding it, since the aversive stimulus which is avoided is not physically present. Consequently, another way of dealing with aversive conditions is to behave in ways which prevent their occurrence—to learn to avoid them. This strategy is referred to as *avoidance* learning. For example, the rat in the Skinner box can learn to bar-press in order to *avoid* onset of an electric shock. Avoidance behavior can also be illustrated by drug addicts who develop clever and adroit schemes to maintain their habits and thereby shun the aversive consequences of being incarcerated.

Skinner (1971) staunchly opposes the application of all forms of behavioral control based on aversive stimuli. For one thing, because of its threatening nature, the tactic of punishing unwanted behavior may generate undesirable emotional and social side effects. Severe and debilitating anxiety, behavioral inhibition, and antisocial actions are just a few of the possible negative by-products of punishment. The threat imposed by aversive controls may also encourage individuals to develop patterns of behavior which are even more objectionable than the ones for which they were initially punished. Consider, for example, the parent who tries to suppress his son's dislike for and poor performance in school by physically punishing him. Later, in the parent's absence, the boy may adopt other behaviors which are more maladaptive— playing hookey, becoming a dropout, vandalizing school property. Regardless of the outcome, it is clear that punishment has failed to instill desirable behavior in the boy. While punishment may temporarily inhibit inappropriate or maladaptive responses, Skinner's main objection is that it does not contribute to the permanent extinction of the responses from a person's behavioral repertoire. Behavior that is punished is likely to reappear as soon as the aversive conditions are withdrawn; therefore, punishment is quite ineffective as a means of thwarting socially undesirable behavior.

In place of aversive types of behavioral control, Skinner recommends alternative techniques to eliminate undesirable behavior. Extinction is one technique of getting rid of objectionable behavior. However, it is usually of limited effectiveness because it is so time-consuming and does not indicate to the person what he must do in order to receive positive reinforcement. Accordingly, the most preferred method advocated thus far by Skinner is to condition incompatible behavior by employing positive reinforcement. He argues that positive reinforcers do not generate the negative by-products associated with aversive stimuli; hence, they are more suitable in shaping the individual's behavior. A brief example suggests a possible application of this method. Convicted felons are subjected to intolerable conditions in many penal institutions (witnessed by several prison riots in the country over the past few years). It is obvious that most attempts to rehabilitate the criminal have failed miserably, a conclusion supported by the high rate of recidivism or recurring offenses. Skinner's approach would be to arrange environmental conditions within prisons so that behavior resembling that of law-abiding citizens is positively reinforced—e.g., reinforcing the criminal for learning socially adaptive skills, values, and attitudes. This type of penal reform would require a team of behavioral experts knowledgeable in the principles of learning, personality, and psychopathology. In Skinner's view, such reform could be effectively implemented with the currently existing resources available to psychologists trained in the methods of behavioristic psychology.

Stimulus Generalization and Discrimination *mark*

A logical extension of the principle of reinforcement is that behavior strengthened in one stimulus situation is likely to recur when the organism encounters other situations that resemble the original one. If this were not so, our behavioral repertoires would be so severely limited and chaotic that we would probably spend most of our waking moments relearning how to respond appropriately in each new stimulus situation. In Skinner's system, the tendency of reinforced behavior to extend to a variety of related settings is called *induction* or *stimulus generalization.* This phenomenon can be readily observed in everyday life. For example, a child who has been rewarded for learning the subtleties of good manners at home will usually generalize this behavior to appropriate situations outside the home environment; he does not need to learn how to behave politely in each new social setting. Stimulus generalization may also result from painful or aversive experiences. A young woman who has been sexually assaulted by a stranger may generalize her shame and hostility to all persons of the opposite sex because they remind her of the physical and emotional trauma imposed by the stranger. Similarly, a single frightening or unpleasant experience with a person belonging to an identifiable ethnic group (blacks, Japanese, whites) may be sufficient grounds for a person to stereotype and thus avoid all future social contact with all such group members.

Although the capacity to generalize responses is an important aspect of much of our everyday social interaction, it is equally apparent that adaptive behavior requires the ability to make fine discriminations in different situations. *Stimulus discrimination,* the obverse of generalization, is the process of learning how to respond appropriately to various environmental stimuli. Examples are legion. A motorist survives the rush hour because he can discriminate red and green traffic lights. A child learns to discriminate between the family pet and a vicious dog. An adolescent learns to discriminate between behavior which results in adult approval and behavior which irritates or alienates others. A diabetic readily learns to discriminate between foods containing high and low amounts of sugar. Indeed, practically all intelligent human behavior is contingent upon the ability to make discriminations.

Discrimination is acquired through reinforcement of behavioral responses in the presence of some stimuli and nonreinforcement of them in the presence of other stimuli. Discriminative stimuli thus enable us to anticipate the probable outcomes associated with emitting a particular operant response in different social situations. Accordingly, individual differences in discriminative ability are dependent upon unique histories of differential reinforcement. Skinner would argue that healthy personality development results from a blend of generalization and discrimination capacities—that is, regulating our behavior so as to maximize positive reinforcement. Let us now turn attention to the philosophic assumptions underlying Skinner's behavioristic-learning theory.

SKINNER'S BASIC ASSUMPTIONS CONCERNING HUMAN NATURE

Because he rejects the traditional concept of internal personality variables as causes of behavior, Skinner presents a conception of man radically different from that of most personologists. Moreover, his basic assumptions concerning

Freedom   ＿＿＿＿＿＿＿＿＿＿ ✓ Determinism
Rationality   ＿＿＿＿ Not applicable ＿ Irrationality
Holism   ＿＿＿＿＿＿＿＿＿＿ ✓ Elementalism
Constitutionalism ＿＿＿＿＿＿＿＿＿＿＿ ✓ Environmentalism
Subjectivity   ＿＿＿＿＿＿＿＿＿＿ ✓ Objectivity
Proactivity   ＿＿＿＿＿＿＿＿＿＿ ✓ Reactivity
Homeostasis   ＿＿＿＿ Not applicable ＿ Heterostasis
Knowability   ✓＿＿＿＿＿＿＿＿＿＿ Unknowability

Figure 5-2 Skinner's position on the eight basic assumptions concerning human nature.

human nature tend to be both strong and explicit. Skinner's positions on these assumptions are graphically depicted in Figure 5-2.

1 Freedom–Determinism Skinnerian man is completely determined by his conditioning history. More specifically, the individual's behavior is a product of prior reinforcements; one does what one has been reinforced to do. Individual differences in behavior result exclusively from variable reinforcement histories, since freedom is not even acknowledged in the experimental analysis of behavior. In fact, Skinner has long argued that the deterministic assumption is an absolute necessity for scientifically studying human behavior:

> If we are to use the methods of science in the field of human affairs, we must assume that behavior is lawful and determined. We must expect to discover that what a man does is the result of specifiable conditions and that once these conditions have been discovered, we can anticipate and to some extent determine his actions (Skinner, 1953, p. 6).

In Skinner's system an infant has an infinite number of possibilities for behavior acquisition. It is parents first who principally reinforce and thus shape development in specific directions; in turn, the infant will behave contingent upon their rewards. Behavior consistently followed by nonreinforcement will not be strengthened. Gradually, as his development proceeds, the child's behavior is "shaped" into patterns as a direct function of his ongoing conditioning experiences. In more traditional, "non-Skinnerian" terms, his "personality" is emerging.

As the child's social world expands, other reinforcement sources are more central in affecting behavioral development. School, athletic, and peer-group experiences are especially powerful sources of reinforcement. The principle of behavior determination by reinforcement remains the same—it is only the kinds and sources of reinforcement that change. Sexual and occupational types of reinforcement occur later. By the time adulthood is reached, the person behaves in a characteristic fashion because of his unique conditioning history; his behavior can be expected to change only as a consequence of the contemporary reinforcement contingencies to which he is exposed. Throughout the entire developmental process, previously reinforced behaviors drop out of the person's response repertoire as a result of either nonreinforcement or punishment from the present social environment. Skinnerian man, then, has no freedom to choose his behavior; rather, his behavior is molded exclusively by external reinforcements.

2 Rationality–Irrationality   As noted previously, Skinner views the human organism as an "unopened box." That the box may eventually prove to contain rational and/or irrational processes may be an interesting speculation—it is just that neither has anything to do with explaining human behavior. For Skinner, behavior is a function only of its consequences or of lawful stimulus-response relationships. What goes into the box, what comes out of the box, and what follows therefrom are the only relevant variables needed in analyzing behavior—not what may or may not occur inside. The principles of behavior, uncovered by means of this functional approach, apply equally to rats, pigeons, and human beings; the latter's presumed more highly developed rational processes are simply not relevant in behavior causation. Because both extremes of the rationality–irrationality dimension refer to hypothetical internal processes that underlie behavior, this assumption plays no important role in Skinner's thinking. It is not really applicable to his position.

3 Holism–Elementalism   What is traditionally referred to by others as "personality" is translated by Skinner to mean nothing more than a collection of behavior patterns that are characteristic of a given individual. These behavior patterns can be further reduced to specific responses—all of which have been acquired via conditioning. An individual's personality, then, is composed of relatively complex but nonetheless independently acquired responses. To understand behavior, one need only understand the person's conditioning history. Most clearly, in Skinner's system behavior is composed of specific elements (responses).

A further indication of Skinner's basic elementalism is revealed in his approach to the study of behavior. He exhaustively examines the conditions under which single responses are acquired and modified, e.g., rats pressing bars, pigeons pecking disks. The unit of analysis in Skinner's experimental work is focused upon single response acquisition. Such an approach demands a commitment to the underlying elementalist assumption that behavior can be understood only by detailed analysis of its constituent parts.

In Skinner's view, individual personality differences are nothing more than what meets the eye—individual differences in behavior. Harry's "personality" is distinguishable from Joe's only insofar as Harry characteristically behaves differently than Joe. Each personality is constructed over time—element by element—people differ only because their individual conditioning histories differ. This elementalistic view is in sharp contrast to holistic conceptions that tend to portray individual uniqueness in terms of some single, unifying, and idiosyncratic factor underlying the person's behavior, e.g., Murray's unity thema. In opposition to Gestalt psychology, then, Skinner believes that the whole is the sum of its parts.

4 Constitutionalism–Environmentalism That Skinner has spent his entire professional life studying how behavior is modified by environmental effects clearly implies wholehearted commitment to environmentalism. While he recognizes that constitutional factors limit a person, these factors are largely ignored in accounting for the individual's behavior. Instead, Skinner portrays the person as supremely subject to environmental whim; characteristic ways in which he learns to behave (his personality) result exclusively from situationally based reinforcement contingencies (his conditioning). The Skinnerian man is a product of the environment.

In explaining how people differ from one another, Skinner places little reliance upon constitutional variation. Following the lead of earlier behaviorists (e.g., Watson), Skinner envisions environmental variation as the basic cause of individual differences. Harry and Joe differ from one another not primarily because of their unique constitutions but because of the different environments to which they have been exposed. If their environments had been interchanged at birth, their personalities at age twenty would also have been interchanged.

5 Subjectivity–Objectivity Skinner's approach to the organism as an unopened box suggests an unequivocal commitment to the objectivity assumption. One does not need to look into the box to explain its behavior. Consistent with much of behaviorism, Skinner argues that human activities can be explained solely in terms of objective stimulus-response relationships. Input occurs, output results—that which follows output (reinforcement) determines the likelihood that it will again follow similar inputs in the future. What the person may presumably think or feel about incoming stimuli or outgoing responses is irrelevant when explaining his or her behavior.

Subjective experience is not only totally irrelevant in Skinner's system but references to it are held to be the main source of confusion in contemporary psychology. Skinner contends that the constructs portraying inner experience used by all other personologists in this text (e.g., Freud's "ego," Erikson's "identity crisis," Murray's "need") simply obfuscate the issue of behavior explanation. These mentalistic concepts are nothing more than explanatory fictions superimposed upon the real external causes of human actions. And the most significant of these fictitious internal agents is the concept of personality itself! While his system allows for the description and explanation of both the similarities and differences among persons (just as does any other personality theory), Skinner can accomplish these objectives without any reference to "personality." Objectivity is an all-important assumption underlying this system; Skinner has taken Watson's earlier rejection of "mind" to its logical conclusion.

6 Proactivity–Reactivity Skinner's account of man's behavior in stimulus-response and response-reinforcement terms emphasizes an underlying commitment to the reactivity assumption. A person's behavior, in his system, is largely a function of external stimulus control. Such reactivity is most evident in classical conditioning, where responses are automatically elicited by stimuli immediately preceding them in time. Pavlov's dogs *react* (salivate) to the sound of a bell; humans *react* in much the same way to the sight and smell of turkey on Thanksgiving.

But even in operant conditioning there is clear evidence of reactivity. While the organism's responses appear to be "freely" emitted, it cannot be assumed that they are proactively based. Certainly the rat bar pressing in a Skinner box is not really internally generating his behavior in a future-oriented fashion. Rather, operant responses seem to suggest the "active" more than the "proactive" nature of the organism. All the individual's actions are triggered by some stimulus events, however subtle or elusive, with the majority of these initiating stimuli being external. As Lundin states, operant responses "are under some form of stimulus control, usually from the external environment, and the problem for the psychologist is to discover what the stimuli are and under what conditions the operant response has developed (1963, pp. 266–267)." On close inspection, people are totally reactive in Skinner's theory.

7 Homeostasis–Heterostasis Both extremes of this dimension refer to the nature and properties of internal motivational states that presumably cause behavior. A person acts to reduce internal tensions or to seek growth and self-actualization. According to Skinner, there is no necessity to speculate about the properties of such hypothetical inner states—they are irrelevant, superfluous concepts used to explain behavior. Only external agents actually cause behavior. Wondering about the nature of motives is like wondering what kind of spirit within a tree causes its branches to bend in the wind. Skinner takes no position on either side of this dimension—both homeostasis and heterostasis are irrelevant assumptions in his system.

How then does Skinner account for motivated behavior? What causes an organism's behavior to change while the environment remains relatively constant? To answer these questions, it is necessary only to examine rat behavior in the Skinner box. Suppose that a rat who has learned to bar-press for food pellets is deprived of food for two days. It can be observed that it will bar-press more often, eat more vigorously when permitted, and prefer food to water. A more "mentalistic" theorist would ascribe the rat's behavior to the hunger motive. To Skinner, however, the term "hunger" has no meaning or status apart from the fact that it designates a relationship between groups of external stimuli and observable responses. Hunger is simply a convenient word to describe the relation of certain objective operations (depriving the animal of food) to the occurrence of certain responses (e.g., more frequent or vigorous bar pressing). Hunger as a presumed internal motivational state does not cause behavior; the environmental operations actually *produce* the behavior. Consistent with his overall position, Skinner does not rely on inner motives to explain behavior. Thus, he assumes nothing about the particular properties (homeostatic versus heterostatic) of such motives.

8 Knowability–Unknowability Skinner's strong stands on the assumptions of determinism and objectivity logically require an equally strong commitment to the knowability assumption. He insists that behavior is determined by external, objective factors; these factors can be elucidated by means of rigorous scientific investigation; therefore, all of human behavior (nature) is ultimately knowable in scientific terms.

Skinner's total commitment to man's knowability through science is unmistakable—he devoted an entire book to the subject (*Science and Human Behavior*), the theme of which is a clear, logically consistent, and exhaustively detailed argument for a natural science of human behavior. In addressing himself to behavior as a scientific subject matter, he stated:

Behavior is a difficult subject matter, not wholly because it is inaccessible, but because it is extremely complex. Since it is a process, rather than a thing it cannot easily be held still for observation. It is changing, fluid, and evanescent, and for this reason it makes great technical demands upon the ingenuity and energy of the scientist. But there is nothing essentially insoluble about the problems which arise from this fact (Skinner, 1953, p. 15).

While studying behavior is difficult, science clearly has the potential to unravel all such problems. Skinner argues further that science can do so only when its practitioners rid themselves of the mythological concept of man as a free, responsible agent who internally initiates his actions. In effect, the *basic assumptions* of scientists concerning human nature hinder them in studying behavior. To apply scientific methodology profitably to human behavior, it is necessary to view people as objectively determined. Stated another way, Skinner seems to believe that a true science of behavior will be fully developed only when other psychologists adopt his particular basic assumptions concerning human nature!

Let us now turn to some illustrative research generated by this highly stimulating and provocative position.

EMPIRICAL VALIDATION OF BEHAVIORISTIC-LEARNING THEORY CONCEPTS

It would be an enormous task just to highlight the vast number of animal and human studies that empirically validate the behavioristic principles of operant conditioning. Skinner, more than any other contemporary theorist, has both provided and stimulated a massive amount of experimental data to support his conceptual formulations of behavior. Furthermore, he has been extremely successful in attracting a large group of adherents who have carried on and extended his efforts to develop a scientifically based approach to behavior. Another indication of the accelerating impact of Skinner's work is the growing number of psychology graduate programs where students are trained in the methods and applications of operant conditioning. The Universities of Kansas, Washington, Oregon, Hawaii, Western Michigan, and the State University of New York at Stony Brook are currently at the forefront of this movement (Goodall, 1972, p. 59). There is no question that Skinner's behavioristic-learning position has generated widespread attention in basic and applied fields of American psychology.

The following discussion examines the methodological characteristics of Skinner's approach to behavioral research concluding with a section on how his principles have been validated in the context of a recent application—behavior therapy and the token economy. Students and interested readers who wish to explore these aspects of Skinner's position in more detail are directed particularly to the following texts: *Operant Learning: Procedures for Changing Behavior* (Williams, 1973); *Behavior Therapy; Techniques and Empirical Findings* (Rimm & Masters, 1974); and *Cumulative Record* (Skinner, 1961). *The Journal of the Experimental Analysis of Behavior, The Journal of Applied Behavior Analysis,* and *Behavior Research and Therapy* also publish reports of experimental research relevant to the empirical verification and behavioral application of Skinnerian concepts.

When compared with the mainstream of present-day behavioral research, Skinner's methodological strategy is quite unconventional. First, as previously noted, his experimental analysis of behavior concentrates on the single subject as opposed to the more prevalent method of selecting a group of subjects as the focus of study. This reliance on a single-subject research design reveals Skinner's fundamental belief that psychological science should ultimately lead to precise and quantifiable laws which are applicable to actual individual behavior.

A second identifiable feature of Skinner's methodological orientation is his automated experimental apparatus and well-defined control over the conditions under which the individual's behavior is observed and recorded. In the typical experimental setting, an investigator would proceed through the following steps: (1) initially establish a baseline measure of stable response rates—e.g., a cumulative record of a rat's rate of bar pressing a lever; (2) introduce a treatment or controlling variable—e.g., a fixed-interval reinforcement schedule; and (3) withdraw that variable after some level of performance has been attained in order to measure and determine its effect upon the behavior under investigation. Any changes in operant behavior which occur as a result of introducing and then withdrawing the treatment variable can thus be reliably attributed to that variable.

Skinner adopts a *molecular* approach to the study of behavior. Reflecting his elementalistic assumption, he believes that the logical place to begin is with the simplest, most basic ingredients of the organism's behavior. Building on his understanding of simple behavioral events, the psychologist can then direct attention to the more complex activity of the organism. Complex behavior in Skinner's approach is nothing more than the summation and integration of its component parts.

Skinner depends primarily on the use of infrahuman species (notably rats and pigeons) as the source of data for establishing empirical laws of learning. As implied earlier in this chapter, he defends his choice of lower organisms as experimental subjects on the grounds that it enables the psychologist to exert greater control over the conditions and variables affecting the behavior under study than would be the case for human subjects. At the same time, Skinner does not hesitate to suggest that principles of behavior demonstrated for infrahumans have direct application to explaining phenomena of interest to the human-oriented psychologist. This assertion reflects an assumption made by practically all Skinnerians, specifically, that laboratory-derived findings are generalizable to the entire animal kingdom, including man. It should come as no surprise that most personologists consider the notion of generalization of principles based on the study of lower organisms to be untenable.

Finally, it should be stressed that the research conducted by Skinner and his followers is exclusively focused on variables amenable to change or modification via manipulation of environmental stimuli. Accordingly, much of the recent research emanating from Skinner's theoretical system is pertinent to our understanding of personality development.

Skinner's current status in psychological science is apparent in the many active domains of research directly affected by his behavioristic principles. The major areas include (1) psychopharmacology or the study of the effects of drugs on behavior; (2) educational technology, including programmed instruction devices and classroom contingency management systems; (3) psycholinguistics and the acquisition of verbal behavior; (4) industrial management, including employee morale and job satisfaction; and (5) therapeutic treatment of psychological problems—e.g., alcoholism, drug addiction, mental retardation, juvenile delinquency, childhood autism, phobias, speech disorders, and sexual disorders. These examples indicate the extent to which operant techniques can be applied effectively outside the "artificial" conditions of the experimentally isolated subject.

Behavior Therapy and the Token Economy: A Research Illustration

Cauleen

Although he is not a clinical psychologist, Skinner's views concerning operant conditioning and behavioral control have had considerable impact on modifying the behavior of severely disturbed individuals (e.g., Ayllon and Azrin, 1965; Atthowe and Krasner, 1968). Indeed, his approach to behavior change or modification has been instrumental in establishing a new breed of behavior therapists in this country.

Coined by Skinner and Lindsley (1954), "behavior therapy" approaches psychotherapy with experimentally established principles and methods derived from behavioristic-learning theory. The details of this form of psychological treatment are well beyond the scope of this book (see Kanfer and Phillips's *Learning Foundations of Behavior Therapy,* 1970, for a comprehensive description of behavior therapy methods and techniques). However, the underlying premise upon which this therapy is practiced is relatively simple—psychological disorders have been *learned* via some faulty history of conditioning. Therefore, the task facing the Skinnerian behavior therapist is to pinpoint those of the patient's maladaptive behaviors ("symptoms") that are to be eliminated, to specify the desired new behaviors, and to determine the reinforcement schedules that are required to shape the desired behaviors. These objectives are accomplished by creating an environment in which the patient's attainment of the "good things in life" are made contingent on performing adaptive or socially desirable behaviors. Thus, behavior therapy is a logical extension of the principles of operant conditioning through which many adjustment problems may be effectively eliminated.

The recent development of what is called a *token economy* illustrates one procedural application of behavior therapy. In a token economy, patients, usually hospitalized adults manifesting severe behavioral disturbances, are rewarded with tokens for engaging in various activities that are deemed desirable. The token is simply a stimulus, like a plastic chip or a numerical rating, which represents something for which certain desired items or activities may be exchanged. Thus, patients might be rewarded for engaging in such routine activities as cleaning their rooms, feeding themselves, or interacting with their fellow patients. The tokens they receive for participating in such activities are then exchanged at a later date for a variety of desired incentives—e.g., candy, cigarettes, clothing, entertainment, or a private audience with the hospital psychologist.

How effective is a token economy in abolishing maladaptive behavior and establishing adaptive behavior? A study conducted by Atthowe and Krasner (1968) suggests a most favorable answer. These two clinicians instituted a token reinforcement program in a psychiatric ward of a Veterans Hospital in

Palo Alto, California. Its purpose "was to change the chronic patients' aberrant behavior, especially that behavior judged to be apathetic, overly dependent, detrimental, or annoying to others (Atthowe and Krasner, 1968, p. 37)." The patients (N = sixty) selected had a median age of fifty-seven and had been hospitalized for a median number of twenty-two years. Most had been previously diagnosed as chronic schizophrenics; the remainder were classified as brain-damaged.

The study extended across twenty months and consisted of three distinct phases. The first six months served as a baseline or operant period during which time the investigators recorded daily the frequency of target behaviors which were to be subsequently extinguished. This was followed by a three-month shaping period during which the patients were gradually prepared to participate in the token economy (i.e., they were instructed as to the types of activities they must perform in order to receive and exchange tokens for items in the hospital canteen). Finally, during the experimental period, continuing for eleven months, patients received tokens for performing specified desirable behaviors involving self-care, attendance at activities, interaction with others, or demonstration of responsibility. The token used was a plastic file card (similar to a credit card) which came in seven colors, with different exchange values assigned to the different colors. Whenever possible, each patient was given a token immediately after completing the desired activity, accompanied by an expression of social approval (e.g., the words "fine job" or a smile).

The results indicated a significant increase in reinforced "desirable" behaviors and a general improvement in patient initiative, activity, responsibility, and social interaction. Figure 5-3 shows, for instance, how attendance at group activities increased and decreased as a function of token reinforcement level. During the operant baseline period the average hourly attendance rate per week was 5.8 hours per patient. With the introduction of the token economy, this rate increased to 8.4 hours for the first month and averaged 8.5 hours throughout the experimental period. Moreover, the rate increased to 9.2 hours during a three-month span within the experimental period when the reinforcing value of the tokens was raised from one to two tokens per hour of attendance.

A second set of findings reported by Atthowe and Krasner focuses on the number of infractions committed by patients. Ordinarily many hospitalized patients refuse to get out of bed in the morning, make their beds, or leave the bedroom area by a specified time, thus necessitating the help of extra personnel. Immediately prior to the introduction of the token economy, the number of infractions in these three areas was recorded for a one-week period. This yielded an average of seventy-five infractions (or a little more than one per patient) per week. A token was then given daily, contingent upon not having a recorded infraction in any of these areas. As seen in Figure 5-4, the number of infractions dropped sharply following the establishment of the contingency program. The unexpected rise in infractions during the fourth week (increased

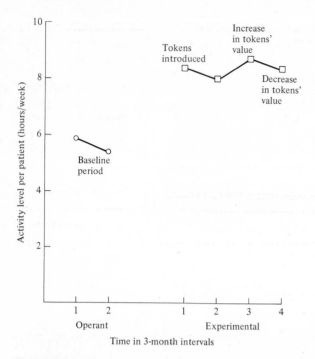

Figure 5-3 Attendance at group activities as a function of tokens given for the activity. *(Adapted from Atthowe and Krasner, 1968, p. 39.)*

to thirty-nine) of the token economy was not explained by the investigators. During the last six months of the experimental period, the frequency of infractions averaged nine per week (not indicated in Figure 5-4).

Atthowe and Krasner also report that significant behavioral gains were made in other areas of the patient's life in the hospital setting. They note:

> At the beginning of the study, there were 12 bed-wetters, 4 of whom were classified as "frequent" wetters and 2 were classified as "infrequent". . . . At the end of the experimental period no one was wetting regularly and, for all practical purposes, there were no bed-wetters on the ward (1968, p. 40).

Despite the impressive behavioral changes demonstrated in this clinical research program, it is not altogether clear whether the changes in behavior were a function of the specific reinforcement procedures used. For example, the possibility exists that patients who participate in a token economy are merely responding to the interest, enthusiasm, attention, and hopeful expectancies of the hospital staff. Advocates of behavior therapy strongly insist that this type of interpretation is not valid, and that the change in patient behavior is a direct result of the shaping and contingency methods they employ. One study which clearly supports this contention is that of Ayllon and

Azrin (1965). They found that performance of desired behaviors directly fluctuated as a function of the presence or absence of token reinforcements. Based on six specific experiments of the token economy, they concluded:

> The reinforcement procedure was effective in maintaining desired performance. In each experiment, the performance fell to a near-zero level when the established response-reinforcement relation was discontinued. On the other hand, reintroduction of the reinforcement procedure restored performance almost immediately and maintained it at a high level for as long as the reinforcement procedure was in effect (1965, p. 381).

Thus, it seems safe to conclude that a token economy can alter the behavior of psychotics in a constructive direction within a hospital setting. More significantly, it illustrates a particularly interesting and rigorous test of the validity of Skinnerian principles in the context of one of humanity's greatest social problems.

APPLICATION: THE WORLD AS A BIG SKINNER BOX

Tom

As noted, Skinnerian principles have been applied to an incredible array of phenomena ranging from teaching machines for schoolchildren to the treat-

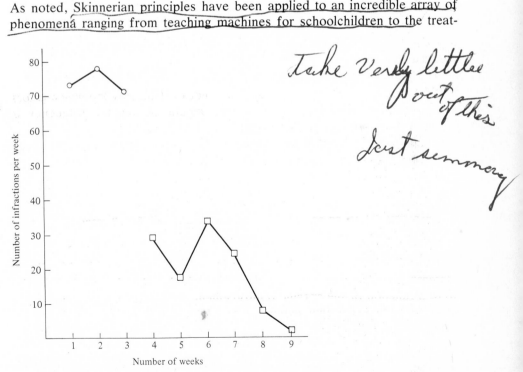

Take Very little out of this dull summary

Figure 5-4 Number of infractions in performing morning routines. *(Adapted from Atthowe and Krasner, 1968, p. 41.)*

ment of hospitalized psychotics. Any of the various applications of his position is sufficiently important to warrant further discussion here. But so far the most significant and far-reaching application of all is spelled out in his 1971 book *Beyond Freedom and Dignity.* In this work, Skinner steps out as a futurist thinker and carefully outlines how entire cultures and social institutions may be consciously designed in strict accordance with his behavioristic principles. Skinner theoretically leaps from simple rat behavior in the operant box to complex human behavior in society with the ease of an Olympic high-jumper. In the words of T. George Harris describing this B. F. Skinner manifesto, "All the world's a box (1971, p. 33)."

Skinner's book, predictably, has stimulated and challenged his many followers while further alienating, outraging, and possibly even frightening his adversaries. It has brought him public attention far beyond the traditional scope of psychology. He appeared on the cover of *Time* magazine (Sept. 20, 1971) and made appearances on several major United States television shows. He has been the center of a storm of controversy, receiving criticisms from poets, philosophers, theologians, psychologists, and even former Vice President Spiro T. Agnew. Others have compared the significance of his work to that of Darwin's. And how does Skinner react to this publicity, unprecedented for a psychology professor? "My hat still fits," he says in a *Psychology Today* interview (Hall, 1972, p. 68). And why shouldn't it? Consistent with his position, anyone with Skinner's genetic endowment and unique conditioning history could have done the same!

Beyond Freedom and Dignity itself is apportioned into nine chapters. Each is briefly discussed below.

Rather the problem is why is there such behavior

1 A Technology of Behavior   In this first chapter, Skinner argues convincingly that all the major problems confronting the modern world involve human behavior. Population, nuclear war, famine, disease, ghettos, and pollution—all these relate to the action or inaction of human beings. While science ultimately holds the keys for solving these problems, physics and chemistry alone will not suffice. What is needed is a technology of behavior.

Yet, even in the face of problems that threaten the very survival of the human race, the science of human behavior progresses at a snail's pace. Why? Skinner contends that the necessary technology of behavior cannot be established until scientists (and the rest of us) discard our outmoded conceptions of human actions as being internally caused:

> Unable to understand how or why the person we see behaves as he does, we attribute his behavior to a person we cannot see, whose behavior we cannot explain either but about whom we are not inclined to ask questions. . . . The function of the inner man is to provide an explanation which will not be explained in turn. . . . He is not a mediator between past history and current behavior, he is a *center* from which behavior emanates. He initiates, originates, and creates. . . . We say that he

is autonomous—and, so far as a science of behavior is concerned, that means miraculous (1971, p. 14).

To properly understand human behavior, we must look toward its antecedents—toward the *environment* (here the basic assumptions of environmentalism, objectivity, and reactivity again rear their heads). A true behavioral technology will emerge only when we put aside the erroneous concept of autonomous man and come to grips with the selective function of the environment in behavior causation (determinism assumption). But the most troublesome features of autonomous man that prevent his conceptual demise are his presumed "freedom" and "dignity."

2 Freedom   The persistent and fallacious belief that people, by nature, are or could be free is nourished by what Skinner terms the "literature of freedom." This literature "consists of books, pamphlets, manifestoes, speeches, and other verbal products designed to induce people to act to free themselves from various kinds of intentional control (p. 30)." In reality, man's perennial struggle for freedom is not due to his will to be free but rather to his behavioral tendency to avoid or escape from aversive environmental stimuli. The literature of freedom has as its targets all "controllers" of human behavior, e.g., governments, organized religions, economic systems, formal education, and parents. While it has encouraged escape from or attack upon all such controllers, the literature of freedom has at the same time erroneously branded any semblance of control as aversive.

Skinner addresses himself to this point as follows:

Those who manipulate human behavior are said to be evil men, necessarily bent on exploitation. Control is clearly the opposite of freedom, and if freedom is good, control must be bad. What is overlooked is control which does not have aversive consequences at any time. Many social practices essential to the welfare of the species involve the control of one person by another, and no one can suppress them who has any concern for human achievements (p. 41).

In brief, Skinner argues that humanity can never be totally freed of environmental control but only from certain kinds of aversive control. To improve the human condition, people must cease the futile search for freedom and focus scientific attention on drastic modification of social structures (reward systems in the culture). In his words, "to make the social environment as free as possible of aversive stimuli we do not need to destroy that environment or escape from it; we need to redesign it (p. 42)."

3 Dignity   Total commitment to Skinner's version of societal redesign rests squarely on the premise that human behavior is environmentally determined. Accordingly, one cannot legitimately be either praised or blamed for one's actions; the human being (whose autonomy is purely mythological) is not responsible for his or her activities—the environment is. And herein lies the downfall of dignity. As long as autonomous man can be credited for achievements and castigated for failures, dignity is possible. But if the environment is responsible for behavior, there is no room for the concept of human dignity or worth. And, as Skinner points out, the more that we know about the real causes of behavior, the less these causes can be attributed to autonomous man:

> It is in the nature of scientific progress that the functions of autonomous man be taken over one by one as the role of the environment is better understood. A scientific conception seems demeaning because nothing is eventually left for which autonomous man can take credit. And as for admiration in the sense of wonderment, the behavior we admire is the behavior we cannot yet explain. Science naturally seeks a fuller explanation of that behavior; its goal is the destruction of mystery (p. 58).

The concept of human dignity is concerned with preserving due credit and admiration. Defenders of the concept (the "literature of dignity") oppose behavioral scientific and technological advances because they directly threaten the illusion of autonomous man's individual responsibility and dignity. Hence, dignity stands in the way of further human achievement. If we are to build the safe, sane, and controlled Skinnerian world of the future, humanity's ego-gratifying but illusory concept of dignity must be discarded along with that of freedom. In short, the salvation of humanity lies only "beyond freedom and dignity."

4 Punishment   An additional negative consequence of the literatures of freedom and dignity is that they have acted in part to preserve the concept of punishment as a perfectly justifiable and effective means of dealing with human behavior. If people are truly responsible for their own behavior, then parents, governments, and religions are justified in meting out all sorts of punishments for bad conduct, crimes, and sins. Skinner argues against punishment systems not only because they stem from a false concept of human behavior but also because they are largely ineffective:

> A person who has been punished is not thereby simply less inclined to behave in a given way; at best, he learns how to avoid punishment. Some ways of doing so are maladaptive or neurotic. . . . Other ways include avoiding situations in which punished behavior is likely to occur and doing things which are incompatible with punished behavior (p. 81).

The issue raised here by Skinner is one of controllability—punishment, in addition to being occasionally horrendous, is simply not all that effective in controlling human behavior. Skinner contends that our task is to make life less punishing by designing a society that need not resort to punishment to control the behavior of its members. But, once again, the literature of freedom and dignity (with their primary emphasis upon autonomous man) stand in the way. Punishment is erroneously seen in these literatures as a means of making "better people." Skinner instead exhorts us to "accept the fact that all control is exerted by the environment and proceed to the design of better environments rather than of better men (p. 82)."

5 Alternatives to Punishment   The champions of freedom and dignity do not confine themselves to punishment as a means of controlling behavior. Other largely ineffective alternatives to punishment are practiced precisely because they allow autonomous man to exercise a presumed freedom and to achieve an illusory dignity. Among the various practices of this type catalogued by Skinner are "permissiveness," "guidance," and "changing minds." Permissiveness, or the abandonment of policy, is ineffective because it simply leaves the control to other aspects of the environment. Guidance fails because behavior actually changes as a result of externally arranged contingencies rather than from the inner unfolding of human potentialities. Attempts to change minds are simply misdirected if the real purpose is to change behavior. Striking at the heart of the matter, Skinner explains why the measures employed by the defenders of freedom and dignity are ineffective:

> The apparent freedom respected by weak measures is merely inconspicuous control. When we seem to turn control over to a person himself, we simply shift from one mode of control to another (p. 97). . . . The fundamental mistake made by all those who choose weak methods of control is to assume that the balance of control is left to the individual, when in fact it is left to other conditions. The other conditions are often hard to see, but to continue to neglect them and to attribute their effects to autonomous man is to court disaster (p. 99).

By their inability to see that behavior is controlled by external contingencies rather than by autonomous man, the advocates of freedom and dignity encourage the misuse of controlling practices and thereby block progress toward an effective technology of behavior. Again Skinner's message is clear—the quality of human life will only be significantly enhanced when people consciously redesign their social environments in accordance with the principles of behavioristic science.

6 Values   But who is to decide what is for the good of humanity? How will the new technology of behavior be used? By whom and for what ultimate purpose? Skinner recognizes in these questions the fundamental issue of *values* raised by his radical proposals for societal redesign. He responds by asserting that questions concerning values are really questions about reinforcements:

> To make a value judgment by calling something good or bad is to classify it in terms of its reinforcing effects (p. 105). . . . Things are good (positively reinforcing) or bad (negatively reinfocing) presumably because of the contingencies of survival under which the species evolved (p. 104). . . . The only good things are positive reinforcers, and the only bad things are negative reinforcers (p. 107).

Supposedly, then, the question of values raised by the proponents of freedom and dignity largely resolves itself. The things that have become "good" in the course of evolution (meaningful work, material possessions) can be scientifically used to induce people to behave for "the good of others." However, Skinner warns that the "good" things must not become excessively available—people will rebel by challenging them and turning to things good only for themselves. He would then react "by intensifying the contingencies which generate behavior for the good of others or by pointing to previously neglected individual gains, such as those conceptualized as security, order, health, wealth, or wisdom (pp. 125–126)." Skinner's broad objective is, from the vantage point of his followers, benign—to create a balanced society in which each person is maximally reinforced.

7 The Evolution of a Culture But the creation of a behaviorist utopia requires an understanding of how cultures, or social environments, evolve. On this score, Skinner seems to be in fundamental agreement with a kind of "social Darwinism":

> A culture, like a species, is selected by its adaptation to an environment: to the extent that it helps its members to get what they need and avoid what is dangerous, it helps them to survive and transmit the culture (p. 129).

Cultural practices, like species traits in Darwin's theory, may be initiated accidentally (mutation), but they persist because they have an adaptation value. The survival of a culture, like that of a species, depends upon evolving practices (traits) which enable it to deal with the physical environment as well as to compete successfully with other cultures. Ultimately, a culture's value can only be judged by one criterion—survival. To ensure survival, the culture must somehow encourage its members to work for this objective; i.e., people must be reinforced for their efforts to help the culture survive. The challenge for the "cultural designer" here is to accelerate the development of practices which bring the remote consequences of an individual's behavior into more direct play. If people are not reinforced by such remote consequences, they will have no reason to work for the survival of the culture. Hence, the culture will fail. The role of behavioral technology in ensuring the survival of the culture is quite clear: "Explicit design promotes that good by accelerating the evolutionary process, and since a science and a technology of behavior make for better design, they are important 'mutations' in the evolution of a culture (p. 144)."

8 The Design of a Culture   In this most lengthy chapter of his book, Skinner argues strongly for the behavioristic design of cultures:

> A culture is very much like the experimental space used in the analysis of behavior. Both are sets of contingencies of reinforcement. A child is born into a culture as an organism is placed in an experimental space. Designing a culture is like designing an experiment; contingencies are arranged and effects noted. In an experiment we are interested in what happens, in designing a culture with whether it will work (p. 153).

All the world is indeed a box! However, Skinner allows that cultures are significantly more complex "boxes" than his operant conditioning chambers and that human behavior, equally, is more complex than rat bar pressing. Be that as it may, the underlying scientific principles governing the variables in both instances remain the same. Skinner emphatically contends that we now know enough about the experimental analysis of behavior to apply its technology to cultural design.

Clearly, objections to this proposal are raised on many sides, and Skinner attempts to answer these criticisms. For example, what of those who simply "wouldn't like" living in a totally controlled culture? Skinner translates this objection as follows: " 'The culture would be aversive and would not reinforce me in the manner to which I am accustomed (p. 163).' " Further, " 'I wouldn't like it' is the complaint of the individualist who puts forth his own susceptibilities to reinforcement as established values (p. 164)." Skinner replies by asserting that "The problem is to design a world which will be liked not by people as they now are but by those who live in it (p. 163)." While there is bound to be resistance to cultural change, people cannot resist positive reinforcement. As the designed culture evolves, individuals will change as their lives become progressively more reinforcing. After all, in the final analysis, happiness is positive reinforcement!   *God*

A danger in this controlled new world is how to control the controller. The answer here, says Skinner, is effective countercontrol. The controller must live fully within the designed culture and thus be wholly susceptible to the important consequences of his behavior. In essence, all control is really reciprocal; the challenge for the cultural designer is to build into the culture effective avenues for such reciprocity. Literally, controllers can never be permitted to get beyond the reach of the countercontrol measures available to the controllees.

Skinner concludes by arguing that scientific cultural design is our only means of survival:

> Our culture has produced the science and technology it needs to save itself. It has the wealth needed for effective action. It has, to a considerable extent, a concern for its own future. But if it continues to take freedom or dignity, rather than its own

survival, as its principal value, then it is possible that some other culture will make a greater contribution to the future (p. 181).

Like Milton's Satan, we will find ourselves in hell with no consolation other than the illusion that "here at least we shall be free (p. 182)."

9 What Is Man?   Skinner devotes the last chapter of his book to the completion of autonomous man's demolition. His basic assumptions of environmentalism and objectivity are strikingly evident when he argues against the existence of autonomous man and his miraculous mental attributes:

> It is in the nature of an experimental analysis of human behavior that it should strip away the functions previously assigned to autonomous man and transfer them one by one to the controlling environment (p. 198). . . . The picture which emerges from a scientific analysis is not of a body with a person inside, but of a body which *is* a person in the sense that it displays a complex repertoire of behavior (p. 199).

But what of the nobility of the human being which has been cherished for centuries?

> . . . whereas the traditional view supports Hamlet's exclamation, "How like a god!," Pavlov, the behavioral scientist, emphasized "How like a dog!" But that was a step forward. . . . Man is much more than a dog, but like a dog he is within range of a scientific analysis (p. 201).

In brief, Skinner argues that "No theory changes what it is a theory about (p. 213)." That there presently is a scientifically outmoded but still prevalent conception of the human being as a free, dignified, and internally responsible agent is no reason to continue to cherish such an ultimately destructive illusion. While Skinner's view of human beings is deeply offensive to those who hold such a conception, he obviously believes his own position to be more accurate. The human being is not demolished in his view—only human autonomy. And this, Skinner argues, is necessary for our survival as a species. A culture based on a scientific conception of humanity is our main hope for a future. As Skinner puts it in concluding his work: "A scientific view of man offers exciting possibilities. We have not yet seen what man can make of man (p. 215)."

What is the real significance of *Beyond Freedom and Dignity?* As we enter the last quarter of this century, we stand on the brink of disaster and possibly even species extinction. Is Skinner a scientific-age savior who alone is pointing the way for humanity to save itself? Or can it be argued that many significant human problems have been brought about precisely because our social, moral, and educational systems have worked against each individual's realization of the full extent of his or her freedom and dignity? Skinner, then, is leading us further down the path of developing a race of human robots in the manner of Huxley's *Brave New World* or Orwell's *1984.*

Psychologists and others differ sharply on the answers to these questions. One might ask why, since the evidence is equally available to all. Our answer is the theme of this book. Individuals react differently to Skinner's proposals fundamentally because they hold different basic assumptions concerning the nature of the human being. One who believes that human beings are free, subjectively oriented, and heterostatically motivated could never accept Skinner's ideas for social reform. Regardless of the ultimate "truth" value of his position, however, B. F. Skinner has made a profound mark upon contemporary personology that will not soon fade away.

SUMMARY

Skinner's behavioristic-learning theory approach to personality is characterized by a rejection of an inner "autonomous" man as the cause of human actions and a disregard for physiological-genetic explanations of behavior. Skinner contends that behavior is lawfully determined, predictable, and environmentally controlled. Further, he holds that the fundamental principles underlying human behavior are most readily discerned by studying lower organisms, e.g., rats, pigeons.

Skinner has focused most of his scientific attention upon operant behavior, i.e., behavior which is emitted by, rather than elicited from, the organism. In a professional lifetime of operant conditioning research, Skinner has shown quantification of such behavior; indicated the lawful control of various reinforcement schedules, conditioned reinforcers, and aversive stimuli; demonstrated its shaping through successive approximation; and indicated its extension and appropriate adaptation to new stimuli (stimulus generalization and discrimination). No other personologist has done more than B. F. Skinner to empirically demonstrate lawful behavior-environment relationships.

Skinner's basic assumptions concerning human nature are strong and explicit. Behavioristic-learning theory reflects a deep commitment to determinism, elementalism, environmentalism, objectivity, reactivity, and knowability. The basic assumptions of rationality–irrationality and homeostasis–heterostasis are not applicable to Skinner's position since he rejects internal sources of behavior.

Behavioristic-learning theory has generated more experimental research than any other personological system. Both the amount and diversity of this research is enormous. Skinner's own approach to behavioral research is characterized by concentration upon single subjects, automated equipment and well-defined control over experimental conditions, emphasis on molecularity, use of infrahumans, and focusing upon environmentally modifiable variables. One research illustration related to Skinner's position deals with behavior therapy and the token economy.

Current applications of Skinnerian principles are numerous and far-reaching. Perhaps the most significant application to date is Skinner's attempt to outline how entire cultures can be designed in accordance with operant conditioning principles. This idea is presented in detail in his highly controversial book *Beyond Freedom and Dignity.*

BIBLIOGRAPHY

Atthowe, J., & Krasner, L. Preliminary report on the application of contingent reinforcement procedures (token economy) on a "chronic" psychiatric ward. *Journal of Abnormal Psychology,* 1968, **73,** 37–43.

Ayllon, T., & Azrin, N. The measurement and reinforcement of behavior of psychotics. *Journal of the Experimental Analysis of Behavior,* 1965, **8,** 357–384.

Dews, P. (Ed.). *Festschrift for B. F. Skinner.* New York: Appleton-Century-Crofts, 1970.

Evans, R. *B. F. Skinner: The man and his ideas.* New York: Dutton, 1968.

Goodall, K. Who's who and where in behavior shaping. *Psychology Today,* June 1972, 58.

Hall, E. "My hat still fits." *Psychology Today,* November 1972, 68.

Harris, T. All the world's a box. *Psychology Today,* August 1971, 33–35.

Isaacs, W., Thomas, J., & Goldiamond, I. Application of operant conditioning to reinstate verbal behavior in psychotics. *Journal of Speech and Hearing Disorders,* 1960, **25,** 8–12.

Kanfer, F., & Phillips, J. *Learning foundations of behavior therapy.* New York: Wiley, 1970.

Lundin, R. Personality theory in behavioristic psychology. In J. Wepman & R. Heine (Eds.), *Concepts of personality.* Chicago: Aldine, 1963, pp. 257–290.

Rimm, D., & Masters, J. *Behavior therapy: Techniques and empirical findings.* New York: Academic Press, 1974.

Skinner, B. F. *The behavior of organisms: An experimental analysis.* New York: Appleton-Century-Crofts, 1938.

Skinner, B. F. *Walden two.* New York: Macmillan, 1948a.

Skinner, B. F. Superstition in the pigeon. *Journal of Experimental Psychology,* 1948b, **38,** 168–172.

Skinner, B. F. Are theories of learning necessary? *Psychological Review,* 1950, **57,** 193–216.

Skinner, B. F. *Science and human behavior.* New York: Macmillan, 1953.

Skinner, B. F., & Lindsley, O. Studies in behavior therapy, status reports II and III, Office of Naval Research Contract N5 ori–7662, 1954.

Skinner, B. F. A case history in scientific method. *American Psychologist,* 1956, **11,** 221–233.

Skinner, B. F. *Verbal behavior.* New York: Appleton-Century-Crofts, 1957a.

Skinner, B. F., & Ferster, C. *Schedules of reinforcement.* New York: Appleton-Century-Crofts, 1957b.

Skinner, B. F. *Cumulative record.* New York: Appleton-Century-Crofts, 1961.

Skinner, B.F. Autobiography of B. F. Skinner. In E. Boring & G. Lindzey (Eds.), *History of psychology in autobiography* (Vol. V). New York: Appleton-Century-Crofts, 1967, pp. 387–413.

Skinner, B. F. *The technology of teaching.* New York: Appleton-Century-Crofts, 1968.

Skinner, B. F. *Contingencies of reinforcement: A theoretical analysis.* New York: Appleton-Century-Crofts, 1969.

Skinner, B. F. *Beyond Freedom and Dignity.* New York: Knopf, 1971.

Skinner, B. F. *About behaviorism.* New York: Knopf, 1974.

Watson, J., & Raynor, R. Conditioned emotional reactions. *Journal of Experimental Psychology,* 1920, **3,** 1–14.

Williams, C. The elimination of tantrum behavior by extinction procedures. *Journal of Abnormal and Social Psychology,* 1959, **59,** 269.

Williams, J. *Operant learning: Procedures for changing behavior.* Monterey, Calif.: Brooks/Cole, 1973.

SUGGESTED READINGS

1 Bandura, A. *Principles of behavior modification.* New York: Holt, Rinehart, and Winston, 1969.

2 Carpenter, F. *The Skinner primer: Beyond freedom and dignity.* New York: Free Press, 1974.

3 Kazdin, A. *Behavior modification in applied settings.* Homewood, Ill.: Dorsey, 1975.

4 Matson. F. *Without/within: Behaviorism and humanism.* Belmont, Calif.: Wadsworth, 1973.

5 Skinner, B. F. Behaviorism at fifty. In T. Wann (Ed.), *Behaviorism and Phenomenology.* Chicago: University of Chicago Press, 1964, pp. 79–108.

Gordon W. Allport

Chapter 6

Gordon Allport: A Trait Theory of Personality

No two people are completely alike. Thus, no two people react identically to the same psychological situation or stimulus. Perhaps this fact is the most compelling and fundamental issue confronting the student of personality. Indeed, every personality theory, in one way or another, must deal with the enigma of individual differences if it is to remain a viable commodity in the marketplace of psychological science. Gordon Allport is a personologist who regards the explanation of an individual's uniqueness as the paramount goal of psychology.

Allport's theory represents a blend of humanistic and personalistic approaches to the study of human behavior. It is humanistic in its attempts to recognize all aspects of the human being, including the potential for growth and transcendence. It is personalistic in that its objective is to understand and predict the development of the real individual person (Allport, 1968a). Further, as a theoretician, Allport may be broadly described as an eclectic because he incorporates insights from philosophy, religion, literature, and sociology, blending such ideas into an understanding of the uniqueness and complexity of personality. In fact, Allport's belief that each person's behavior derives from a particular pattern of personal *traits* is the trademark of his orientation to personology.

BIOGRAPHICAL SKETCH

Gordon Willard Allport, the youngest of four brothers, was born in Montezuma, Indiana, in 1897. His father, a country doctor, moved the family to Ohio shortly after Gordon's birth, and the youngest Allport received his early education in the Cleveland public schools. The Protestant work ethic dominated Allport's home life:

> My mother had been a school teacher and brought to her sons an eager sense of philosophical questing and the importance of searching for ultimate religious answers. Since my father lacked adequate hospital facilities for his patients, our household for several years included both patients and nurses. Tending office, washing bottles, and dealing with patients were important aspects of my early training. . . . Dad was no believer in vacations. He followed rather his own rule of life, which he expressed as follows: "If every person worked as hard as he could and took only the minimum financial return required by his family's needs, then there would be just enough wealth to go around." Thus it was hard work tempered by trust and affection that marked the home environment (Allport, 1967, pp. 4–5).

Allport pursued undergraduate study at Harvard University at the urging of his brother Floyd, who was then a graduate student in psychology. Going to college produced almost instant culture shock for Allport:

> Almost overnight my world was remade. My basic moral values, to be sure, had been fashioned at home. What was new was the horizon of intellect and culture I was now invited to explore. . . . First and foremost was the pervading sense of high standards. . . . At the first hour examinations I received an array of D's and C's. Profoundly shattered, I stiffened my efforts and ended the year with A's (Allport, 1967, p. 5)

He majored in economics and philosophy and was awarded the B.A. degree in 1919. During the following academic year, he taught English and sociology at Robert College, Istanbul, Turkey. He then returned to Harvard where he secured his M.A. degree in 1921 and his Ph.D. in psychology in 1922. From 1922 to 1924, supported by a Sheldon Traveling Fellowship, Allport studied at the Universities of Berlin and Hamburg in Germany and the University of Cambridge in England. Returning from Europe, he served as an instructor for two years in Harvard's Department of Social Ethics. He married Ada Lufkin Gould in 1925. They had one child, Robert. Allport next accepted the position of assistant professor of psychology at Dartmouth College, where he stayed until 1930. In that year, he was invited by Harvard to return at the same rank in the Department of Social Relations. He was promoted to Professor of Psychology in 1942 and held this position until his death in 1967.

Allport actively participated in numerous professional and honorary organizations. During World War II he served on the Emergency Committee in Psychology, an organization specializing in problems of civilian morale and rumor. He was a representative of the American Psychological Association (APA) on both the National and Social Science Research Council, and a director of the National Commission for the United Nations Educational, Scientific, and Cultural Organization. Between 1937 and 1949, Allport was editor of the *Journal of Abnormal and Social Psychology*. He was president of the APA in 1937, of the Eastern Psychological Association in 1943, and of the Society for the Psychological Study of Social Issues in 1944. He was a recipient of the Gold Medal from the American Psychological Foundation in 1963 and received the APA's Distinguished Scientific Contribution Award in 1964, which had the following citation:

> For reminding us that man is neither a beast nor a statistic, except as we choose to regard him so, and that the human personality finds its greatest measure in the reaches of time. This is to say that, while life may have its crude beginnings, it has its noble endings too, and there is a line that leads from one to the other—a line that graphically portrays the character of the individual, and of mankind as well. This is what he taught his students. He taught them also to respect scholarship and to abhor the massive ignorance of the fortuitous researcher. And because so many of them learned their lessons well, the name of Gordon Allport has become a hallmark of the well-turned curriculum vitae (*American Psychologist*, 1964, p. 942).

Allport was a prolific writer. Among his widely known publications are *Personality: A Psychological Interpretation* (1937); *The Individual and His Religion* (1950); *Becoming: Basic Considerations for a Psychology of Personality* (1955); *Personality and Social Encounter* (1960); *Pattern and Growth in Personality* (1961); and *Letters from Jenny* (1965). He also coauthored two widely used personality tests; *The A-S Reaction Study* (with F. H. Allport, 1928) and *A Study of Values* (with P. E. Vernon, 1931; revised with G. Lindzey in 1951 and again in 1960). A complete list of his writings may be found in *The Person in Psychology* (Allport, 1968b). His autobiography is presented in Volume 5 of *A History of Psychology in Autobiography* (1967, pp. 3–25).

PERSONALITY AS A "SOMETHING" *Weber*

The term "personality" is not easily defined. In fact, its precise meaning varies considerably from theory to theory. According to some theorists (e.g., Skinner), personality as such does not even exist—it is really a superfluous term that some people unfortunately find useful in describing behavior. For other theorists (e.g., Freud), personality includes deep, dark recesses of the mind that very few people, including the subject, even know about. Allport was quite dissatisfied with this state of affairs and expended a great deal of energy in constructing his own definition of personality. If he was going to spend a professional lifetime studying the functioning of personality, he first wanted to at least have a preliminary idea of what it is!

In his first book, *Personality: A Psychological Interpretation,* Allport devoted an entire chapter to a review of the many different notions offered by authorities in the field and concluded that an adequate synthesis of existing definitions might be something like the phrase "what a man really is (1937, p. 48)." What this definition possesses in the way of comprehensiveness, it certainly lacks in precision. Recognizing this, Allport went a step further and asserted that "personality is something and does something. . . . It is what lies behind specific acts and within the individual (1937, p. 48)." Eschewing the notion of personality as merely a hypothetical entity, then, Allport argued that it definitely is an existent "something" within the person. At least in Allport's system, personality is alive, well, and functioning.

The overriding, looming, and remaining question, however, is "What is the nature of this *something?"* Allport (1937) answered this question by offering a precise definition of personality which he subsequently modified slightly to read as follows: "Personality is the dynamic organization within the individual of those psychophysical systems that determine his characteristic behavior and thought (1961, p. 28)." What does all this verbiage mean? First, the phrase "dynamic organization" suggests that human behavior is constantly evolving and changing; the person is not a static entity in Allport's theory, although there is an underlying mental system that integrates and organizes the various elements of personality. As Allport used the phrase, "psychophysical systems" means that both physical and mental factors must be considered when describing and studying personality. Personality, then, reflects all of what a human being is. The inclusion of the term "determine" is a logical consequence of Allport's psychophysical orientation. Basically, the implication is that personality is made up of "determining tendencies" which, when aroused by appropriate stimuli, give rise to actions through which the individual's true nature is revealed. (These "determining tendencies"—traits in Allport's theory—will subsequently be discussed at length.) The word "characteristic" in Allport's definition simply highlights the paramount importance that he attached to individual uniqueness. Each person is truly an entity unto himself in this personological system. Finally, the phrase "behavior and thought" is a blanket designed to cover everything the person does. Allport believed that personality may express itself in some way in virtually all observable human actions.

In arriving at his conceptual definition, Allport noted that the terms *character* and *temperament* have often been used as synonyms for personality. This seems particularly true when considering the layman's use of these terms. Allport explains how each may be readily distinguished from the concept of personality. The word "character" traditionally connotes a moral standard or value system against which the individual's actions are evaluated. For example, whenever another person is considered of "good character," a personal judgment as to the ethical desirability of his personal qualities is really the topic. Character thus is really an ethical concept. Or, as Allport (1961) put it, character is personality *evaluated;* personality is character *devaluated.* Character, then, should not be considered as some special region contained within personality.

Temperament, by contrast, is the "raw material"—along with intelligence and physique—out of which personality is fashioned. Allport considered the term particularly useful in referring to the characteristic and largely hereditary aspects of a person's emotional nature, e.g., his or her susceptibility to emotional stimulation, customary strength and speed of response, prevailing mood state, fluctuation and intensity of moods (Allport, 1961). Representing one aspect of an individual's genetic endowment, temperament limits the development of personality. Temperamentally speaking, you certainly "can't make a silk purse out of a sow's ear" in Allport's system. Like any good definition of personality, then, Allport's concept states clearly both what it *is* and what it *is not.*

WHAT A PERSONALITY THEORY SHOULD BE

Before considering those concepts that are most uniquely identified with Allport's theory, it will be instructive to examine his five requirements for an adequate personality theory. Specifically, Allport (1960) insisted that:

1 A truly adequate theory of human behavior must *regard the human personality as centered in the organism.* This raises the question "Where else would it be?" In fact, other theorists have in effect placed personality outside the person by equating it with social roles or interpersonal relationships. Concerning the former, *role theory,*—as proposed by sociologists and anthropologists,—explains personality as nothing more than one's membership in a group and the situationally defined roles one is expected to adopt. According to this approach, any given person, say, Adam, for example, is known only by the roles he enacts—Adam is only a college student, son, consumer, church attender, part-time drug pusher, and so on. Allport was quick to chide such theorists, arguing that these situational factors should not obscure the more central idea that Adam's traits, values, and other internal factors account for his conduct in everyday life. If Adam is to be truly understood, he must be considered as a self-contained unit rather than as the social impression he makes on others, his reputation, or how people react to him.

2 A complete theory of personality *regards the organism as replete, not empty.* Readers who have been converted to Skinner's view of the human being by the previous chapter would find Allport's second requirement patently absurd. Representing the antithesis of Skinner's position, Allport argued that we must assume a "well-stocked" organism, not an empty one, if we are to advance in personality theorizing. Whereas Skinner believes environmental events shape the "empty" organism, Allport believes personality is something that is located within the organism: "Any theory of personality pretending adequacy must be dynamic and, to be dynamic, must assume a well-stocked organism (Allport, 1960, p. 26)." To explain Adam's behavior, then, the personologist must postulate some set of dispositions existing within him. In other words, one must understand what's happening psychologically within Adam in order to comprehend his observable behavior. Most major personality theories today, Allport's included, represent highly systematic attempts to accomplish such a person-centered objective.

   3   An adequate theory must *regard motivation as normally a fact of present structure and function, not simply as an outgrowth of earlier forces or experience.* Motivationally speaking, Adam is not a prisoner of his past. He does not forever drag the chains of his early childhood experiences to rattle through his every adult action. Instead, Allport believed that an adequate personality theory should portray Adam as he is now, as a twenty-year-old college student, and interpret his motivation accordingly. Suppose, for example, that Adam is a psychology major contemplating clinical psychology as a career. Some Freudians would have us believe that this vocational preference is due to Adam's frustrated and now repressed childhood curiosity about sex. He is unconsciously motivated to pursue clinical psychology so that he can spend a professional lifetime probing the intimate and lurid details of patients' sex lives.

   In Allport's scheme of things, this is, in a word, nonsense. While Allport would admit that childhood experiences certainly contribute to the direction of personal development, he also would argue that a psychologically healthy Adam has a vocational preference understandable in terms of more contemporary and adult motives, e.g., a desire to help disturbed individuals therapeutically, a keen interest in simply understanding human behavior for its own sake, or wanting to fulfill oneself as a person. Allport elaborated this requirement considerably in his theoretical concept of "functional autonomy" (to be discussed subsequently). Basically, as will be seen, Allport believed that the confusion between the historical roots of motives and the contemporary functioning of motives is the most stultifying of all misconceptions that mar current personality theories. The motives of people must be understood as they are now rather than as they were in the historical then. Thus, an adequate theory must allow for the forward thrust or futuristic bent of personal motives that normally characterizes healthy adults.

   4   In order for a theory to be adequate it must *employ units of analysis capable of living synthesis.* This requirement stipulates that personality must somehow be broken down into definable units (segments, aspects, factors) for study, but that the units themselves must be of such a nature as to permit their reconstruction, capturing that holistic quality of "dynamic organization" which is at the heart of Allport's definition of personality. For example, to account for the personality of Humpty Dumpty, it would indeed be necessary for a theory first to break him into pieces. However, unlike all the king's horses and all the king's men, an adequate personality theory would be able to put Humpty Dumpty together again, and dynamically—into a "living synthesis."

   But what of the "pieces"—what is their nature? Allport rejected units of analysis such as attitudes, values, needs, and drives because they fail to reconstruct, when synthesized, the vital and intrinsic nature of personality organization within the individual. Instead, Allport remained true to his own definition of personality involving an enduring psychophysical organization *unique* to each person. Consequently, he suggested that theorists have no choice but to rely upon units of analysis which are *peculiar to the individual*— specifically, a system of generalized action tendencies or traits. Adam, then, can be best understood by studying the individual trait system representing the unique, dynamic pattern of organization characterizing his life.

5 Finally, a theory must *allow adequately for, but not rely exclusively upon, the phenomenon of self-consciousness.* To portray Adam accurately an adequate personality theory must recognize that he is consciously aware of himself. In fact, this self-consciousness is the most concrete evidence Adam has of his personal identity. Further, Adam's awareness of himself, at least to some extent, makes him an active agent in shaping his own destiny. To the extent that he knows the ship, he can navigate it through various seas. Finally, it is precisely this aspect of personality, self-consciousness, that most clearly separates Adam from other species. Man is conscious of his own consciousness; lower organisms are not. A truly human theory of personality, while not overwhelmed by this fact, recognizes it fully.

CONCEPT OF TRAIT

This chapter started with the assertion that no two people are completely alike. Any one person behaves in a consistent and different fashion from all others. Why? Allport's answer is found in his concept of *trait,* which he regarded as the most valid "unit of analysis" for representing what people are like and how they differ from one another psychologically.

What is a trait of personality? Allport begins by defining it as a "neuropsychic structure having the capacity to render many stimuli functionally equivalent, and to initiate and guide equivalent (meaningfully consistent) forms of adaptive and expressive behavior (1961, p. 347)." In simpler terms, *a trait is a predisposition to respond in an equivalent manner to various kinds of stimuli.* Traits, in effect, are psychological entities that render many stimuli as well as many responses equivalent. Many stimuli may evoke the same response, or many responses (perceptions, interpretations, feelings, actions) have the same functional meaning in terms of the trait. To illustrate this concept, Allport (1961) cites the case of a fictitious Mr. McCarley whose leading trait is a "fear of communism." For him, this trait renders equivalent the social stimuli of Russians, black and Jewish neighbors, liberals, most college professors, peace organizations, the United Nations, and so forth. All are perceived and labeled as communists. In addition, such a trait triggers hostile response sequences which are equivalent in their capacity to reduce the perceived threat of communism. Mr. McCarley might support nuclear war against Russians, write hostile letters to the local newspaper about blacks, vote for extreme right-wing political candidates and policies, join the Klu Klux Klan or John Birch Society,

Stimuli

1. Communists

2. Books by Marx

3. Black and Jewish neighbors

4. Immigration

5. Intellectuals and liberals

6. Left-wing organizations

Fear of Communism— a trait

Responses

1. Advocating nuclear war against Communist countries

2. Voting for extreme right wing political candidates

3. Joining the Klu Klux Klan

4. Criticizing the United Nations

5. Rioting against the objectionable stimulus persons

6. Writing protest letters to newspapers

Figure 6-1   The generality of a trait as determined by equivalence of stimuli that arouse it and by equivalence of responses that it produces. *(Adapted from Allport, 1961, p. 322.)*

criticize the UN, and/or participate in any one of a number of other equivalent hostile responses. Figure 6-1 shows schematically the range of possibilities.

Needless to say, an individual may sincerely adopt a number of these positions without necessarily possessing undue hostility or fear of communism. Additionally, everyone who votes for right-wing candidates or opposes the UN does not necessarily fall in the same personological category. However, this example shows that one's traits are organized and expressed on the basis of perceived similarities. That is, many stimulus situations, because of their perceived equivalence, arouse a certain trait which then initiates a variety of behavioral responses which are equivalent in giving expression to the trait. It is this conception of equivalence of stimuli and responses (united and mediated) by a trait that constitutes Allport's theory of personality organization. In essence, traits theoretically serve to integrate what would otherwise be dissimilar stimuli and responses.

According to Allport, traits are not linked to a small number of specific stimuli or responses; rather, they are relatively generalized and enduring. By uniting responses to numerous stimuli, traits produce fairly broad consistencies in behavior. A trait is what accounts for the more permanent, enduring, transsituational features of our behavior. It is a vital ingredient of our "personality structure." At the same time, traits may also be focal in nature. For example, the trait of dominance may be aroused only when the individual is in the presence of specific others, his or her children, spouse, or intimate acquaintances. In each case he or she immediately becomes ascendant. However, the trait of dominance is not activated in the event that the individual discovers a missing $10 bill on the floor of a friend's home. Such a stimulus would arouse the trait of honesty (or dishonesty as the case may be). It would not arouse dominance. Allport thus admits that personality traits are embedded within social situations, adding: "any theory that regards personality as stable, fixed, invariable is wrong (1961, p. 175)." As an analogy, water can have the shape and texture of a liquid, a solid (ice), or some substance along the continuum (snow, hail, sleet). It is the degree of environmental warmth that determines its physical form.

It should be emphasized, however, that traits do not lie dormant waiting to be aroused by external stimuli. In fact, the individual may actively seek stimulus situations that encourage the expression of his traits. The person with a strong disposition toward sociability not only responds in a charming manner when in a group of people but also seeks out company when he is alone. In other words, the individual is not a passive "reactor" to the situation as B. F. Skinner might suggest; rather, the situations in which he is likely to find himself are often those in which he has actively placed himself. Specifically, Allport suggests that traits and the situation interact to produce behavior. The two components are functionally interdependent.

The "Traits" of Traits

In Allport's system, traits themselves may be said to have "traits" or defining characteristics. Shortly before his death, Allport (1966) published an article entitled "Traits Revisited" in which he summarized all that he had learned in response to the question "What is a trait of personality?" In this article, he proposed that eight basic criteria define a personality trait:

1 *A trait has more than nominal existence.* Personality traits are not fictions; they are a very real and vital part of man's existence. Every person possesses inside his or her skin these "generalized action tendencies"—it is the psychologist's task to discover what they are. Aside from "fear of communism," other readily defined traits would be such things as "fear of capitalism," "introversion," "extraversion," "aggressiveness," "meekness," "honesty," "dishonesty," and a whole possible host of others. Allport's main point here is that these personal characteristics are *real*—they actually exist in people and are not simply theoretical make believe.

2 *A trait is more generalized than a habit.* Traits tend to cut across situations and thereby account for the more permanent, enduring, and general features of our behavior. Habits, while enduring, refer to more narrow and limited types of determining tendencies and are thus less generalized in terms of the situations which may arouse them or the responses which they evoke. For example, a child learning to brush her teeth may continue to do so for some time only because she is encouraged by her mother. This is a habit. However, with the passing of years, brushing one's teeth not only becomes habitual but is woven into a broader system of habits, viz., a *trait* of personal cleanliness. To some extent, then, a trait is the product of integrating numerous specific habits that serve the same adaptive function for the person. Traits embrace two or more interdependent habits.

3 *A trait is dynamic or at least determinative in behavior.* Traits underlie behavior—they *cause* behavior. In Allport's system, traits do not lie dormant waiting to be aroused by external stimuli. Rather, they motivate the person to seek stimulus situations in which he can manifest his traits. For example, a college student with a strong "sociability" trait does not just sit around and wait to go to parties to be sociable. He actively seeks out parties so that he can express his sociability trait. Traits, then, guide and direct an individual's actions. Because traits can, in effect, cause behavior, they can be considered "derived motives."

4 *A trait's existence may be established empirically.* If they're real, somebody ought to be able to prove that they are. While traits as such can never be directly observed (how can you "see" sociability?), Allport believed that they could be verified scientifically. Specifically, evidence for the existence of traits may be derived from observations of repeated actions by the subject, case histories or biographies, or statistical techniques that determine the degree of coherence among separate responses. Some interesting approaches to establishing a trait's existence empirically will be discussed in the "Empirical Validation" section of this chapter.

5 *A trait is only relatively independent of other traits.* To paraphrase a well-known saying, "No trait is an island." They overlap. There is no rigid boundary separating one trait from another. Rather, the personality is comprised of a network of overlapping traits only *relatively* independent of one another. To illustrate, Allport (1960) cites a study in which it was found that the traits of insight and humor are highly correlated with one another. Clearly, these are separate traits, but they nonetheless are somehow related. While it is scientifically impossible to draw causal conclusions from such correlational data, one might speculate that if a person possessed a high degree of insight, he would undoubtedly perceive the ludicrous aspects of the human condition and be led to develop a well-rounded sense of humor. Much more likely from Allport's viewpoint, however, is that traits overlap primarily because of the organism's tendency to react to events in an integrated fashion.

6 *A trait is not synonymous with moral or social judgment.* Despite the fact that many traits (e.g., sincerity, loyalty, greediness), are bound by conventional social meaning, they still represent true traits of personality. Ideally, it would be preferable first to discover traits as they exist in a given individual and then seek devaluated words to identify them. In Allport's opinion, personologists should be studying *personality,* not *character.*

7 *A trait may be viewed either in light of the personality that contains it or in light of its distribution in the population at large.* Take autoeroticism as an illustration. Like any other trait, it has both *unique* and *universal* aspects. When viewed uniquely, autoeroticism could be studied in terms of the role it plays in a given individual's personality, e.g., Alexander Portnoy. Conversely, this trait could be studied "universally" by constructing a reliable and valid "autoeroticism scale" and determining how people differ on it. This latter approach is called "differential psychology" or the psychology of individual differences.

8 *Acts or even habits that are inconsistent with a trait are not proof of the nonexistence of the trait.* As an illustration, consider Eve Smith who is characteristically neat in terms of her personal appearance; never a hair out of place and her attire impeccable, she possesses the trait of neatness. But one

could never tell this just by examining her desk, room, or car. Her personal belongings in each case are carelessly arranged, cluttered, and downright sloppy. Why the apparent contradiction? From an Allportian frame of reference, there are three possible explanations. First, not everyone will show the same degree of integration in respect to a given trait—what is a major trait for one person may either be a minor or nonexistent trait for another person. Here, Eve's trait of neatness is less major than it might be for someone else in terms of its pervasiveness within personality. In Eve's case, neatness may be restricted only to her person. Second, the same individual may possess contradictory traits; e.g., Eve is *neat* with respect to her personal appearance and *slovenly* with regard to her belongings. Usually, however, contradictory traits are of unequal strength—considered as a whole, Eve should be able to be characterized as more neat than slovenly. Third, there are instances where a person's actions are simply unrelated to the trait; rather, they are products of stimulus situations or momentary attitudes. If Eve is running to catch a plane, for example, she may not care whether her hair blows all over the place or her clothing becomes disheveled in the process. Therefore, to observe that not all of Eve's actions are consistent with an underlying disposition of neatness is no proof that the disposition does not exist within her.

Types of Traits: Pervasiveness within a Personality *Donna*

As has been indicated, traits are determining tendencies or predispositions to respond consistently over time and across situations. Even Eve Smith's rather circumscribed trait of neatness in her personal appearance should be manifested practically any time she "personally appears" any place. But must a person who has a certain trait *always* exhibit it? If he or she does not, how are the varying degrees of a trait's generality judged?

Facing this issue, Allport proposed that traits may be classified into a threefold and somewhat overlapping category system according to the degree to which they pervade and influence individual behavior:

1 Cardinal Traits If a trait is extremely pervasive, so pervasive that almost all a person's activities can be traced to its influence, it is a *cardinal trait* in Allport's system. This highly generalized disposition cannot remain hidden unless, of course, it happens to be something like seclusiveness, in which case its possessor might become a hermit and eventually no one would ever hear of him, much less his cardinal trait. In other instances, however, this kind of master sentiment or ruling passion makes its possessor famous. Allport insisted that very few people possess a cardinal trait.

The meaning of a cardinal trait may be readily grasped by considering the many trait adjectives derived from historical and fictional characters; e.g., when someone is referred to as being a chauvinist, sadist, Machiavellian, Don Juan, Scrooge, or Joan of Arc. Or consider that Albert Schweitzer was said to have had one cardinal disposition in his life—"reverence for every living organism." Similarly, Leo Tolstoy was said to have been endowed with a burning passion for the "oversimplification of life." Finally, most of Sigmund Freud's adult life could be said to be characterized by a consuming "interest in psychology," in uncovering the nature of man's deepest motivations. The theme of the lives of these three individuals reveals the all-pervasive quality of cardinal traits.

2 Central Traits   Less pervasive but still quite generalized dispositions of the individual are what Allport termed *central traits*—the so-called building blocks of personality. These traits might best be regarded as those attributes which would be stressed in writng a carefully defined letter of recommendation—e.g., outgoing, sentimental, attentive, sociable, and vivacious. Specifically, central traits are those tendencies that a person often expresses which people around him can readily discern. In a rather hypothetical manner, Allport asked: "How many central traits does the average individual possess?" He approached this question by asking ninety-three students "to think of some one individual of your own sex whom you know well" and "to describe him or her by writing words, phrases, or sentences that express fairly well what seem to you to be the essential characteristics of this person (1961, p. 366)." Ninety percent of the students listed between 3 and 10 essential characteristics: the average number listed was 7.2. Allport thus concluded that the number of central dispositions by which a personality can be described is surprisingly small, perhaps no more than five to ten. Sometimes from the vantage point of the person himself, his central traits may be perceived as very few indeed. H. G. Wells once commented that there were only two dominant themes in his life: interest in an ordered world society and sex. This example should shed light on the meaning of central as opposed to cardinal traits (and also on H. G. Wells).

3 Secondary Traits   Dispositions which are less conspicuous, less generalized, less consistent, and thus less relevant to the definition of a personality are called *secondary traits*. Food preferences, specific attitudes, and other situationally determined characteristics of the person would be classified under this rubric of traits. Consider, for instance, a person whose central traits are dominance and assertiveness, which he manifests in practically every interpersonal encounter. This person might also have as a secondary trait submissiveness, which he displays only in relation to police who dutifully-stop him for speeding, running red lights, and ignoring stop signs ("Yes, officer," "No, officer," "You're right, officer," etc.). According to Allport, an individual possesses a great many more of these than of the other trait types; hence, an individual must be known quite intimately in order to discern his secondary traits.

Common versus Individual Traits   *Pauleen*

Allport also distinguished between *common* and *individual* traits. The former, *common traits* (also called *dimensional* or *nomothetic* traits) includes any generalized disposition to which most people within a given culture can be reasonably compared. The logic for assuming the existence of common traits is that members of a given culture are subject to similar evolutionary and social influences; therefore, they develop somewhat roughly comparable modes of adjustment. Examples include proficiency in the use of language, political and/or social attitudes, value orientations, anxiety, and conformity. The majority of people within our own culture could be measurably compared with one another on these common dimensions.

According to Allport, what usually (but not invariably) results from such trait comparisons among individuals is a normal distribution curve. That is, when common trait test scores are plotted on a graph, they approximate a bell-shaped curve, with the bulk of cases piling up as average scores in the middle and the rest tapering off toward the extremes. Figure 6-2 illustrates this situation for the common trait "dominance–submission." The dimensionality of common traits, then, allows the personologist to compare one individual with another along meaningful psychological dimensions (such as he might for common physical characteristics such as height and weight).

While regarding such cross comparisons as legitimate and useful, Allport (1968a) also believed that traits never occur in any two people in exactly the same way. The psychological pervasiveness and expression of dominance for Linda is unique to her. To this extent, Linda's dominance cannot really be compared with Susan's. *Individual traits* (also called *personal dispositions* or *morphological traits*), then, designate those characteristics peculiar to the individual which do not permit comparisons among individuals. It is these "genuine and neuropsychic units that guide, direct, and motivate specific acts of adjustment (1968a, p.3)." Always operating in unique ways within each person, this category of traits most accurately pinpoints the personality structure of any given individual, the organized focuses of his life. For Allport, then, the true personality surfaces only when individual traits are examined, using such resources as a person's case history, diary, letters, and other such

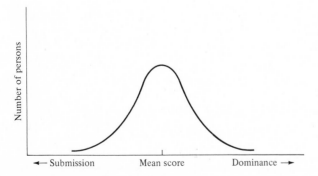

Figure 6-2 The distribution of scores based on a test measuring the dominance—submission trait continuum.

personal documents. Consequently, the common trait of dominance can be profitably studied by comparing Linda, Susan, and everybody else on some meaningful yardstick (e.g., a dominance test or scale). But dominance as an individual trait can only be understood by studying its unique functioning in Linda, in Susan, and in everyone else considered one at a time, which, for Allport, was the only real way to understand individual personalities.

THE PROPRIUM: A REAL SELF?   *Mary Belot*

No personologist, least of all Allport, believes that personality is a mere bundle of unrelated traits. Personality embodies a unity, consistency, and integration of traits. It is therefore reasonable to suppose that there is an overall principle that unifies traits, attitudes, values, motives, and experiences. For Allport, the problem of identifying and describing the nature of personality integration requires an all-inclusive construct such as the self, ego, or style of life. In older, less scientific days, people called it a soul. But all these terms had accumulated too many ambiguous connotations and semantic ambiguities for Allport's taste. So he introduced a new term—the *proprium.*

Allport's humanistic orientation toward personality is nowhere more clearly revealed than in his concept of proprium, defined as "the self-as-known—that which is experienced as warm and central, as of importance (1968a, p. 4)." It's the "me" part of subjective experience. It's selfhood.

For Allport, the proprium represents the positive, creative, growth-seeking, and forward-moving quality of human nature. This point is highly significant, for this view of the person represented a radical departure from the dreary, dark, and deterministic portrait painted by many psychoanalysts or the stimulus-response robot image promulgated by many behaviorists. The influence of the true humanists in psychology—e.g., Abraham Maslow—was yet to reach its heyday, and much that Allport wrote about selfhood has a contemporary humanist-Maslowian ring to it. This important turn in the development of personality theory will be more fully appreciated when the reader proceeds to Chapters 8 and 9 (Maslow and Rogers).

While Allport conceived of the proprium as including all aspects of personality that contribute to a sense of inward unity, as marking the consistency associated with the individual's traits, intentions, and long-range goals, he did not regard it as a "thing." It is not separable from the person as a whole. Above all, it is not a homunculus. Rather, Allport (1955) used the term to refer to those functions that make for the peculiar unity and distinctiveness of personality. Moreover, he identified at least seven different aspects of "selfhood" which are involved in the development of the proprium. These so-called *propriate functions* develop gradually (are not innate), and their eventual synthesis constitutes the "me" as an object of subjective knowledge and feeling. Presented in order of their sequential appearance in the growing child, the propriate functions of personality follow. (When studying these, the reader is urged to attempt to relate them to *him- or herself,* so that Allport's concept of proprium will become intuitively more clear.)

1 The Sense of Bodily Self A sense of one's own body, including bodily sensations, attests to one's existence and therefore remains a lifelong anchor for self-awareness. Allport notes that one's bodily sense is so basic that most adults are unaware of it—it assumes importance only when pain or illness strikes (e.g., a man is usually unaware of his little finger until it is smashed in a door). A dramatic example of how the natural intimacy of bodily functions can readily become alien is seen in the following exercise. First, imagine yourself sucking blood from a cut in your finger; then picture yourself sucking blood from a bandaid around your finger. What was formerly perceived as belonging intimately to your body instantly becomes cold and disgusting. Presumably, most adults retain a very infantile conception of their bodies; otherwise examples of this sort would not be so unpalatable.

2 The Sense of Self-Identity The second aspect of the proprium to unfold, self-identity, is most evident when the child, through acquiring language, recognizes himself as a distinct and constant point of reference. Unquestionably, the most important anchorage for a child's self-identity is his own name. Clothing, toys, and other precious possessions also strengthen his sense of identity, but identity is not firmly established all at once. For instance, a two-year-old may be unaware that he is cold, feels tired, or needs to eliminate. Fantasy and reality are often blurred and the former often dominates play life.

3 The Sense of Self-Esteem or Pride Essentially, self-esteem is an individual's evaluation of himself. The urge to want to do everything for oneself and take all the credit is one of the most conspicuous aspects of a two-year-old's behavior. Parents frequently consider this as the age of negativism, since the child resists almost any adult proposal as a threat to his integrity and autonomy. By the age of four or five, self-esteem acquires a competitive flavor, reflected by the child's delighted "I beat you!" when he wins a game.

4 The Sense of Self-Extension During the third year of life, the proprium is elaborated through self-extension, that is, the sense that although other people and things are not inside my physical body, they are still very much a part of me—they are "mine." With it comes jealous possessiveness—e.g., "This is *my* ball," "I *own* the doll house." *My* mommy, *my* sister, *my* dog, *my* house are regarded as warm parts of oneself and are things to be guarded against loss, especially against takeover by another child.

5 The Self-Image How others view "me" is another aspect of selfhood that emerges during childhood. Now is the time when the child realizes that parents expect him to be "good" while at times he is "naughty." As yet, however, the child has no clearly developed conscience nor any image of himself as he would like to be as an adult. Allport writes: "In childhood the capacity to think of oneself as one is, as one wants to be, and as one ought to be is merely germinal (1961, p. 123)."

6 The Sense of Self as a Rational-Coper   Between six and twelve years of age the child begins to realize fully that he has the rational capacity to find solutions to life's problems so that he can cope effectively with reality demands. Reflective and formal thought appear and the child begins to think about thinking. But the child does not yet trust himself to be an independent moral agent. He dogmatically believes that his family, his religion, and his peer group are *right;* this stage of propriate development reflects intense moral and social conformity.

7 Propriate Striving   Allport believed that the core problem for the adolescent is the selection of an occupation or other life goal. The adolescent knows that the future must follow a plan and, in this sense, his selfhood assumes a dimension entirely lacking in childhood (Allport, 1961). Pursuing long-range goals, having a sense of directedness and intentionality in striving for defined objectives, imparting to life a sense of purpose—this is the essence of propriate striving, although it may be quite elementary in the adolescent.

Examples of propriate striving include all forms of behavior that serve self-enhancement. The artist, the scientist, the parent—all strive for goals that are, strictly speaking, unattainable but which unify personality to make life meaningful. In Allport's words:

> Propriate striving confers unity upon personality, but it is never the unity of fulfillment, of repose, or of reduced tension. The devoted parent never loses concern for his child; the devotee of democracy adopts a life-long assignment in his human relationships. The scientist, by the very nature of his commitment, creates more and more questions, never fewer. Indeed the measure of our intellectual maturity, one philosopher suggests, is our capacity to feel less and less satisfied with our answers to better and better problems (1955, p. 67).

FUNCTIONAL AUTONOMY: THE PAST IS PAST   *Debbie*

Basic to Allport's trait theory is the underlying idea that personality is a dynamic (motivated), growing system. In fact, Allport held that "any theory of personality pivots upon its analysis of the nature of motivation (1961, p. 196)."

Allport proposed that an adequate theory of human motivation must meet four requirements. First, it must recognize the *contemporaneity of motives.* While knowledge about a person's past helps to reveal the present course of his life, Allport believed that such historical facts are useless unless they can be shown to be dynamically active in the present. In his words, "Past motives explain nothing unless they are also present motives (1961, p. 220)." Second, it must be a *pluralistic theory, allowing for motives of many types*. Many theorists, hoping to unravel the complex nature of human motivation, have suggested that all motives are reducible to one type—e.g., to a few basic drives, to the unconscious, or to self-actualization. Being a true eclectic, Allport felt that there is some truth in all these formulations of motivation, adding "Motives are so diverse in type that we find it difficult to discover the common denominator (1961, p. 221)." Thus, many motivational concepts must be used if we are to understand motivation. Third, such a theory must *ascribe dynamic force to the individual's cognitive processes*, especially to the individual's long-range intentions and plans. For Allport, the most significant question one can ask a person in order to understand his personality is "What do you want to be doing five years from now?" or "What are you trying to do with your life?" An adequate theory of motivation must therefore address itself to what sort of future a person is trying to bring about. And fourth, the theory must *allow for the concrete uniqueness of motives*. In contrast to theorists who assume a schedule of motives common to all men, Allport insisted that the study of motivation must focus on how motives function in unique ways in the individual organism.

The concept of *functional autonomy* of motives provides, in Allport's view, the necessary foundations for a theory of motivation which satisfies the four criteria specified above. This is undoubtedly the best-known and most controversial of the concepts contained within Allport's theoretical system. In many ways it constitutes the core of his trait theory.

The principle of functional autonomy states that adult motives are not related to the earlier experiences in which they originally appeared. The past is past—no strings. A person's motives today are functionally autonomous, *independent* of whatever might have brought them into existence originally. The personality is therefore divorced from its past; any bond to the past is purely historical, not functional. What you are today, you are today—you are not motivationally bound to your past history. Obviously, one can see how such a view of motivation would anger psychoanalysts and behaviorists alike, with their respective strong emphases upon early childhood developmental stages and conditioning experiences as crucial to contemporary adult personality functioning.

Functional autonomy clearly means that a given form of behavior may become an end or goal in itself despite the fact that it may have been originally adopted for some other reason. As an example, consider a young man who wants to become a veterinarian. As a youngster he liked to catch frogs, dissect them, and examine their organs. Furthermore, his father unfortunately happened to look like a frog. Finally, to complete the example, his peers would bring their pet frogs to him for advice in frog care. His teachers praised him for such knowledge and encouraged its development, so that he eventually became a celebrity in the local frog-raisers' subculture.

Now it may be quite true that our young man first began cutting up frogs as an outlet for the repressed hostility he felt toward his father as residue from his Oedipal days. It's also quite conceivable that all that praise from teachers and recognition from peers could have powerfully reinforced his interest in animals, thus leading him in the direction of broadening and deepening it. But now he is twenty-three years old, in veterinary school, has taken numerous courses in biology and animal behavior, and is simply interested in veterinary medicine for its own sake. He lives it and is self-motivated to pursue it as a career. In Allport's system, it is assumed that the original motives are entirely lost. What was formerly a means to an end has now become an end in itself. The young man's present drive to become a veterinarian is functionally autonomous of earlier motives.

Other illustrations of functional autonomy include (1) the retired sailor who aches to return to the salt air and sea; (2) the dedicated craftsman who perfects his product even though his income no longer depends on the extra effort; (3) the musician who yearns to blow his trumpet again after an enforced absence; (4) the miser who continues to amass money while living in poverty; and (5) the economically secure businessman who drives himself sick for the sake of further expanding his business and grossing $20 million a year. In each example the original basis for the motive has been removed or displaced, yet the motive remains. In other words, the original reason for the behavior is missing, yet the behavior persists. This is the essence of functional autonomy.

Two Kinds of Autonomy

Allport eventually distinguished between two levels or types of functional autonomy. The first, *perseverative functional autonomy*, refers to reverberatory or feedback mechanisms in the nervous system which are governed by simple neurological principles. Processes in this category of functional autonomy are neurologically self-maintaining; they help to keep the organism going. Illustrations are infrahuman perseverative activity (e.g., molluscs that burrow in the sand on the beach as a function of the movements of the tide and continue the same rhythm when placed in a laboratory); "circular mechanisms," such as the infant's babbling and other repetitive actions, and the marked inclination of people to satisfy their drives in familiar and routine ways (e.g., eating at the same times each day, sleeping in a familiar bed, suffering from acute homesickness during vacations).

In contrast to the "circular-feedback" processes that characterize perseverative autonomy, *propriate functional autonomy* refers to the individual's acquired interests, values, attitudes, and intentions. Propriate autonomy, essential to the integration of adult personality, significantly contributes to the person's striving for a congruent self-image and enriching style of life. It is what impels an individual to respond to life's challenges, resulting in his attainment of progressively higher levels of authentic maturity and growth. Once again, Allport proposed a concept that is a precursor to much of the contemporary humanistic thinking about man's nature. For example, propriate autonomy clearly suggests that man need not be constantly rewarded (rein-forced) to sustain his efforts:

> How hollow to think of Pasteur's concern for reward, or for health, food, sleep, or family, as the root of his devotion to his work. For long periods of time he was oblivious of them all, losing himself in the white heat of research. And the same passion is seen in the histories of geniuses who in their lifetimes received little or no reward for their work (Allport, 1961, p. 236).

Propriate functional autonomy, then, is a distinct step above merely "keeping the person going." It represents the adult's striving for goals, perception of the world in terms of those goals and values, and the sense of responsibility he takes for his life. Again, the concept is quite in line with a humanistic conception of man.

As might be expected, the notion of functional autonomy of motives has been the target of considerable controversy and attack. Not only are those of psychoanalytic and behavioristic persuasion ruffled by it, but personologists of other theoretical persuasions would simply like to see some of the issues that this concept raises adequately addressed. For example, how does functional autonomy evolve? Precisely how does a motive divest itself of its childhood origin and still continue on as a motive; e.g., how did Johnny begin by draining off hostility killing frogs and end up genuinely interested in veterinary medicine? In actuality, Allport never explained this developmental process so central to the viability of the functional autonomy concept.

Another problem is that Allport never specified exactly what, if any, relationship there was between childhood and adult functionally autonomous motives. Is there a relation between childhood experience and adult motivation? If so, what is it? If not, what prevents everything one does as a child from somehow becoming a propriate striving in adulthood—why do certain developmental experiences in the lives of people seem important? Besides killing frogs, Johnny liked to fly kites too. Why isn't he interested in becoming an airplane pilot today?

Allport's posture in response to such questions was that the phenomenon of functional autonomy will never be clearly understood until the neurophysiological processes involved are established. However, he did attempt a clarification of the psychological processess underlying the incorporation of motives into the proprium. Specifically, the process of propriate autonomy is governed by three principles. The first of these is the *principle of organizing the energy level*. This principle states that propriate autonomy is possible because the energy level possessed by an individual is in excess of that required to satisfy survival needs, drives, and demands for immediate adjustment. Here Allport asserted that man's nature necessitates adequate outlets to consume his available energies to supplement routine motives for survival and drive satisfaction. The second principle, the *principle of mastery and competence*, states that the essence of human nature is to master and extract meaning from the environment and to orient oneself toward future aspirations. Hence, whatever increases or enhances one's competence will become functionally autonomous. Allport's third principle, that of *propriate patterning,* asserts that the autonomy of motives emerges *because the self-structure of man demands it*—the essential nature of the human being innately presses toward a relative unification of life. As a consequence of this trend toward unification, Allport noted that human behavior is primarily proactive, intentional, and unique. In brief, then, functional autonomy is:

> a way of stating that men's motives change and grow in the course of life because it is the nature of man that they should do so. Only theorists wedded to a reactive, homeostatic, quasi-closed model of man find difficulty in agreeing (Allport, 1961, pp. 252–253).

Turning the coin on the other side, however, only theorists wedded to a *proactive, heterostatic,* quasi-open model of man would easily agree with the functional autonomy concept. Once again, then, it becomes evident that regardless of the important but surface theoretical disagreement among personologists concerning a given theory or concept, the fundamental difference among them lies in the realm of their respective basic assumptions concerning human nature.

WHAT IS A HEALTHY PERSON?

Unlike many personologists whose theories grew out of their work with neurotic or deviant personalities, Allport never practiced psychotherapy nor did he consider clinical observations as relevant to personality theorizing. He simply refused to believe that neurotics and psychologically healthy people really had much in common. In fact, he seemed to feel that most other personologists of his day could not even identify a healthy personality. And worse, there was little concerted theoretical effort to define or describe the healthy personality. A person was "healthy" if he or she did not have enough evident neurotic symptoms or money to consult a psychoanalyst. So Allport began a long search to uncover an adequate definition and description of the healthy personality or what he termed the "mature personality." When viewed historically, Allport pioneered efforts that ultimately led to the rejection by many contemporary personologists of the concept of personality built around psychopathology. He helped to focus attention on some of man's *positive* attributes, such as self-esteem and competence.

During his search it rather quickly became obvious to Allport that different cultures have different concepts of what constitutes healthy behavior. Despite this fact, Allport maintained that some people approximate an "ideal" personality more closely than others, at least as far as the value conceptions of Western culture are concerned. He gradually came to view healthy personality development as a growing and active process by which an individual assumes responsibility for his life and develops in a unique and personal way. The emergence of personal maturity is a continuous and lifelong process of *becoming* (Allport, 1955). He concluded that positive mental health is comprised of six components:

1 The mature person will have a *widely extended sense of self.* Healthy people can get "outside" of themselves. They are not forever stuck in the psychological rut of narrow activities related only to their own needs and desires. Instead, they *care.* They participate meaningfully in work, family, various human relationships, hobbies, political and social issues, religion, or whatever else they experience as valuable. Each activity requires authentic ego-involvement and commitment resulting in some direction to life. For Allport, self-love is a prominent factor in everyone's life, but it need not dominate the person's life-style.

2 The social adjustment of the mature person is characterized by a *warm relating of self to others.* There are two kinds of interpersonal warmth subsumed under this criterion—*intimacy* and *compassion.* The intimacy aspect of warmth is seen in the person's capacity to show deep love for family and friends unencumbered by possessive and jealous feelings. Compassion is reflected in the person's ability to tolerate differences (concerning values, attitudes) between self and others, thus allowing the person to show profound respect and appreciation for the human condition.

3 *Emotional security* or *self-acceptance* is another feature of the mature personality. The well-rounded individual has a fundamentally positive image of himself so that he can tolerate frustrating or irritating events as well as his own shortcomings without becoming inwardly bitter or hostile. He *accepts* himself as a person. Such an individual also deals with his emotional states (e.g., depression, anger, ineptness) in such a way that they do not interfere with the well-being of others. For example, if his sex drive is up that day, he doesn't go out and rape somebody; if he is angry, he doesn't fly off the handle at the first person he sees. Finally, the healthy person expresses his beliefs and feelings considering those of others; he is secure enough not to be threatened by his own emotional expressions or by theirs.

4 The mature person is also marked by *realistic perception, skills, and assignments.* Healthy persons see things as they are, not as they wish them to be. They are in full contact with reality; they do not distort it perceptually to fit their needs and fantasies. Moreover, healthy people possess appropriate skills for solving objective problems. By being problem-oriented, they can lose themselves in their work, setting aside personal desires and impulses for indeterminate amounts of time while a task takes precedence. Allport quotes Harvey Cushing, the famous brain surgeon, in conveying this aspect of maturity: "The only way to endure life is to have a task to complete (1961, p. 290)." Mature people, then, perceive other persons, objects, and situations for what they are; they possess skills adequate to deal with reality; and they strive for personally important and realistic goals.

5 The mature person is capable of *self-objectification* and of *insight in* *humor.* Socrates observed that there is one paramount rule for achieving the good life: "Know thyself." Allport called this "self-objectification." By it, he meant that the mature person will know herself as an "object" and will understand the differences between what she is, what she would like to be, and what others think of her. Humor is an important ingredient in self-insight because it prevents pompous self-glorification and just plain phoniness. It allows the person to see and appreciate the utterly ludicrous aspects of her own or anyone else's life situation. Humor, as Allport saw it, is the ability to laugh at the things one cherishes (including oneself) and still cherish them.

6 Finally, a *unifying philosophy of life* earmarks the healthy adult. Healthy people can "put it all together" with a clear, consistent, and systematic way of seeing meaning in their lives. A person does not have to be an Aristotle to do this—one simply needs a value system that will present one with a dominant goal, theme, or objective that makes one's life meaningful. Different people may develop different central values around which their lives can purposefully revolve (see "Application" section of this chapter for further discussion of this point). They may choose the pursuit of truth, social welfare, religion, or whatever—there is no one best value or philosophy in Allport's opinion. Rather, Allport's point is that a mature person has a set of deeply held values which serves as a unifying foundation for his or her life. A unifying philosophy of life therefore provides a kind of overriding value orientation which gives meaning and significance to practically everything one does.

Allport admits that not all adults achieve full maturity in the ways he describes. However, he did consider these six criteria as offering a reasonably accurate and comprehensive picture of what personal maturity is like in our culture.

Attention is now shifted to the basic assumptions underlying this trait theory of personality.

ALLPORT'S BASIC ASSUMPTIONS CONCERNING HUMAN NATURE

Allport waged a life long battle against the basic psychoanalytic and behavioristic conceptions of human nature. Reflecting his humanistic persuasion, he wrote:

> Some theories of becoming are based largely upon the behavior of sick and anxious people or upon the antics of captive and desperate rats. Fewer theories have derived from the study of healthy human beings, those who strive not so much to preserve life as to make it worth living (Allport, 1955, p. 18).

The reasons underlying Allport's objections to psychoanalysis and behaviorism are readily apparent when considering his basic assumptions concerning human nature (graphically depicted in Figure 6-3).

X X   2-26-81

Freedom	_ _ ✓ _ ✓ _ _ _ _ _ _ _	Determinism
Rationality	✓ _ _ _ _ _ _ _ _ _ _ _	Irrationality
Holism	_ _ ✓ _ _ _ _ _ _ _ _ _	Elementalism
Constitutionalism	_ _ _ _ _ ✓ _ _ _ _ _	Environmentalism
Subjectivity	_ _ _ _ ✓ _ _ _ _ _ _	Objectivity
Proactivity	✓ _ _ _ ✓ _ _ _ ✓ _ _ _	Reactivity
Homeostasis	_ _ _ _ _ _ _ ✓ _ _ ✓ _	Heterostasis
Knowability	_ _ _ ✓ _ _ _ _ _ _ _	Unknowability

Figure 6-3 Allport's position on the eight basic assumptions concerning human nature.

1 Freedom–Determinism. Allport supported the concept of human freedom more than any other personologist examined thus far in this volume. This position is illustrated by an excerpt from a published conversation Allport had with Richard Evans:

> I would say that we have more freedom than most of today's psychology admits. I would not, however, argue for the absolute, untrammeled freedom espoused by some of the existentialists. The answer lies somewhere in the middle course (Evans, 1971, p. 59).

The emphasis on freedom found in Allport's theory is most clearly revealed in his portrayal of personality development. Specifically, Allport viewed human growth as an active process of "becoming," in which the individual takes some responsibility for charting the course of his life. At least part of the "dynamic organization" so essential to Allport's definition of personality is thus self-determined.

However, Allport's trait concept puts serious limits on the absolute degree of freedom in human behavior. That is, once traits are formed in a person, they largely determine his or her perceptions and actions. As explained earlier, traits are potent governors of both stimulus selection and responses made to various stimuli. Human actions are thus initiated and guided by specific traits. Allport further believed that situational determinants play a central role in influencing an individual's behavior. Thus, while granting significantly more free choice to man than characteristically encountered in either psychoanalysis or behaviorism, Allport's overall commitment to freedom in human behavior is best judged as slight.

2 Rationality–Irrationality Allport was extremely committed to the assumption that human beings are rational organisms. In fact, he spent considerable effort disputing the Freudian emphasis upon unconscious, irrational elements in human behavior (Allport, 1961). He agreed with Freud that such forces dominate the mental lives of the emotionally disturbed—this, in fact, is what distinguishes disturbed from healthy individuals. But Allport argued that Freud erred in assuming that unconscious processes dominate the functioning of sound and healthy people. Mature, well-balanced people are fully capable of conscious, rationally based actions; they live their lives in terms of goals, long-range plans, and an overall philosophy—all of which are founded upon rationality.

The belief in human rationality underscores practically all Allport's theoretical formulations. For example, he insisted that one important criterion for an adequate theory of motivation is that it must ascribe dynamic force to the individual's cognitive processes, such as thinking, planning, and intending (Allport, 1961). Allport also considered the self as rational coper (i.e., the recognition that one can solve problems by thinking) as being an integral part of proprium development. Finally, it will be recalled that Allport described the mature person as one who possesses realistic perception, skills, and assignments. This clearly implies that such people know where they are going and how to get there. If he or she develops and functions along normal lines, the Allportian person is exquisitely rational.

3 Holism–Elementalism Allport's theory reflects an intricate interweaving of the holism and elementalism assumptions, although the former is considerably stronger in his system. To appreciate this counterbalance of forces, consider that Allport's unit of analysis is the "trait." People are studied largely in terms of their exhibited traits, which seems to be a straightforward, elementalist approach to personological research. Yet Allport argued that personality will never be totally understood by examining each trait separately. While he believed that some system of dimensions or conceptual schemata (traits) was necessary to study personality, Allport maintained that a trait must ultimately be related to the total pattern of personality of which it is a part (Evans, 1971).

Underlying the various elements (traits), then, is a unifying, holistic entity—the proprium, which includes all aspects of personality that contribute to inward unity (Allport, 1955). Moreover, the most essential ingredient in this totality of personality is propriate striving (Allport, 1961). Rather than being viewed as merely a static unity at any given time, man is depicted as continually seeking inward unity by striving for distant goals, objectives, and ideals. While he recognized the empirical necessity of studying "elements" in personology, Allport believed that such elements can never be properly understood apart from the more holistic frame of reference of propriate striving.

4 Constitutionalism–Environmentalism Allport strikes a near-perfect balance between constitution and environment in his conception of human nature. Specifically, he believed that genetic and environmental factors are equally influential in determining human behavior. In fact, Allport (1961) argued that no feature or act of the human personality is without both genetic and environmental influences.

According to Allport, neither heredity alone nor environment alone determines the way in which personality is fashioned. Instead, it is through the reciprocal influence of heredity and environment that intelligence, interests, aptitudes, values, or any other personality characteristics emerge. Also, Allport suggested that one's temperament (representing consitutional factors) sets limits upon external influences, while broad social and cultural forces, in turn, modify temperament. Although he conceded that psychology still has much to learn about the precise operations of constitutional and environmental influences upon behavior (Evans, 1971), Allport regarded both as of equal importance in human functioning.

5 Subjectivity–Objectivity While Allport was passionately interested in the uniqueness of the individual personality, he did not regard man's subjective experience (subjectivity) as particularly critical in understanding individuality. Specifically, in his morphogenic approach to personality study (to be elaborated upon in the following section), he considered uniqueness to be of paramount importance, but in his system it is to be found in the dynamic organization of individual *traits* rather than in the quality of one's subjective experience. There is, then, a difference between the concepts of *uniqueness* and *subjectivity*. Allport strongly emphasizes the former in his theory while manifesting at best only a slight commitment to the latter.

The subjectivity assumption surfaces when Allport's concept of the proprium is examined. Referring to the focal point of one's personal sense of existence, the proprium identifies all the regions of personal life that one regards as peculiarly one's own. In effect, the proprium aids the individual in drawing distinctions between matters of subjective importance and matters of fact. Yet, while Allport's "proprium" contains within it the seeds of subjectivity, he did not regard subjectivity as the key to understanding a person. For him, the world of subjective experience is only one component of many that constitute the complexity of personality. Psychology, in Allport's opinion, will become truly scientific only when it can deal fully with the issue of individual uniqueness.

6 Proactivity–Reactivity In describing the concept of propriate striving, Allport (1961) noted that directedness or intentionality is the cement which holds a person's life together. That is, in order to function well, an individual needs a defining objective toward which he or she is striving. The assumption of proactivity evident in this description is even more unmistakable when Allport speaks of propriate patterning:

> . . . the essential nature of man is such that it presses toward a relative unification of life (never fully achieved). . . . As a consequence of this quest—which is the very essence of human nature—we note that man's conduct is to a large degree proactive . . . (Allport, 1961, p. 252).

Allportian man, then, lives in a world of future goals, life ambitions, and strivings which are generated from within. Functional autonomy serves to demolish reactive ties to the past; propriate striving negates any account of behavior merely in terms of reactions to present stimuli. Allport's commitment to the proactivity assumption is strong and explicit.

7 Homeostasis–Heterostasis   Allport recognized the validity of homeostatic drives as the primitive and animal-like part of human motivation. But he (1961) cited Cannon, the originator of the homeostasis concept, as acknowledging that tension reduction does not account for all human conduct. Basically, Cannon believed that once the person's essential needs were answered through homeostasis, he or she was free to seek the "priceless unessentials." Allport, revealing his heterostatic assumption, felt that these "priceless unessentials" are the most conspicuous features of the human personality. More specifically, he writes:

> The healthy child and adult are continually building up tensions . . . and are going way beyond the basic, safety level of homeostasis. New experiences, which most of us crave, cannot be put in terms of tension-reduction, nor can our desire to acquire knowledge for its own sake, to create works of beauty and usefulness, nor to give and receive love . . . (Allport, 1961, p. 90).

Allport's assumption of heterostasis is further expressed in his theoretical account of propriate functional autonomy which, as you may recall, involves the principles of "organizing the energy level," "mastery and competence," and "propriate striving." If these previously discussed principles are now considered within a heterostatic framework, Allportian man must be viewed as motivated toward growth and unification. In fact, this sort of motivation is one identification of man as phylogenetically unique. There is a strong commitment to heterostasis throughout Allport's theory.

8 Knowability–Unknowability   Like most other humanistically minded personologists, Allport was less than optimistic about the ultimate power of psychological method and theory to unravel the mystery of human behavior. More to the point, he believed that although it is possible to study empirically specific aspects of human behavior and functioning, science alone could not provide total knowability of human nature. As an illustration, Allport (1966) advocated what he termed "heuristic realism" as the basic empirical approach to personality study. Briefly, this doctrine holds that since, within every individual there inhere generalized action tendencies or traits, it is psychology's task to discover what they are. Because traits are never directly observed but only inferred, however, there are major scientific hurdles to overcome in uncovering their true nature. Yet the persistent "heuristic realist" presses onward. While he knows that his efforts probably will not wholly succeed, owing partly to the complexity of personality and partly to the inadequacy of present methods for its study, he prefers to believe that the nature of personality is partly or approximately knowable (Allport, 1966).

In effect, Allport maintained that personality can be studied empirically— but one defined "limb" at a time. The degree to which science can eventually put these appendages together to form the complete person, which Allport holistically believes is there, remains a largely unanswered question. Furthermore, Allport's morphogenic approach to personality research renders it scientifically difficult to grasp human nature as a whole by studying people one at a time. Perhaps Allport said it best in concluding his discussion of the "heuristic realism" approach to the study of the person: "Along the way we regard him as an objectively real being whose tendencies we can succeed in knowing—at least in part . . . (Allport, 1966, pp. 8–9)." Thus, Allport's commitment to the knowability assumption is less than complete.

EMPIRICAL VALIDATION OF TRAIT THEORY CONCEPTS

To what extent have psychologists demonstrated the empirical validity of Allport's theoretical conceptions of personality? An exhaustive search of the relevant literature indicates that Allport has stimulated almost no research bearing on the empirical validation of his trait theory concepts. Several sophisticated writers in personology agree (Bischof, 1970; Hall and Lindzey, 1970; Maddi and Costa, 1972). Although Allport's is certainly a comprehensive personological system, it seems that almost no one has taken the time or trouble to test the empirical validity of its concepts. In an empirical discipline like psychology, no theory will endure unless it generates testable predictions based on its major constructs. Allport's theory is no exception.

Although trait theory has failed in the heuristic sense, Allport's theory has definitely been of considerable stimulus value for other domains of psychological study. Through collaboration with colleagues and students, for example, he contributed significantly to the literature on expressive behavior (e.g., Allport and Vernon, 1933; Allport and Cantril, 1934; Estes, 1938; Huntley, 1940; Zweigenhaft and Marlowe, 1973). "Expressive behavior" refers to the style in which the individual performs behavioral acts, e.g., facial expression, gait, voice, and handwriting. More recent research focusing on the criteria of psychological maturity, children's imagery, self-esteem, humor, social perception, rumor, and prejudice also partially reflects, although only indirectly, the influence of Allport's theoretical interests. These and other empirical contributions are listed in the extensive bibliography accompanying Allport's *Personality and Social Encounter* (1960). The Allport-Vernon-Lindzey (1960) *Study of Values* (3d ed.), a scale designed to assess six separate value orientations possessed by an individual, also documents the continuing influence of Allport. This scale, to be discussed in the "Application" section, is still regarded as a highly respectible method of measuring values having been used extensively in various research in recent years.

If frequency of citations in major texts on personality theory is a valid measure of stimulus value, Allport would receive a gold star. In scanning the author indexes of fifteen personality textbooks published since 1967, each contains no fewer than five references to Allport. He may not have inspired much empirical study in direct reference to his theoretical concepts, but contemporary personologists seem unable to ignore the total impact of his thinking.

Allport's Approach to Research: Illustrative Studies

Allport argued that personality research should always be guided by methods which allow for the reliable and valid study of individual life styles. Specifically, he advocated the *morphogenic* (also called *idiographic*) approach to personality study whereby the uniqueness of each person is the primary goal of psychological understanding and prediction. While not abandoning the usefulness of *nomothetic* approaches which study people in groups (e.g., psychological tests measuring common traits), Allport (1968b) argued for the increased study of individual patterns of growth to shed light on the nature of personality.

Although morphogenic methods are neither easy to devise nor to employ. Allport (1962) considered such things as personal documents—including diaries, autobiographies, letters, open-ended questionnaires, and verbatim recordings of interviews—as having obvious research applicability. However, he insisted that procedures should not be used to exclusion of proved nomothetic methods. Indeed, the bulk of his own empirical investigations followed the more conventional nomothetic approach. In the remaining pages of this section, two studies illustrating Allport's orientation toward personality research will be discussed. The first reveals how personal documents may be used to establish the existence of individual traits, while the second deals with the relationship between religiosity and prejudice, a topic that captivated Allport's theoretical imagination.

1 Letters from Jenny: A Morphogenic Trait Study The value of morphogenic methods as a means of determining an individual's outstanding traits is best illustrated in Allport's *Letters from Jenny* (1965). This case study was based on the personal correspondence of a middle-aged woman named Jenny Grove Masterson who wrote, during an eleven-year period, some 300 letters to a young married couple living and teaching in an eastern college town:

> The tie of friendship extended back to the time when the husband (Glenn) had been the roommate of Jenny's son (Ross) at college, about ten years before the beginning of the correspondence. . . . The correspondence begins in earnest in

March, 1926, and continues without interruption . . . until Jenny's death in October, 1937 (Allport, 1965, p. v).

Allport acquired Jenny's letters in the 1940s and he subsequently used them as pedagogical material for stimulating class discussions in his personality course at Harvard. Of specific interest here, however, are the various clinical and quantitative analyses of these personal documents made by Allport and his students.

Allport's (1942) first empirical assessment consisted of listing Jenny's essential characteristics as perceived by thirty-nine clinical judges who read her letters in sequence. Labeled *content analysis,* this procedure resembles a commonsense or impressionistic approach to personality study. The results were expressed in the form of a series of 198 descriptive adjectives that clustered into eight distinct groups of "commonsense" traits. Baldwin (1942), one of Allport's students, extended the content analysis of Jenny's letters to include a more elaborate and statistical treatment of the data. Using a method that he called *personal structure analysis,* he instructed raters to count the number of times particular topics and themes (e.g., money, art, women, nature) occurred in each of the letters and to correlate such categories of thought that clustered together. In brief, Baldwin's study revealed that Jenny's personality was described quite accurately in terms of the eight central traits which had emerged from Allport's prior analysis.

More recently, Paige (1966), yet another of Allport's proteges, conducted a still more quantified analysis of Jenny's letters. He used a computer program (called the General Inquirer) specifically designed to recognize and "tag" certain designated adjectives in the letters that were used in conjunction with each other. For example, any terms Jenny used to express aggression, hostility, and opposition were coded together under the tag category ATTACK. The program also provided the frequency with which various tag words in a given letter were associated with all others in the same letter. Paige then subjected these to a statistical technique known as factor analysis. Based on this computerized evaluation of the document, eight highly stable trait factors were identified as descriptive of Jenny. These factorially derived traits are very similar to those which were obtained from the previous studies. Table 6-1 lists in parallel fashion the clusters obtained by content analysis based on a careful reading of the series, along with the factors, obtained by Paige in his factorial study.

Allport interpreted the similarity of the two lists (derived from two divergent types of analysis) as indicative of the validity of his conclusions about Jenny's personality trait structure:

> In spite of the differences in terminology the general paralleling of the two lists establishes some degree of empirical check on both of them. We can say that the direct common-sense perception of Jenny's nature is validated by quantification, coding, and factoring (Allport, 1966, pp. 7–8).

**Table 6-1   Central Traits in Jenny's Personality as
Determined by Impressionistic and Factor-Analytic
Methods of Assessment**

Commonsense traits		Factorial traits	
1	Quarrelsome-suspicious, aggressive	1	Aggression
2	Self-centered (possessive)	2	Possessiveness
3	Sentimental	3	Need for affiliation, need for family acceptance
4	Independent-autonomous	4	Need for autonomy
5	Esthetic-artistic	5	Sentience
6	Self-centered (self-pitying)	6	Martyrdom
7	(No parallel)	7	Sexuality
8	Cynical-morbid	8	(No parallel)
9	Dramatic-intense	9	("Overstate")

Source: Adapted from Allport, 1966, p. 7.

2 Religion and Prejudice: Are They Related?   During the latter years
of his career, Allport became vitally interested in the individual's religious life,
particularly as it relates to ethnic prejudice. As noted earlier, Allport considered religion as one source of a unifying philosophy of life. The research
problem is this—many investigations have established that church attenders
harbor more ethnic prejudice, on the average, than nonattenders. This finding
might suggest that religion encourages prejudice. At the same time, however, it
is assumed that all great religions teach equality, brotherhood, and compassion.
Indeed, many ardent workers for civil rights (Mahatma Gandhi, Albert
Schweitzer, Martin Luther King, Jr., and several recently martyred clergy in
the United States) were known to be religiously motivated. This could suggest
that religion as such breaks down prejudice. The paradox, then, is that
"Religion makes for prejudice; it also unmakes prejudice (Allport, 1966, p. 5)."
     In attempting to resolve this paradox, Allport (1966) tentatively assumed
that two contrasting but measurable forms of religious orientation exist. An
extrinsic orientation involves religious devotion not as a value in its own right
but rather as instrumental in serving the motives of personal comfort, security,
status, or social support. Extrinsically oriented religious people use religion to
satisfy other needs. Contrariwise, an *intrinsic* orientation regards faith as a
supreme value in its own right. An intrinsically religious person, Allport adds,
"takes seriously the commandment of brotherhood that is found in all religions,
and seeks a unification of being (1966, p. 6)." A self-report questionnaire (called
the Religious Orientation Scale) was constructed to measure these two

orientations toward religion. Two scale items follow, with possible response alternatives ranging from strongly agree to strongly disagree. Endorsement of the first statement is indicative of an extrinsic religious orientation, while endorsement of the second is indicative of an intrinsic religious orientation:

> One reason for my being a church member is that such membership helps to establish a person in the community.

> I try hard to carry my religion over into all my other dealings in life.

The utility of Allport's distinction between extrinsic and intrinsic orientations was determined by correlating religious orientation scores with various measures of ethnic prejudice for several different samples of Protestant and Catholic churchgoers. As shown in Table 6-2, for each sample studied extrinsicness of orientation is positively related to prejudice (i.e., those who agree with extrinsically worded items tend toward greater prejudice), whereas intrinsicness of orientation is negatively related to prejudice (i.e., those who agree with intrinsically worded items tend toward absence of prejudice).

Ironically, an earlier study by Wilson (1960) found that subjects who endorse both intrinsic and extrinsic items are the most prejudiced of all! Allport designated such individuals "inconsistently proreligious," noting that they simply like religion; for them, it has social desirability. This interesting research area, although not a direct outgrowth of Allport's trait theory, provides a basis

Table 6-2 Correlations between Measures of Religious Orientation among Churchgoers and Various Scales of Ethnic Prejudice

Denominational sample	Religious orientation	Target of prejudice	r
Unitarian ($N = 50$)	Extrinsic type	Anti-Catholic	+.56
	Intrinsic type	Anti-Catholic	−.36
	Extrinsic type	Anti-Mexican	+.54
	Intrinsic type	Anti-Mexican	−.42
Catholic ($N = 66$)	Extrinsic type	Anti-Negro	+.36
	Intrinsic type	Anti-Negro	−.49
Nazarene ($N = 39$)	Extrinsic type	Anti-Negro	+.41
	Intrinsic type	Anti-Negro	−.44
Mixed* ($N = 207$)	Extrinsic type	Anti-Semitic	+.65

Source: Adapted from Allport, 1966, p. 7.
*From Wilson (1960).

for evaluating the religious sentiment and its role in the dynamics of ethnic prejudice.

APPLICATION: THE STUDY OF VALUES *Alicia & Donna*

Allport stressed that the mature person needed a unifying philosophy of life to make sense of his existence. An individual's philosophy is founded upon his *values*—basic convictions that he holds about what is and is not of real importance in life. Believing that a person's efforts to find order and meaning in his or her existence are governed by values, Allport worked hard to identify and measure basic value dimensions. The success of his effort is evident in the well-known personality test that he helped significantly to develop—the *Study of Values*—which was originally published in 1931 and is currently in its third edition (Allport, Vernon, and Lindzey, 1960). Within the context of trait theory, this instrument illustrates Allport's ability to dissect an enormously complex component of personality (values) into empirically measurable terms.

To accomplish this difficult task, Allport needed a conceptual model to account for value differences among persons. He found the required model in the work of Eduard Spranger, a European psychologist. In his book *Types of Men,* Spranger (1922) outlined six major value-types. Conceived as the basic alternative value directions evidenced in human life, not as six main types of people, these values appeal in varying degrees to persons who construct the unity of their lives around them (Allport, 1961). Hence, no one person falls exclusively under any one value category; rather, different value combinations are more or less salient in the lives of different individuals. From an Allportian perspective, these values are best described as deep-level traits.

Following are Spranger's basic value types, as depicted in the *Study of Values* manual (Allport, Vernon, and Lindzey, 1960).

1 The Theoretical The theoretical person is primarily concerned with the discovery of *truth.* He or she assumes a "cognitive" attitude in pursuing this objective, seeking only to observe and to reason. In so doing, the theoretical individual searches for fundamental identities and differences, rejecting any considerations of beauty or utility. Since his or her interests are basically rational, critical, and empirical, the theoretical person is necessarily an intellectual, frequently a scientist or philosopher. Such a person need not, however, attain a high level of achievement, since Spranger believed that one's true values are revealed in interests and intentions rather than through concrete achievements. What theoretical persons want most is to order and systematize their knowledge.

2 The Economic The economic individual places highest value upon what is *useful.* He or she is thoroughly "practical" and conforms closely to the stereotype of the successful American businessman. Rooted originally in the satisfaction of bodily needs (self-preservation), the economic value gradually extends to the everyday affairs of the business world—the production, marketing, and consumption of goods, the elaboration of credit, and the accumulation of tangible wealth. The economic person is interested in making money.

In their personal lives, economic individuals are likely to confuse luxury with beauty. Moreover, when relating to others, economic persons tend to be more interested in surpassing them in wealth than in understanding (theoretical), serving (social), or dominating (political) them. But, above all, the economic individual values what is practical and useful. He or she wants education to be such and regards unapplied knowledge as waste. Many great feats of engineering and technology have resulted from the demands that economic persons have made upon science.

3 The Aesthetic   The aesthetic person places highest value on *form* and *harmony.* Judging each single experience from the standpoint of grace, symmetry, or fitness, he or she perceives life as a procession of events, with each individual impression enjoyed for its own sake. Such an individual need not be a creative artist but is aesthetic to the degree that his or her chief interest is in the artistic episodes of life.

In direct opposition to the theoretical value, the aesthetic individual agrees with Keats that truth is equivalent to beauty and with Mencken that to make a thing charming is a million times more important than to make it true. Such persons oppose the economic value, seeing manufacturing, advertising, and trade as wholesale destructions of their most primary values. In social affairs, aesthetic individuals are interested in persons but not in their welfare; they tend toward individualism and self-sufficiency in their dealings with others.

4 The Social   The highest value of the social type is *love of people.* Since the *Study of Values* focuses only upon the altruistic or philanthropic aspects of love (as opposed, for example, to conjugal or familial love), social persons prize others as ends, themselves being kind, sympathetic, and unselfish. Such a person is likely to experience the theoretical, economic, and aesthetic attitudes as cold and inhuman, regarding love as the only suitable form of human relationship. In its purest form, the social attitude is selfless and is closely related to the religious value.

5 The Political   The dominant interest of the political individual is *power.* Vocational activities of this type of person are not necessarily confined to the realm of politics, since leaders in any field generally place a high value on power. Because competition and struggle are inherent in all life, many philosophers have argued that power is the most universal and fundamental human motive. In fact, some of the writings of Alfred Adler, a well-known neo-Freudian theorist, reflect this point of view. However, for Spranger there are clear individual diffferences in the power value. For certain personalities, direct expression of this motive overrides all others in that they yearn for personal power, influence, and renown above all else.

6 The Religious Religious individuals place their highest value upon *unity.* Being fundamentally mystical, they seek to understand and experience the world as a unified whole. Spranger describes the religious person as one who is permanently oriented toward the creation of the highest and absolutely satisfying value experience. There are, however, different modes of seeking this level of experience. For instance, some religious persons are "immanent mystics" (i.e., individuals who find their religious meaning in the affirmation and active participation in life), while others are "transcendental mystics," striving to unite themselves with a higher reality by withdrawing from life (e.g., monks). Regardless of the particular type of expression, the religious man basically seeks unity and higher meaning in the cosmos.

To concretize these six types, consider the following. Suppose that six individuals, each representing one of the dominant value orientations, are walking together through the woods on a sunny fall afternoon. The theoretical individual might be contemplating the basic biological principles underlying tree growth; the economic person could be wondering how much money could be made by chopping down some of the trees, converting them to toothpicks, and marketing same; the aesthetic would probably be having a peak experience running to and fro among the leaves proclaiming the beauty of the surroundings; the social person might just be happy that five other people are present; the political individual would undoubtedly be walking in front of the group periodically insisting that the others follow his or her path through and out of the woods; and the religious person might be sublimely contemplating the nature of the underlying ultimate reality of which these people and woods are a profound expression.

It is again worth noting that, while Spranger described these six in terms of "ideal types," he did not imply that a given person falls exclusively under any single one of them. Rather, they are to be understood as basic ways in which persons in varying degrees orient, perceive, experience, and evaluate their personal world. Each individual can be characterized by a specific *pattern* of values as well as by his dominant value orientation.

Allport attempted to assess the relative strength of these six values in any given individual by means of the *Study of Values* test. Developed and standardized with college students, the test consists of forty-five questions and requires about twenty minutes to complete. Two sample questions are found in Figure 6-4. As a self-administered pencil-and-paper inventory, it can be taken in a group or individually.

Part I of the test consists of thirty relatively "controversial" statements or

Sample item from Part I

If you should see the following news item with headlines of equal size in your morning paper, which would you read more attentively? (*a*) PROTESTANT LEADERS TO CONSULT ON RECONCILIATION; (*b*) GREAT IMPROVEMENTS IN MARKET CONDITIONS

Sample item from Part II

In your opinion, can people who work in business all the week best spend Sunday
a. trying to educate themselves by reading serious books.
b. trying to win at golf or racing.
c. going to an orchestral concert.
d. hearing a really good sermon.

Figure 6-4   Sample items from the Study of Values Test. *(Allport, Vernon, and Lindzey, 1960.)*

questions with two possible alternative answers provided for each. The subject's task is to select the alternative in each instance that is relatively more acceptable to him. In so doing, the testee has three points to distribute between the two alternatives for each item. For example, if he *strongly* agrees with alternative *a* and disagrees with *b*, he assigns three points to the former and zero points to the latter. Should the subject *slightly* prefer *a* to *b*, he would assign two points to *a* and one to *b*. These two situations would of course be reversed if the person's relative preference was for alternative *b* over *a*. In this fashion, the subject is permitted to indicate not only what his preferences are but also, in at least approximate form, the *relative* strength of these preferences. To clarify this procedure, the reader is advised to reexamine the first item in Figure 6-4 and then answer it personally. As one might imagine, alternative *a* reflects the religious value while *b* reflects the economic.

Part II of the test is made up of the remaining fifteen questions. Four alternatives, much like a multiple-choice examination, are provided for each question. Unlike the typical "multiple-guess" test, however, the *Study of Values* asks the subject to order the four alternatives in terms of his relative preferences, assigning a numerical value of 4 to his first choice, 3 to the alternative appealing to him second best, and so on. Consistent with Part I of the test, this response format is designed to elicit the relative strengths of the person's preferences. Again, the reader is advised to carry out this process with the second item in Figure 6-4 to gain a more intuitive sense of what this test is like.

Since there are basically two alternative answers to each of the first 30 questions and four alternatives to each of the remaining 15 items, there are 120 possible responses in Parts I and II of this instrument, 20 of which refer to each of the six values. When the subject's scores on each value dimension are summed, they may be plotted on a profile so that he can see his standing on the six values simultaneously. These profiles are particularly helpful for classroom demonstration and counseling.

How adequate is the *Study of Values* as a personality test? Allport himself noted that Spranger's conception of values, while useful, tends to present a flattering view of human nature. For example, it does not allow for valueless, hedonistic, expedient, or sensuous philosophies that obviously pervade the lives of some people. Referring again to the second question in Figure 6-4, some subjects may really believe that a person who works hard all week might best spend Sundays drinking beer or watching pornographic films! But given this limitation, how well does the *Study of Values* measure what it was designed to measure? To answer this question, psychologists resort to data on the *reliability* (consistency or freedom from chance error of measurement) and *validity* (the degree to which a test measures what it purports to measure) of the instrument. Generally, the reliability and validity data reported by the test authors are acceptable. For instance, subjects who retake the *Study of Values* one or two months after an original testing tend to achieve scores quite similar to their original ones (reliability) while average scores on the six values differ in expected directions for different occupational groups (validity); e.g., business students score highest on the economic value, art and design students on the aesthetic value, and clergymen on the religious value (Allport, Vernon, and Lindzey, 1960).

Another aspect in evaluating a personality test is its utility. Allport, Vernon, and Lindzey (1960) suggest various ways that the *Study of Values* can be used in classroom demonstration, counseling, research, vocational guidance and selection. In fact, this test has been widely employed over the years in these diverse areas. In sum, this instrument is a deceptively simple, straightforward, and highly useful approach to the assessment of certain fundamental and broad personality traits (values), based on the assumption that the subject is largely consciously motivated and rational. In this respect, it accurately reflects Gordon Allport's theory of personality and basic view of man.

SUMMARY

Gordon Allport's trait theory represents a blend of humanistic and personalistic approaches to the study of human behavior. Believing that the explanation of an individual's uniqueness is the paramount goal of psychology, Allport viewed personality as the dynamic organization of those internal psychophysical systems that determine a person's characteristic behavior and thought. Within the individual, personality is real; it is "what a person really is."

Allport regarded the *trait* as the most valid unit of analysis for understanding and studying personality. In his system, traits are predispositions to respond in an equivalent manner to various kinds of stimuli. In short, traits account for a person's behavioral consistency over time and across situations. They may be classified under one of three headings—cardinal, central, or secondary—according to their degree of pervasiveness within a personality. Allport also distinguished between common and individual traits, the former being generalized dispositions to which most people within a given culture can be compared, whereas the latter refer to personal dispositions peculiar to an individual which do not permit comparisons with others.

The overall construct that unifies traits and provides direction for the person's life is termed the *proprium*. This concept essentially refers to the "self-as-known," including all aspects of personality that contribute to an inward sense of unity. Another of Allport's personality concepts, his best-known and most controversial, is that of *functional autonomy*. This principle asserts that adult motives are not related to the earlier experiences in which they originally appeared. Allport further distinguished between perseverative functional autonomy (reverberatory or feedback mechanisms in the nervous system) and propriate functional autonomy (the individual's acquired interests, values, attitudes, and intentions). In essence, the latter allows for the development of the truly mature person, the salient characteristics of which Allport carefully delineated.

Allport's profound disagreements with the psychoanalytic and behavioristic conceptions of human nature are clearly evident in his basic assumptions concerning it. Trait theory reflects (1) a strong commitment to the assumptions of rationality, proactivity, and heterostasis; (2) a moderate commitment to the holism and knowability assumptions; (3) a slight commitment to the assumptions of freedom and subjectivity; and (4) a "middle of the road" position on the constitutionalism–environmentalism dimension.

While trait theory has stimulated almost no research to date in support of its core constructs, Allport himself made some interesting empirical contributions to the personological literature. He advocated the morphogenic approach to personality study, which is directed toward uncovering the uniqueness of each individual. One such study, *Letters from Jenny*, was described along with an illustration of Allport's more traditional, nomothetic research in the area of personal religious orientation and prejudice.

One useful application of Allport's theory, the *Study of Values*, is a self-report personality test. Based upon Spranger's value types, it assesses the relative strength of each of six basic values in the individual's life: theoretical, economic, aesthetic, social, political, and religious. Persons can be characterized by their dominant value orientation or by their particular patterns of values.

BIBLIOGRAPHY

Allport, G. *Personality: A psychological interpretation.* New York: Holt, Rinehart and Winston, 1937.

Allport, G. *The use of personal documents in psychological science.* New York: Social Science Research Council, Bulletin 49, 1942.

Allport, G. *The individual and his religion.* New York: Macmillan, 1950.

Allport, G. *Becoming: Basic considerations for a psychology of personality.* New Haven, Conn.: Yale University Press, 1955.

Allport, G. *Personality and social encounter: Selected essays.* Boston: Beacon Press, 1960.

Allport, G. *Pattern and growth in personality.* New York: Holt, Rinehart and Winston, 1961.

Allport, G. (Ed.). *Letters from Jenny.* New York: Harcourt, Brace & World, 1965.

Allport, G. Traits revisited. *American Psychologist,* 1966, **21,** 1–10.

Allport, G. Autobiography. In E. Boring & G. Lindzey (Eds.), *A history of psychology in autobiography,* Vol. 5. New York: Appleton-Century-Crofts, 1967, 1–25.

Allport, G. Personality: Contemporary viewpoints (I). In D. Sills (Ed.), *International encyclopedia of the social sciences.* New York: Macmillan and Free Press, 1968a, Vol. 12, pp. 1–5.

Allport, G. *The person in psychology: Selected essays.* Boston: Beacon Press, 1968b.

Allport, G., & Allport, F. *A–S reaction study.* Boston: Houghton Mifflin, 1928.

Allport, G., & Cantril, H. Judging personality from voice. *Journal of Social Psychology,* 1934, **5,** 37–55.

Allport, G., & Vernon, P. *Studies in expressive movement.* New York: Macmillan, 1933.

Allport, G., Vernon, P., & Lindzey, G. *A study of values.* Boston: Houghton Mifflin, 1960 (3d ed.).

American Psychologist, 1964, **19,** 942–945.

Baldwin, A. Personal structure analysis: A statistical method for investigating the single personality. *Journal of Abnormal and Social Psychology,* 1942, **37,** 163–183.

Bischof, L. *Interpreting personality theories.* New York: Harper & Row, 1970 (2d ed.).

Estes, S. Judging personality from expressive behavior. *Journal of Abnormal and Social Psychology,* 1938, **33,** 217–236.

Evans, R. Gordon Allport: A conversation. *Psychology Today,* April 1971, 55–59, 84, 86, 90, 94.

Hall, C., & Lindzey, G. *Theories of personality.* New York: John Wiley & Sons, 1970 (2d ed.).

Huntley, C. Judgments of self based upon records of expressive behavior. *Journal of Abnormal and Social Psychology,* 1940, **35,** 398–427.

Maddi, S., & Costa, P. *Humanism in personology: Allport, Maslow, and Murray.* Chicago: Aldine–Atherton, 1972.

Paige, J. Letters from Jenny: An approach to the clinical analysis of personality structure by computer. In P. Stone (Ed.), *The general inquirer: A computer approach to content analysis.* Cambridge: M.I.T. Press, 1966.

Spranger, E. *Lebensformen* (3d ed.). Halle: Niemeyer, 1922. (Translated: P. Pigors. *Types of men.* Halle: Niemeyer, 1928).

Wilson, W. Extrinsic religious values and prejudice. *Journal of Abnormal and Social Psychology,* 1960, **60,** 286–288.

Zweigenhaft, R., & Marlowe, D. Signature size: Studies in expressive movement. *Journal of Consulting and Clinical Psychology,* 1973, **40,** 469–473.

SUGGESTED READINGS:

1 Allport, G. *The nature of prejudice.* Cambridge, Mass.: Addison-Wesley, 1954.
2 Allport, G. The open system in personality theory. *Journal of Abnormal and Social Psychology,* 1960, **61,** 301–310.
3 Allport, G. The general and the unique in psychological science. *Journal of Personality,* 1962, **30,** 405–422.
4 Gormly, J., & Edelberg, W. Validity in personality trait attribution. *American Psychologist,* 1974, **29,** 189–193.
5 Maddi, S. Humanistic psychology: Allport and Murray. In J. Wepman & R. Heine (Eds.), *Concepts of personality.* Chicago: Aldine, 1963, pp. 162–205.

George A. Kelly

George Kelly: A Cognitive Theory of Personality

It is a fundamental fact of life that human beings are thinking animals. Indeed, man's intellectual processes are so intuitively self-evident that all personality theories in some way must acknowledge their effects on behavior. George Kelly was the first personologist to emphasize the cognitive or knowing aspects of human existence as the dominant feature of personality. According to his theoretical system, entitled the *Psychology of Personal Constructs,* man is basically a *scientist* in that he strives to understand, interpret, anticipate, and control his personal world of experience for the purpose of dealing effectively with that world. This scientist-like nature of human behavior is the hallmark of Kelly's theory.

> Mankind, whose progress in search of prediction and control of surrounding events stands out so clearly in the light of the centuries, comprises the men we see around us every day. The aspirations of the scientist are essentially the aspirations of all men (Kelly, 1955, p. 43).

BIOGRAPHICAL SKETCH *Cauleen*

George Alexander Kelly was born in Perth, Kansas, on April 28, 1905, the only child of farm parents. His father was a Presbyterian minister who turned to farming because of ill health. Kelly's early education was limited to a one-room country school. His parents later sent him to Wichita, Kansas, where in the course of four years he attended four different high schools. Kelly's parents were religiously devout, hardworking, and firmly opposed to such evils as drinking, card playing, and dancing. Kelly's family was imbued with traditional Mid-western American values and aspirations, and Kelly himself was afforded considerable attention as an only child.

Kelly pursued undergraduate study for three years at Friends University, followed by one year at Park College, where he received his B.A. degree in physics and mathematics in 1926. Originally he had sought a career in mechanical engineering but, partly because of his experience in intercollegiate debates, he shifted his interests to social problems. Thus, he majored in educational sociology at the University of Kansas, minoring in labor relations and sociology. He wrote a thesis based on a study of the distribution of leisure-time activities of workers in Kansas City and was awarded an M.A. degree in 1928. The following year Kelly had divergent teaching responsibilities; he was a part-time instructor in a labor college in Minneapolis; he conducted classes in public speech for the American Bankers' Association; and he taught an Americanization class for prospective citizens. He next joined the faculty of a new public junior college in Sheldon, Iowa, where he met Gladys Thompson. (They were married in 1931 and subsequently had two children.) After a year and a half in Iowa, including a brief spell as an aeronautical engineer in Wichita, Kelly obtained an exchange fellowship to study at the University of Edinburgh in England. There, in 1930, he earned a Bachelor of Education degree, being permitted to take examinations over two years of graduate work after only nine months in residence. Under the direction of Sir Godfrey Thomson, a prominent statistician and educator, his thesis dealt with the prediction of teaching success. That same year he returned to the United States to enroll as a psychology doctoral candidate at the State University of Iowa. In 1931 Kelly was awarded the Ph.D. degree, having written a dissertation on common factors in speech and reading disabilities.

Kelly's career as an academic psychologist began at Fort Hays Kansas State College. There he rose to become an associate professor of psychology in 1943. During this twelve-year period he developed a program of traveling psychological clinics that allowed both him and his students opportunities to implement new approaches to behavior problems encountered in the state's school system. This experience also stimulted numerous ideas that were later incorporated into his formulations of personality and psychotherapy. During World War II, as a naval aviation psychologist, Kelly headed a training program for local civilian pilots. His interest in aviation continued at the

Bureau of Medicine and Surgery of the Navy in Washington, D. C., where he remained in the Aviation Branch until 1945. That year he was appointed associate professor at the University of Maryland.

The war's end created considerable demand for clinical psychologists because countless United States servicemen were returning home plagued with all types of personal problems. Indeed, World War II was the single most important factor contributing to the development of clinical psychology as an integral part of the health sciences. Kelly became a prominent figure in this evolution. In 1946 he attained national status when he became professor and director of clinical psychology at Ohio State University. In his twenty years there, Kelly completed his major theoretical contributions to psychology. For the first few years of this period, his efforts focused on the organization and administration of the graduate program in clinical psychology. Within a few years he piloted this program into the forefront of graduate training centers in the United States.

In 1965 Kelly departed for Brandeis University, where he was appointed to the Riklis Chair of Behavioral Science. This position, a professor's dream come true, allowed him complete freedom to pursue his own scholarly interests. One year later, on March 6, 1966, he died at the age of sixty-two. At the time of his death, Kelly was assembling a volume composed of the numerous papers he had delivered in the previous decade. Under the editorship of Brendan Maher, a former student, a revised version of this work appeared posthumously in 1969.

In addition to his distinguished career as a teacher, scientist, and theorist, Kelly held many leadership positions in American psychology. He served as president of both the Clinical and Counseling Divisions of the American Psychological Association. He also was instrumental in formulating the American Board of Examiners in Professional Psychology, an organization devoted to the further upgrading of professional psychologists, and served as its president from 1951 through 1953. He received invitations to teach and lecture at countless universities throughout the world. During the concluding years of his life, Kelly contributed much of his time to international affairs. For example, financed by the Human Ecology Fund, he and his wife traveled around the world during 1960–1961 applying his personal construct theory to certain international problems.

Although he published less extensively than other major personologists, Kelly exerted a lasting influence through his training of clinical psychologists. In the short span of three years (1952–1955), for instance, twelve doctoral dissertations at Ohio State were addressed to research implications and applications of his theory. Kelly's best known scholarly contribution is a two-volume work published in 1955 entitled *The Psychology of Personal Constructs*. These volumes describe his theoretical formulations of personality and their clinical ramifications. Students who wish to pursue other aspects of Kelly's work might be interested in the following books: *Inquiring Man: The Theory of*

Personal Constructs (Bannister and Fransella, 1971); *Clinical Psychology and Personality: The Selected Papers of George Kelly* (edited by Maher, 1969); *Perspectives in Personal Construct Theory* (edited by Bannister, 1970).

CORNERSTONES OF COGNITIVE THEORY *Judy*

The central theme of this volume is that any personality theory necessarily involves certain philosophical assumptions about human nature. That is, the way a personologist chooses to view his subject matter, the human organism, will largely determine his model of the person. Unlike most personologists, George Kelly explicitly adknowledged that all conceptions of human nature, including his own, are founded on basic assumptions. Kelly developed his personal constructs theory on the basis of a single philosophical assumption— constructive alternativism.

Constructive Alternativism

In the present age, where young people are experimenting with alternative life-styles and ways of understanding things, George Kelly's vintage-1955 theory now appears to have been curiously ahead of its time. Kelly's underlying philosophy, constructive alternativism, furnishes a dazzling array of options for people seeking alternatives to the commonplace. In fact, the philosophy practically demands that people do so.

As a doctrine, constructive alternativism asserts that all present interpretations of the universe are subject to revision or replacement. Nothing is sacred. There are no politics, religions, social mores, or even college adiministrative policies that are absolutely and unalterably "right." All could be changed if people could only learn to see them differently. And why? Because Kelly argues that there is no such thing as an "interpretation-free" view of the world. A person's perception of reality is always subject to interpretation; in Kelly's philosophy, objective reality or absolute truth are figments of man's imagination. Truth, like beauty, exists in the mind of the beholder.

Since events exist only in man's mind, it follows that there are many alternative ways to construe them. To illustrate, consider the event of a girl taking money from her mother's purse. What does it signify? The event is simply that money has been removed from the purse. However, if we ask a child analyst to interpret the event, he may give an elaborate account of the girl's unconscious resentment toward her mother—resentment resulting from an unresolved Electra conflict. If we ask the mother, she may say that her daughter is "naughty" and untrustworthy. The girl's father may suggest that she is "undisciplined." Grandfather may construe the event as a childish prank. The girl herself may consider the event as reflecting her mother's unwillingness to provide her with a sufficient allowance. While the event itself obviously cannot be undone—the money was taken—its meaning is open to several alternative interpretations. Any event, then, can be viewed from a wide variety of perspectives. Persons have a dazzling choice of options available when interpreting the inner world of experience or the outer world of practical affairs. Kelly summarized his commitment to constructive alternativism in the following way:

> . . . whatever nature may be, or howsoever the quest for truth will turn out in the end, the events we face today are subject to as great a variety of constructions as our wits will enable us to contrive (1970, p. 1).

The intriguing nature of constructive alternativism can be understood more clearly if it is contrasted with one of Aristotle's traditional philosophic principles. Aristotle first put forth the principle of identity: *A is A.* A thing is itself in objective reality; it is open to only one valid interpretation. For example, assume that a person's behavior is produced by one motive or set of motives only. If the personologist does not understand that person's motives, that is his problem (and mistake) rather than the subject's. By contrast, Kelly would argue that *A is what one construes as A!* Reality is what one construes as reality; events can always be viewed from a wide variety of perspectives. In this scheme of things, then, there is no one true or valid way of interpreting a person's behavior. Whether one is attempting to understand another's behavior, oneself, or the nature of the universe, there are always "constructive alternatives" open for consideration.

Man the Scientist

Kelly's theory is a contemporary cognitive approach to the study of personality—an approach that emphasizes the manner in which individuals perceive and interpret people and things in their environments. Construct theory thus focuses on the processes which enable people to understand the psychological terrain of their lives. From this cognitive perspective, Kelly proposed a model of personality based on the analogy of *man as a scientist.* Specifically, he theorized that just like the scientist who studies him, the human subject also generates working hypotheses about reality with which he tries to anticipate and control events in his life. To be sure, Kelly did not propose that every person is literally a scientist who attends to some limited aspect of the world and employs sophisticated methods to gather and assess data. That analogy would have been foreign to his outlook. But he did suggest that all persons are scientists in that they formulate hypotheses and follow the same psychological processes to validate or invalidate them that characterize the scientific enterprise (Kelly, 1955). Thus, the basic premise underlying personal construct theory is that science constitutes a refinement of the aims and procedures by which each of us works out a way of life. The aims of science are to predict, to modify, and to understand events. Not only the scientist, but every person shares these same aims. All of us are motivated to anticipate the future and make plans based on expected outcomes.

To concretize this model of the human being, consider the example of a student who encounters a new professor on the first day of class (assuming that she has no previous knowledge of the professor's "reputation"). Based on limited data (perhaps fifty minutes of class time), the student perceives and interprets the professor to be "fair." Kelly's word for this process is *construe;* the student "construes" fairness in the professor. Essentially, what's happening is that the student is generating a hypothesis about the professor that will help her anticipate and control events concerning that course. Specifically, if the student's hypothesis proves "valid," the professor can be expected to assign a reasonable amount of reading, give decent examinations, and grade fairly. Should the professor's subsequent behavior be sharply otherwise, then the student would be in need of an alternative hypothesis; e.g., the prof is unfair, the prof is a dingbat, or whatever. The point here is simply that the student (like all of us) needs a useful and consistent means of anticipating events affecting her life.

In developing this theory of personal constructs based on the analogy of the person as a scientist, Kelly was amazed to discover the contrast between views the psychologist uses to explain his own behavior and those used to explain the behavior of his research subjects. He described this discrepancy as follows:

> It is as though the psychologist were saying to himself, "I, being a psychologist, and therefore a scientist, am performing this experiment in order to improve the prediction and control of certain human phenomena; but my subject, being merely a human organism, is obviously propelled by inexorable drives welling up within him, or else he is in gluttonous pursuit of sustenance and shelter" (1955, p. 5).

Kelly rejected the tunnel-vision notion that only the psychological scientist wearing a white lab coat and behaving like a scientist is concerned with predicting and controlling the course of events in life. Rather than viewing the human organism as some kind of unwilling and unthinking blob of protoplasm, Kelly credited the human subject with having the same aspirations as the so-called scientific psychologist. This notion, namely that the psychologist is no different from the subject he studies, epitomizes Kelly's personal construct theory of personality. It reveals Kelly's belief that no one being can lay claim to more intellectual and rational powers than any other.

To treat all persons as if they were scientists leads to a number of important consequences for Kelly's theory. Foremost, it suggests that people are fundamentally oriented toward future rather than past or present events taking place in their lives. In fact, Kelly (1955) maintained that all behavior can be understood as anticipatory in nature. He also noted that one's outlook on life is transitory insofar as it is rarely the same today as it was yesterday or will be tomorrow. In attempting to anticipate and control future events, one's view of reality is constantly being tested:

Anticipation is not merely carried on for its own sake; it is carried on so that future reality may be better represented. It is the future which tantalizes man, not the past. Always he reaches out to the future through the window of the present (Kelly, 1955, p. 49).

A second consequence following from the analogy of the person as a scientist is that this person has the capacity to actively represent his or her environment rather than merely passively respond to it. Just as the psychologist rationally formulates and revises theoretical notions about phenomena, so also can a lay person interpret and reinterpret, construe and reconstrue, his or her environment. For Kelly, then, life is characterized by the person's continuous struggle to make sense of his or her tangible world of experience; it is this quality of life that enables persons to shape their own destiny. One need not be an enslaved victim of his past history or present situation—unless he decides to construe himself in such a way. In short, a person is not controlled by present events (as Skinner suggests) or past ones (as Freud proposed) but controls events depending on the questions asked and the answers found.

PERSONAL CONSTRUCT THEORY

The heart of Kelly's cognitive theory lies in the manner in which individuals perceive and interpret people and things in their environments. Labeling his approach *personal construct theory,* Kelly focused on the processes which enable the person to order and understand the events of his or her life.

Constructs: Templets for Reality

Scientists formulate theoretical constructs to describe and explain the events with which they are concerned. In Kelly's personological system, the key-theoretical construct is the term *construct* itself:

Man looks at his world through transparent patterns or templets which he creates and then attempts to fit over the realities of which the world is composed. The fit is not always very good. Yet without such patterns the world appears to be such an undifferentiated homogeneity that man is unable to make any sense out of it (Kelly, 1955, pp. 8–9).

It is these "transparent patterns or templets" which Kelly designated *personal constructs.* Stated otherwise, a construct is a category of thought by which the individual construes or interprets his or her personal world of experience. It represents a consistent way for the person to make sense of some aspect of reality. Examples of personal constructs include "refined versus vulgar," "intelligent versus stupid," "good versus bad," "religious versus nonreligious," and "friendly versus hostile." These constructs are ones which many people use to construe events in their daily lives.

As an illustration of constructs in action, let's examine how different people might construe the same event. The event in question is that a recent college graduate, instead of pursuing his earlier plans to attend medical school, packs up his guitar and goes off with his woman to live in a hippie commune. The young man's father might construe this event as "distressing" or "embarrassing" while his mother construes him to be "living in sin" ("sinful"). His college counselor, well-grounded in Eriksonian theory, thinks that he is "searching for his identity," and his sociology prof believes that he's simply "rejecting the norms of a materialistic society." The young man himself construes the event as "natural," as "the right thing for me to do at this time." Which is it? In Kelly's theory, there is no way to tell. Kelly's point is simply that, for all of us, reality is filtered through different templets—constructs— that we need in order to understand the world in a consistent fashion.

According to Kelly, one predicts and controls personal experiences by construing their replications. This process is significant in that it provides the person with a tangible basis for expecting what kinds of events are likely to occur and for interpreting their meaning. In the initial stages of construing, the individual notes the general flow of events and tentatively interprets them. He or she then recognizes a pattern or repetition of the events within his or her field of experience. Finally, one places a structure and meaning on the events that have been experienced. This temporal process of experiencing, interpreting, and structuring is called *construing:* it accounts for a person's capacity to generalize experiences in an orderly and meaningful fashion. Constructs are thus relevant to prediction and control because they provide the person with expectations for anticipating subsequent events. In the absence of constructs, an individual's life would be chaotic; he or she would have no consistent way to make sense of the world. Unable to form expectations about the future, current events would also be incomprehensible. The existence of personal constructs thus enables one to impose some order and predictability in one's world.

Consistent with his model of man as scientist, Kelly maintained that once the person hypothesizes that a given construct will adequately anticipate and predict some event in his or her environment, he or she will then test that hypothesis against events that have not yet occurred. If the construct leads to an accurate prediction of the environment (i.e., helps the person to anticipate events correctly), the person retains it. Conversely, if a prediction is disconfirmed, the construct from which it was derived is likely to undergo some revision or may even be eliminated altogether (recall our earlier example of the professor initially construed as "fair"). The validity of a construct, then, is tested in terms of its *predictive efficiency,* of which there are varying degrees.

Kelly also theorized that all personal constructs are inherently *bipolar* and *dichotomous* in nature—that the essence of human thought is to perceive life's experiences in black versus white terms, not shades of gray. More specifically, in experiencing events, the person observes that certain events seem similar to

having more than one part

each other (they share common properties) and different from other events. One notices, for example, that some people are fat and some are skinny, that some are black-skinned and some are white-skinned, that some are affluent and some are poor, that some things are dangerous to touch and some are not. It is this cognitive process of observing similarities and contrasts which leads to the formation of personal constructs. Thus, at least three elements (events or things) are needed to form a construct: two of the construct elements must be perceived as similar to each other, while the third element must be perceived as different from these two; e.g., Danny and Betty are *honest;* Dick is not.

The way in which two elements are construed to be similar or alike is called the *construct* or *similarity* pole of the construct dimension; the way in which they are contrasted with the third element is called the *contrast* pole of the construct dimension. Every construct thus has a similarity pole and a contrast pole. The thrust of personal construct theory is to discover how people interpret and anticipate their experiences in terms of similarities and contrasts.

However, Kelly neglected to elaborate on the processes by which an individual comes to construe his or her experiences along particular lines; i.e., *why* are John's constructs different than Burt's? He simply did not consider the issue of individual differences vis á vis the origin and development of personal constructs. This is understandable insofar as Kelly's theory is *ahistorical,* thereby placing no special emphasis upon the individual's early experiences. However, constructs must come from somewhere, and it seems most reasonable to assume that they are a product of the individual's past history. It is likely that differential histories of environmental experiences account for the variability among individual construct systems.

Formal Properties of Constructs

Kelly proposed that certain formal properties characterize all constructs. First, a construct resembles a theory in that it encompasses a particular domain of events. This *range of convenience* consists of all events for which a particular construct may be relevant or applicable. The construct dimension "scholarly versus not scholarly," for example, is quite applicable to understanding a vast array of intellectual and scientific accomplishments but is hardly appropriate for construing the relative merits of being married or single. Kelly noted that the predictive efficiency of a construct is seriously jeopardized whenever it is generalized beyond the range of events for which it was intended. Thus, all constructs have a limited range of convenience, though the scope of the range may vary widely from construct to construct. The construct "good versus bad" has a wide range of convenience since it applies to most situations requiring personal evaluation. In contrast, the construct "virginity versus prostitution" is substantially narrower in its breadth of application.

Each construct also has a *focus of convenience,* that is, a point or area within the construct's range of convenience where it is maximally useful in construing certain events. For instance, one person's construct of "honest versus dishonest" might have as its focus of convenience keeping one's hands off other people's money and property. Another person may apply the same construct to politics. Hence, a construct's focus of convenience is always specific to the individual employing the construct.

Permeability–impermeability is another dimension along which constructs vary. A permeable construct admits to its range of convenience new elements not yet construed within its boundaries, whereas an impermeable one, while embracing events that made up its original formulation, remains closed to the interpretation of new experiences. There are relative degrees of permeability and impermeability. One student's construct of "competent versus incompetent" teachers might be sufficiently permeable to account for any new instructor he encounters. That is, after interacting with any new instructor for some time, the student could construe him as either competent or incompetent, rendering the construct completely permeable. But another student may use the same construct in a totally impermeable way, insisting that competent teachers no longer exist—that the last competent one was her third grade teacher who is now dead. Thus, the distinction between competent and incompetent teachers is no longer relevant for her. All teachers are incompetent! Note that permeability is relevant only to a given construct's range of convenience; a construct is impermeable by definition to any experience beyond its range of convenience. Hence, "competent versus incompetent" has no meaning when judging the ripeness of one's favorite fruit.

Types of Constructs   Kelly also suggested that personal constructs can be classified according to the nature of the control they implicitly exercise over their elements. A construct which freezes ("preempts") its elements for membership exclusively in its own realm Kelly termed a *preemptive* construct. This is a type of pigeonhole construct; what has been placed into one pigeonhole mutually excludes its placement into any other. Preemptive construing may be likened to the "nothing but" kind of thinking characteristic of a rigid person. Ethnic labels illustrate the use of preemptive constructs. For instance, if a person is identified as a Jew, then he may be thought of by some as nothing but a Jew. Or, to a lesser degree, once a professor has been labeled as "hard-nosed," some students may disregard the possibility of thinking of him or her in other ways; e.g., as a person with tender feelings for his or her children, artistic hobbies, and social reform pursuits. Preemptive thought represents a kind of denial of the right of both others and ourselves to re-view, reinterpret, and see in a fresh light some part of the world around us (Bannister and Fransella, 1971).

A *constellatory* construct permits its elements to belong to other realms concurrently but fixes their realm memberships. That is, once an event is subsumed under one construct, its other characteristics are fixed. Sterotyped or typological thinking illustrates this type of construct. For example, constellatory thinking accepts "if this man is a Jew he must therefore be assertive, money-hungry, and dishonest." Here, a Jew may be considered as something other than a Jew, but there is no latitude as to what else he may be considered. By definition, constellatory constructs restrict one's chances of adopting alternative views.

A construct which leaves its elements open to alternative constructions is called a *propositional* construct. This type of construct directly contradicts preemptive or constellatory constructs since it allows the person to be open to new experiences and adopt alternative views of the world. In this instance, construing someone as a Jew is propositional to the extent that other personal attributes do not necessarily follow. While it is tempting to "construe" preemptive and constellatory constructs as undesirable and propositional constructs as desirable, Kelly clearly stated that such is not necessarily true. Essentially, if a person used propositional constructs only, he would have an extremely difficult time getting along in the world since he could not reach pressing decisions.

As an illustration, consider a baseball game in which the ball is speedily coming in the direction of your head. You could begin to construe the ball propositionally, considering and reconsidering it from all conceptual angles. As it smacked you in the face, you might then see that it would have been far better in this circumstance to construe the ball preemptively; i.e., this event is a baseball coming at my head and nothing else! However, Kelly believed that, to avoid intellectual rigor mortis, one must be able to engage in propositional thinking. Without it, a person would be doomed to a sterile, unchanging, and stereotyped mode of perceiving reality. Hence, preemptive, constellatory, and propositional forms of thinking are necessary to construe events. Propositional thinking is simply a contrast to preemptive and constellatory ways of making sense of reality.

There are several other ways in which constructs can be categorized or typed. For example, there are *comprehensive* constructs which subsume a relatively wide spectrum of events, and *incidental* constructs which subsume a small range of events (i.e., have a much narrower range of convenience). There are *core* constructs that govern the person's basic functioning and *peripheral* constructs that may be altered without serious modification of the core structure. Finally, some constructs are *tight* insofar as they lead to unvarying predictions, whereas others are *loose* in that they lead the individual to arrive at different predictions under very similar conditions.

Personality: The Personologist's Construct? *mary*

Kelly never offered an explicit definition of the term "personality." However, he discussed the concept in general terms in one paper stating that personality is

Our abstraction of the activity of a person and our subsequent generalization of this abstraction to all matters of his relationship to other persons, known and unknown, as well as to anything else that may seem particularly valuable (1961, pp. 220–221).

Kelly thus believed that personality is an abstraction made by personologists of the psychological processes they observe in others. It is not a separate entity to be discovered by them. Furthermore, Kelly argued that personality is by its very nature inextricably linked to the person's interpersonal relationships. Meshing these two ideas and adding one of our own, a more pointed definition of personality within Kelly's system is possible; specifically, an individual's personality is nothing more or less than his or her construct system. A person uses constructs to interpret his or her world of experience and to anticipate future events. Indeed, personality consists of constructs the individual uses to anticipate his or her future. To understand another person involves knowing something about the constructs he or she employs, the events subsumed under these constructs, and the way in which they are organized in relation to one another to form a construct system. In short, to know someone's personality is to know how he or she construes personal experience.

Motivation: Who Needs It?

Psychologists have traditionally used the concept of motivation to explain two aspects of behavior: (1) why people are active (behave) at all and (2) why their activity takes one direction rather than another. In Kelly's judgment, the term "motivation" assumes that humans are by nature static beings and act only when some force prods them. In contrast, Kelly outrightly repudiated the notion that *humans are inactive or reactive* by nature and behave only when set into motion by some internal or external force. For Kelly (1958), people are motivated for no other reason than they they are alive. In fact, life itself is seen as a form of process or movement; human beings represent one specific species of such all-pervasive movement. Following from this reasoning, no special concepts (e.g., drives, needs, instincts, rewards, motives) are required to understand what makes or motivates human behavior.

Kelly summarized the state of modern motivation theories and contrasted them with his own position in the following way:

> Motivational theories can be divided into two types, push theories and pull theories. Under push theories we find such terms as drive, motive, or even stimulus. Pull theories use such constructs as purpose, value, or need. In terms of a well known metaphor, there are pitchfork theories on the one hand and the carrot theories on the other. But our theory is neither of these. Since we prefer to look to the nature of the animal himself, ours is probably best called a jackass theory (1958, p. 50).

Accordingly, personal construct theory construes the human being as an active and struggling organism simply by virtue of being alive—a person is like a "jackass" when it comes to being active. Motivation is thus a redundant construct—who needs it?

Since Kelly rejected motivation to account for human activity, how did he explain its directionality? The explanation is presented in his fundamental postulate, discussed below.

A POSTULATE AND SOME COROLLARIES

The formal structure of personal construct theory is both economical and parsimonious in that Kelly advanced his central tenets by using one fundamental postulate and eleven elaborative corollaries. After we describe his basic postulate, discussion will be focused upon those corollaries that appear most to add to our account of Kelly's position presented up to now.

Channelizing Processes

Each personality theorist seems to have a language of his own when describing human behavior. Kelly is no exception to this principle, as can be seen in his *fundamental postulate: "A person's processes are psychologically channelized by the ways in which he anticipates events (1955, p. 46)."* A typical response to this postulate by an uninitiated Kelly reader might be "Huh?"—so let's break it down for better understanding since it is so critically central to his formal system.

Roughly translated, the fundamental postulate stipulates that how the person predicts future occurrences determines his or her behavior. It also means that Kelly is primarily interested in the whole individual rather than any part of him or her (e.g., intergroup relations). The word "processess" suggests that the person is basically a behaving organism, not an inert substance pushed and pulled by internal or external forces. To clarify this idea, one need only recall Kelly's "jackass" view of human motivation. Kelly's fundamental postulate also reveals that his system is psychological in scope, that its range of convenience is limited to understanding human behavior. "Channelized" means that behavior is relatively stable across time and situations. Kelly (1955) conceived of a person's processes as operating through a network of pathways as opposed to fluttering about in an unpredictable void. The word "ways" is synonymous with *constructs,* while the pronoun "he" highlights the individuality of construing. Concerning this latter point, Kelly (1955) noted that each individual erects and characteristically uses different ways (constructs), and it is the way that one chooses which channelizes one's processes. Finally, the phrase "anticipates events" conveys the predictive and motivational features intrinsic to cognitive theory. Like the scientist, the person seeks prediction of reality to facilitate the anticipation of events affecting his or her life. This notion is what accounts for the directionality of human activities in Kelly's scheme. In this system, persons look at the present so that they may anticipate the future through the unique templet of their personal constructs.

Individuality and Organization

The basic theme set forth in Kelly's fundamental postulate is elaborated upon in various corollaries. Of these, the *individuality corollary* appears particularly pertinent for understanding the uniqueness of personality: "Persons differ from each other in their construction of events (Kelly, 1955, p. 55)." For Kelly, no two people, whether they be identical twins or supposedly similar in outlook, will approach and interpret the same event in exactly the same way. Each person construes reality through his or her unique personal construct goggles. Hence, differences between people are rooted in their construing of events from different perspectives.

Examples abound. Consider the traditional differences of opinion between political liberals and conservatives on such issues as welfare, military spending, taxation, forced racial integration, pornography, and capital punishment. Or reflect on why students may disagree with professors, professors with department chairpersons, department chairpersons with deans, and everybody with college presidents. Or what is popularly called the "generation gap"—the fundamental differences of viewpoint between parents and their offspring—a situation which, in Kelly's theory, might more properly be labeled a "personal construct gap." In all these instances, persons are in disagreement because each is operating from a different construct system. No wonder there is such lack of accord among people—from Kelly's vantage point, they are not even talking about the same things!

In addition to the individuality of personal constructs, Kelly also maintained that constructs are organized within persons in different ways. This conviction is most clearly asserted in his *organization corollary:* "Each person characteristically evolves, for his convenience in anticipating events, a construction system embracing ordinal relationships between constructs (1955, p. 56)." This corollary indicates that persons organize their personal constructs hierarchically to minimize incompatibilities and inconsistencies. Perhaps even more importantly, it implies that people differ not only in the number and kinds of constructs they use to view the world but also in the ways in which they organize their constructs.

For Kelly, the organization of systems of constructs is essentially a logical one: constructs are ordered in a pyramidal structure so that some constructs are either superordinate or subordinate in relation to other parts of the system. (Of course, a construct may be quite independent of all others in the person's repertoire.) A *superordinate* construct subsumes other constructs within its context, whereas a *subordinate* construct is one that is included in the context of another (superordinate) construct. For example, for some people, the construct "good versus bad" subsumes within its two poles, respectively, the two poles of the construct "sexy versus nonsexy." In this instance, the former construct is superordinate to the latter. To illustrate, consider a male chauvinist type in the process of construing the playmate of the month in *Playboy* magazine. He would most probably construe her as "sexy" and hence, superordinately speaking, "good." But even in the most blatant male chauvinist's construct system, "good" usually incorporates more than "sexy." For example, he may also construe the interview of the month in this same magazine as "good" because, to him, it is "insightful." In this case, then, the constructs "sexy versus nonsexy" and "insightful versus noninsightful" are both subordinate to the "good versus bad" superordinate construct. The basic point here is simply that people evolve different hierarchies of personal constructs. What is a superordinate-subordinate construct relationship in one person's system is not necessarily the same as that in another's system. According to Kelly, only by knowing the individual's mode of organizing constructs can one make meaningful statements about his or her behavior.

To Construe or Not to Construe: That Is the Question

From Kelly's perspective, the translation of cognition into behavior in any situation depends upon what construct the person will use to construe the relevant events and which end of the dichotomous construct he or she will apply. Kelly put forth the *choice corollary* to describe how people make these selections: "A person chooses for himself that alternative in a dichotomized construct through which he anticipates the greater possibility for extension and definition of his system (1955, p. 64)." Specifically, an individual confronted with a choice situation (i.e., she must use her constructs in one way or another) will opt for the alternative that is most likely either to enhance her understanding of the world or to better clarify her present construct system. In other words, she will choose that construct pole which renders the event most understandable to her—the one that will contribute most to the predictive efficiency of her construct system. Kelly called this the *elaborative choice.*

The choice corollary also suggests that one's construct system is elaborated in the direction of either *definition* or *extension.* In the case of definition, the person chooses that alternative which has the greater probability of validating aspects of experience which have already been fairly accurately construed. That is, he wagers a relatively safe bet as to how he thinks things will turn out based on previous experience and then he observes the evidence. If the anticipated event does occur and his construct system is confirmed, then the construct becomes more consolidated and clear-cut by virtue of its having led to a correct prediction. In extension, the person chooses that alternative which has the greater likelihood of broadening his understanding of events (increasing the construct's range of convenience) in new and different ways. If the prediction is correct, then the construct is validated and becomes, at least temporarily, more comprehensive. Thus, if enough is known about the structure of a person's construct system to predict his choices in terms of that system, then it is also possible to predict his behavior to some extent.

Kelly characterized the difference between definition and extension as one between security and adventure. Persons must continuously decide which of these two modes will further articulate their personal constructs. College students, for example, must often choose whether to take courses similar to ones they have previously taken—courses in which satisfactory grades are somewhat assured—or whether to take unfamiliar courses where failure is a risk but which offer possibilities of broadening their knowlege and understanding of the world. A "snap" course in a familiar subject represents "security" while organic chemistry, for most students, is an "adventure." In this instance, if the student chooses the alternative that minimizes risk, then his construct system (if validated) is further consolidated and defined. However, if he opts for the alternative that will extend his system, then he invites greater risk insofar as he may not be able to correctly anticipate events; i.e., he might flunk. Of course, the likelihood of acquiring additional understanding which will serve him in future predictions is increased substantially.

Kelly did not suggest that the individual seeks certainty, reinforcement, and/or the avoidance of pain in elaborating personal constructs. Instead, people seek to anticipate events while validating and extending construct systems. Literally, they strive to increase the range of convenience of their construct systems.

Although Kelly detailed the basis for recognizing whether a person defines or extends his or her construct system, there is scant empirical evidence or theoretical rationale as to why or when one kind of choice will be favored over the other. Possibly when a person feels secure and confident of predicting events correctly even at the risk of being wrong, he or she will then more likely choose to extend his construct system. In contrast, if the person feels insecure and inadequate in correctly predicting events, then he or she will be more likely to choose definition.

C-P-C Cycle   Kelly presented various models to illustrate the process of how cognition is translated into action. One of particular importance is called the *circumspection-preemption-control* (C-P-C) *cycle,* which involves a sequential progression from construction to overt behavior. In the first phase of the C-P-C cycle, the *circumspection* phase, the individual considers a number of different constructs as they relate to the particular situation—that is, she contemplates the various possibilities facing her in a propositional fashion. This is analogous to looking at all sides of the question. (Recall that a propositional construct is open to new experiences.) The *preemption* phase follows when the individual reduces the number of alternative constructs (hypotheses) to ones most appropriate to the problem. Here she decides which of the preemptive alternatives to use. Finally, during the *control* phase of the cycle, she decides on a course of action and its accompanying behavior. The choice is made, in other words, based on an estimate as to which alternative construct is most likely to lead to extension and definition of the system. As an illustration of the C-P-C cycle, consider the case of a young woman just entering college. She surveys her situation, considering a wide variety of constructs. There are a great many ways in which she *could* construe herself in relation to this new situation (circumspection). However, if she is eventually to graduate, the situation must be preempted in terms of the construct "student"; she must predominately construe herself as a college student before she can consistently act accordingly, e.g., study, seriously attend classes, pass examinations (preemption and then control). However, if, instead, the young woman continues to think of herself only as "Mary Highschooler, the goof-off," or "Daddy's little girl," or "Star local lover—seducer of men," she will never get to engage in the behaviors necessary to the successful completion of college.

Kelly noted that a person may go through a number of C-P-C cycles before he or she decides to act. He cites Hamlet as the classic example of a person who, after preemption ("To be, or not to be; that is the question. . . ."), could not decide to make the final choice and instead returned to the circumspection phase of the cycle. The notion of the C-P-C cycle is consistent with Kelly's conviction that the alternatives each person sees before him are of his own making and reflect the constructs he uses to construe the situation. Thus, if one could only change his constructs, he could literally change his life; the options in Kelly's system are dazzling. Kelly also contended, however, that since the world is multidimensional and a person possesses a number of different dimensions in his construct system, the dimensions must be sorted out until there is a single dichotomous choice to be made before the person can act. In Kelly's view, only when the person says "this and this only is the important dimension" is he ready to act. Ultimately, then, one must construe in order to behave intelligently.

Change in a Construct System

A construct system enables the individual to anticipate events as accurately as possible. It follows, then, that a construct system changes in relation to its inability to correctly anticipate the unfolding sequence of events. In this regard, Kelly postulated that a construct system change occurs most often when the individual is exposed to novel or unfamiliar events which do not conform to his or her existing system of constructs. Accordingly, the *experience corollary* states: "A person's construct system varies as he successively construes the replication of events (1955, p. 72)."

Also called the learning corollary, it suggests that a personal construct system is a set of hypotheses about the world which are perpetually being tested by experience. The feedback one receives as to how adequately these hypotheses have predicted future events leads to a modification of constructs which in turn are used as new hypotheses to progressively change the system.

Those constructs found to be useful are retained, whereas those that are not are either revised or discarded. Thus, for Kelly, a construct system undergoes successive revision in light of its varying validational fortunes.

For Kelly, a person's *experience* is the reconstruction of his or her life based upon revisions of his or her constructs as they are affected by events taking place over time. This means that the person gains little or no experience if after having observed a succession of events he or she still construes the events in the same way. If, for example, a professor has been teaching for ten years and is still presenting the same lectures in the same way as she did in her first year, Kelly would question whether she has really had ten years of teaching experience. On the other hand, if what she taught during her first year led her to alter and better her teaching in her second year, and successively through the tenth year, then she could legitimately claim to have had a decade of teaching experience.

Kelly's *modulation corollary* delineates the conditions under which changes occur in a construct system: "The variation in a person's construction system is limited by the permeability of the constructs within whose range of convenience the variants lie (1955, p. 77)." As discussed earlier, "permeability" refers to the degree to which a construct can assimilate novel experiences and events within its range of convenience. Thus, this corollary implies that the more permeable (open) the person's superordinate constructs are, the greater the amount of possible variation (systematic change) within the substructures they subsume. If the person has no superordinate constructs for construing change, then change cannot occur within his system. He is psychologically rigid. Consequently, the person must not only be capable of construing new events or reconstruing old events, but he must also be capable of construing change itself. In other words, since modification of a construct or a set of constructs is an event for the individual, he must have some conceptual framework in which the changes in his system can be construed. Otherwise, change cannot take place, although chaos might.

By way of illustration, consider a twenty-one year-old male who construes his relationship to his mother in such a way that he still reacts to her as "Mommy's little boy," i.e., overdependently. Obviously, he is going to have a great deal of trouble going through life unless he can change this construction of the relationship. The young man is in luck if he happens to have a permeable superordinate construct like "mature versus immature" which he can apply to this situation. If so, he should begin to construe himself as "mature" and thus start to respond differently toward his mother, i.e., less dependently. In essence, he reconstrues his relationship to his mother in terms of his application of the construct "mature" to himself.

Social Relationships and Personal Constructs

If, as Kelly asserted in his individuality corollary, people differ as a result of the way they interpret situations, then it logically follows that people may be similar to others to the extent that they construe experiences in similar ways. Birds of a feather construe together. This idea is made explicit in Kelly's *commonality corollary:* "To the extent that one person employs a construction of experience which is similar to that employed by another, his psychological processes are similar to those of the other person (1955, p. 90)." Thus, if two people view the world in the same way (i.e., are similar in their constructions of personal experiences), they are likely to behave in similar ways. The essential point to note in this corollary is that people are not similar because they have experienced similar events nor because they manifest similar behavior; rather, they are similar because events have approximately the same psychological meaning for them. In line with his cognitive orientation, Kelly's emphasis is upon construing rather than past experience or observable behavior.

Interestingly, this notion implies that the similarities evident among members of a particular culture are not behavioral similarities alone. More fundamentally, Kelly (1955) believed that people belong to the same cultural group because they construe their experiences in much the same way. So, for example, in understanding the culture of a primitive tribe that practices rain dances, it is not enough to observe the peculiarities of the rain dance alone. One must see that the members of this culture all possess the construct "Rain God," who happens occasionally to respond favorably to their ritualistic gyrations. Or, closer to home, the differences in our own society between members of the "middle class" and "counterculture" cannot be explained in terms of dress, hair length, music preferences, and other such behaviors alone. In Kelly's system, the basic difference lies in the way each group commonly construes its experience. Consider, for example, the classic "middle class" versus "counterculture" constructions of drugs, money, work, religion, morality, material goods, the meaning of life, etc., etc., etc. These are fundamental differences in construing, not just overt behavior.

Another and one of the most important aspects of Kelly's theory of personal constructs deals with relationships between people and their construct system. This is formally defined in the *sociality corollary* which specifies the conditions necessary for an interpersonal relationship: "To the extent that one person construes the construction processes of another, he may play a role in a social process involving the other person (1955, p. 95)." This corollary stipulates that social interaction consists primarily of one person trying to understand how another person perceives and interprets his or her environment. This differs from the assumption that people can only interact when they have similar construct systems or are in some sense similar people. For Kelly, effective social interaction requires that one person psychologically place himself or herself in the shoes of another so that he or she is better able to understand and predict the other's present and subsequent behavior. To "role play" your father, for instance, it would be necessary to understand how he views things (including yourself) "through his constructs" and to structure your actions appropriately. Playing a role in relation to another person does not necessarily mean agreeing with him, as parent-child relationships readily attest. As indicated by the commonality corollary, it is far easier to understand how another person thinks if one shares similar outlooks, but it is not essential for effective role playing.

Kelly's use of "role" should not be confused with sociologists' usage of the word. A role in Kelly's system is defined as a "pattern of behavior that follows from a person's understanding of how the others who are associated with him in his task think (1955, pp. 97–98)." This definition suggests that significant social interaction does not automatically exist because two or more people are communicating with one another or are involved in a common task. Role enactment requires that at least one of the interacting individuals have some preception of the other person's ways of seeing things. Thus, based on the understanding of what the other person is doing and thinking in relation to him, he engages in an interpersonal activity. Roles need not be reciprocal (i.e., the person enacting the role need not be construed by the person or persons toward whom the role is directed) in order for a person to become involved in a social relationship. The other person need not enter into a role relationship with the construing individual. Indeed, our society is dominated by one-sided role relationships (e.g., teacher-student, doctor-patient, lawyer-client, employer-employee). In this regard, Kelly noted that an optimal relationship involves a mutual understanding of one another's views on life, as is the case in a healthy husband-wife relationship.

Kelly's sociality corollary has profound relevence for the field of human relations. In particular, it offers a potentially unifying link between individual and social psychology. The implicit notion that a lasting and genuine human relationship cannot develop until at least one person attempts to see another person through the other's glasses may explain those problems people have in communicating with each other in situations ranging from everyday discourse (parents, relatives, friends, teachers) to international affairs. A better world may ultimately depend upon the capacity of human beings (particularly heads of state) to sensitively and accurately construe one another's construction processes.

KELLY'S BASIC ASSUMPTIONS CONCERNING HUMAN NATURE

Kelly's philosophic position of constructive alternativism denies any objective reality independent of human construction systems. Reality is what we construe it to be. When applied to human nature, Kelly's doctrine asserts that persons are fundamentally whatever they construe themselves to be. Differences among personality theorists concerning human nature, then, were seen by Kelly as reflections of the unique construct systems with which they construed their subject matter. Kelly himself, of course, was no exception to this principle. Using the approach taken to all theorists in this text, however,

Freedom	_ _ _ _ _ ✓ _ _ _ _ _	Determinism
Rationality	✓ _ _ _ _ _ _ _ _ _ _	Irrationality
Holism	_ _ ✓ _ _ _ _ _ _ _ _	Elementalism
Constitutionalism	_ _ _ _ _ _ _ _ ✓ _ _	Environmentalism
Subjectivity	✓ _ _ _ _ _ _ _ _ _ _	Objectivity
Proactivity	_ _ Not applicable _ _ _	Reactivity
Homeostasis	_ _ Not applicable _ _ _	Heterostasis
Knowability	_ _ _ _ _ _ _ _ _ _ ✓	Unknowability

Figure 7-1 Kelly's position on the eight basic assumptions concerning human nature.

Kelly's constructs about humanity may be construed as actually reflecting his basic assumptions concerning human nature. His positions, discussed below, are depicted in Figure 7-1.

1 Freedom–Determinism In Kelly's theory, man is both free *and* determined. Paradoxically, man is depicted as *freely determining* his own behavior. As Kelly neatly puts it:

> This personal construct system provides him with both freedom of decision and limitation of action—freedom, because it permits him to deal with the meaning of events rather than forces him to be helplessly pushed about by them, and limitation, because he can never make choices outside the world of alternatives he has erected for himself (1958, p. 58).

In other words, human beings have an enormous range of constructs from which to choose in interpreting events, but—once selected—their constructions determine their behavior. Humans operate behaviorally only within the boundaries of the constructs they employ. A person facing a new event, for example, is free to use or not use the construct "good-bad" in construing it. Should she decide to employ it, she will automatically use that pole of the construct through which she anticipates greater extension and definition of her system *(choice corollary)*, and her behavior will necessarily follow therefrom. However, she is free not to use the "good-bad" construct; she may opt to construe the new event in other terms, thereby establishing different self-imposed boundaries resulting in different behaviors. Of course, the person may construe and reconstrue the event throughout her lifetime, thus allowing the freedom-determinism cycle underlying her behavior to manifest itself again and again. Freedom and determinism are inextricably interwoven in Kelly's theory.

2 Rationality–Irrationality Kelly's exceptionally strong commitment to the rationality assumption pervades every aspect of his theory. This assumption plays a more central part in Kelly's system than in any other presented in this text. Fundamentally regarding man as "man the scientist," Kelly portrays the human being as constantly engaged in the process of intellectually construing the world around him. Kelly's man does not desire to love the world, nor to conquer it; he basically wants to *know* the world or at least to construe it. For Kelly to construe individuals in this fashion, for him to regard personality as a construct system, absolutely requires as a philosophical precursor the basic assumption of rationality. In fact, Kelly's cognitive theory could not exist as a viable "constructive alternative" without the rationality assumption as its base.

3 Holism–Elementalism   Kelly is moderately committed to a holistic view of human nature. While his unit of analysis, the construct, appears at first glance to reflect an elementalist approach to the study of humanity, Kelly does not suggest that a person can ever adequately be understood "one construct at a time." Instead, he refers repeatedly to a construct system, unique to each person, in which constructs are related to one another in an organized individual manner. The person is depicted as forever using his or her total system in construing the events of everyday life. Thus, to understand a person, it is necessary to understand his or her entire construct system.

Student A's construct of "good," for example, as applied to his or her psychology professor, might merely be subordinate to his or her construct of "entertaining," whereas the "good" construct of student B in this same situation may be subordinate to "intellectually stimulating." One could never appreciate this difference simply by studying in isolation the "good" constructs of A and B. The myriad of additional construct interrelationships within a system would also be missed in an element-by-element approach. Nevertheless, constructs can in fact be studied individually; in this sense, Kelly adopts a less than complete commitment to the holistic assumption.

4 Constitutionalism–Environmentalism   Kelly is noticeably inclined toward the environmentalism pole of this dimension. While he never addressed himself directly to the constitutional versus environmental origins of personal constructs, there is simply no acknowledgement of constitution in Kelly's theory. On the other hand, the environment is theoretically ubiquitous; Kelly's person is construing and reconstruing it all the time. Personal constructs presumably are abstracted from experience, employed to anticipate environmental events, and modified or discarded if they do not serve to accurately predict these events. Thus, the ultimate function of the individual's personal construct system is to interpret the surrounding world.

Yet in Kelly's theory, the environment is not invested with the awesome determinative power that it is in Skinner's system. The cognitive person interprets, evaluates, hypothesizes about, construes, and reconstrues the environment rather than simply being molded by its effects. This is because this person is, unlike Skinner's, fundamentally cognitive and rational. The environment is certainly there in Kelly's system, but never to the point of being overwhelming to the construer. Kelly's commitment to environmentalism is thus best described as moderate.

5 Subjectivity–Objectivity   Kelly contended that human beings live in a highly subjective world of personal constructs. People may construe and reconstrue external events however they wish, but they nonetheless remain encapsulated within their subjective construction systems. Each individual views reality through a templet of personal constructs, and the templets are unique to each person.

Objective external factors can have no uniform or standardized effects upon the individual because they are always construed by him or her in idiosyncratic ways. What is a "worthwhile" experience to one person is "anxiety-provoking" to another; what is "relevant" to one may be simply "superficial" to another's construct system. Objective reality (assuming there is such a thing) is always filtered through one's constructive apparatus—reality is what one construes as reality. Thus, each person lives in a unique constructive world of his or her own making. To be sure, that world can change, but only to the extent that one is willing to reconstrue it. Kelly is firmly committed to the subjectivity assumption. In fact, the particular blend of the rationality and subjectivity assumptions appears to contribute heavily to the unique character of Kelly's theory.

6 Proactivity–Reactivity   The proactivity-reactivity assumption is fundamentally an issue of *motivation:* Do human beings internally generate their own behavior or is their behavior a reaction to external stimuli? Since Kelly regards motivation as a redundant construct, he makes no assumption about its proactive versus reactive nature. For Kelly, humans are neither proactive nor reactive—they are simply alive. To be alive is to be active; life *is* a form of movement. Hence, Kelly's person finds it unnecessary to internally generate his or her behavior since, by simply being alive, he or she is already behaving. Relying on the environment to reactively stimulate behavior is equally unnecessary. Because of Kelly's unique position on motivation, then, the proactivity-reactivity assumption is not applicable.

7 Homeostasis–Heterostasis   This assumption also refers essentially to a basic motivational question: Do people behave to reduce drives and maintain internal harmony or is their behavior directed toward growth and self-actualization? For Kelly, neither category applies. Instead, in Kelly's view, people seek to develop and organize coherent construct systems so that they can accurately anticipate future events. In so doing, the person engages in *elaborative choice;* i.e., he or she always chooses that alternative which seems to lead to the greater extension and definition of his or her construct system *(choice corollary).* To the heterostatically oriented, this depiction may sound suspiciously like growth and self-actualization. On the other hand, champions of homeostasis might argue with equal cogency that persons always choose in this fashion because they are attempting to reduce inner uncertainties about the world. Kelly himself, however, took no position on this motivational issue. Motivation is a nonessential concept in his view. As a basic assumption about human nature, then, the homeostasis-heterostasis issue is not applicable to Kelly's system.

8 Knowability–Unknowability   For all practical purposes, human nature is scientifically unknowable in Kelly's theory. He rejects the prevalent philosophical position of *realism,* which asserts that there is an objective reality independent of our perception of it. Within the framework of realism, the ultimate task of science is to discover the nature of that reality. Each science has a "range of convenience"—for personology, it is the nature of human beings. Eschewing realism, Kelly put forth his own epistemological doctrine of constructive alternativism (actually a version of philosophical nominalism) which holds that only individual events have reality. Objective reality has no existence apart from our constructions of it. Launched from this basic premise, science can never "discover" objective reality, since there is none to discover! For psychology, human nature can never really be known but only alternatively construed.

The obvious question, then, becomes why bother with science? Kelly's answer is that scientific theories serve as differentially useful construct systems in the process of explaining events. Some are more efficacious than others in this regard—only future events will tell—but the more durable theories have served well as constructive alternatives. Consider personality theories as an example. Freud construed man in terms of unconscious motivation; Erikson discovered psychosocial stages of ego development; Murray perceived needs; Skinner observed instrumentally conditioned responses; and Allport saw traits underlying behavior. And Kelly? Kelly construed constructs.

By implication, Kelly's personal construct theory carries within it the seeds of its own demise. Since reality remains open to alternative constructions, there will come a day when the events presently construed by Kelly's theory will be better anticipated by some other personological construct system. He recognized this and, with disarming candor, admitted it. In discussing the various ways in which personal construct theory has been categorized by responsible scholars, he concluded that "It has also been classified as nonsense, which indeed, by its own admission, it will likely some day turn out to be (Kelly, 1970, p. 10)." By virtue of his philosophic position, then, Kelly assumes that human nature is unknowable through science.

EMPIRICAL VALIDATION OF COGNITIVE THEORY CONCEPTS *Donna*

To what extent has the psychology of personal constructs generated evidence supporting the empirical validity of its major theoretical concepts? This question was the focus of a comprehensive literature survey conducted by Bonarius (1965) who, on the basis of evaluating more than ninety published studies stimulated by Kelly's ideas or directly related to them, concluded that it would be premature to assume that Kelly's basic theory had been validated at that point. However, close inspection of these studies reveals that most pertain to a test that Kelly developed, the Role Construct Repertory Test (commonly called the Rep Test), rather than to his theoretical concepts per se. The truth is that the Rep Test has captured more research attention than the theory of which it is an integral part. While Kelly's theory has not been subjected to much empirical test, then, he has exerted a significant influence upon persono-logical research primarily through the development of the Rep Test.

More recent sources also support the impression that Kelly's theory itself has not received much research attention. For instance, the personality chapters in the *Annual Review of Psychology* (published yearly, it consists of evaluations by experts of progress in both traditional and new areas of psychology), 1964 through 1972, cite Kelly in the author index of only three issues. *The Handbook of Personality Theory and Research* (edited by Borgatta and Lambert, 1968), a lengthy volume reflecting the current status of personality theory and research, does not mention any work by Kelly or his followers. Accordingly, it appears that there has been no systematic attempt to test the validity of Kelly's major theoretical concepts. Since the vast majority of the existent Kelly-related research employs the Rep Test, let's briefly examine its rather interesting nature before considering any investigations prompted by Kelly's theory.

Role Construct Repertory Test: Assessing Personal Constructs

Kelly (1955) developed the *Role Construct Repertory Test* to identify the important constructs a person uses to construe significant people in his life. More particularly, the Rep Test was originally devised as a diagnostic instrument to assist the therapist in understanding a client's construct system and the way the client uses it to structure his or her personal and material environment. Unfortunately, the format of the Rep Test does not readily lend itself to traditional psychometric assessment; no data for its reliability, validity, or standardization are in a form that enables a potential user to apply the test routinely. But then, there was very little that was ever really traditional about Kelly. Thus, although the Rep Test was developed out of Kelly's theory,

Table 7-1 Role Title List Definitions for the Grid Form of the Rep Test

	Role titles	Definitions
1	*Self*	Yourself
2	*Mother*	Your mother or the person who has played the part of a mother in your life
3	*Father*	Your father or the person who has played the part of a father in your life
4	*Brother*	Your brother who is nearest your own age, or if you have no brother, a boy near your own age who was most like a brother to you during your early teens
5	*Sister*	Your sister who is nearest your own age or, if you have no sister, a girl near your own age who was most like a sister to you during your early teens
6	*Spouse*	Your wife (or husband) or, if you are not married, your closest present friend of the opposite sex
7	*Accepted teacher*	The teacher who influenced you most when you were in your teens
8	*Rejected teacher*	The teacher whose point of view you found most objectionable when you were in your teens
9	*Boss*	An employer, supervisor, or officer under whom you worked during a period of great stress
10	*Doctor*	Your physician
11	*Pitied person*	The person whom you would most like to help or for whom you feel most sorry
12	*Rejecting person*	A person with whom you have been associated, who, for some unexplained reason, appeared to dislike you
13	*Happy person*	The happiest person whom you know personally
14	*Ethical person*	The person who appears to meet the highest ethical standards whom you know personally
15	*Intelligent person*	The most intelligent person whom you know personally

Source: Adapted from Kelly, 1955, p. 227.

studies pertaining to its clinical and research applications are not indicative of the underlying validity of the theory itself.

Many forms of the Rep Test, individual and group, exist, but one procedure is basic to all of them. The subject is presented a *Role Title List* which contains twenty to thirty different role definitions of persons assumed to be of personal importance to him. For each role, the subject is asked to write the name of a person he knows personally who best fits the role description. Some of the roles that typically appear on a role title list are shown in Table 7-1.

The names assigned to these designated roles are called *figures*. After the role title list has been completed, the examiner presents the subject with the names of three figures whom he mentioned as filling these roles, asking him to state which two are alike in some important way but different from the third.

For example, the subject might be asked to compare and contrast the persons he has named for sister, brother, and mother. In considering the triad, he might decide that brother and sister are similar in that they are "calm" but different from mother, who is "hyperactive." Thus, the construct dimension elicited from this "sort" is that of "calm versus hyperactive." This procedure is repeated with several other triads (usually twenty to thirty), the purpose being to determine how the subject categorizes and differentiates these persons. All the roles are used approximately equally in triads, so that the sampling of the subject's construction system is not biased. Based on the verbal content of the elicited constructs, the psychologist can then formulate hypotheses about the way the subject perceives and copes with significant persons in his life. This form of the Rep Test is called the *Listform* and is administered individually.

Kelly also devised a *Grid Form* of the Rep Test (illustrated in Figure 7-2). The procedure for administering this form of the test consists of presenting the subject with a specially prepared grid or matrix in which the significant figures in his life are listed on one axis and the various sorts he is required to make are listed on the other axis. The subject inserts persons' names who fit each role in

Self	Mother	Father	Brother	Sister	Spouse	Accepted teacher	Rejected teacher	Boss	Doctor	Pitied person	Rejecting person	Happy person	Ethical person	Intelligent person	Sort No.	Construct pole	Contrast pole
1	2	3	4	5	6	7	8	9	10	11	12	13	14	15			
							✓	⊗	⊗		○			✓	1	Authorities	Nonauthority
○	○	○													2		
	○						○				○				3		
			○								○		○		4		
				○				○				○			5		
○					○	○									6		
	○	○								○					7		
○		○	○												8		
												○	○	○	9		
					○		○					○			10		
						○				○			○		11		
											○	○	○		12		
	○		○										○		13		
					○		○	○							14		
○		○								○					15		

Figure 7-2 Illustration of Grid Form of the Rep Test. *(Adapted from Kelly, 1955, p. 270.)*

the space on the form corresponding to those illustrated at the top of Figure 7-2 (i.e., after reading the brief role definition of each). He is then instructed to enter the first row of the matrix to the columns where three people designated by circles are located. These circles designate the three figures whom the subject is to consider in the first sort.

In Figure 7-2, for instance, row 1 of the matrix contains circles in the squares under columns 9, 10, and 12 (i.e., "Boss," "Doctor," and "Rejecting Person"). The subject is instructed to decide how two of them are alike in some important respect that differentiates them from the third. Once he has decided how two of the figures are alike but different from the third, he inserts an "X" in the two circles which correspond to the two persons who are similar. The third circle is left blank. Next, the subject writes a word or brief phrase that indicates how these two figures are alike in the column marked "Construct pole." In the column marked "Contrast pole" he writes a word or brief phrase that tells how the third figure is different from the other two. As depicted in Figure 7-2, Boss and Doctor are seen as alike in terms of being "authorities" whereas Rejecting person is seen as being a "nonauthority." Finally, the subject examines the remaining figures in the first row (those not considered in the sort which elicited the construct dimension) and puts a check mark in the square of each if the construct pole characteristic can be used to construe that figure. This procedure is continued until the subject has completed each of the remaining rows. Each succeeding presentation of a triad generates a construct dimension. The end result is a grid with the figures at the top, the various constructs in the right-hand columns, and a pattern of voids and check marks inside the rectangle. The reader may find it an intellectually interesting and self-revealing exercise to complete Figure 7-2 with his or her own constructs.

How to Construe Rep Test Results   The end product of the Rep Test, regardless of the way in which it is administered, is a sample of the individual's personal construct system and of the way it is used. Results of the Listform are generally subjected to a clinical analysis in which the examiner considers *(a)* the number and variety of constructs elicited, *(b)* the substance and tone of the constructs, *(c)* the way in which various figures are related to the constructs and to one another, and *(d)* additional characteristics of the subject's constructs such as their permeability, looseness or tightness, and communicability. This is fundamentally a subjective interpretation of Rep Test results allowing the examiner to become acquainted with the ways the subject construes others in his life and how he anticipates the future. Kelly (1961) devised a mathematical scheme (nonparametric factor analysis) for analyzing the Grid Form so that it is less susceptible to interpretative error or bias. In brief, this type of statistical analysis reduces the grid to a few basic construct dimensions which capture most succinctly the dominant world views of the subject.

Schizophrenic Thought Disorder: A "Destructive" Alternative

One illustrative use of the Rep Test is found in studies of schizophrenic thought disorders. Clinical descriptions of schizophrenia generally stress that it is marked by language and thought disturbances. Confusion and vagueness of ideas, use of new words with idiosyncratic meanings *(neologisms)*, and unusual shifts in the direction of thought are quite commonly observed. In construct theory terms, schizophrenics are employing an overly loose and inconsistent construct system for construing their experiences. Their ideas about people are both poorly integrated and unstable in that they suffer from a relative lack of structure and consistency. Since the Rep Test provides a method of assessing degree of cognitive structure and organization in construing other people, it offers a promising approach for understanding the nature of the disordered thinking characteristic of schizophrenia.

Bannister and Fransella (1966) hypothesized that schizophrenics use overloose and highly inconsistent constructs. Additionally, they sought to establish a clinically economic and adequately standardized grid test for detecting the presence of schizophrenic thought disorder. The subjects for this study consisted of six different groups: *(a)* thought-disordered schizophrenics, *(b)* non-thought-disordered schizophrenics, *(c)* normals, *(d)* neurotics, *(e)* organics (i.e., organic brain damage), and *(f)* depressives. Each subject was individually presented with an array of eight passport-type photographs of strangers and instructed to rank-order them on six constructs that normal people usually consider highly interrelated. Specifically, subjects were asked to rank all eight photographs from the *most kind* to the *least kind.* This procedure was then repeated with the same photos using the constructs *stupid, selfish, sincere, mean,* and *honest.* Immediately after the subjects completed the test, they were asked to retake it, using the same photographs and rank-ordering them for the same constructs. They were also told that this was not to test their memory but that they should undertake the second test as if they were doing it for the first time.

Bannister and Fransella computed two statistical measures from each subject's test protocol—one for *intensity* and one for *consistency.* The intensity score reveals how closely the subject ranked the photos on one construct relative to his rankings on the other constructs. A high intensity score indicates that the subject has rank-ordered as if the constructs he has judged are related, whereas a low intensity score indicates that he has treated them as relatively independent characteristics. The consistency score reflects the degree to which the subject has maintained the pattern of relationships between his constructs from Grid Test I to Grid Test II. In effect, it is a test-retest correlation indicating the degree to which the subject on retest uses the constructs in the same way as he did on the original test.

It was predicted that thought-disordered schizophrenics would have lower intensity and consistency scores than subjects in the other groups. The results provided substantial support for these predictions. Table 7-2 presents the means and standard deviations for intensity and consistency for the six groups. This table reveals that the constructs of the thought-disordered schizophrenics were considerably less highly interrelated (i.e., lower intensity) than were those of the other groups, and that their immediate test-retest reliability (i.e., consistency) was also significantly lower.

A second experiment conducted by Bannister and Salmon (1966) examined the question of whether schizophrenics are disordered across their entire construct system (i.e., are equally perplexed by every aspect of the world in which they live) or whether they are disordered in a more focal sense (i.e., are perplexed by some things more than others). This question was investigated by administering two grid forms of the Rep Test to thought-disordered schizophrenics and normal controls. The first, a "people" form, used passport-type photographs of strangers and, as in the preceding study, subjects ranked the photos on each of six psychological constructs. The second form of the test, an "object" form, required subjects to rank a set of fifteen objects (e.g., English bowler hat, loaf of bread) on six constructs (e.g., curved-straight, heavy-light). Subjects completed both forms of the test in the same experimental session so that both the degree of structure and stability of the pattern of construct interrelationships across elements could be assessed.

Bannister and Salmon reported that while schizophrenics did not differ from normal controls in their construing of objects, they were vastly less stable and consistent in their construing of people. This finding suggests that schizophrenic thought disorder may not be diffuse but, rather, may be particularly related to interpersonal constructs. That is, it is interpersonal construing that has been damaged in thought disorder. Contemplating results such as those considered in these two experiments, Bannister (1963) proposed a theory of schizophrenic thought disorder based on a *serial invalidation* hypothesis. In brief, this theory suggests that thought disorder is the outcome

---

Table 7-2 Means and Standard Deviations of Intensity and Consistency Scores for Six Groups of Subjects

	Thought-disordered schizophrenics	Normals	Nonthought-disordered schizophrenics	Depressives	Neurotics	Organics
Intensity X	728	1,253	1,183	1,115	1,383	933
Standard deviation	369	339	390	456	517	524
Consistency X	0.18	0.80	0.73	0.75	0.74	0.73
Standard deviation	0.39	0.34	0.34	0.41	0.45	0.47

Source: Adapted from Bannister and Fransella, 1966, p. 98.

of being consistently wrong in one's predictions so that a gross loosening of one's construct system is the ultimate form of psychological adjustment. This type of research is just one example of the heuristic value of Kelly's theory.

APPLICATION: EMOTIONAL STATES, PSYCHOLOGICAL DISORDERS, AND FIXED-ROLE THERAPY

Kelly's personal construct theory represents a cognitive view of behavior; the human being is depicted as a scientist, that is, as someone who is continously engaged in predicting and controlling the events that occur in his or her environment. Yet this personological system emerged, in the main, from *clinical psychology,* a professional discipline devoted to the understanding and treatment of psychological disturbances. Kelly's ultimate goal was to create a more scientific approach to the difficult work of clinical psychology. In fact, Volume 2 of *The Psychology of Personal Constructs* (1955) is subtitled "Clinical Diagnosis and Psychotherapy," while an entire chapter in Volume 1 describes Kelly's own particular psychotherapeutic approach, fixed-role therapy. How, then, does a fundamentally *cognitive, intellectually* oriented theory of personality apply to the everyday realities encountered by a clinical psychologist— emotional states, psychological disorders, and psychotherapy?

Emotional States   Kelly retained but redefined several traditional psychological concepts of emotion in terms relevant to cognitive theory. For example, he defined *anxiety* as the awareness "that the events with which one is confronted lie outside the range of convenience of one's construct system (1955, p. 495)." Thus, the vague feeling of apprehension and helplessness commonly labeled as anxiety is, for Kelly, a result of being aware that one's available constructs are not applicable to anticipating the events he encounters. Kelly emphasized that it is not the fact that one's construct system is not functioning that is anxiety-provoking; one is not anxious merely because his anticipations are inaccurate. Anxiety is created (experienced) only when one realizes that one has no constructs by which to interpret an event. Kelly often facetiously referred to this state as being "caught with his constructs down." Under such circumstances the individual cannot predict; hence, he cannot fully comprehend what is happening or solve his problems.

This view of anxiety is far different from the Freudian conception of the neurotically anxious individual as a victim of unconscious conflicts and dammed-up instinctual energy. Rather than being threatened by the breakthrough of sexual and aggressive impulses into consciousness, the anxious person is really overwhelmed by events which he can neither understand nor anticipate. Viewed in this latter manner, psychotherapy assists a client in acquiring new constructs which will more accurately enable him to predict the troublesome events or make his existing constructs more permeable so they admit new experiences to their range of convenience.

Guilt, another emotional state often alluded to in personality theories, is defined by Kelly as the perception of apparent dislodgment of the self from one's core role structure. The guilty person is aware of having deviated from the important roles (self-images) by which he maintains his relationships to others. For example, the college student who construes himself as a scholar will feel guilty if he spends too much time at the local beer house with his roommates, thus violating the most basic aspect of his role as a scholar, namely studying. Presumably a student who construes himself as a playboy would not experience such guilt.

Still another familiar emotional experience, *threat,* is viewed by Kelly as the awareness that one's construct system is about to be drastically altered by what has been discovered. One feels threatened when a major shakeup in his personal constructs is imminent. Threat does psychological violence to the person. The thought of one's own death is perhaps the most formidable type of threat, unless the person construes it as basic to his life's meaning.

Hostility, a final illustration of emotional states, is defined as the "continued effort to extort validational evidence in favor of a type of social prediction which has already proved itself a failure (Kelly, 1955, p. 510)." Traditionally considered as a disposition to behave vindictively toward or inflict harm upon others, hostility in Kelly's system is merely an attempt to hold onto an invalid construct in the face of contradictory (invalidating) evidence. The hostile person, rather than resign himself to the fact that his expectations about other people are unrealistic and therefore in need of revision, tries to make others behave in ways which fit his expectations. Consider, for example, the reaction of a father who discovers that his college-aged daughter is living the life of a "sexually liberated" woman. No matter how compelling the contrary evidence is, the angry father persists in his belief that she is his "little baby girl." Changing one's constructs is difficult, threatening, and sometimes even impossible. How much better it would be if one could change the world, rather than his way of viewing it, so that it would conform to his preconceptions. Hostility represents just such an attempt.

Psychological Disorders   Kelly also took a unique stance in relation to psychological disorders, reconstruing them in terms of cognitive theory. For him, a psychological disorder is "any personal construction which is used repeatedly in spite of consistent invalidation (1955, p. 831)." Psychological disturbances thus represent the apparent failure of a person's construct system to achieve its purpose. Or, more to the point, psychological disorders involve anxiety and the individual's repeated efforts to regain the sense of being able to predict events. Caught up in his lack of capacity to predict, the disturbed individual searches about frantically for new ways of construing the events of his world. Or he may swing in the opposite direction and rigidly adhere to the same predictions, thereby keeping his personal construct system intact in the face of repeated failures. In either case, the maladjusted person cannot anticipate events with much accuracy and hence fails to learn or cope adequately with the world.

Kelly interpreted psychological disturbances in accordance with his own unique set of diagnostic constructs.

Dilation serves as a good example of one such construct in terms of which psychological disorders can be viewed. In Kelly's theory of psychopathology, dilation occurs when the person has no superordinate constructs to organize his perceptual field. Having abandoned or lost governing constructs, the individual then attempts to broaden (dilate) his constructs and to reorganize them at a more bizarre and comprehensive level of plausibility. What happens then? Kelly suggested that the disorders traditionally labeled as *mania, depression,* and *paranoia* result. Traditionally, *mania* has been understood as a psychotic state in which the patient's thinking is overinclusive (i.e., inability to preserve conceptual boundaries so that thought becomes less accurate, more vague, and overly general) while his affect often appears euphoric. Manic patients are forever frantically beginning a variety of projects and activities that they will never finish, all the while talking feverishly about their plans in grandiose terms. They jump from topic to topic and make sweeping generalizations with few substantive ideas. In Kelly's view, the manic person's exploration has simply outrun his conceptual organization. He is left with "loose construc- tions" of reality, and his excitement represents a kind of frenzied attempt to cope with his rapidly dilating perceptual field.

Another psychopathological response to anxiety is *depression.* Depression tends to occur in people who have *constricted* their perceptual field (i.e., who have narrowed their interests to a smaller and smaller area). The depressed patient has profound difficulty in making even the simplest everyday decisions. Overwhelmed by the immensity of his problems, the depressed person often contemplates suicide—the ultimate act of constriction. Depression, then, represents a psychological disorder in which people attempt to construe their experiences from the opposite side of the dilation construct—constric- tion.

Dilation is also focal in the case of the paranoid patient. As classically conceived, *paranoia* is a serious disorder involving only one cardinal symp- tom—an extremely well-systematized delusion, usually of persecution. The paranoid earnestly but erroneously believes that others are intentionally "out to get him," a feeling often accompanied by a delusion of grandeur, the false belief that one is a special or divine person. Why else would so many people be actively plotting against him? Considering that there are alternative ways of construing reality, paranoia is simply one of the less fortunate and predictively efficient alternatives. The paranoid has a well-developed persecution construct; as he elaborates upon it, he is led farther and farther afield. Armed with such a comprehensive persecution construct, the paranoid simply proceeds to dilate his whole perceptual field, gradually construing most people and events in persecution terms.

Other diagnostic constructs and descriptions of related disorders may be found in Volume 2 of Kelly's 1955 major work.

Connie

Fixed-Role Therapy   While many of the therapeutic methods described by Kelly (1955) are compatible with those used in other clinical schemes (including psychoanalysis), there are two distinguishing features of his own approach: first, his conception of what the goal of psychotherapy should be and, second, the development and practice of fixed-role therapy.

Kelly discussed the nature and task of therapeutic change in terms of the development of better construct systems. Since disorders involve using constructs in the face of consistent invalidation, psychotherapy is directed toward the psychological reconstruction of the client's construct system so that it is more workable. But more than this, it is an exciting process of scientific experimentation. The therapy room is a laboratory in which the therapist encourages the client to develop and test new hypotheses, both within and outside the clinical situation. The therapist is highly active—constantly prodding, pushing, and stimulating the client to try new constructs on for size. If they fit, the client can use them in the future; if not, further hypotheses are generated and tested. Science is thus the model for clients to use in construing their lives. Along with this, it is the therapist's task to make validating data (information feedback) available, against which the client can check his own hypotheses. By providing this data in the form of responses to a wide variety of the client's constructions, the clinician actually gives the client an opportunity to validate his constructs, an opportunity which is not normally available to him (Kelly, 1955).

Kelly went beyond this unique interpretation of psychotherapy to develop his own specific brand, *fixed-role therapy.* Fixed-role therapy maintains that, psychologically, human beings are not only what they construe themselves to be but also what they do. In general terms, the therapist sees his role as one of encouraging and helping the client to perceive and construe himself in new ways, to act accordingly, thereby becoming a new, more effective person.

How does fixed-role therapy actually work? It begins by having the client write a sketch of himself in the third person. The sketch has no detailed outline, the client being given only the following instructions. Note how the instructions elicit objectivity, minimize threat, and allow the client freedom of expression.

> I want you to write a character sketch of Harry Brown, just as if he were the principal character in a play. Write it as it might be written by a friend who knows him very *intimately* and very sympathetically, perhaps better than anyone even really could know him. Be sure to write it in the third person. For example, start out by saying, Harry Brown is . . . (Kelly, 1955, p. 323).

Careful study of Harry Brown's self-characterization will uncover many of the constructs he habitually uses in construing himself and his relationships to significant others. What is then needed is a tailor-made means of helping Harry to revise his personal construct system. The vehicle for accomplishing this objective is called the *fixed-role sketch.* Based on the self-characterization, it is essentially a personality role description of a fictional individual, preferably compiled by a group of experienced clinicians. The fictional person is given a name other than the client's, and he is furnished with a construct system that is judged therapeutically beneficial for Harry to act out. The sketch is not designed to "remake" Harry but, rather, to invite him to explore, experiment, and—more to the point—*reconstrue* himself and his life situation. In short, the fixed-role sketch is designed to stimulate the client into reconstruing his experiences so that he will become better able to deal with them constructively.

In the next phase of fixed-role therapy, the therapist presents the fixed-role sketch to the client, making an *acceptance check* to determine if the client understands and accepts it as representing a person he would like to be (Patterson, 1966). The client is then directed to *act as if he were that person* for the next two weeks. He reads the sketch at least three times a day and tries to think, act, talk, and *be* like the fictional character portrayed in the sketch. If, for instance, the character is Archie Bunker, then the client is told the following: "For a few weeks you are to try to forget who you are or who you ever were. You *are* Archie Bunker. You behave like him. You think and feel like him. You do the things you think he would do. You even have his interests and you enjoy the things he would enjoy." While we will refrain from speculating as to precisely who could possibly benefit therapeutically by aspiring to Archie Bunker's construct system, the point here is simply that the client is asked to temporarily suspend being himself so that he can discover new aspects of himself. During this period, the therapist and client meet often to discuss the latter's problems in enacting the role sketch. There may also be some rehearsing of the sketch during therapy sessions so that both the therapist and client together are able to examine the new construct system firsthand. Through techniques such as role playing, the client is encouraged to apply the sketch character's constructs in his social relationships, work situation, family pattern, and other important life areas. Throughout this period, the therapist treats the client as if he were actually the character in the sketch.

To what end? As is the case with most forms of psychotherapy, the results are mixed. While some clients respond favorably to Kelly's unorthodox approach, others do not. Ideally, the Kellian client is provided with a golden opportunity to begin to reconstrue herself and her life under expert therapeutic guidance. She can explore constructive alternatives, retaining useful constructs and rejecting unworkable ones. Rather than dredge up her past history, she need only learn to reconstrue the present (including herself) so that she can better anticipate the future. Kelly remained optimistic that a more functional construct system would emerge from this entire therapeutic process.

Clearly, then, the psychology of personal constructs is applicable to realms of human experience far removed from that traditionally considered as cognitive. For instance, emotional states, psychological disorders, and psychotherapy can all be construed from Kelly's novel perspective. And who knows what else? If George Kelly's purpose in developing his theory was, as he sometimes noted, to stimulate, excite, and open people's minds to the incredible array of life's possibilities, he has indeed succeeded amply.

SUMMARY

George Kelly's cognitive theory is based on the philosophical position of constructive alternativism, which holds that reality is what one construes as reality. Accordingly, an individual's perception of reality is always subject to interpretation and modification. Man is a "scientist," constantly generating and testing hypotheses about the nature of things so that adequate predictions of future events can be made.

Persons comprehend their worlds through transparent patterns or templets called constructs. Each individual has a unique construct system (personality) which he or she uses to construe or interpret experience. Kelly theorized that all constructs possess certain formal properties: range of convenience, focus of convenience, and permeability-impermeability. Kelly also recognized various types of constructs: preemptive, constellatory, propositional, comprehensive, incidental, core, peripheral, tight, and loose.

Kelly's theory is formally stated in terms of one fundamental postulate and eleven elaborative corollaries. The former stipulates that a person's processes are psychologically channelized by the ways in which he or she anticipates events, while the corollaries explain how a construct system functions, changes, and influences social interaction.

Kelly was much more explicit and cognizant of the philosophical underpinnings of personality theory than most personologists. Nonetheless, his position still is founded upon his basic assumptions concerning human nature. Cognitive theory reflects (1) a strong commitment to the assumptions of rationality, subjectivity, and unknowability; (2) a moderate commitment to the assumptions of holism and environmentalism; and (3) a "middle of the road" position on the freedom-determinism dimension. The proactivity-reactivity and homeostasis-heterostasis assumptions do not apply to Kelly's position since he regarded motivation as a redundant construct.

Although Kelly's theoretical concepts have directly stimulated little research to date, he devised a personality instrument, the Rep Test, which has been widely employed in a variety of studies. The Rep Test assesses personal constructs; in this chapter, its use is illustrated in two investigations of schizophrenic thought disorder.

Kelly's personal construct theory is applicable to behavioral domains far beyond that traditionally defined as cognitive. In the concluding chapter section, Kelly's theory was applied to the everyday concerns of the clinical psychologist—emotional states, psychological disorders, and psychotherapy.

BIBLIOGRAPHY

Bannister, D. The genesis of schizophrenic thought disorder: A serial invalidation hypothesis. *British Journal of Psychiatry,* 1963, **109,** 680–686.

Bannister, D. (Ed.). *Perspectives in personal construct theory.* New York: Academic Press, 1970.

Bannister, D., & Fransella, F. A grid test of schizophrenic thought disorder. *British Journal of Social and Clinical Psychology,* 1966, **5,** 95–102.

Bannister, D., & Fransella, F. *Inquiring man: The theory of personal constructs.* Baltimore: Penguin Books, 1971.

Bannister, D., & Salmon, P. Schizophrenic thought disorder: Specific or diffuse? *British Journal of Medical Psychology,* 1966, **39,** 215–219.

Bonarius, J. Research in the personal construct theory of George A. Kelly: Role construct repertory test and basic theory. In B. Maher (Ed.), *Progress in experimental personality research.* New York: Academic Press, 1965, pp. 1–46.

Borgatta, E., & Lambert, W. (Eds.). *Handbook of personality theory and research.* Chicago: Rand McNally, 1968.

Kelly, G. *The psychology of personal constructs,* Vols. 1 and 2. New York: Norton, 1955.

Kelly, G. Man's construction of his alternatives. In G. Lindzey (Ed.), *Assessment of human motives.* New York: Rinehart and Winston, 1958, pp. 33–64.

Kelly, G. *A nonparametric method of factor analysis for dealing with theoretical issues.* Unpublished manuscript. Mimeograph, Ohio State University, 1961.

Kelly, G. A brief introduction to personal construct theory. In D. Bannister (Ed.), *Perspectives in personal construct theory.* New York: Academic Press, 1970, pp. 1–29.

Maher, B. (Ed.). *Clinical psychology and personality: The selected papers of George Kelly.* New York: Wiley, 1969.

Patterson, C. *Theories of counseling and psychotherapy.* New York: Harper and Row, 1966.

Sechrest, L. The psychology of personal constructs: George Kelly. In J. Wepman & R. Heine (Eds.), *Concepts of personality.* Chicago: Aldine, 1963, pp. 206–233.

SUGGESTED READINGS

1 Bannister, D. A new theory of personality. In B. Foss (Ed.), *New horizons in psychology.* Baltimore: Penguin Books, 1966.

2 Kelly, G. Europe's matrix of decision. In M. Jones (Ed.), *Nebraska symposium on motivation,* 1962, pp. 83–125.

3 Kelly, G. *A theory of personality.* New York: Norton, 1963.

4 Kelly, G. Personal construct theory as a line of inference. *Journal of Psychology,* 1964, **1,** 80–93.

5 Kelly, G. The language of hypotheses: Man's psychological instrument. *Journal of Individual Psychology,* 1964, **20,** 137–152.

6 Kelly, G. A threat of aggression. *Journal of Humanistic Psychology,* 1965, **5,** 195–201.

Abraham H. Maslow

Abraham Maslow:
A Humanistic
Theory of
Personality

Three distinct psychological revolutions which dominate psychology today have occurred in the twentieth century. The first, that of *psychoanalysis,* presents an image of man as a creature of instinct and conflict. This bleak conception of human nature emerged from Freud's study of mentally disturbed individuals and, at least until recently, emphasized unconscious and irrational forces as the controlling factors in behavior. *Behaviorism,* the second revolution, characterizes man as a flexible, malleable, and passive victim of external stimuli—the permanent pawn of environmental fate. As epitomized by B. F. Skinner, behaviorism emphasizes the essential similarity of men and animals, stressing learning as the major explanation for human behavior. More recently, a third revolution has swept psychology. This new brand, the *humanistic or third force* movement, has given rise to a radically different image of human nature. It is generally acknowledged that Abraham Maslow is the spiritual father of humanism in American psychology. His self-actualization theory of personality, based on the study of healthy and creative individuals, clearly illustrates the humanistic perspective, namely that:

Human life will never be understood unless its highest aspirations are taken into account. Growth, self-actualization, the striving toward health, the quest for identity and autonomy, the yearning for excellence (and other ways of phrasing the striving "upward") must now be accepted beyond question as a widespread and perhaps universal tendency (Maslow, 1970, pp. xii–xiii).

BIOGRAPHICAL SKETCH

Abraham Harold Maslow was born April 1, 1908, in New York City. His parents were uneducated Jewish immigrants from Russia who dreamed of something better for their son than what their own lives had been. Maslow was strongly encouraged by his parents to be academically successful, yet by his own admission he experienced considerable loneliness and suffering during most of his childhood and early adolescence:

> With my childhood, it's a wonder I'm not psychotic. I was a little Jewish boy in the non-Jewish neighborhood. It was a little like being the first Negro enrolled in the all-white school. I was isolated and unhappy. I grew up in libraries and among books, without friends (Maslow, 1968, p. 37).

One might speculate that Maslow's desire to help people live more enriching lives had its origins in his desire to live better himself. Not only did he spend numerous hours in cloistered study, he also experienced the practical side of life working many summers for his family's barrel manufacturing company, which his brothers still operate today.

Maslow began his college education by trying to specialize in law because of pressure from his father. Two weeks of study convinced him that he couldn't become a lawyer, and with his father's reluctant approval, he undertook a more eclectic course of study at Cornell University. His junior year Maslow transferred to the University of Wisconsin, where he subsequently received all his formal academic training in psychology, obtaining his B.A. degree in 1930, his M.A. in 1931, and his Ph.D. in 1934. While still an undergraduate, Maslow married Bertha Goodman, his high school sweetheart. Getting married was an extremely important event in Maslow's life. "Life didn't really start for me," he reported, "until I got married and went to Wisconsin (1968, p. 37)."

Maslow's decision to study psychology at Wisconsin was largely affected by the behaviorism of John Watson. Maslow explains:

> I had discovered J. B. Watson and I was sold on behaviorism. It was an explosion of excitement for me. . . . Bertha came to pick me up and I was dancing down Fifth Avenue with exuberance; I embarrassed her, but I was so excited about Watson's program. It was beautiful. I was confident that here was a real road to travel, solving one puzzle after another and changing the world. . . . I was off to Wisconsin to change the world. But off to Wisconsin because of a lying catalog. I went there to study with Koffka, the psychologist; Dreisch, the biologist; and

Meiklejohn, the philosopher. When I showed up on campus, they weren't there. They had just been visiting professors, but the school put them in the catalog anyway (1968, p. 37).

Despite the intense disappointment and disillusionment he must have felt, Maslow completed his doctoral work under the guidance of Harry Harlow. Incredible as it may seem today, his Ph.D. dissertation was an observational study of sexual and dominance characteristics of *monkeys!* Actually, this study marked the beginning of Maslow's abiding interest in sexuality and affection, which later shifted to humans. Maslow always considered sex research, especially the study of homosexuality, as essential to a profound understanding of humanity.

After serving on the Wisconsin faculty as Assistant Instructor in Psychology (1930–1934) and Teaching Fellow in Psychology (1934–1935), Maslow became a Carnegie Fellow at Columbia University, remaining there from 1935 through 1937. He next served as Associate Professor at Brooklyn College until 1951. Maslow described New York City during this period, particularly the late 1930s and early 1940s, as the center of the psychological universe. It was here that he personally encountered the very cream of European intellectuals who were forced to flee from the clutches of Hitler. Erich Fromm, Alfred Adler, Karen Horney, Ruth Benedict, and Max Wertheimer were just a few of those whom Maslow sought out to enhance his understanding of human behavior. The informal conversations and challenging experiences afforded by such distinguished scholars played an enormous role in shaping the intellectual foundations for Maslow's later humanistic views. He was also psychoanalyzed during this time.

Maslow's enthusiasm for behaviorism literally vanished when his first of two daughters was born. "Our first baby changed me as a psychologist. It made the behaviorism I had been so enthusiastic about look so foolish I could not stomach it anymore. . . . I'd say that anyone who had a baby couldn't be a behaviorist (Maslow, 1968, p. 55)." Evidently, the complex behavior displayed by Maslow's own children convinced him that behavioristic psychology was more relevant to understanding rodents than humans.

World War II markedly changed the direction of Maslow's professional life. For him the war epitomized the prejudice, hatred, and baseness of mankind. The experience of witnessing a parade shortly after Pearl Harbor was the turning point in Maslow's career.

As I watched, the tears began to run down my face. I felt we didn't understand— not Hitler, nor the Germans, nor Stalin, nor the communists. We didn't understand any of them. I felt that if we could understand, then we could make progress. I had a vision of a peace table, with people sitting around it, talking about human nature and hatred and war and peace and brotherhood. . . . That moment changed my whole life and determined what I have done since. Since that moment in 1941 I've devoted myself to developing a theory of human nature that could be tested by experiment and research (Maslow, 1968, p. 54).

In 1951 Maslow was appointed chairman of the Psychology Department at Brandeis University and held that position until 1961, after which he continued as professor of psychology. During this period Maslow became the foremost spokesman of the humanistic movement in American psychology. In the spring of 1969 he took a leave of absence from Brandeis to become the first resident fellow of the W. P. Laughlin Charitable Foundation, Menlo Park, California. This nonacademic post allowed him complete freedom to pursue his interests in the philosophy of democratic politics and ethics. But on June 8, 1970, at the age of sixty-two, Maslow died of a heart attack, after a chronic history of heart disease.

Maslow was affiliated with a number of professional and honorary societies. He served on the council of the Society for the Psychological Study of Social Issues and was president of the Massachusetts State Psychological Association. As a member of the American Psychological Association he was president of the Division of Personality and Social Psychology, president of the Division of Esthetics, and was elected president of the entire association for 1967–1968. Maslow was also a founding editor of both the *Journal of Humanistic Psychology* and the *Journal of Transpersonal Psychology*, and he served as consulting editor of numerous other scholarly periodicals.

The majority of Maslow's books were written within the last ten years of his life and include *Toward a Psychology of Being* (1962); *Religions, Values, and Peak-Experiences* (1964); *Eupsychian Management: A Journal* (1965); *The Psychology of Science: A Reconnaissance* (1966); *Motivation and Personality* (1970, 2d edition); and *The Farther Reaches of Human Nature* (1971, a collection of articles previously published by Maslow in various psychological journals). A volume compiled with the assistance of his wife and entitled *Abraham H. Maslow: A Memorial Volume* was published posthumously in 1972.

Donna

BASIC TENETS OF HUMANISTIC PSYCHOLOGY

The term "humanistic psychology" was coined by a group of psychologists who in the early 1960s joined under the leadership of Abraham Maslow to establish a viable theoretical alternative to the two most influential intellectual currents in psychology—psychoanalysis and behaviorism. Unlike the others, humanistic psychology is not a single organized theory or system but might better be characterized as a movement (i.e., a collection or convergence of a number of lines and schools of thought). Maslow called it *third force psychology*. Although proponents of this movement represent a wide range of views, they do share certain fundamental conceptions of human nature. Practically all these shared concepts have deep roots in the history of Western philosophical thinking. More specifically, humanistic psychology is heavily steeped in European existential philosophy and psychology as developed by such thinkers and writers as Kierkegaard, Sartre, Camus, Binswanger, and Boss.

Existential philosophy is concerned with man as an individual and the unique problems of his existence. Man is literally one who exists as being-in-the-world, consciously and painfully aware of his own existence and eventual nonexistence (death). Rejecting the notion that the person is either a product of hereditary (genetic factors) or environmental influences (particularly early ones), existentialists believe that each person carves out his or her own destiny; one creatively fashions *essence* (what one is) from the fact of *existence* (that one is). Since there are no cause-effect relationships in human behavior, the individual has complete freedom of choice, and each person alone is responsible for his or her own existence. In a profound sense, then, "life is what you make it."

Human beings, determining what they will or will not do, are free to be whatever they want to be. This does not mean that given freedom of choice, one will necessarily act in one's own best interest. The individual's freedom to choose does not ensure that all the choices that are made will be wise ones. If this were so, then people would not be afflicted with misery, alienation, anxiety, boredom, guilt, and a host of other ailments. For the existentialists, it is a question of whether or not one can live an authentic (honest and genuine) life. Because existential philosophy believes each person is responsible for his or her own actions, it appeals to humanistic psychology. Humanistic theorists also stress that each individual is the chief determinant of his or her own behavior and experience. The human being is a conscious agent—experiencing, deciding and freely choosing his or her actions. Humanistic psychology, then, takes as its basic model the responsible human being freely making choices among the possibilities that are open.

Perhaps the most important concept which humanistic psychologists have extracted from existentialism is that of *becoming*. A person is never static; he or she is always in the process of becoming something different. A college student is decidely different from the record-swapping, giggling teenager of four years ago. And four years from now he or she may be radically different as a contributing member of society. Accordingly, it is the individual's responsibility as a free agent to realize as many of his or her human potentialities as possible. For only by actualizing these can one live a truly authentic life. Thus, in the existential-humanistic view, the human being is one whose quest for an authentic existence requires more than the fulfillment of biological needs and of sexual and aggressive instincts. Conversely, people who refuse to become have refused to grow; they have denied themselves the full possibilities of human existence. Humanistically speaking, this is a tragedy and a distortion of what the human being can be, since Maslow regarded this process of becoming, or self-actualization, as inherent to human nature.

What about the future

Finally, existentialism stresses human consciousness, subjective feelings and moods, and personal experiences as they relate to one's existence in the world of other people. This outlook may be designated in a shorthand way as the *phenomenological* or "here-and-now" perspective. Existentialists and humanists alike emphasize subjective experience as the primary phenomenon in the study of human nature. Both theoretical explanations and overt behavior are secondary to experience itself and its meaning to the experiencing person. In this vein, Maslow (1966) wrote: "The basic coin in the realm of knowing is direct, intimate, experiential knowing (p. 46)" and "There is no substitute for experience, none at all (p. 45)."

Scattered throughout his various theoretical writings Maslow set forth his brand of humanistic psychology. As will become increasingly evident, Maslow's personological theory sharply contradicts theories dominant for the past half century.

Sandy

1 The Individual as an Integrated Whole One of the most funda-
mental aspects of humanistic psychology—and Maslow's version of it—is that each individual must be studied as an integrated, unique, organized whole. Maslow felt that for too long psychologists had concentrated upon minute analyses of separate events, neglecting the basic aspects of the whole person and his human nature. In a commonplace metaphor, psychologists studied the trees, not the forest. In fact, Maslow's theory was primarily developed as a revolt against those theories (especially behaviorism) which deal in bits and pieces of behavior while ignoring the person as a unified whole.

Viewed in the context of Maslow's motivational theory, the individual is motivated as a *whole* rather than just in part:

> In good theory there is no such entity as a need of the stomach or mouth, or a genital need. There is only a need of the individual. It is John Smith who wants food, not John Smith's stomach. Furthermore, satisfaction comes to the whole individual and not just to a part of him. Food satisfies John Smith's hunger and not his stomach's hunger. . . . when John Smith is hungry, he is hungry all over (Maslow, 1970, pp. 19–20).

For Maslow, then, the central core of personality lies in its unity and totality.

2 Irrelevance of Animal Research Advocates of humanistic psychol-
ogy recognize a profound difference between human and animal behavior. In other words, human beings are more than just animals; they are special kinds of animals. This tenet is in sharp contrast to behaviorism, which relies heavily on infrahuman research. Unlike the behaviorists, who emphasize humanity's continuity with the animal world, Maslow regarded the human being as uniquely different from all other animals. He believed that behaviorism and its

accompanying philosophies have "dehumanized" the individual, leaving little more than a machine composed of chains of conditioned and unconditioned reflexes. Hence, animal research is irrelevant to the understanding of human behavior because it ignores those characteristics that are uniquely human, e.g., ideals, values, shame, humor, art, jealousy, and, very importantly, what it takes to produce poetry, music, science, and other works of the mind. Highly significant from a humanistic perspective, then, is the fact that there are no rat, pigeon, monkey, or even dolphin personologists represented in this text. There are none—only humans have the capacity to theorize about humans. *not so* *God has a bigger right*

3 Man's Inner Nature Freud's theory implicitly assumed that man basically has an evil character, that human impulses, if not controlled, will lead to the destruction of others as well as the self. Whether this view is accurate or not, Freud placed little faith in human virtue, pessimistically speculating on the course of human destiny. Those who endorse a humanistic view advocate quite another position: specifically, that human nature is essentially good, or at the very least, neutral. One might not be able to appreciate this view while being mugged in Central Park. However, from the humanistic perspective, evil, destructive, and violent forces in the behavior of muggers arise from a bad environment rather than from any inherent rottenness on their part. *Both natures are present—which will prevail*

4 Man's Creative Potential The primacy of human creativity is perhaps the most significant concept of humanistic psychology. Maslow (1950) merits the distinction of being the first to call attention to the fact that the most universal characteristic of all the people he studied or observed was their creativeness. Describing it as a fundamental characteristic common to human nature, Maslow (1970) viewed creativity as a potentiality present in all people at birth. It's natural—trees sprout leaves, birds fly, humans create. However, sad to say, Maslow also recognized that most human beings lose it as they become "enculturated" (formal education stamps out a lot of it). Happily, some few individuals hold onto this fresh, naïve, and direct way of looking at things or, if they number among the majority who lose it, they are able to recover it later in life. Maslow theorized that since creativity is potential in anyone, it requires no special talents or capacities. One need not write books, compose music, or produce art objects to be creative. Comparatively few people do. Creativity is a universal human function and leads to all forms of self-expression. Thus, for example, there can be creative homemakers, disc jockeys, shoe salesmen, stripteasers, and even college professors!

5 Emphasis on Psychological Health Maslow consistently argued that none of the available psychological approaches to the study of behavior does justice to the "healthy human being's functioning," "modes of living" or his "life's goals." In particular, he strongly criticized Freud's preoccupation with the study of neurotic and psychotic individuals. Quite simply, Maslow considered Freudian theory as a one-sided psychology lacking in comprehensiveness, since it was grounded on the abnormal or "sick" part of human behavior. He felt that psychology had exclusively dwelled on the negative side of human nature (i.e., its frailties and shortcomings), ignoring humanity's strengths and virtues. For example, the nature of graduate students would hardly become evident by studying high school dropouts exclusively. In fact, such a study would be much more likely to discover what graduate students are *not* like than what they are like. To correct this deficiency, Maslow and those sympathetic to the humanistic movement focused attention on the psychologically healthy person and the understanding of such a person in terms other than comparison with the mentally ill. In short, it was Maslow's belief that one cannot understand mental illness until one understands mental health. Stated more baldly, Maslow (1970) argued that the study of crippled, stunted, immature, and unhealthy specimens can yield only a "crippled" psychology. He strongly urged the study of self-actualizing, psychologically healthy persons as the basis for a more universal science of psychology. In brief, humanistic psychology considers self-fulfillment as the main theme in human life—a theme never uncovered by studying neurotics alone.

therefore they most certainly should have included a study of God.

MASLOW'S HIERARCHICAL THEORY OF MOTIVATION

Maslow believed that much of human behavior can be explained by the individual's tendency to seek personal goal states that make life rewarding and meaningful. In fact, motivational processes are the heart of his personality

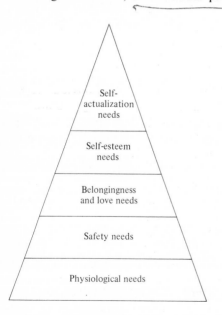

Self-
actualization
needs

Self-esteem
needs

Belongingness
and love needs

Safety needs

Physiological needs

Figure 8-1 A schematic representation of Maslow's need-hierarchy theory.

theory. Maslow (1970) depicted the human being as a "wanting animal" who rarely reaches a state of complete satisfaction except for a short time period. If Nirvana exists, it is strictly temporary. In Maslow's system, as one personal desire is satisfied, another will surface to take its place. When the person satisfies this one, still another will clamor for satisfaction. It is characteristic of human life that people are almost always desiring something.

Maslow proposed that human desires (i.e., motives) are innately given and are arranged in an ascending hierarchy of priority or potency. Figure 8-1 is a schematic representation of this need-hierarchy conception of human motivation. The needs are, in order of their potency: (1) basic physiological needs; (2) safety needs; (3) belongingness and love needs; (4) self-esteem needs; and (5) self-actualization needs or the need for personal fulfillment. Underlying this scheme is the assumption that low-order, prepotent needs must be at least somewhat satisfied before an individual can become aware of or motivated by higher-order needs. That is, as one general type of need is satisfied, another higher-order need emerges and becomes operative in the person's life. For example, if one is starving to death, one urgently needs food and drink (e.g., pizza and beer) before one is able to worry about satisfying higher order needs. Gratification of needs lower in the hierarchy allows for awareness of and motivation by needs occurring higher in the hierarchy; i.e., physiological needs must be met before the safety needs become salient and are attended to; both the physiological and safety needs must be satisfied *to some degree* before the needs for belongingness and love emerge and press for satisfaction, and so forth. For Maslow, this sequential arrangement of basic needs in a hierarchy of lesser or greater potency is the chief principle of organization underlying human motivational life. He posited that the hierarchy of needs is specieswide and that the farther up the hierarchy a person is able to go, the more individuality, humanness, and psychological health he or she will display. A description of each need category is presented below.

1 Physiological Needs The most basic, powerful, and obvious of all human needs is the need for physical survival. Included in this group are the needs for food, drink, oxygen, activity-sleep, sex, protection from extreme temperatures, and sensory stimulation. These physiological drives are directly concerned with the biological maintenance of the organism and must be gratified at some minimum level before the individual is motivated by higher-order needs. Put another way, the person who fails to satisfy this basic level of needs just won't be around long enough to attempt satisfaction of higher need levels.

Admittedly, the social-physical environment in American culture provides for the satisfaction of primary needs for most persons. However, if one of these needs remains unsatisfied, the individual rapidly becomes dominated by that need, so that all other needs quickly become nonexistent or decidedly secondary. The chronically hungry person will never strive to compose music, construct personological theories, or build a brave new world. Such a person is much too preoccupied with getting something to eat. Maslow adds:

> For our chronically and extremely hungry man, Utopia can be defined simply as a place where there is plenty of food. He tends to think that, if only he is guaranteed food for the rest of his life, he will be perfectly happy and will never want anything more. Life itself tends to be defined in terms of eating. Anything else will be defined as unimportant. Freedom, love, community feeling, respect, philosophy, may all be waved aside as fripperies that are useless, since they fail to fill the stomach. Such a man may fairly be said to live by bread alone (1970, p. 37).

bread is his God.

Physiological needs are crucial to the understanding of human behavior. The devastating effects on behavior produced by a lack of food or water have been chronicled in numerous experiments and autobiographies. One terrifying example of the behavioral effects brought about by prolonged food deprivation occurred when a Peruvian airliner crashed deep in the jungle of South America in 1970. Trapped with a dwindling supply of food, the survivors, including a Catholic priest, resorted to eating the victims of the crash. This incident illustrates how deeply ingrained social and moral taboos can give way to biological drives under stressful conditions. Without a doubt, physiological needs dominate human desires, forcing themselves on one's attention before higher-order goals can be pursued.

alecia

2 Safety Needs Once the physiological needs have been sufficiently satisfied, the individual becomes concerned with a new set, often called the *safety* or *security* needs. The primary motivating force here is to ensure a reasonable degree of certainty, order, structure, and predictability in one's environment. Maslow suggested that the safety needs are most readily observed in infants and young children because of their relative helplessness and dependence on adults. Infants, for instance, respond fearfully if they are suddenly dropped or startled by loud noises or flashing lights. Later learning and education tend to neutralize such apparent dangers through knowledge; e.g., "I am not afraid of thunder and lightning because I know something about them." The urgency of safety needs is also evident when a child experiences bodily illnesses of various kinds. A child with a broken leg will temporarily experience fears, have nightmares, and manifest a need for protection and reassurance not evident before the accident.

Another indication of the need for safety is the child's distinct preference for some kind of dependable, undisrupted routine. According to Maslow, young children function more effectively in a system which has at least a skeletal outline of rigidity, which can be anticipated not only for the present but also into the future. If such elements are absent in the environment, he will feel insecure, anxious, and mistrustful, seeking out those areas of life which offer the most stability and Maslow further noted that parents who apply the theory of unrestricted, permissive child-rearing practices do not satisfy the child's safety needs. Not to require a child to go to bed at a certain time or to eat at somewhat regular intervals will only cause confusion or fright. The child then has nothing stable in the environment upon which to depend. Maslow singled out parental quarreling, physical assault, separation, divorce, and death within the family as being particularly harmful to the child's sense of well-being. In effect, these factors render the child's environment unstable, unpredictable, and hence unsafe.

Safety needs also exert an active influence beyond childhood. The preference for a job with tenure and financial protection, the establishment of savings accounts, and the acquisition of insurance (e.g., medical, unemployment, old age) may be regarded as motivated in part by safety seeking. At least in part, religious and philosophic belief systems may also be interpreted in this fashion. Religions and philosophies help a person to organize his or her world and the people in it into a coherent and meaningful whole, thus making the person feel "safe." Other expressions of the need for safety occur when individuals are confronted with real emergencies, e.g., war, crime waves, floods, earthquakes, riots, societal disorganizations and similar conditions.

Maslow further maintained that certain types of neurotic adults (especially obsessive-compulsive neurotics) are predominantly motivated by the search for safety. Some neurotics behave as if a great catastrophe were imminent, frantically attempting to stabilize their world in a neat, disciplined, orderly fashion so that new contingencies may not appear. The neurotic's safety needs "often find specific expression in a search for a protector, or a stronger person on whom he may depend, perhaps a Fuehrer (Maslow, 1970, p. 42)."

3 Belongingness and Love Needs   The *belongingness* and *love* needs constitute the third hierarchical level. These needs arise primarily when the physiological and safety needs are relatively quiescent. An individual motivated on this level longs for affectionate relationships with others, namely for a place in his or her family and/or reference groups. Group membership becomes a dominant goal for the individual. Accordingly, the person will feel keenly the pangs of loneliness, social ostracism, friendlessness, and rejection, especially when induced by the absence of friends, relatives, a spouse, or children. Students who attend college far from home fall prey to the effects of belongingness needs, striving with great intensity to be recognized as somebody within a group regardless of its size.

Despite the sparsity of empirical data concerning the belongingness and love needs, Maslow insisted that their behavioral effects are potentially disruptive in a highly fluid society such as the United States. Specifically, America has become a land of nomads (approximately 40 million Americans, about one-fifth of the population, change their addresses at least once a year), a nation of people who are rootless, alienated, indifferent to community and home problems, and afflicted with shallowness in personal relationships. In Maslow's view, the widespread social mobility brought about by industrialization is a key factor in accounting for the tremendous increase in *sensitivity groups* and other forms of personal growth groups. Such groups, he writes, are:

> . . . motivated by this unsatisfied hunger for contact, for intimacy, for belonging-ness and by the need to overcome the widespread feelings of alienation, aloneness, strangeness, and loneliness, which have been worsened by our mobility, by the breakdown of traditional goupings, the scattering of families, the generation gap, the steady urbanization and disappearance of village face-to-faceness, and the resulting shallowness of American friendship (Maslow, 1970, p. 44).

Maslow also held that rebellious youth groups are motivated to some extent by the profound need for "groupiness," for intimate contact, for real togetherness "in the face of a common enemy, any enemy that can serve to form an amity group simply by posing an external threat (Maslow, 1970, p. 44)." University administrators often serve as excellent "common enemies" in this respect.

Maslow rejected the Freudian notion that love and affection are derived from sublimated sexual instincts; that is, to Maslow, love is not synonymous with sex. Rather, he contended that love involves a healthy, loving relationship between two people, which includes mutual respect, admiration, and trust. Maslow also stressed that love needs involve both giving and receiving love. Being loved and accepted is instrumental to healthy feelings of worth. Not being loved leads to feelings of futility, emptiness, and hostility.

In brief, it was Maslow's contention that the belongingness and love needs are often frustrated in American society, resulting in maladjustment and pathology. Love and affection are regarded with ambivalence or as if a taboo existed on tenderness. Many people are reluctant to disclose themselves in intimate relationships, since they fear rejection. Maslow concluded that there is a mounting mass of evidence to prove a substantial correlation between affectionate childhood experiences and a healthy adulthood. Such data, in his judgment, add up to the generalization that love is a basic need condition for healthy development of the human being: "we can say that the organism is so designed that it needs . . . love, in the same way that automobiles are so designed that they need gas and oil (Maslow, 1970, p. 176)."

4 Self-Esteem Needs   When one's needs for being loved and for loving others have been reasonably gratified, their motivating force diminishes, paving the way for *self-esteem* needs. Maslow classified these needs into two subsidi-ary sets: self-respect and esteem from other people. The former includes such things as desire for competence, confidence, personal strength, adequacy, achievement, independence, and freedom. An individual needs to know that he or she is worthwhile—capable of mastering tasks and challenges in life. Esteem from others includes prestige, recognition, acceptance, attention, status, reputation, and appreciation. In this case individuals need to be appreciated for what they can do; i.e., they must experience feelings of worth because their competence is recognized and valued by others.

Again, the hierarchical nature of Maslow's view of motivation needs to be kept in mind. One seeks self-esteem only after one's love and belongingness needs are satisfied. One quickly reverts back from level four to level three if level three need satisfaction is suddenly jeopardized. For example, consider a person who, thinking her love needs are in good order, busies herself with becoming a recognized business tycoon. Suddenly and unexpectedly, her husband leaves her for another woman. Immediately she casts aside all aspects of self-esteem, behaving like an utter fool in order to regain her husband, i.e., satisfy her love needs. Once this relationship is restored or a suitable alternative is developed, however, she is free to reconcern herself with "conquering" the business world.

Satisfaction of the self-esteem needs generates feelings and attitudes of self-confidence, worth, strength, capability, and of being useful and necessary in the world. In contrast, the thwarting of these needs leads to feelings and attitudes of inferiority, ineptness, weakness, and helplessness. These negative self-perceptions, in turn, may give rise to basic discouragement, a sense of futility and hopelessness in dealing with life's demands, and a low evaluation of self vis-à-vis others. Maslow emphasized that the most healthy self-esteem is based on earned *respect* from others rather than on fame, status, or adulation. Esteem is the result of effort—it is earned. Hence, there is a real psychological danger of basing one's esteem needs on the opinions of others rather than on real ability, achievement, and adequacy. Once a person relies exclusively upon the opinions of others for his own self-esteem, he places himself in psychological jeopardy. To be solid, self-esteem must be founded on one's *actual* worth rather than on external factors outside of one's control.

5 Self-Actualization Needs   Finally, if all the foregoing needs are satisfied, the need for self-actualization comes to the fore. Maslow characterized *self-actualization* as the desire to become everything that one is capable of becoming. The person who has achieved this highest level presses toward the full use and exploitation of his talents, capacities, and potentialities. Otherwise phrased, it is the person's desire for self-improvement, namely, his or her drive to become actualized in what he or she is potentially. In short, to self-actualize is to become the total kind of person that one wants to become—to reach the peak of his or her potential: "A musician must make music, an artist must paint, a poet must write, if he is to be at peace with himself. What a man can be, he must be. He must be true to his own nature (Maslow, 1970, p. 46)."

Self-actualization need not take the form of creative and artistic endeavors. A parent, an athlete, a student or teacher, or an ardent laborer may all be actualizing their potential abilities in doing well what they each can do best, since specific forms of self-actualization vary greatly from person to person. It is at this level of Maslow's need hierarchy that individual differences are greatest.

As an illustration of self-actualization in action, suppose that Mark is taking this personality course as part of a long-term plan to become a clinical psychologist. Other theorists could probably explain why he's selected this vocational alternative. For example, Freud might say it's related to his deeply repressed childhood curiosity about sex. Murray might argue that it's an outgrowth of his attempts to satisfy nAchievement and nNurturance. Skinner, on the other hand, may say it's a product of his conditioning history, while Kelly may feel that it all depends on how he construes it. However, Maslow could argue that Mark just might sense in becoming a clinical psychologist the kind of person that he really wants to become; i.e., he is impelled toward this career objective by the need for self-actualization.

Now, further, suppose that Mark has successfully gone through the long, hard, tortuous process of taking all those psychology graduate courses, completing the required 2,000-hour internship, doing a doctoral dissertation, and finally obtaining his Ph.D. in clinical psychology. Then somebody offers him a job as a police detective in Brooklyn. But the job pays extremely well, provides excellent fringe benefits (Blue Cross, Blue Shield, great vacation time, etc.), and *guarantees* steady employment and security for life. Think about it—would he take it? If his honest answer is yes, go back three spaces to level two (safety needs), because that's where he's at—psychologically anyway. If he wouldn't take it, why not? Certainly not because the job lacks social value. Brooklyn could function better and longer without psychologists than without police detectives. No, it's more than that—we repeat, from Maslow's perspective, "what a man can be, he must be." Given his interests and aspirations, Mark would simply have no chance for self-actualization in this job. At that point, he would instead opt for a job as a clinical psychologist so that he could develop his capacities, become the kind of person that he really wants to become, and, in brief, self-actualize. Maslow's doctrine of self-actualization is exciting and refreshing because it makes a person *look up*—look up to what he or she *can be* and thus live with zest and purpose.

Why Can't All People Achieve Self-Actualization?

According to Maslow, most, if not all, of mankind has a need for and strives toward inner fulfillment. His own research led him to conclude that the impulse toward realizing one's potentialities is both natural and necessary. Yet only a few—usually the gifted—ever achieve it (Maslow estimated less than 1 percent of the population). In part, Maslow believed that this extremely unfortunate state of affairs exists because many people are simply blind to their potential; they neither know that it is possible nor understand the rewards of self-enhancement. Rather, they tend to doubt and even fear their own abilities, thus precluding a fair chance at becoming self-actualized. In addition, the social environment often stifles development toward self-fulfillment.

One example is the cultural stereotype of what is masculine and what is not. Such human qualities as sympathy, kindness, gentleness, and tenderness are frequently discouraged because of the cultural tendency to consider such characteristics "unmasculine." Or worse, consider the overwhelming and stifling effects that the traditional cultural female role has upon the psychological development of women. Following from such considerations, actualization of the highest potentials—on a mass basis—is possible only under "good conditions." Or, more directly, people will generally need a "facilitative" society in which to maximize their human potentials to the fullest degree. At this point in history, there is no one society that fully facilitates the self-actualization of all its members; although, admittedly, some are far superior to others in terms of providing opportunities for individual self-fulfillment.

A final obstacle to self-actualization mentioned by Maslow is the strong negative influence exerted by the safety needs. The growth process demands a constant willingness to take risks, to make mistakes, to break old habits. This requires courage. It logically follows that anything that increases the individual's fear and anxiety also increases his tendency to regress toward safety and security. It is also evident that most people exhibit strong tendencies to continue specific habits—to persist in past behavior. Realization of one's full potential therefore requires an openness to novel ideas and experiences. Maslow maintained that children reared in a secure, warm, friendly atmosphere are more apt to acquire a healthy taste for the growth process. All of the foregoing can be summed up in the statement that under healthy conditions (where the individual's basic need satisfactions are not endangered), growth is rewarding and the individual will become the best that he or she is able to become. In other words, people who fail to develop their true potential—to become what they as individuals could become—are reacting to the deprivation of their basic needs. If more people are to achieve self-actualization, then, the world needs to be changed to permit more widespread opportunities for people to satisfy their lower-level needs. Quite obviously, this task would require a major reorganization of many of our social institutions and political structures.

DEFICIT MOTIVATION VERSUS GROWTH MOTIVATION

In addition to his hierarchical conception of motivation, Maslow (1955) distinguished two broad categories of human motives: *deficit* motives and *growth* motives. The former (also designated *deficiency* or *D motives* by Maslow) reflect little more than the lower needs in Maslow's motivational hierarchy, especially those concerned with the organism's physiological and safety requirements. The aim of deprivation motivation is to fend off organismic tension arising through deficit states, e.g., hunger, cold. In this sense, D motives are urgent determiners of behavior. According to Maslow (1962), deficit motives are identifiable based on the following five criteria: (1) Their absence produces illness (using hunger as an example, if a man does not eat, he will get sick); (2) their presence prevents illness (if he eats properly, he won't get sick because of it); (3) their restoration cures illness (there's no cure for starvation like food); (4) under certain complex free-choice conditions, they are preferred by the deprived person over other gratifications (if he is starving, he will choose food over sex anytime); and (5) they are found to be inactive or functionally absent in the healthy person (healthy people are fortunate enough to be in a life situation in which their behavior is not constantly dominated by a quest for food).

In contrast to D-type motives, growth motives (also designated as *metaneeds* and *being* or *B motives*) are distant goals associated with the inborn urge to actualize one's inherent potentials. The objective of growth motives or metaneeds is to enrich living by enlarging experiences, thus increasing the joy of being alive. Growth motivation does not involve the repairing of deficit states (i.e., tension reduction) as much as the expansion of horizons (i.e., tension increase). Taking a course in organic chemistry, for example, just because a person wants to know about it, is more reflective of *B-* than *D*-type motivation. Growth or B-type motives come into play chiefly after the D motives have been satisfied. A person would certainly not be interested in taking organic chemistry if she were starving to death.

More recently, Maslow (1967a) proposed that metaneeds are as instinctive or inherent in people as the D motives. Thus, they must be adequately fulfilled if psychological health is to be maintained and the fullest growth achieved. Otherwise, the individual may become psychologically "sick." Interestingly, the "illnesses" resulting from failure to achieve one's fullest humanness or growth Maslow labeled "metapathologies" (Maslow, 1967a). Such psychological states as apathy, alienation, depression, and cynicism are just a few examples of what Maslow meant by this higher level of psychic disturbances. In humanistic psychology, not only is the person more highly regarded than in psychoanalysis or behaviorism, but he or she is even endowed with *psychological disorders* of a distinctly higher class!

Maslow also theorized that metaneeds or growth motives possess equal value; thus, they have no generalized hierarchy. Consequently, one can be easily substituted for another when a person's life circumstances so dictate. People who are metamotivated are devoted to working for truth, for beauty, for goodness, for law and order, for justice, and for perfection. Maslow described metamotivated people as follows:

> For more highly evolved persons, "the law" is apt to be more a way of seeking justice, truth, goodness, etc., rather than financial security, admiration, status, prestige, dominance, masculinity, etc. When I ask the questions: which aspects of

The discussion as to what will best fullfill we should be made on God's standards not the standards of the world.

Freedom	_ ✓ _ _ _ _ _ _ _ _ _ _	Determinism
Rationality	_ ✓ _ _ _ _ _ _ _ _ _ _	Irrationality
Holism	✓ _ _ _ _ _ _ _ _ _ _ _	Elementalism
Constitutionalism	_ _ _ _ ✓ _ _ _ _ _ _	Environmentalism
Subjectivity	_ ✓ _ _ _ _ _ _ _ _ _ _	Objectivity
Proactivity	✓ _ _ _ _ _ _ _ _ _ _ _	Reactivity
Homeostasis	_ _ _ _ _ _ _ _ _ ✓ _	Heterostasis
Knowability	_ _ _ _ _ _ _ _ _ _ ✓	Unknowability

Figure 8-2 Maslow's position on the eight basic assumptions concerning human nature.

your work do you enjoy most? What gives you your greatest pleasures? When do you get a kick out of your work? etc., such people are more apt to answer in terms of intrinsic values, of transpersonal, beyond-the-selfish, altruistic satisfactions, e.g., seeing justice done, doing a more perfect job, advancing the truth, rewarding virtue and punishing evil, etc. (1971, p. 310).

In sum, the motivational life of self-actualizers is not only quantitatively different but also qualitatively different from that of non-self-actualizers. Whereas ordinary people are motivated by basic need gratifications that they lack, self-actualizing people strive to grow to perfection and to develop more and more fully in their own style. In sharp contrast to Skinner's *Beyond Freedom and Dignity*, then, Abraham Maslow's view of man might aptly be termed "beyond determinism and homeostasis." *serving God rather than self*

MASLOW'S BASIC ASSUMPTIONS CONCERNING HUMAN NATURE

Kim and Mary

As was emphasized earlier, humanistic psychology differs sharply from both psychoanalysis and behaviorism in terms of its basic image of human nature. In fact, the contemporary movement of humanistic psychology was born largely out of protest against the images of humanity prevalent in psychoanalytic and behavioristic circles. The profound differences separating these other "forces" from humanistic theory are most evident when considering the basic assumptions concerning human nature espoused by each. Careful examination of Maslow's basic assumptions (depicted in Figure 8-2), particularly when contrasted with those of Freud and Skinner, should prove illuminating in this respect.

1 Freedom–Determinism Although hesitant to accept the untrammeled freedom propounded by influential existentialists, Maslow pretty much approximates their belief. In his system, the human being is fundamentally free and responsible for his or her own behavior. This freedom is manifest in whether one decides to satisfy one's needs, how one chooses to satisfy them, and, specifically, how one gropes toward self-actualization. A person *decides* what his or her potentialities are and how he or she will actualize them.

In Maslow's theory it appears that the older a person becomes and the higher he or she climbs on the need ladder, the more freedom that person has available. For example, infants aren't really "free" because they are dominated by physiological needs; they don't actually "decide" when to eat, sleep, or eliminate. But the potential is there in their nature. As people mature, they move up the need hierarchy and progressively fashion their own individuality. In effect, they begin to create themselves—they carve out the kind of person they wish to become from a whole host of possibilities. And the higher they progress on the need ladder, the more free they are of pressing D-type motivation and hence the more free they are as persons to create their own destinies. However, in Maslow's system, *each person* has the potential to actualize himself or herself in his or her own unique way. Maslow's commitment to the underlying freedom assumption is really very strong indeed.

2 Rationality–Irrationality   When considering Maslow's position on the rationality assumption, it is highly relevant that he regards animal research as largely irrelevant for human psychology. One major reason for this rejection is that an animal lower on the phylogenetic scale does not consciously review his past experiences, think about present circumstances, consider future possibilities, and then cognitively decide on a course of action. An average human being, however, engages in this activity daily. So, in Maslow's theory, rationality is a central feature of the human being's makeup and conduct.

While Maslow allows for irrationality—evidenced in conflict among needs, compulsions, inconsistencies in behavior, and unconscious processes—human conduct, to him, is largely governed by rational forces. As one instance of this conviction, Maslow (1968) considered a person's conscious self-report of his or her own subjective experience as valid data for scientific study. No personologist supports an "introspective method of inquiry" unless he thinks that the person is sufficiently rational and self-aware to understand and report the reasons for his or her behavior. At the same time, however, Maslow (1970) accepted data from projective techniques (e.g., Thematic Apperception Test and Rorschach) which are designed to tap unconscious, irrational aspects of personality. But irrational processes do not dominate most people's lives. The basic thrust of Maslow's theory presents a picture of human beings who *rationally* make decisions and strive to actualize their potential. Maslow's commitment to rationality is strong.

3 Holism–Elementalism   It is difficult to imagine a theorist more committed to the holism assumption than Abraham Maslow. As noted earlier, one of the basic tenets of humanistic psychology is "The individual as an integrated whole." And even among humanistic psychologists, Maslow stands out in terms of the extent to which holism characterizes his theory (Maddi and Costa, 1972).

Earlier Maslow was quoted in this respect as noting that "It is John Smith who wants food, not John Smith's stomach (Maslow, 1970, pp. 19–20)." It can now be observed that, in Maslow's theory, it is also *John Smith* who wants safety, *John Smith* who wants self-esteem, and, above all, *John Smith* who wants self-actualization. All aspects of personality are intertwined and fused in Maslowian man. The individual as a totality is the only valid object for psychological study—no bits and pieces for Maslow! Maslow's position on the holism assumption is indeed extreme.

4 Constitutionalism–Environmentalism The heavy existentialist-type emphasis upon freedom running throughout Maslow's theory almost makes the issue raised by this assumption irrelevant. If people are largely free to shape themselves and creatively determine their own destinies, then neither constitution or environment play a significant role in molding human behavior. Of the two, however, Maslow is inclined to give constitution slightly more weight. *Physiological needs,* obviously constitutional in origin, are the basis for his entire need hierarchy conception of human motivation. Yet he seems to use this concept more to recognize the biological communality of humanity rather than to explain individual differences in personality; e.g., Germaine and Raquel are similar in that they both have physiological needs, but the essential personality difference between them is not constitutional; it lies much more in the realm of how each freely chooses to satisfy needs and to self-actualize.

Further traces of constitutionalism are found in Maslow's concepts of B-motives and self-actualization itself. In discussing these earlier in the chapter, terms like "inborn urge," "instinctive," and "inherent in humanity" were used. Indeed, Maslow regarded the drive toward actualizing one's potentialities as an inherent aspect of *what the person is,* rather than what he or she learns to become as a result of environmental learning factors. In brief, it's inborn. Maslow (1962) also recognized the influences of early environment on personality development, but he seemed to give weight to this factor only when it has been a devastatingly destructive force in contributing to a person's later emotional disturbance. On balance, Maslow leans slightly toward constitutionalism, but in no way does he theoretically emphasize it. Because of his strong position on the freedom assumption, his commitment to constitutionalism is only slightly greater than it is to environmentalism.

5 Subjectivity–Objectivity The existential, phenomenological, "here-and-now" perspective in Maslow's theory clearly reveals his strong allegiance to the subjectivity assumption. While not elevating it to the mountain peak of importance that his fellow humanistically inclined colleague Carl Rogers does (see next chapter), Maslow obviously believed that man's subjective experience constitutes the cardinal data of psychological science. People cannot be understood without reference to their private world; subjective experience is more important than observable behavior for psychology.

While he posited a hierarchical set of needs common to humanity, Maslow (1964) argued that these needs are specific to each indivudual and will thus be expressed in a unique way. For example, while both Ayn and Betty have a need for self-esteem, each will *subjectively experience* and attempt to satisfy this need in different ways. One may enhance her position as a mother so that others will recognize her outstanding parenthood, while the other may derive self-esteem satisfaction via a career in business. Finally, it should be noted that the word "self" in Maslow's key phrase "self-actualization" is firmly rooted in the subjectivity assumption. According to humanistic psychology, each person is constantly working toward the actualization of a unique self which only he or she alone can subjectively experience and appreciate.

6 Proactivity–Reactivity   Rejecting practically any kind of situational determinism, Maslow (1970) clearly advocates a proactive view of humanity. The Maslowian person does not behave in response to external stimuli; he or she *acts* rather than *reacts*. More specifically, the person is depicted as attempting to satisfy broad internal need states which serve to generate his or her behavior.

Maslow's exceedingly strong adherence to the proactivity assumption is most clearly evident in his central concept of self-actualization. Think about it for a minute—*there can be no external stimuli* for this all-important human characteristic. *By its nature,* self-actualization is a proactive concept. The person is pictured as oriented toward the future, aware of his or her potentialities, and forever striving to bring them into being. In fact, the only way that a person can self-actualize is through his or her own internally generated actions. To achieve self-actualization, the person *must act*. Persons, then, are highly proactive in Maslow's system.

7 Homeostasis–Heterostasis   Maslow is strongly inclined toward the heterostatic assumption; the image of the individual pushing on to greater and greater heights of psychological growth is an integral Maslow's theory. Yet Maslow recognizes two categories of human motivation—D- and B-type motives. Examination of these clearly indicates that D (deficit) motives are homeostatically based, while B (growth) motives are obviously heterostatic. So the human being doesn't just strive for growth all the time—part of human life necessarily involves tension reduction.

But Maslow did not achieve recognition in psychology because of his account of D motives. Others, particularly animal psychologists, had already studied these thoroughly. No—instead, Maslow seems to treat D motives as almost a necessary theoretical evil. They are something that have to be recognized, worked through, and dealt with successfully on one's way to becoming fully human. And how does one become fully human? By rising above D-level functioning and working toward growth and self-realization. In Maslow's theory, the human being is an animal that has its eyes on the sky. The entire thrust of his theory is the individual rising above those motives that form a link with the rest of the animal kingdom and seeking growth and personal fulfillment. Such a conception of personality could not exist without a solid foundation in the heterostasis assumption.

8 Knowability–Unknowability   D. O. Hebb (1974) has observed that humanistic psychology as a totality tends to confuse two very different ways of knowing about man—science and literature. The first is objective, careful, and circumscribed; the second is intuitive, immediate, and perhaps overly global. Whether one agrees or disagrees with Hebb's assessment, it is clear that a theory which regards the human being as free and subjective will have a difficult time achieving ultimate knowledge of its subject matter through traditional scientific methodology. Maslow's is precisely such a theory.

Implicit in Maslow's writings is a humanistic image of man that cannot be fully captured by traditional modes of scientific inquiry. Man is unknowable in this sense. And so, to approach a more comprehensive understanding of human nature, we will either have to look beyond the traditional ken of science or restructure psychological science to incorporate subjective, intuitive concepts befitting the nature of the subject. As a psychologist, Maslow unequivocally favored the latter. In fact, he chastised psychology and its graduate training for studying "Dry bones. Techniques. Precision. Huge mountains of itty-bitty facts, having little to do with the interests that brought the student into psychology (Maslow, 1956, p. 229)." Instead, as the "spiritual father" of the humanistic movement, Maslow wanted a drastically redefined psychology— one that would address itself squarely to his own image of humanity. One is forced to conclude that this is because the Maslowian person is simply unknowable within the traditional domain of psychological science. Thus the third force movement emerged.

EMPIRICAL VALIDATION OF HUMANISTIC THEORY CONCEPTS

Efforts aimed at verifying Maslow's humanistic conceptions of personality have focused primarily on two areas: (1) the hierarchy of needs and (2) the concept of self-actualization. Empirical attention highlights only these two areas, since they constitute the bulk of Maslow's contributions to personology.

1 Are Needs Arranged in a Hierarchy?   As previously discussed, Maslow proposed that human needs are arranged in a dominance hierarchy with the gratification of lower, deficit needs as a prerequisite to the emergence of higher, growth-related needs. This idea has received considerable attention in theoretical and applied writings on human motivation (e.g., McGregor, 1960; Porter, 1961), yet relatively few attempts have been made to test it empirically. Many studies have included measures of the needs described by Maslow, but most investigators, having assumed the validity of need-hierarchy theory, used the measures only to examine other issues.

With few exceptions, empirical support for Maslow's need-hierarchy conception of motivation is based on the study of physiological and safety needs. For example, numerous psychological reports substantiate the dominating and disrupting effects of severe cold, hunger, thirst, and fear. It seems well documented that survival needs and those involving pain and threat (e.g., anxiety and insecurity) under severe conditions can dominate the organism's behavior, remaining secondary at other times. To this extent, then, Maslow's hierarchy of needs has received support. However, hierarchical needs lying above the physiological and safety levels (e.g., belongingness and love, self-esteem) have seldom been studied by personologists within the context of validating Maslow's concepts.

Other evidence to support Maslow's views of motivation comes from organizational research. To illustrate, Porter (1961) found that high-level executives are more concerned with esteem needs and self-actualization than lower-status managers in an industrial setting. Most personologists question the value of such research since it relies upon cross-sectional methodology which excludes the study of behavior *over a period of time.* And, as Maddi and Costa (1972) point out, the crucial test of Maslow's theory would require a longitudinal design (one that examines behavior over time), since Maslow's view states that as a lower-level need in the hierarchy becomes progressively satisfied, the next higher-level need comes to the fore. Studies involving such longitudinal assessment of need-hierarchy theory are not yet evident in psychological journals and texts.

In one of the few direct empirical tests of need-hierarchy theory, Graham and Balloun (1973) advanced two hypotheses. The first hypothesis stated that "the level of satisfaction of any given need should be negatively correlated with desire for satisfaction of that need (p. 99)." The second predicted that "in any pairwise comparison of needs at different levels in the hierarchy, satisfaction with the lower order need should be greater than for the higher order need (p. 99)."

Table 8-1 Product-Moment Correlations between Satisfaction and Desire for Maslow's Needs

	Desire			
Satisfaction	Physiological	Security	Social	Self-actualization
Physiological	−.57	−.21	−.24	−.20
Security	−.40	−.66	−.25	−.11
Social	−.22	−.27	−.72	−.18
Self-actualization	−.09	−.04	−.17	−.42

Source: Adapted from Graham & Balloun, 1973, p. 103.

Table 8-2   Mean Scores for Interview Protocol and Satisfaction Ratings

Need	Mean Interview protocols	Satisfaction
Physiological	14.23	4.14
Security	12.69	3.35
Social	9.09	3.73
Self-Actualization	7.20	3.00

Source: Adapted from Graham & Balloun, 1973, pp. 104 and 106.

The subjects ($N = 37$) for this study were preselected to represent the general population in terms of such variables as age, education, and income. Home interviews with each subject were then conducted by trained interviewers. Two methods were used to collect data specific to the hypotheses. First, subjects were asked to *describe the most important things in their lives*. Answers to this open-ended question, recorded verbatim, were subsequently rated by several psychology graduate students in terms of the amount of desire expressed for physiological, security, social, and self-actualization needs. Ratings were made separately for each need level and were expressed on a five-point scale ranging from "very high" to "little or no" desire. An example of an interview protocol rated high on desire for self-actualization follows: "I feel that self-growth, self-improvement is a lifetime challenge for myself as an individual (p. 100)." A concern for the fulfillment of security needs is reflected in the following statement: "I think the most important thing is money, house, food, clothing and transportation (p. 101)."

A second measure consisted of having subjects provide self-report ratings of present *satisfaction and of improvement wanted* for each of the four needs. Subjects expressed their level of satisfaction on a five-point scale ranging from "very satisfied" to "very unsatisfied." A four-point scale ranging from "none" to "very much" was used to assess the amount of improvement desired.

The first hypothesis was tested by computing product-moment correlations between level of satisfaction and desire for satisfaction as furnished by the direct self-report rating scales (measure 2). Table 8-1 presents the correlation matrix obtained from these indexes. It can be readily seen that the direction and magnitude of the diagonal correlations confirmed the predicted relationship between satisfaction and desire. For example, the more satisfied the subjects reported being about their security needs, the less improvement they desired ($r = -.66$). Hypothesis 1, therefore, was supported.

The second hypothesis was examined independently for each measure. Mean scores computed from ratings of the interview protocols (measure 1) are shown in Table 8-2.

These data are based on ratings of the degree of concern shown for physiological, security, social, and self-actualization needs in subjects' descriptions of the most important things in their lives. Since low mean values indicate high levels of expressed concern, it can be seen that level of concern follows a hierarchical pattern which corresponds to the ordering of needs as proposed by Maslow. Table 8-2 also contains mean scores computed from subjects' ratings of their present level of satisfation with each need (measure 2). Again, it is readily apparent that the ordering of mean values approximates what would be expected from need-hierarchy theory, although the mean satisfaction rating for the social need did not conform to the predicted pattern. In sum, the results of Graham and Balloun's investigation support Maslow's theory concerning the relationships between satisfaction and desire as well as the hierarchical ordering of human needs. Such results, however, require replication before confidence can be placed in these aspects of Maslow's theory.

Susan Caulen

2 Is Self-Actualization Real or Not?   The basic view of human nature espoused by Maslow and other humanistic psychologists is highly positive (some might say "rosy"). They not only emphasize humanity's innate potential for creativity and personal growth but also are optimistic as to the realization of these human potentialities given suitable environmental conditions. Allied to this image is the belief that the person is imprisioned by different layers of circumstances which do not always allow him or her to attain full humanness. Thus, if self-actualization is to be achieved, the individual must transcend the restraints of society and his or her deficit needs and assume responsibility for becoming whatever he or she is capable of becoming. Empirical validation for this conception of human nature is tenuous at best, with what little that does exist coming from Maslow's (1950) own study of self-actualizing people.

In a modestly conducted informal study (regrettably informal considering the speculative weight it was subsequently required to support), Maslow examined the characteristics of forty-nine famous and prominent people who he felt personified the ideal of psychological health. The individuals studied were selected from his personal acquaintances and friends, from public figures living and dead, and from among college students. These were people who by all conventional standards appeared to have lived self-actualized lives and thus achieved genuine maturity. Notably, they showed no tendencies toward neuroses, psychoses, or other gross psychological problems. At the same time, there was considerable evidence of self-actualization—loosely defined by Maslow as evidence that the person appeared to be fulfilling himself and to be doing the best that he was capable of doing. Maslow justified his lack of methodological rigor in selecting subjects this way:

> If we want to answer the question how tall can the human species grow, then
> obviously it is well to pick out the ones who are already tallest and study them. If

we want to know how fast a human being can run, then it is no use to average out the speed of a "good sample" of the population; it is better to collect Olympic gold medal winners and see how well they can do. If we want to know the possibilities for spiritual growth, value growth, or moral development in human beings, then I maintain that we can learn most by studying our most moral, ethical, or saintly people (Maslow, 1969, p. 726).

Abiding by this rationale, Maslow's research relied heavily upon observation rather than hypothesis testing, with the resulting observations admittedly subjective in nature. Moreover, by focusing on a relatively small and select group of subjects, he deviated markedly from the orthodox conception of statistics, specifically sampling theory. Nonetheless, his assessment of the self-actualized person and the kinds of motives which characterize him or her has captured the imagination of personologists.

Maslow divided his subjects into three categories. Examples of the first category, "fairly sure cases," included Jefferson, Lincoln, Spinoza, Einstein, and Eleanor Roosevelt. Category two of "partial cases" consisted of five contemporary individuals who fell short somewhat of self-actualization but still could be used for study. Their names were not revealed. Finally, a "potential or possible cases" category included people who appeared to be striving toward self-actualization but who never quite attained it, e.g., Franklin, Whitman, G. W. Carver, Renoir, and Adlai Stevenson. Maslow regarded all these individuals as rare specimens of psychological health who could be used as touchstones to explore the farther reaches of human nature.

The data accumulated on these persons did not consist of the usual gathering of discrete facts; rather it involved the gradual development of global or holistic impressions of the sort that one forms of friends and acquaintances. Specifically, Maslow obtained biographical information relevant to each subject (much like a case history) and, whenever possible, he questioned friends and relatives. In many cases it was impossible for him to question or test his older subjects, although such measures were carried out with the younger ones. Hence, quantitative analysis of the data was impossible. This procedure yielded a list of fifteen salient characteristics or traits of self-actualizing people which will be discussed in the "Application" section of this chapter. Despite its inadequacies and technical flaws (discussed next), this study serves as the foundation for Maslow's idea of the self-actualizing person as a model of optimal psychological health.

The crucial flaw in Maslow's study is the procedure he used to select his sample of self-actualizers (Smith, 1973). In effect, Maslow chose people for whom he personally had the highest admiration as human specimens. His empirical definition of self-actualization thus rests solely on his own implicit values that underlie this global judgment. One may well question whether these characteristics pertain to a psychological process called self-actualization or are merely the reflections of Maslow's particular value system. The array of characteristics that he reports must then be considered not as a factual description of self-actualizing people but rather as a reflection of Maslow's personalized conception of ideal human values. In short, the dice are loaded in favor of Maslow's own values.

Other methodological problems also make it difficult to evaluate Maslow's claim that his self-actualizing subjects represent the best possible specimens of the human race. Foremost is the question of *how* they were studied. What were their ages, sex distributions, marital status, number of children, socioeconomic levels, and places of residence? Were they exceedingly bright, highly educated, favorably employed? Is it possible that some factor such as intelligence, talent, or employment may have made them unrepresentative of the general populace and, therefore, a biased sample from which to generalize about the species? Unfortunately, basic questions such as these cannot be answered from the available data. In light of these problems, it is easy to see why Maslow's descriptive account of the metapsychology of the self-actualizing being has been criticized for the relative vagueness of its concept, "looseness" of its language, and sheer lack of evidence related to its basic contentions (Cofer and Appley, 1964).

Lack of an adequate instrument to measure self-actualization originally blocked any attempts to validate Maslow's major assertions. However, with the recent development of the Personal Orientation Inventory (POI: Shostrom, 1965, 1966) as a reliable and valid measure of self-actualization, empirical research relating to Maslow's theory is now being pursued at an accelerating rate. The POI, a self-report questionnaire, was devised in strict accordance with Maslow's theorizing and provides an assessment of the individual's degree of self-actualization. Specifically, the POI consists of 150 two-choice comparative value and behavior judgments. For each set of items, the subject must choose one of the two as most relevant to him. The response format and sample items are illustrated as follows:

> **a** I live by the rules and standards of society.
> **b** I do not always need to live by the rules and standards of society.
> **a** It is better to be yourself.
> **b** It is better to be popular.

The items are scored to measure two major areas of personal and interpersonal development: one dealing with effective use of time *(time competence)* and the other with inner-directedness *(inner-support)*. In addition, there are ten complementary subscales designed to measure conceptually important elements of self-actualization: *Self-actualizing values, existentiality, feeling reactivity, spontaneity, self-regard, self-acceptance, nature of man, synergy, acceptance of aggression,* and *capacity for intimate contact.*

Since the POI first appeared, there has been increasing evidence of its construct validity (Fox, Knapp, and Michael, 1968; Shostrom, 1966). These

studies have shown that the test does differentiate between groups of individuals nominated by personologists as representing different categories of self-
actualization and non-self-actualization. A study by McClain (1970) illustrates
how the POI has been validated as a measure of an individual's level of positive
mental health. He examined the personalities of thirty guidance counselors
who were attending a summer counseling institute. Their scores on the POI,
administered during the first week of the institute, indicated that they were a
psychologically healthy group. A composite self-actualization score for each
counselor was then derived from the evaluations of the three staff members
who knew him or her most intimately. One of these was a practicum supervisor
who supervised only six counselors. He reviewed the taped counseling sessions
with his counselors and thus was able to become acquainted with each one in
terms of his or her personality dynamics and ways of behaving in personal
confrontations. Second was a group process leader who also had six counselors
in his group. The group sessions focused on sensitivity training, enabling the
staff leader to know the counselors in his group in depth. Third was a clinical
psychologist who studied each of the thirty counselors by means of self-report
and projective personality instruments.

At the end of the nine-week session, these staff members reviewed a long
list of characteristics of self-actualizers summarized from Maslow's various
writings. Based on these characteristics, each staff member rated each counselor in his charge along a six-point scale for overall self-actualization. The
three staff ratings for each counselor were summed for a composite rating
which was then correlated with the POI scales. The correlations between the
POI scores and the composite behavioral ratings for self-actualization by staff
members are given in Table 8-3. Of a total of twelve correlations, nine were

**Table 8-3   Product-Moment Correlations between Counselor Personal Orienta-
tion Scores and Composite Ratings for Self-Actualization**

POI scale	r	p
Time competence	.40	.05
Inner-support	.69	.01
Self-actualizing value	.41	.05
Existentiality	.43	.02
Feeling reactivity	.45	.02
Spontaneity	.53	.01
Self-regard	.36	ns
Self-acceptance	.56	.01
Nature of man constructive	.23	ns
Synergy	.32	ns
Acceptance of aggression	.42	.05
Capacity for intimate contact	.42	.05

Source: Adapted from McClain, 1970, p. 22.

statistically significant in the predicted direction. These data are offered as evidence that the POI does measure self-actualization among normal adults.

The POI has also been studied in relationship to other standardized measures of personality. For instance, the inner-support scale (measuring whether one's orientation is toward self or others) correlates positively with the autonomy scale and negatively with the abasement scale of the Edwards Personal Preference Schedule (Grossack, Armstrong, and Lussiev, 1966). Further, certain POI scales correlate positively with various measures of creativity (Braun and Asta, 1968). The majority of the POI scales also are positively correlated with academic achievement among college students (LeMay and Damm, 1968). In sum, the POI seems well suited for research on self-actualization; as data continue to accumulate, it is hoped that more empirical light can be shed on Maslow's central theoretical construct.

APPLICATION: FOOD FOR THOUGHT ON HOW TO SELF-ACTUALIZE

For anyone attracted to humanistic psychology, the attainment of self-actualization epitomizes the ideal life-style. In this section some ideas will be offered as to how one might accomplish this laudable objective for oneself. Of course, as with any ideal psychological state—e.g., absolute mental health, nirvana, cosmic consciousness, etc.,—one can never attain it simply by following pat prescriptions propounded by "experts." Nonetheless, to the extent Maslow's concept of self-actualization is real, there should be clear ways of thinking about how it might apply to each person. It is in this spirit that this chapter section is offered—food for thought, not "prescriptions."

The first requirement for becoming a self-actualized person is to satisfy the first four levels of needs in Maslow's hierarchy. That, for many of us, would take the rest of our lives! But, for those who do go on from there, developing self-actualization on one's own can best be facilitated by studying the characteristics of healthy, self-actualizing adults. In this way, individuals can compare their progress against this objective; in effect, they would know what to modify in their own personality development. Maslow (1950, 1970) listed fifteen salient characteristics of self-actualizers in his unique study discussed earlier. In spite of the sound methodological criticisms of this study, the characteristics that emerged from it make intuitive sense when related to the concept of psychological well-being.

What Are Self-Actualizers Really Like?

Maslow lists fifteen notable characteristics of his self-actualizing persons, some which may or may not be applicable to each reader. They are presented as follows along with appropriate examples.

1 Efficient perception of reality Perhaps the most universal characteristic of these superior people is their unusual ability to perceive other people correctly and efficiently, to see reality *as it is* rather than as *they wish it to be.* They have a better perception of reality and more comfortable relations with it. They are less emotional and more objective about their perceptions; they do not allow their desires and hopes to distort their observations. Because of their superior perception, self-actualizing people are more readily able to detect the fake, the phony, and the dishonest in others. Maslow discovered that this ability to see more efficiently extended to many other areas of life, including art, music, science, politics, and philosophy. For example, an informal survey indicated that self-actualizers are more accurate in their predictions of future events.

The self-actualized or psychologically healthy (Maslow equated the two) individual's perception is also less distorted by expectations, anxieties, stereotypes, false optimism, or pessimism. Maslow labeled this nonjudgmental type of perception *"being cognition."* Self-actualizers are really "with it" in a profound sense; they are *realists.* Finally, the self-actualizer is able to tolerate ambiguity and uncertainty more easily than others. He is generally unthreatened and unfrightened by the unknown; he accepts it, is comfortable with it, and often is even more attracted by it than by the known.

2 Acceptance of Self, Others, and Nature The healthy person displays a sense of respect for self and others. Without feeling undue concern, he or she accepts his or her own nature in a stoic style, with all its shortcomings, frailties, and weaknesses. There is also freedom from overriding guilt, crippling shame, and debilitating anxiety. Maslow writes:

> One does not complain about water because it is wet, or about rocks because they are hard, or about trees because they are green. As the child looks out upon the world with wide, uncritical, undemanding, innocent eyes, simply noting and observing what is the case, so does the self-actualizing person tend to look upon human nature in himself and in others (1970, p. 156).

Self-acceptance is also vividly expressed at the physiological level. Self-actualizers have hearty appetites, sleep well, and enjoy their sexual lives without unnecessary inhibition. Basic biological processes (e.g., urination, pregnancy, menstruation, growing old) are considered as part of nature and are graciously accepted.

3 Spontaneity, Simplicity, Naturalness The behavior of self-actualizing people is marked by spontaneity and simplicity, by an absence of artificiality or straining for effort. This does not imply consistently unconventional behavior. It is the person's *inner life* (thoughts, impulses, etc.) that is unconventional, natural, and spontaneous. Their unconventionality is not intended to impress others and may even be suppressed in order not to distress others, so that they may even abide by ceremonies and rituals. Thus, they may conform if it means protecting themselves or others from hurt or injustice. For this reason, if it suits their purposes, self-actualizers may in fact tolerate practices within educational institutions that they regard as unnecessary, repetitive, or mind-debilitating. However, the self-actualizer refuses to be hampered or inhibited by social convention when it seems to interfere with some act he or she sees as important or basic. In other words, if the self-actualizer becomes keenly absorbed in a personally vital project or task, he or she may, for its sake, ignore normally accepted rules. One consequence of this characteristic is that such a person's ethical codes do not necessarily correspond to those of the person's milieu.

4 Problem Centering   Without exception, Maslow found his subjects to be committed to some task, duty, vocation, or beloved job which they regarded as important. That is, they are not ego-centered but rather oriented toward problems beyond their immediate needs, problems to which they are dedicated in the sense of a mission in life. In this sense, they live to work rather than work to live; their work is subjectively experienced as a defining characteristic of themselves.

Self-actualizers are also deeply concerned with philosophic and ethical issues. Accordingly, they live and work within the widest frame of reference, tending to devote themselves to nonpersonal "missions" or tasks. Such a life-style denotes a lack of concern for the trivial and petty, thus making life far more bearable not only for the self-actualizers but for all who are associated with them.

5 Detachment: Need for Privacy   This kind of individual prefers solitude and privacy and even seeks it to a greater extent than the average person. In social encounters he or she is often viewed by "normal" people as being aloof, reserved, snobbish, and cold. This is because self-actualizers do not *need* other people in the usual sense of friendship. They rely completely upon their inner resources and remain unruffled by that which produces turmoil in others.

This quality of detachment encompasses other aspects of behavior as well. For instance, since they are able to concentrate more intensely than ordinary people, they may become absent-minded and oblivious to outer surroundings. They remain calm and serene during periods of personal misfortune. Maslow explained that this comes in part from the self-actualizer's tendency to stand by his or her own interpretation of situations instead of relying upon what other people think or feel about matters.

Katherine

6 Autonomy: Independence of Culture and Environment As prior characteristics would suggest, self-actualizing people are not dependent for their main satisfactions on the physical and social environment. Rather, they rely on their own potentialities and latent resources for growth and development. For example, truly self-actualizing college students do not really *need* the "right" academic atmosphere on campus to learn. They can learn anywhere they want because they have *themselves.* Of course, some campus "atmospheres" may be better than others in this respect; the point here is simply that the self-actualizer does not require a certain type of environment before he or she can learn, or, for that matter, do almost anything else. In this sense, the self-actualizer is a self-contained unit.

Healthy people also have a high degree of self-direction and "free will." They regard themselves as self-governed, active, responsible, and self-disciplined agents in determining their own destinies. They are strong enough to be oblivious to others' opinions and affection; thus, they shun honors, status, prestige, and popularity. Such extrinsic satisfactions are perceived as less significant than self-development and inner growth. Of course, attaining this point of relative independence depends upon having been loved and respected in the past, e.g., satisfying lower-level needs.

7 Continued Freshness of Appreciation Maslow discovered that healthy, mature adults exhibit a capacity to appreciate even the most ordinary events in their lives with a sense of newness, awe, pleasure, and even ecstasy. They seldomly become bored with life experiences:

> Thus for such a person, any sunset may be as beautiful as the first one, any flower may be a breathtaking loveliness, even after he has seen a million flowers. The thousandth baby he sees is just as miraculous a product as the first one he saw. . . .
> For such people, even the casual workaday, moment-to-moment business of living can be thrilling, exciting, and ecstatic (Maslow, 1970, p. 163).

8 Peak or Mystic Experiences Maslow observed that self-actualizing individuals commonly had what he called *peak experiences* (also termed "oceanic feeling"). This term refers to moments of intense excitment and high tension as well as to those of relaxation, peacefulness, blissfulness, and stillness. Representing the most ecstatic moments of life, such occurrences usually come from love and sexual climax, bursts of creativity, insight, and discovery, and fusion with nature. These people can "turn on" without artificial stimulants. Just being alive turns them on.

For Maslow, peak or mystic experiences are not necessarily religious or spiritual in nature. He found that persons undergoing peak experiences ("peakers") feel more in harmony with the world, lose their self-awareness or transcend it, feel simultaneously more powerful and also more helpless than before, and become less conscious of time and space.

"Streaking," for some, could represent such an experience. As many readers undoubtedly know, streaking refers to a fad which reached national attention early in 1974 when many people stripped and ran naked in public. Here "streakers" may very well be "peakers." Of course, there are also somewhat less humanistically based and flattering explanations that could be offered for such behavior. And, for those who prefer the more mundane world of clothing, peak experiences can also be found through books, music, art, intellectual endeavors, and human relationships generally.

9 Social Interest   Even though self-actualizers are sometimes troubled, saddened, and even enraged by the shortcomings of the human race, they experience a deep feeling of kinship with humanity. Consequently, they have a genuine desire to help improve the lot of their fellows. This nurturant attitude is evidenced by a feeling of compassion, sympathy, and affection for all humanity.

10 Interpersonal Relations   Self-actualizing people tend to form deeper and closer personal relationships than those of the "average" adult. Similarly, those with whom they associate are likely to be healthier and closer to self-actualization than the average person. That is, self-actualizers are more inclined to associate closely with others of similar character, talent, and capacity ("birds of a feather flock together"). Usually their circle of intimate friends is small, since befriending in the self-actualizing style demands a great deal of time. One of Maslow's subjects said it this way: "I haven't got time for many friends. Nobody has, that is, if they are to be real friends (Maslow, 1970, p. 166)." They also have especially tender feelings for children and are easily touched by them.

Maslow noticed that many of the relationships that these people develop are one-sided. It is not unusual for them to attract admirers, disciples, and worshipers—individuals who, in effect, demand more than they give. When forced into these distressing and distasteful relationships, self-actualizers are kind and pleasant but try to avoid them as gracefully as possible. However, this does not imply a lack of social discrimination. In fact, they may become very harsh with those who deserve it, particularly people who are hypocritical, pretentious, or unduly indignant.

11 Democratic Character Structure   Maslow described his subjects as being "democratic" in the deepest sense. Since they are free of prejudice, they tend to have basic respect for all persons. Further, they are willing to learn from anybody who is able to teach them, irrespective of class, education, age, race, or political beliefs. At the same time, Maslow discovered that self-actualizers do not indiscriminately equalize all human beings:

These individuals, themselves elite, select for their friends elite, but this is an elite of character, capacity, and talent, rather than of birth, race, blood, name, family, age, youth, fame, or power (Maslow, 1970, p. 168).

12 Discrimination between Means and Ends In their day-to-day living, self-actualizing individuals show less confusion, inconsistency, and conflict than the average person about what is right or wrong, good or bad. They have definite moral-ethical standards, although very few of them are religious in the orthodox sense of the term. Maslow's subjects also showed a keen ability to discriminate between the end goal (what they are striving for) and the means for accomplishing that goal to an extent that most people do not. On the other hand, they often enjoy the means or instrumental behavior leading to a goal, which more impatient persons would dislike. That is, they are more likely to appreciate doing something for its own sake, the "doing itself" (Maslow, 1970).

13 Sense of Philosophical Humor Another characteristic common to all Maslow's subjects was a distinct preference for philosophical or cosmic humor. Whereas the average person may enjoy humor that pokes fun at another's inferiority, that hurts or ridicules someone, or that is "off-color" (i.e., smutty or dirty jokes), the healthy person typically finds humor expressing the foolishness of humanity in general most appealing. Lincoln's humor serves as a relevant example. His jokes always had something to convey, a purpose beyond just producing a laugh. They often dealt with a parable or fable. According to Maslow, philosophical humor usually elicits more of a smile than a laugh.

14 Creativeness Not surprisingly, Maslow found that without exception creativity was more prominent in self-actualizers than in others. However, the creativeness manifested by his subjects was different from unusual talent or genius as reflected in poetry, art, music, or science. Maslow likened it to the natural creativeness found in children. This kind of self-actualizing creativity appears in everyday life as an expression of a personality which is perceptive, spontaneous, and "childlike." It does not necessarily involve the writing of books, composing of music, or production of art objects. Rather, it may be much more humble in nature and can touch virtually all the person's activities. Basically, it revolves around the discovery of things new and novel that depart from conventional ideas.

15 Resistance to Enculturation Finally, Maslow observed that his superior subjects are in harmony with their culture while maintaining a certain inner detachment from it. As essentially autonomous beings, they make their own decisions despite contrary popular opinion. This resistance to enculturation does not mean that self-actualizers are unconventional in all realms of behavior. For instance, they remain well within the limits of conformity concerning choice of clothes, speech, food, and the manner of doing things, which are not really important enough to prompt objection. However, they can become extremely independent and unconventional when they feel basic issues are involved. Self-actualizers also manifest a calm, long-term commitment to cultural improvement. Although cognizant of society's imperfections, they accept the fact that social change can be slow and painstaking but is best achieved by working within the system.

Self-Actualizers Aren't Angels

The preceding discussion may have invited the illusion that self-actualizers are a race of supermen and wonder women so far above the rest of humanity as to approach perfection. Maslow clearly refuted this. As *imperfect* human beings, self-actualizers are just as susceptible to silly, nonconstructive, and wasteful habits as the rest of humanity. They, too, can be obstinate, irritable, boring, petulant, selfish, or depressed, and they are by no means immune from superficial vanity, undue pride, and partiality to their own friends, family, and children. Temper outbursts are not unusual. Maslow also found his subjects capable of displaying a certain "surgical coldness" when confronted with interpersonal difficulties:

> The man who found that a long-trusted acquaintance was dishonest cut himself off from this friendship sharply and abruptly and without any observable pangs whatsoever. Another woman who was married to someone she did not love, when she decided on divorce, did it with a decisiveness that looked almost like ruthlessness. Some of them recover from the death of people close to them so easily as to seem heartless (Maslow, 1970, p. 175).

Moreover, self-actualizers are not free from guilt, anxiety, sadness, and self-doubt. Their intense concentration may produce a lack of tolerance for idle gossip and light conversation. In fact, they may use language or engage in behavior that is distressing, shocking, or insulting to others. Finally, their kindness toward others may leave them vulnerable to exploitative relationships, e.g., becoming deeply involved with neurotics, bores, and unhappy people. Despite such imperfections in their makeup, Maslow's healthy subjects remind us that humanity's potential for psychological growth is far greater than what has yet been attained.

Perhaps the more fundamental question to consider is whether it is even possible to become a healthy person in an imperfect society! Or, as Maslow asked, "How good a human being does society permit?" While this question is open to empirical research, the mere presence of self-actualizing people alone suggests that human beings are more improvable than most people believe. And that is precisely the legacy that Maslow wished to leave to psychology. He desperately wanted a better world, an improvement in the human condition, and a society that would allow us to elevate ourselves and our treatment of one another to a truly *humanistic* level based on knowledge gained from psychology. In fact, for Maslow, this is the ultimate value of psychology:

> If we die in another war or if we continue being tense and neurotic and anxious in an extended cold war, then this is due to the fact that we don't understand ourselves and we don't understand each other. Improve human nature and you improve all. . . . We need psychology . . . (Maslow, 1956, p. 227).

SUMMARY

Humanistic psychology, or the third force movement, has given rise to an image of humanity in psychology radically different from that of either psychoanalysis or behaviorism. Heavily influenced by existential philosophy, humanistic psychology has as its basic tenets the individual as an integrated whole; the irrelevance of animal research; the perception of the person as a basically good, creative being; and an emphasis on the study of psychological health.

One major statement of humanistic psychology, the theory of Abraham Maslow, depicts human motivation in terms of an ascending hierarchy of priority or potency. Lower needs (more basic) in the hierarchy must be satisfied before higher-level needs emerge as dominant energizing forces in the individual's behavior. In order of their potency, Maslow's hierarchy of human needs is: (1) physiological; (2) safety; (3) belongingness and love; (4) self-esteem; and (5) self-actualization. The humanistic nature of Maslow's theory is epitomized in the self-actualization need level or the highest fulfillment of self.

Maslow's basic assumptions concerning man's nature are reasonably strong and generally explicit. Maslow's humanistic theory reflects (1) a strong commitment to the assumptions of freedom, rationality, holism, subjectivity, proactivity, heterostasis, and unknowability and (2) a slight commitment to the constitutionalism assumption.

Empirical research generated by Maslow's theory has tended to fall in one of two main areas: (1) the hierarchy of needs or (2) the concept of self-actualization. Illustrative studies reflecting each of these two areas, including one of Maslow's own, were discussed in this chapter.

In the concluding chapter section, some ideas stemming from Maslow's work were offered to further detail his self-actualization concept. Fifteen notable characteristics of self-actualizing persons were listed and discussed.

BIBLIOGRAPHY

Abraham H. Maslow: A memorial volume. Monterey, Calif: Brooks/Cole, 1972.
Braun, J., & Asta, P. Intercorrelations between the Personal Orientation Inventory and the Gordon Personal Inventory Scores. *Psychological Reports*, 1968, **23**, 1197–1198.

Cofer, C., & Appley, M. *Motivation: Theory and research.* New York: Wiley, 1964

Conversation with Abraham H. Maslow, *Psychology Today,* 1968, **2,** pp. 35–37; 54–57.

Fox, J., Knapp, R., & Michael, W. Assessment of self-actualization of psychiatric patients: Validity of the Personal Orientation Inventory. *Educational and Psychological Measurement,* 1968, **28,** 565–569.

Graham, W., & Balloun, J. An empirical test of Maslow's need hierarchy theory. *Journal of Humanistic Psychology,* 1973, **13,** 97–108.

Grossack, M., Armstrong, T., & Lussiev, G. Correlates of self-actualization. *Journal of Humanistic Psychology,* 1966, **6,** 87.

Hebb, D. What psychology is about. *American Psychologist,* 1974, **29,** 71–79.

LeMay, M., & Damm, V. The Personal Orientation Inventory as a measure of self-actualization of underachievers. *Measurement and Evaluation in Guidance,* 1968, 110–114.

McClain, E. Further validation of the Personal Orientation Inventory: Assessment of self-actualization of school counselors. *Journal of Consulting and Clinical Psychology,* 1970, **35,** 21–22.

McGregor, D. The human side of enterprise. New York: McGraw-Hill, 1960

Maddi, S., & Costa, P. *Humanism in personology: Allport, Maslow, and Murray.* Chicago: Aldine Atherton, 1972.

Maslow, A. *Self-actualizing people: A study of psychological health. Personality symposia: Symposium* #1 on values. New York: Grune & Stratton, 1950, pp. 11–34.

Maslow, A. Deficiency motivation and growth motivation. In M. Jones (Ed.), *Nebraska Symposium on motivation.* Lincoln, Nebraska: University of Nebraska Press, 1955.

Maslow, A. A philosophy of psychology. In J. Fairchild (Ed.), *Personal problems and psychological frontiers.* New York: Sheridan House, 1956.

Maslow, A. *Toward a psychology of being.* Princeton: Van Nostrand, 1962.

Maslow, A. *Religions, values and peak experiences.* Columbus, Ohio: Ohio State University Press, 1964.

Maslow, A. Criteria for judging needs to be instinctoid. In M. Jones (Ed.), *Human motivation: A symposium.* Lincoln, Nebraska: University of Nebraska Press, 1965, pp. 33–47.

Maslow, A. *Eupsychian management: A journal.* Homewood, Ill.: Irwin-Dorsey, 1965.

Maslow, A. *The psychology of science: A reconnaisance.* New York: Harper & Row, 1966.

Maslow, A. A theory of metamotivation: The biological rooting of the value-life. *Journal of Humanistic Psychology,* 1967a, **7,** 93–127.

Maslow, A. Self-actualization and beyond. In J. Bugental (Ed.), *Challenges of humanistic psychology.* New York: McGraw-Hill, 1967b.

Maslow, A. Toward a humanistic biology. *American Psychologist,* 1969, **24,** 724–735.

Maslow, A. *Motivation and personality* (2d ed.). New York: Harper & Row, 1970.

Maslow, A. *The farther reaches of human nature.* New York: Viking, 1971.

Porter, L. A study of perceived need satisfactions in bottom and middle management jobs. *Journal of Applied Psychology,* 1961, **45,** 1–10.

Shostrom, E. An inventory for the measurement of self-actualization. *Educational and Psychological Measurement,* 1965, **24,** 207–218.

Shostrom, E. *Manual: Personal Orientation Inventory.* San Diego: Educational and Industrial Testing Service, 1966.

Smith, B. On self-actualization: A transambivalent examination of a focal theme in Maslow's psychology. *Journal of Humanistic Psychology,* 1973, **13,** 17–33.

SUGGESTED READINGS

1 Chiang, H., & Maslow, A. *The healthy personality.* New York: Van Nostrand, 1969.

2 Child, I. *Humanistic psychology and the research tradition: Their several virtues.* New York: Wiley, 1973.

3 Goble, F. *The third force: The psychology of Abraham Maslow.* New York: Pocket Books, 1970.

4 Greening, T. *Existential humanistic psychology.* New York: Harper & Row, 1970.

5 Hampden-Turner, C. *Radical man: The process of psycho-social development.* Garden City, N.Y.: Anchor Books, 1971.

6 Jourard, S. *Healthy personality: An approach from the viewpoint of humanistic psychology.* New York: Macmillan, 1974.

7 King, M. *For we are: Toward understanding your personal potential.* Reading, Mass.: Addison-Wesley, 1975.

8 May, R. *Psychology and the human dilemma.* New York: Van Nostrand, 1971.

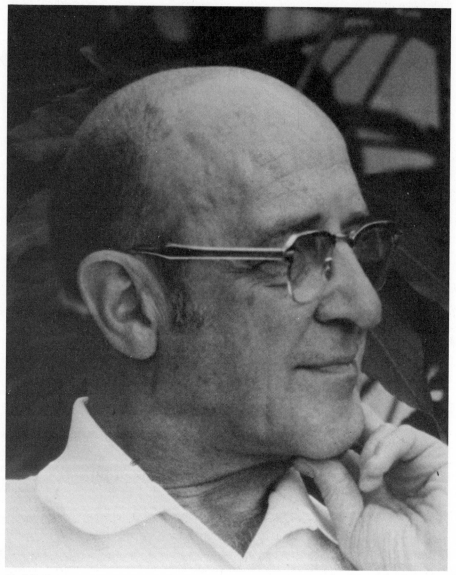

Carl R. Rogers

Carl Rogers:
A Phenomenological
Theory of Personality

Phenomenology is the study of the individual's subjective experience, feelings, and private concepts as well as his or her personal views of world and self. As a disciplined effort to explain why each of us experiences the world as we do, phenomenological psychology today has one of its most articulate spokesmen in Carl Rogers. For Rogers, behavior is utterly dependent upon how one perceives the world—that is, behavior is the result of immediate events as they are actually perceived and interpreted by the individual. Such an approach to personology emphasizes the self and its characteristics. Rogers' theory is no exception. Indeed, his theory is often referred to as a *self* theory of personality because "the best vantage point for understanding behavior is from the internal frame of reference of the individual himself (Rogers, 1951, p. 494)."

BIOGRAPHICAL SKETCH

Carl Ransom Rogers was born January 8, 1902, in Oak Park, Illinois, a Chicago suburb. He was the fourth of six children, five of whom were boys. His father was a civil engineer and contractor who achieved financial success in his profession, so the family was economically secure throughout Rogers' childhood and early youth. When he was twelve years old, Rogers' parents moved to a farm west of Chicago, and it was in this rural setting that he spent his adolescence. Although the family members were self-reliant and yet inwardly dependent upon one another, there is no impression of actual joy and contentment among its members. Rogers recalls his boyhood years structured by a strict and uncompromising religious and ethical atmosphere. He describes his parents as having been sensitive and loving, but nonetheless devoutly and dogmatically committed to fundamentalist religious views:

> I think the attitudes toward persons outside our large family can be summed up schematically in this way: Other persons behave in dubious ways which we do not approve in our family. Many of them play cards, go to movies, smoke, drink, and engage in other activities—some unmentionable. So the best thing to do is to be tolerant of them, since they may not know better, and to keep away from any close communication with them and live your life within the family (Rogers, 1973, p. 3).

Rogers recalls that his parents' condescending attitude toward others outside the home characterized his own behavior throughout elementary school. Having no close friends beyond the family, he spent much time in solitary pursuits, especially reading books. This pattern of social isolation continued throughout Rogers' high school years. He attended three different high schools, none for more than two years, commuting long distances by train to each one, so that he was never able to participate in any extracurricular activities with other students. However, Rogers was an outstanding student during his preparatory years. He received straight "A" grades in almost all his courses and did his best work in English and science. Despite his election as president of his junior class, he had only one date in high school—to attend a senior class dinner. Summer vacations were consumed by long hours of tiring work on the farm:

> . . . I rode a cultivator all day long, usually being assigned to the cornfield at the far end of the farm which was full of quack grass. It was a lesson in independence to be on my own, far away from anyone else. . . . It was a type of responsibility experienced by few young people today (Rogers, 1967, p. 347).

College represented the first break in this solitary existence. Rogers enrolled at the University of Wisconsin in 1919, the school which both his parents and three older siblings had attended. He chose scientific agriculture as his initial field of study and roomed with his older brother Ross at a YMCA dormitory. Following his family's religious tradition, he became very active in church work and was the leader of a boys' club. During his sophomore year, Rogers attended a Christian youth conference which had its slogan "Evangelize the world in our generation." This experience encouraged him to study for the ministry. The following year a major event occurred which changed the direction of his life: He was selected as one of ten United States college students to attend a World Student Christian Federation Conference in Peking, China. Abroad for more than six months, he observed a broad range of religious and cultural attitudes far different from his own. This experience not only liberalized Rogers' outlook on life but caused him to question seriously the divinity of Jesus. This trip also marked Rogers' declaration of independence from the intellectual and religious ties with his home, which was done, it might be noted, with a minimum of emotional upheaval. Following his sojourn in the Orient, Rogers returned to Wisconsin and completed his B.A. degree in history in 1924. At this point he had had only one psychology course—by correspondence!

Following graduation, despite strong parental objections, Rogers married Helen Elliott, a Wisconsin coed whom he had known since childhood. (They subsequently had two children, David and Natalie.) That summer the newlyweds set out in a Model-T Ford for Union Theological Seminary, a liberal religious institution in New York City. Rogers found life in New York stimulating and exciting: "I made friends, found new ideas, and fell thoroughly in love with the whole experience (Rogers, 1967, p. 353). While at Union Seminary, Rogers first realized the common goal of helping distressed persons that the ministry and mental health professions shared. About then he became disenchanted by the academic courses in religion—a disenchantment that was further enhanced by his growing skepticism about specific doctrines. At the end of his second year he transferred from the seminary to Teachers College, Columbia University, to pursue graduate study in clinical and educational psychology. He received a fellowship at the emerging Institute of Child Guidance and spent a rewarding year there from 1927 to 1928. Rogers obtained his M.A. in 1928 and his Ph.D. in clinical psychology in 1931. Under the supervision of Goodwin Watson, his doctoral dissertation culminated in a test for measuring personality adjustment in children which, incredibly according to Rogers (1974), is still being sold by the thousands today.

Upon receiving his doctoral degree, Rogers accepted a position as staff psychologist at the Child Study Department of the Society for the Prevention of Cruelty to Children in Rochester, New York. For the next decade Rogers was very active in applied psychological service for delinquent and underprivileged children. He was also instrumental in forming the Rochester Guidance Center, of which he emerged as director despite strong opposition that the office should be held by a psychiatrist. As a result of publishing a highly successful volume entitled *Clinical Treatment of the Problem Child* in 1939, Rogers accepted a faculty appointment in the psychology department at Ohio

State University in 1940. The move into academia brought Rogers wide recognition in the burgeoning field of clinical psychology. He attracted many talented and critical graduate students and began to publish numerous articles detailing his views on psychotherapy and how it might be empirically investigated. Rogers' text *Counseling and Psychotherapy: Newer Concepts in Practice* (1942) represented the first major alternative to psychoanalytic therapy.

From 1945 to 1957 Rogers was Professor of Psychology and Director of Counseling at the University of Chicago. This position enabled him to establish a counseling center for undergraduates where professional staff and graduate students worked as equals. During this period he completed his major work, *Client-Centered Therapy: Its Current Practice, Implications, and Theory* (1951), a book detailing the theory underlying his approach to interpersonal relations and personality change. All in all, it was a very active period of both clinical work and research in psychotherapy with a strong client orientation.

In 1957 Rogers returned to his alma mater, the University of Wisconsin, where he held joint appointments in the departments of psychology and psychiatry except for the year 1962–1963, which he spent as a fellow at the Center for Advanced Study in the Behavioral Sciences at Stanford. He subsequently initiated an intensive research program utilizing psychotherapy with schizophrenic patients in a state mental hospital. Unfortunately, this research program encountered several problems and proved to be far less successful than Rogers had anticipated. Several staff members were opposed to Rogers' client-centered approach, data mysteriously disappeared, and findings indicated that schizophrenics in the program showed little improvement when compared with patients exposed to routine hospital activities. Rogers' major disappointment, however, focused on the university's psychology department and its narrow and, to him, punitive approach to the training of doctoral students. He discovered that psychology graduate students were required to memorize vast amounts of trivia that had nothing to do with the real world of professional psychology.

Rogers resigned from his academic post in 1964 to become a resident fellow at the Western Behavioral Sciences Institute (WBSI) in La Jolla, California, a nonprofit organization devoted to humanistically oriented research in interpersonal relationships. In 1968 he left WBSI to take a position with the Center for Studies of the Person, also situated in La Jolla. He continues there at the present time. Rogers' affiliation with this group has led him to apply his theoretical concepts of personality growth to industrial organizations and school systems. He is also actively involved in the encounter group movement as a means of facilitating human growth and potential.

Like many other personality theorists, Carl Rogers is a member of numerous scholarly societies. He was president of the American Academy of Psychotherapists in 1956, vice president of the Orthopsychiatric Association in 1944, president of the American Association for Applied Psychologists in 1944, and president of the American Psychological Association in 1946–1947. Rogers was awarded the APA's Distinguished Scientific Contribution Award in 1956 and was the recipient of the APA Distinguished Professional Contribution Award in 1972. The citation for the latter reads:

> His commitment to the whole person has been an example which has guided and challenged the practice of psychology in the schools, in industry, and throughout the community. By devising, practicing, evaluating, and teaching a method of psychotherapy and counseling which reaches to the very roots of human potentiality and individuality, he has caused all psychotherapists to re-examine their procedures in a new light. Innovator in personality research, pioneer in the encounter movement, and a respected gadfly of organized psychology, he has made a lasting impression on the profession of psychology (*American Psychologist*, 1973, p. 71).

Rogers has written several books on counseling and personality, including *Psychotherapy and Personality Change* (with R. Dymond, 1954), *On Becoming a Person: A Therapist's View of Psychotherapy* (1961), *Freedom to Learn: A View of What Education Might Become* (1969), and *Becoming Partners: Marriage and Its Alternatives* (1972). His autobiography appears in *A History of Psychology in Autobiography* (Volume 5, 1967, pp. 341–384). Carl Rogers is unquestionably one of the most influential American psychologists living today.

ROGERS' VIEW OF HUMAN NATURE

Rogers' ideas of human nature, like Freud's, grew out of his experiences in working with emotionally disturbed people. The major impetus to his psychological thinking, he admits, is

> . . . the continuing clinical experience with individuals who perceive themselves, or are perceived by others to be, in need of personal help. Since 1928, for a period now approaching thirty years, I have spent probably an average of 15 to 20 hours per week, except during vacation periods, in endeavoring to understand and be of therapeutic help to these individuals. . . . From these hours, and from my relationships with these people, I have drawn most of whatever insight I possess into the meaning of therapy, the dynamics of interpersonal relationships, and the structure and functioning of personality (Rogers, 1959, p. 188).

On the basis of his clinical experience, Rogers has concluded that the innermost core of human nature is essentially purposive, forward-moving, constructive, realistic, and quite trustworthy. He regards the person as an active force of energy oriented toward future goals and self-directed purposes rather than a creature pushed and pulled by forces beyond his or her control. Such a point of view clearly implies a Rousseauean faith in the inherent goodness of human nature—a belief that, if this nature is allowed to unfold and blossom forth in terms of its own innate potential, optimum personal development and effectiveness will result.

Rogers contends that Christianity has nourished the belief that man is innately evil and sinful. Moreover, it is his contention that this negative view of humanity has been reinforced by Freud, who presented us with a portrait of the person with an id and an unconscious which would, if permitted expression, manifest itself in incest, homicide, thievery, rape, and other horrendous acts. According to this view, humanity is basically and fundamentally irrational, unsocialized, selfish, and destructive of self and others. Rogers (1957a) agrees that people occasionally express all kinds of bitter and murderous feelings, abnormal impulses, bizarre and antisocial actions, but he contends that at such times they are not behaving in concert with their true inner natures. Thus, when people are functioning as *fully human beings,* when they are free to experience and to satisfy their inner natures, they show themselves to be positive and rational creatures who can be trusted to live in harmony with themselves and others. Aware that his view of human nature may be considered by others as nothing more than naïve optimism, Rogers indicates that his conclusions are based on almost thirty years of psychotherapeutic experience. He declares:

> I do not have a Pollyanna view of human nature. I am quite aware that out of defensiveness and inner fear individuals can and do behave in ways which are incredibly cruel, horribly destructive, immature, regressive, anti-social, and harmful. Yet one of the most refreshing and invigorating parts of my experience is to work with such individuals and to discover the strongly positive directional tendencies which exist in them, as in all of us, at the deepest levels (Rogers, 1961, p. 27).

In sum, Rogers has a profound (almost religious) sense of respect for human nature. He posits that the human organism has a natural tendency to move in the direction of differentiation, self-responsibility, cooperation, and maturity. The expression of this basic nature, according to Rogers, allows for the continuation and enhancement of the individual and the species. It should be noted that such assumptions about the nature of man are interwoven throughout Rogerian theory and are closely identified with the humanistic movement in personology.

ACTUALIZING TENDENCY AS LIFE'S MASTER MOTIVE

In line with his positive view of human nature, Rogers hypothesizes that all behavior is energized and directed by a single, unitary motive which he calls the *actualizing tendency.* This represents "the inherent tendency of the organism to develop all its capacities in ways which serve to maintain or enhance the person

(Rogers, 1959, p. 196)." Thus, the primary motive in people's lives is to actualize, maintain, or enhance themselves—to become the best that their inherited natures will allow them to be. This basic actualizing tendency is the *only* motivational construct postulated in Rogers' theoretical system. Rogers (1963) felt that there was nothing to be gained from postulating specific motives—such as hunger, sex, and competence—and using these hypothetical motives to explain the why of behavior. Take hunger as an illustration. Traditionally, psychology has regarded it as a separate drive or motive, a thing unto itself. In Rogers' system, hunger is just one specific expression of the master motive underlying human existence; specifically, it serves to "maintain" the person. If you don't believe this, just stop eating. You will then come to believe this principle in less than one week—or you will die trying. Or consider sex as a motive. Sex serves to "enhance" the person. This point requires no elaboration to anyone over twelve years old. Or the need for achievement— Murray's nAchievement. In Rogers' system, such a need can easily be construed as one expression of the actualizing tendency. A person seeks achievement as a way of fulfilling his or her potential as a human being.

Certain definitive characteristics mark the actualizing tendency. First, it is rooted in the physiological processes of the entire body (i.e., it is a *biological fact* and not a psychological tendency). At an organic level this inborn tendency involves not only the maintenance of the organism by meeting deficiency needs (air, food, water, and the like) but also the enhancement of the organism by providing for development and differentiation of the body's organs and functions, its growth and continual regeneration. But of greater significance for the human personality is the motivating force which the actualizing tendency provides for increased autonomy and self-reliance, for enlarging one's field of experience, and for being creative.

Secondly, the actualizing tendency does not merely aim at tension reduction (the preservation of life processes and the pursuit of comfort and quiescence). It also involves *tension increase.* Instead of seeing all behavior as having the discharge of tensions as its goal, Rogers views behavior as motivated by the individual's need to develop and improve. The person is governed by a growth process in which potentialities and capacities are brought to realization. Additionally, Rogers maintains that the actualizing tendency is common to *all* forms of life—it is characteristic not only of human beings, not only of animals, but of all living things. It is the essence of life.

Rogers himself neglects to give many concrete behavioral examples of the actualizing tendency, but it might be characterized in terms of wanting to achieve or accomplish something that makes one's life more enriching and satisfying (e.g., getting good grades, obtaining a job promotion, striving to be imaginative, helping underprivileged children). One can think of numerous other examples of Rogers' actualizing principle. For instance, a young child learning to walk is impressive by virtue of his tenacity—he really "hangs in there" and actualizes. He falls backward, buckles his knees, bumps his head, and smashes his nose. Yet he eventually walks. Similarly, tennis players strive to perfect their forehand and backhand, golfers their putting and driving, college professors their publication records, and adolescents their identities. This movement toward self-development is often accompanied by struggle and hurt, but because the urge is so compelling, the person perseveres despite the pain he or she may have to endure. In short, it is Rogers' conviction that virtually everything which humans do is aimed at increasing their competency or actualizing themselves.

According to Rogers, the actualizing tendency serves as a criterion against which all of one's life experiences are evaluated. Specifically, in the course of actualizing themselves, individuals engage in what Rogers describes as an *organismic valuing process*. Experiences which are perceived as maintaining or enhancing the person are sought after and valued positively. The person derives a feeling of satisfaction from such positive experiences. Conversely, experiences which are perceived as negating or opposing the maintenance or enhancement of the person are valued negatively and are avoided. The organismic valuing process enables the person to evaluate experiences in light of whether they facilitate or impede his or her basic actualizing tendency. Accordingly, the individual's natural tendency is to approach actualizing experiences while avoiding those not so perceived.

The most critical aspect of the actualizing tendency from the standpoint of personality is the individual's drive toward self-actualization. In the context of Rogerian theory, the *self-actualizing tendency* is what gives a forward thrust to life, involving all movement of a person in the direction of complexity, self-sufficiency, and maturity. Self-actualization is the process of becoming a more adequate person. For Rogers, no special motivational constructs (i.e., specific drives) are required to understand why the human being is active; every person is inherently motivated simply by being alive. Motives and drives do not account for the activity and goal-directedness of the organism. Humanity is basically active and self-actualizing by virtue of its nature.

ROGERS' PHENOMENOLOGICAL POSITION

It has already been noted that Rogers' theory is illustrative of the phenomenological approach to personality. A *phenomenological* position holds that what is real to an individual (i.e., what reality is thought, understood, or felt to be) is that which exists within that person's *internal frame of reference* or subjective world, including everything in his or her awareness at a given point in time. It follows that the individual's perceptions and experiences not only constitute that person's reality but also form the basis for his or her actions; one responds to events in accordance with how one perceives and interprets them. For example, a thirsty man stranded in the desert will run as eagerly to a pool of water which is only a mirage as he will to a real pool. Similarly, two people observing an identical set of circumstances may later recall two very different outcomes, which is often the case with "eyewitness" accounts of unidentified flying objects, traffic accidents, and other unexpected events.

Phenomenological psychology asserts as its basic doctrine that the psychological reality of phenomena is exclusively a function of the way in which they are perceived. A person's senses do not directly mirror the world of reality; instead, effective reality is reality as it is observed and interpreted by the reacting organism. Each individual, then, according to Rogers (1959, pp. 222–223), construes reality in accordance with his or her private world of subjective experience. Furthermore, this experiential world is a private world that can be completely known only to the individual. A final point here is that Rogers (1951), unlike Kelly, avoids making any assertions about the nature of "objective" reality. He concerns himself only with *psychological reality* (i.e., how the person perceives and experiences the world), leaving objective reality for philosophers to fight about.

One important implication of a phenomenological perspective for a theory of personality is that the best understanding of a person's behavior is obtained through observation of his or her internal frame of reference. To explain why an individual thinks, feels, and behaves in a given way, it is necessary to know how that person perceives and interprets the world. Subjective experience is thus the key to understanding behavior. This means that the most important object of psychological study is the person's subjective experiences, because it is these experiences alone that are the causal agents in behavior.

Subjective Experience and Behavior

The relationship between experience and behavior is vividly illustrated in the case of paranoia. As may be recalled from our brief mention of it in the Kelly chapter, *paranoia* is a serious disturbance marked by a *fixed delusion,* typically of persecution. Now paranoiacs have been known to go out and start shooting people for no apparent reason (unlike most mental patients, classic paranoiacs are often dangerous to others). For instance, a paranoid individual may believe that "the communists" are actively plotting to do her in, to kill her. She perceives communists all over the place, reading into the behavior of others various innuendoes and cryptic "messages" reflecting the fact that they are "in" on the conspiracy. But the fact of the matter is that this individual is a shoe clerk in the middle of Kansas and, most probably, the Kremlin is just not all that interested in her. But *she* thinks so, and she interprets the world accordingly. So finally, out of this truly frightening world of subjective experience populated by imaginary enemies conspiring against her, she decides to shoot some of them first either to protect herself or to teach them a lesson.

Newspapers frequently report these tragic incidents as inexplicable, and upon some digging, they finally describe the perpetrator as a "loner." You'd be a "loner" too if you perceived most people around you as enemies plotting to kill or otherwise harm you. And the behavior *is* inexplicable—unless one happens to look at the world from the subjective frame of reference of the paranoid person herself. Her behavior is a direct product of, and cannot be understood without reference to, that private world in which she lives. While this example may seem to overstate the case because of its extreme nature, Rogers' position is that we *all* live in private worlds of subjective experience and that the relationship between these worlds and our overt behavior is precisely the same as that of the unfortunate paranoiac. This experience-behavior relationship is the essential point in Rogers' phenomenological position.

In terms of predicting behavior, Rogers maintains that a person acts in accordance with his impression of events. He thus advocates abandoning Skinner's notion that the regularities of behavior can be explained in terms of the person's response to the objective stimulus situation—rather, it is *his* *interpretation* of the stimulus situation impinging upon him, its personal meaning for him, that governs his behavior. What is critical in a person's life is his perception of things. It is what eggnog tastes like to me, what love and anger feel like to me, what a particular person means to me.

For the most part, Rogers rejects Freud's position that historical aspects or derivatives of behavior are the primary causative factors underlying personality. Behavior is not determined by something which occurred in the past. Instead, Rogers emphasizes the necessity of understanding the individual's relationship to his environment as he now exists and perceives his world. It is man's present interpretation of past experiences rather than their factual existence that influences current behavior. If Rogers were asked, for instance, "What causes that person to act in such a hostile way?" he would respond "Because he views the world as a dangerous place and considers himself unloved and unlovable." Rogers would not respond "Because he was deprived and neglected when he was a child."

The significance of this *ahistorical* view is that it is unnecessary to retrace a distant past in order to discover why the individual is behaving as he is today. To be sure, Rogers recognizes that past experiences exert an influence on the meanings of present experiences. However, he insists that current behavior is always affected by present perception and interpretation. Moreover, Rogers believes that ongoing behavior is strongly affected by how the person foresees his future (note the similarity to Kelly's personal construct system here). For instance, if a young woman regards herself as a socially unappealing person who has experienced difficulty in attracting males, her present dilemma is not so much due to past failures as it is to her perceived anticipation of future failures. She is governed by a self-fulfilling prophecy, namely, that she will be unable to interest men because of her lack of social charm. Changing her negative self-image would presumably result in more rewarding heterosexual experiences in the future. Thus, Rogers favors the notion that personality should be studied within a "present-future" framework.

Finally, Rogers' choice of a phenomenological approach to personality theory reflects his belief that the complexity of behavior can only be understood by reference to the entire person. In other words, Rogers espouses a *holistic* view of personality, the view that the person reacts as an integrated organism and that his unity cannot be derived from atomistic (i.e., reductionistic) approaches to behavior. As will become evident in the ensuing discussion, Rogers' commitment to a holistic point of view is manifest in practically every facet of his theorizing.

Concept of Self: Who Am I Anyway?

The self is the most important structural construct in Rogers' theory of personality; indeed, the concept of self is indispensable to appreciating Rogers' view of human behavior. Surprisingly, however, this emphasis on self was not always so evident. Rogers recalls that he first began his clinical work with the firm notion that the concept of self was a vague, scientifically meaningless word which had disappeared from the psychologist's vocabulary with the departure of the introspectionists. However, his clients persisted in expressing their problems and attitudes in terms of the self, and slowly he realized that self was a significant element in human experience and that the client's goal was to become his or her "real self."

The self or self-concept (Rogers uses the terms synonymously) is defined as an

> organized, consistent, conceptual gestalt composed of perceptions of the characteristics of the "I" or "me" to others and to various aspects of life, together with the values attached to these perceptions. It is a gestalt which is available to awareness though not necessarily in awareness (Rogers, 1959, p. 200).

Roughly translated, the self is a differentiated portion of the individual's *phenomenal* or *perceptual field* (defined as the totality of experience) and consists of the conscious perceptions and values of the I or me. The self-concept denotes the individual's conception of the kind of person he or she is. The self-concept is one's image of oneself. Especially included are awareness of being (what "I" am) and awareness of function (what "I" can do).

A person's self-concept includes not only his perceptions of what he is really like but also what he thinks he ought to be and would like to be. This latter component of the self is called the *ideal self*. The ideal self represents the self-concept the individual would most like to possess. It is basically equivalent to the superego in Freudian theory.

Rogers' notion of the self may be further understood in terms of its various properties and functions. To begin, Rogers posits that one's self-conception follows the general laws and principles of perception established in scientific psychology. This means that the concept of self is consistent with what has traditionally been a basic domain of experimental psychology. Second, Rogers views the self-concept as being configurational in nature, meaning that it represents an organized, coherent, and integrated pattern of self-related perceptions. Thus, for example, although the individual's self is fluid and constantly changing as a result of new experiences, it always retains a patterned, gestaltlike quality to it. No matter how much people change over time, they always retain a firm internal sense that they are still the same persons at any given moment in time. Rogers goes on to suggest that the self-concept is not a homunculus or "little man in the head" which controls a person's actions. The self does not regulate behavior; instead, it serves to symbolize the individual's existing body of conscious experience. Finally, the conglomeration of experiences and perceptions known as the self is, in general, conscious and admissible to awareness. Rogers believes that a definition of the self that incorporates unconscious mentation could not result in operational definition and accordingly would not be amenable to research, a necessity in his system.

Development of the Self-Concept

Unlike such other clinic-based theorists as Freud and Erikson, Rogers does not devote much attention to development per se and has not worked out a specific timetable of critical stages through which a person passes in acquiring a self-concept. Instead, he concerns himself with the ways in which evaluations of an individual by others, particularly during childhood, tend to promote the development of a positive or negative self-image.

The neonate perceives all experience, whether it is produced by bodily sensations or by external stimuli such as the rotating movement of a mobile in the crib, as unitary. The infant is not aware of himself or herself as a separate being, as an "I"; therefore he or she makes no distinction between what is "me" and what is "not me." Hence, early in life self is a non-entity (does not exist); only the unitary, all-encompassing, and undifferentiated phenomenal field is present. However, out of the general tendency toward differentiation which is a part of the organismic actualizing tendency, the child gradually begins to distinguish himself or herself from the rest of the world. It is this process of differentiating the phenomenal field into that which is recognized and felt as part of oneself and that which is not part of oneself that accounts for the emergence of the individual's self-concept in Rogers' theory.

Rogers postulates that when the self is first formed, it is governed by the organismic valuing process alone. In other words, the infant or child evaluates each new experience in terms of whether it facilitates or impedes his or her innate actualizing tendency. For instance, hunger, thirst, cold, pain, and sudden loud noises are negatively valued, since they seriously interfere with the maintenance of biological integrity. In contrast, food, water, security, and love are positively valued, since they favor the enhancement of the organismic tendency. In a true sense the organismic valuing process is a monitoring system which keeps the human infant on the proper course of need satisfaction. Infants evaluate their experiences according to whether or not they like them, whether they are pleasing or displeasing to them, and so on. Such evaluations result from their spontaneous responses to direct experiences; i.e., they are completely "natural."

The structure of self is subsequently shaped through interaction with the environment, particularly the environment composed of significant others (e.g., parents). In other words, as the child becomes socially sensitive and as his or her cognitive-perceptual abilities mature, his or her self-conception becomes increasingly differentiated and complex. To a large extent, then, the content of one's self-concept is a social product. Elements important in self-concept development follow.

Need for Positive Regard Rogers contends that all persons possess a basic desire to experience attitudes such as warmth, respect, admiration, love, and acceptance from significant people in their lives. This *need for positive regard* develops as the awareness of self emerges, and in the individual is pervasive and persistent. It is first seen in the infant's need for being loved and cared for and thereafter reflects the person's satisfaction at receiving the approval of others and frustration at receiving disapproval. Rogers indicates that positive regard may be either learned or innately given to all persons, and although he prefers the former explanation (i.e., that it is a secondary, learned motive), its origin is irrelevant to his theory. An intriguing aspect of positive regard is its reciprocal nature; that is, when an individual views himself or herself as satisfying another's need for positive regard, he or she necessarily experiences satisfaction of his or her own need.

Rogers' fundamental position is that the child will do almost anything, even sacrifice his organismic valuing process, to satisfy his need for positive regard. For example, if a parent insists that a child behave like a "nice little boy" in order to receive love and affection, the child will begin to value experiences in terms of the parental image of "niceness" rather than in terms of his own organismic reaction to them. Instead of being free to discover how it would feel to say a "naughty" word, put a frog in his sister's bed, or steal a candy bar from the drugstore, he prejudges these experiences as "bad" and condemns them. Hence, the child's behavior comes to be regulated not by the degree to which experiences maintain or enhance his self-concept but instead by the likelihood of receiving positive regard. Rogers describes this state of incongruity between self and experience in the following way:

> This, as we see it, is the basic estrangement in man. He has not been true to himself, to his own natural organismic valuing of experience, but for the sake of preserving the positive regard of others has now come to falsify some of the values he experiences and to perceive them only in terms based upon their value to others.

Yet this has not been a conscious choice, but a natural—and tragic—development in infancy. The path of development toward psychological maturity . . . is the undoing of this estrangement in man's functioning . . . the achievement of a self which is congruent with experience, and the restoration of a unified organismic valuing process as the regulator of behavior (Rogers, 1959, pp. 226–227).

According to Rogers, the person needs positive regard not only from others but also from himself. The need for *positive self-regard* is a learned need which develops out of the association of self-experiences with the satisfaction or frustration of the need for positive regard. It refers to the individual's satisfaction at approving and dissatisfaction at disapproving himself. Viewing it from another perspective, it is as if the self had become its own "significant social other." The development of positive self-regard assures that the tendency toward becoming an independent person, which is part of the tendency toward self-actualization, will take the form of following behavior and development that is compatible with the self-concept. Consequently, the person is unlikely to behave in ways which are inconsistent with his self-concept because this would frustrate his need for positive self-regard.

Conditions of Worth Given the fact that the child has a compelling need for positive regard, she becomes increasingly sensitive to, or influenced by, the attitudes and expectations toward her of the important people in her life. This is not surprising insofar as most adults in the child's life make their positive regard for her *conditional* (i.e., I will love, respect, and accept you *only if* you are the kind of person I expect you to be). Such *conditional positive regard* (also designated as "conditions of worth") represents the situation in which the child receives praise, attention, approval, and other forms of reward for behaving in accordance with others' conceptions of what she ought to be.

For example, such is the case when a father tells his son that bringing home a straight "A" report card will not only earn him a bonus to his weekly allowance but also excuse him from having to wash the family car and mow the grass. Conditional positive regard is also manifest in many other types of human relationships involving the giving or withholding of approval and support. Football coaches frequently award a gold star (pasted to the helmet for all spectators to see) to the player who gains the most yardage or makes the most tackles in a game. The college president awards or denies promotions to faculty members on the basis of their demonstrated excellence in teaching or research activities. In each instance, the individual's view of his self-importance (self-esteem) is contingent upon fulfilling the demands or standards imposed by others.

Rogers states, rather forcefully, that conditions of worth imposed on a child are *detrimental* to his becoming a fully functioning person. This is because the child tries to attain standards others set for him rather than identifying and attaining what he really is or wants to be. Thus, he comes to evaluate himself and his worth as an individual (what is valuable and what is not valuable about himself) in terms of those of his actions, thoughts, and feelings that received approval and support. He will feel that in some respects he is prized and in others not. This process results in a self-concept which is out of kilter with organismic experience and hence does not serve as a solid foundation for psychological health.

Unconditional Positive Regard   While it is obvious that no person is completely devoid of conditions of worth, Rogers feels that it is possible to give or receive positive regard irrespective of the worth placed on specific aspects of a person's behavior. This means that the person is accepted and respected for what he or she is—without any ifs, ands, or buts. Such *unconditional positive regard* is strikingly evident in a mother's love for her child when,— regardless of the child's actions, thoughts, and feelings—he or she is genuinely loved and respected. She loves her child because it is her child, not because the child has fulfilled any specific condition or lived up to any specific expectation.

Rogers postulates that if the maturing individual experiences only unconditional positive regard

> . . . then no conditions of worth would develop, self-regard would be unconditional, the needs for positive regard and self-regard would never be at variance with organismic evaluation, and the individual would continue to be psychologically adjusted, and would be fully functioning. This chain of events is hypothetically possible, and hence important theoretically, though it does not appear to occur in actuality (Rogers, 1959, p. 224).

Rogers feels that nothing in the child's behavior is so objectionable as to give the parent a reason to say, "If you do this, or if you feel this way, then I can no longer value and love you." Admittedly, for the average parent, this is a difficult principle to remember while his three-year-old is systematically kicking in the family's new color TV screen. However, it is important to understand that unconditional positive regard does not literally mean that significant others must condone or approve everything the child does. For instance, if a young child tries to play with Daddy's power saw, he must be restrained. Otherwise, he could saw the color TV, the house, himself, or (for Freudians) even Daddy! But if his need to experience positive regard is to be continued even though he is being restrained, it must be perfectly clear from the parent's method of restraining that there is no loss of approval and respect for him as a person. If the child is spanked or told he is a bad boy for wanting to play with Daddy's tools, then he is not being positively regarded. If, on the other hand, he is told in simple words appropriate to his age level that while it may be fun to play with Dad's power saw, such an activity is unsafe, then he is still being respected as a person.

It can be seen, then, that Rogers' emphasis on unconditional positive regard as the ideal approach to child rearing does not imply an absence of discipline, social contraints, or other forms of behavioral control. What it does mean is providing an *atmosphere* in which the child is valued and loved for exactly what he or she is—a precious human being. When children perceive themselves in such a way that no self-experience is more or less worthy of positive regard than any other, they are experiencing *unconditional positive self-regard*. For Rogers, the existence of unconditional positive self-regard enables the individual to become a fully functioning person.

Experience of Threat and the Process of Defense

Rogers has argued that most ways of behaving which an individual adopts are those which are consistent with the structure of his or her self-concept. In other words, the individual seeks to maintain a state of consistency among self-perceptions and experience. It logically follows that experiences which are in accord with the individual's self-concept and its conditions of worth are permitted entry to awareness and are perceived accurately. Conversely, incoming experiences which conflict with the self and its conditions of worth constitute a threat to the self-concept; they are prevented from entering awareness and being accurately perceived. It should be noted here that the individual's conception of himself or herself is the criterion against which experiences are compared and either symbolized in awareness or denied symbolization.

Suppose a young woman has been taught by her parents to believe that it's a grave sin to engage in premarital intercourse. However, while attending college she is exposed to attitudes and values which give unqualified support to sexual relations, especially when one feels genuine love for another person. Although she continues to accept her earlier introjected values, the young woman is about to marry a man who feels that "making love" presents no moral dilemma since they are committed to each other. She complies and finds it pleasant. For Rogers, this experience is in direct violation of her self-image; she regards this behavior as immoral and definitely out of line with who she really is. Consequently, engaging in sexual behavior in these circumstances is threatening to her. It simply does not fit her self-concept.

In Rogers' theory, *threat* exists when a person recognizes an incongruity between his or her self-concept (and its incorporated conditions of worth) and actual experience. Experiences incongruent with the self-concept are perceived as threatening; they are kept from entering awareness because the individual's personality is no longer a unified whole. Thus, if an individual views himself as an honest person and he behaves dishonestly, he is in a state of threat. Or, as in the earlier example, the young woman who believes that premarital sex is wrong and yet experiences it as pleasant is threatened. The individual's response to such a state of incongruence is one of tension and internal confusion.

Incongruity between self and experience need not be perceived at a conscious level. In fact, Rogers postulates that it is quite possible for an individual to discriminate an experience as threatening without the threat being symbolized in awareness. Consequently, whenever incongruity between the self-concept and experience exists and the individual is unaware of it, he or she is potentially vulnerable to anxiety and personality disorganization. *Anxiety* is thus an emotional response to threat which signals that the organized self-structure is in possible danger of becoming disorganized if the discrepancy between it and the threatening experience reaches awareness. The anxiety-ridden individual is one who dimly perceives (without full awareness) that the recognition or symbolization of certain experiences would force a drastic change in his or her current self-image. Thus, the awareness of deep feelings of aggression and hostility would demand a major reorganization in the self-concept of an individual who conceives of himself or herself as a totally loving person. This individual will experience anxiety whenever he feels and acknowledges anger and hostility.

For Rogers, as long as the individual is in no way threatened, he or she is open to experience and does not need to exhibit defensiveness. When, however, some experience is perceived or *subceived* (discriminated without awareness) to be incongruent or inconsistent with the self-concept, threat exists, which, in turn, is followed by a defensive response. Rogers (1959) defines the process of *defense* as the behavioral response of the organism to threat, the goal of which is the maintenance of the current self-structure:

> This goal is achieved by the perceptual distortion of the experience in awareness, in such a way as to reduce the incongruity between the experience and the structure of the self, or by the denial of any experience, thus denying any threat to the self (Rogers, 1959, pp. 204–205).

In essence, the organism erects defenses in order to preserve its self-consistency and to protect itself from the impending danger of threatening experiences.

The Defense Mechanisms

Rogers proposes only two basic mechanisms of defense: *perceptual distortion* and *denial*. Perceptual distortion is operative whenever an incongruent experience is allowed into awareness but only in a form that makes it consistent with the person's current self-image. For instance, suppose that a college student perceives herself as quite bright but receives an unexpected and yet fully justified grade of "F" on an examination. She can maintain her self-concept intact by distorting the symbolized conceptualization of this failure by saying "The professor is unfair in his grading practices" or "I just had bad luck." Rogers occasionally refers to such selective perceptions or distortions as *rationalizations*. In the case of denial, a far less common defensive response, the individual preserves the integrity of her self-structure by completely avoiding any conscious recognition of threatening experiences. That is, the individual ignores the actual existence of those experiences which are inconsistent with her self-concept. An example of denial familiar to many professors is that of a student who fails four of the required five examinations in a course and then appears on the morning of the fifth and final examination to ask what he needs on the final to pass the course. Because it is incompatible with his self-concept, the student has denied to awareness the mounting evidence that he is mathematically unable to pass the course. Quite obviously, when denial is carried to an extreme, it can have psychological consequences far more grave than flunking a course.

Personality Disorganization and Psychopathology

Thus far in our presentation of Rogers' phenomenological theory of personality we have described events which apply to every individual in a greater or lesser degree. Even the most psychologically healthy individual is periodically threatened by an experience which is discrepant from his self-concept and which forces him to distort or deny the experience. Anxiety is a conspicuous aspect of everyday life in modern society. Correspondingly, most individuals possess adequate defenses for dealing with moderate levels of anxiety. When, however, experiences become more than moderately inconsistent with the self-structure or when incongruent experiences occur frequently, then the individual experiences a level of anxiety that is distinctly offensive and may seriously disrupt his daily routine. A person in such an incongruent state is typically labeled "neurotic" (although not by Rogers himself, since he avoids the use of such labels, maintaining that they cloud rather than clarify one's perception of the person involved). In such instances, the person's inner discomfort is such that he is likely to seek the help of a psychotherapist as a means of alleviating his anxiety. Nonetheless, the neurotic's defenses are still partially effective in preventing threatening experiences from being accurately symbolized in awareness. The result is that the neurotic's self-structure is allowed to remain in a whole, if somewhat tenuous, state.

According to Rogers, if there is a significant degree of incongruence between the individual's self-concept and his evaluation of experience, then his defenses may become inoperable. In his "defenseless" state, with the incongruent experience accurately symbolized in awareness, the self-concept becomes shattered. Thus, personality disorganization and psychopathology occur when the self is unable to defend itself against threatening experiences. Persons undergoing such disorganization are commonly tagged "psychotic." They manifest behaviors which to an objective observer seem bizarre, irrational, or even "crazy." Rogers posits that psychotic behaviors are often times congruent with the denied aspects of experience rather than congruent with the self-concept. For example, a person who has kept his sexual impulses under rigid control, denying that they were a part of his self-image, may make obvious sexual overtures toward those whom he encounters during his psychotic break with reality. Many irrational behaviors associated with psychosis are of this nature.

Rogers' *client-centered therapy* attempts to reestablish a more harmonious relationship between the self-concept and the total organism and to facilitate a greater degree of congruence between the self-concept and the phenomenal field of experience. The details of this therapeutic approach will be discussed in the "Application section" of this chapter.

ROGERS' VIEW OF THE GOOD LIFE: THE FULLY FUNCTIONING PERSON

Rogers, like most other therapy-oriented personologists, has advanced certain ideas as to what constitutes the "good life" in terms of concrete personality characteristics. Such views are largely based on his experiences gleaned from working with disturbed and troubled people who struggled to achieve that life.

The Rogerian view of the good life begins with an assessment of what it is not. Specifically, the good life is neither a fixed state of being (i.e., it is not a state of virtue, contentment, happiness) nor a condition in which the individual is adjusted, fulfilled, or actualized. Nor is it, to use psychological terms, a state of drive reduction, of tension reduction, or of homeostasis. The good life is not a destination but a direction. Rogers explains:

> It is a process of movement in a direction which the human organism selects when it is inwardly free to move in any direction. . . . the general qualities of this selected direction appear to have a certain universality. . . . the person who is psychologically free moves in the direction of becoming a more fully functioning person (1961, pp. 187–191).

"Fully functioning" is a term used by Rogers to designate individuals who are using their capacities and talents, realizing their potentialities, and are moving toward complete knowledge of themselves and their full range of experiences. Rogers specifies five major personality characteristics pertaining to people who are fully functioning. They are enumerated and briefly discussed below.

1   The first and foremost characteristic of the fully functioning person is *openness to experience.* To be open to experience is the polar opposite of defensiveness. Individuals who are completely open to experience are able to listen to themselves, to experience what is going on within themselves without threat. They are acutely aware of their own feelings (but not self-consciously), they do not try to suppress them, they often act upon them, and even if they do not act upon them, they are able to admit them to awareness.

For example, the fully functioning person may suddenly, while sitting in a personality class, strongly experience the feeling that he would like to have sex right now with the young woman seated in front of him. If he has any sense, he won't follow through with this feeling—it would disrupt the class and not, in the long run, facilitate his actualizing tendency. But the point is that he would not be threatened by the feeling itself—there are no internal barriers or inhibitions preventing conscious awareness of his feeling states. The fully functioning person is sufficiently rational to recognize his feelings and is able to make judgments as to the prudence of acting on them at any given time. Feeling something does not automatically mean that one acts upon that feeling. Thus, the person in this instance would probably recognize and accept the sexual impulse for what it is, realize that it would be damaging to himself and others (particularly the young woman who is unknowingly its "object"), and thus put it aside and turn his attention to other matters (like the personality lecture that is going on at the time). For the fully functioning person, then, no internal experience or emotion is threatening in its own right—he is truly *open* to all.

   2 The second characteristic of the optimally functioning person listed by Rogers is what he terms *existential living*. This is the global quality of living fully in each and every moment of one's existence. By doing so, each moment of one's life is new and different from that which existed before. Thus, as Rogers (1961) describes it, what a person is or will be in the next moment grows out of that moment and cannot be predicted in advance by either the person or others (the correspondence with existential philosophy is quite clear here). A related aspect of existential living is that the individual's self and personality emerge from experience, rather than experience being translated or twisted to fit some preconceived self-structure. Hence, people living the good life are flexible, adaptable, tolerant, and spontaneous. They discover the structure of their experiences in the process of living them.

   3 Still another attribute of the fully functioning person is what Rogers calls *organismic trusting*. This dimension of the good life is best illustrated in the context of decision making. Specifically, in choosing what course of action to take in any situation, many people rely upon a code of social norms laid down by some group or institution (e.g., the church), upon the judgment of others (from spouse and friends to Ann Landers), or upon the ways they have behaved in other similar situations. In short, their decision-making capacities are strongly if not totally dominated by external sources of influence. Conversely, fully functioning persons attend to their organismic experiences as the valid sources of information for deciding what they should or should not do. Or, as Rogers says, "doing what 'feels right' proves to be a competent and trustworthy guide to behavior which is truly satisfying (1961, p. 190)." Organismic trusting thus signifies the ability to consult and abide by one's inner experiences as the major basis for reaching decisions.

   4 The fourth characteristic of the fully functioning person noted by Rogers is *experiential freedom*. This facet of the good life involves the sense that one is free to live one's life in any way one chooses. It is subjective freedom, a *feeling* that one, of his or her own volition, is able to play a responsible part in shaping his or her own world. At the same time, Rogers does not deny that the person's behavior is heavily influenced by his or her biological makeup, social forces, and past experiences, which, in fact, determine the choices that are made. Indeed, Rogers contends that there can be no freedom in accounting for human choice. Yet he also believes that fully functioning people operate as free choice agents, so that whatever happens to them depends on themselves exclusively. Experiential freedom thus refers to the inner feeling that "I am solely responsible for my own actions and their consequences."

Rogers' overall position on the freedom versus determinism issue will be discussed more fully in the ensuing section of this chapter.

5   The final characteristic associated with optimal psychological maturity is *creativity.* For Rogers, the person who is involved in the good life would be the type of person from whom creative products (ideas, projects, actions) and creative living emerge. Creative people would also tend to live constructively in their culture while at the same time satisfying their own deepest needs. They would be able, creatively, to make adequate adjustments to changing environmental conditions. However, Rogers adds that such people are not necessarily fully adjusted to their culture and are almost certainly not conformists. Their relation to the society around them might best be put this way—they are in and of the society of which they are members, but they are *not* prisoners of that society.

Rogers attempts to weld these various qualities of the fully functioning person into a composite picture when he writes:

> . . . the good life involves a wider range, a greater richness, than the constricted living in which most of us find ourselves. To be a part of this process means that one is involved in the frequently frightening and frequently satisfying experience of a more sensitive living, with greater range, greater variety, greater richness.
>
> I believe it will have become evident why, for me, adjectives such as happy, contented, blissful, enjoyable, do not seem quite appropriate to any general description of this process I have called the good life, even though the person in this process would experience each one of these feelings at appropriate times. But the adjectives which seem more generally fitting are adjectives such as enriching, exciting, rewarding, challenging, meaningful. This process of the good life is not, I am convinced, a life for the faint-hearted. It involves the stretching and growing of becoming more and more of one's potentialities. It involves the courage to be. It means launching oneself into the stream of life (1961, pp. 195–196).

It is evident, then, that Rogers, like Maslow and to some extent Allport before him, wants the person to look up to what he *can be.* For Rogers, this means being fully alive, fully aware, fully involved in what it really means to be a human being—in brief, "fully functioning." Upon further analysis, one cannot help but notice the basic communalities of Rogers' "fully functioning person," Maslow's "self-actualizer," and, to a degree, Allport's "mature personality." These three theorists (particularly Rogers and Maslow) are in general agreement about what humanity can be because they share certain basic convictions about what humanity is. It is to Carl Rogers' basic assumptions concerning human nature, then, that we now turn.

ROGERS' BASIC ASSUMPTIONS CONCERNING HUMAN NATURE

At the beginning of the 1970s, B. F. Skinner and Carl Rogers were the two most influential living American psychologists. With all psychologists exposed

Freedom	✓ _ _ _ _ _ _ _ _ _ _	Determinism
Rationality	✓ _ _ _ _ _ _ _ _ _ _	Irrationality
Holism	✓ _ _ _ _ _ _ _ _ _ _	Elementalism
Constitutionalism	_ _ _ ✓ _ _ _ _ _ _ _	Environmentalism
Subjectivity	✓ _ _ _ _ _ _ _ _ _ _	Objectivity
Proactivity	✓ _ _ _ _ _ _ _ _ _ _	Reactivity
Homeostasis	_ _ _ _ _ _ _ _ _ _ ✓	Heterostasis
Knowability	_ _ _ _ _ _ _ _ _ _ ✓	Unknowability

Figure 9-1 Rogers's position on the eight basic assumptions concerning human nature.

to the thinking of each, they have both attracted numerous followers. As the symbolic figureheads of the deep split in contemporary American psychology, that between behaviorism and phenomenology, Skinner and Rogers differ from one another on many important issues. But *nowhere* do they differ more profoundly than in their respective images of humanity. And *nowhere* is this difference more apparent than in the basic assumptions that each makes concerning the nature of human beings. Examination of Rogers' assumptions (depicted in Figure 9-1) should make this profound philosophic difference quite evident. In fact, on practically every assumption on which Skinner and Rogers can legitimately be compared, the reader will find that they are virtually *polar opposites!*

1 Freedom–Determinism In discussing his differences with behavioristic psychology in general and B. F. Skinner in particular, Rogers (1974) noted that his experience in therapy and in groups made it impossible for him to deny the reality and significance of human choice. For years, Rogers has observed all kinds of persons in both individual therapy and encounter group situations struggling to grow, facing difficult life decisions, and ultimately making these decisions. And the choices that an individual makes, much as in existential philosophy, help to create the kind of person he or she will eventually become. For Rogers, then, people are to some extent architects of themselves.

Freedom, in Rogers' theory, is an integral part of his master motive, the actualizing tendency. The natural course of that tendency is away from control of the person by external forces toward progressively greater internal and autonomous behavioral directions (Rogers, 1959). That is, the more the actualizing tendency can operate, (1) the more people can overcome the "conditions of worth" placed upon them in early life, (2) the more aware and open they are to experience, and (3) the more free they will be in creating themselves and charting the courses of their lives. The actualizing tendency is maximally operative in "fully functioning persons" who, as has already been noted, can be described by such characteristics as experiential freedom, organismic trusting, and existential living. Here, human freedom reaches its peak; these individuals know they are free, look toward themselves for the fountainhead of that freedom, and really "live it" every minute. Rogers' commitment to the freedom assumption is indeed strong.

2 Rationality–Irrationality   At the deepest level of being, the Rogerian person is rational. The irrationalities in human actions so apparent in everyday life—e.g., murder, rape, war, college administrative policies—result from humanity's being "out of tune" with its true inner nature. Again, as in the case of human freedom, humanity's true rationality rises to its highest level when the actualizing tendency is operating maximally. When social conditions permit people to behave in accordance with their true nature, rationality will guide their conduct.

As Rogers clarifies in a published interview with Willard Frick (Frick, 1971), freedom, rationality, and the actualizing tendency are all inextricably interwoven in his basic image of humanity. When the operation of the actualizing tendency is facilitated, an individual progressively becomes more free and aware in directing his or her behavior. As one becomes more aware, one is correspondingly more able to select the course of one's self-actualization rationally. In the ideal situation, this point-counterpoint relationship results in a fully functioning person whose behavior is exquisitely rational. Such a conception of human beings would not be possible without the rationality assumption firmly implanted at its base.

3 Holism–Elementalism   Rogers is very much committed to understanding and studying the person as a gestalt or unified whole. As noted earlier, Rogers' holistic emphasis is evident throughout his theorizing. But it is perhaps most evident in his central theoretical construct of self. For a theorist to find it necessary to posit such a global, all-inclusive, and unitary construct to explain behavior requires as a precursor the holistic assumption.

Moreover, in Rogers' system, the self is always moving in the direction of greater wholeness (Rogers, 1963). This view is a salient feature of Rogers' account of human development, which begins with the infant's undifferentiated phenomenological field, continues as that field becomes differentiated into self and environment—as the self-concept emerges—and culminates in the organism's continuing efforts to achieve a unity of self and self-consistency. Developmentally speaking, then, the person, if he or she is healthy, is always moving towards progressively greater wholeness and unification. Holism is a basic assumption commonly found among humanistically oriented personologists; Rogers' theory epitomizes this principle.

4 Constitutionalism–Environmentalism   Rogers is moderately committed to constitutionalism in its very broadest sense. That is, in reading his theoretical writings, one is struck by the relative frequency of his use of such phrases as "human nature," "man's inner nature," "man's true self," "man's innate potential," all of which imply a biological base of human development and personality. This constitutional leaning is perhaps most evident in Rogers' concept of the actualizing tendency. It cannot be forgotten that life's master motive is inherent, rooted in the physiological processes of the body, and, in brief, a biological fact of life. To describe the unitary motive underlying all human activity in such terms reflects, quite simply, the constitutionalism assumption.

But that is not the whole story. As the self unfolds, it is significantly influenced by environmental variables. "Unconditional positive regard" from others who count in the environment facilitates healthy self-development; imposition of "conditions of worth" impedes it. Thus, the person's emergent self-concept is laden with environmental influences. So Rogers' theory is by no means devoid of the environmentalism assumption.

Yet, to place Rogers' position on the constitutionalism-environmentalism assumption in proper perspective, one must see its relationship to his position on the freedom and rationality assumptions. As noted in Chapter 1, the eight basic assumptions are not entirely independent from one another; the same most certainly holds true for the position of any given theorist on them. In this instance, Rogers contends that human beings are the only animals who really can be aware of both their past and present life situations, thus making it possible for them to make choices about their futures (Frick, 1971). Thus, because people are rational and free, they are able (at least to some extent) to rise above the constitutional and particularly the environmental influences upon their development. In brief, Rogers' belief that human beings, as in existential philosophy, considerably shape their own destinies moderates the potency of his position on the constitutionalism-environmentalism question.

5 Subjectivity–Objectivity Without a doubt, subjectivity is the key assumption in Rogers' system. In fact, the entire structure of phenomenological theory is based squarely upon it. For Rogers, each person lives entirely in a rich, ever-changing, private, subjective world of experience of which he or she is the center. Each person perceives the world in his own terms and responds to it accordingly. And at the very heart of the individual's perceptual system is his perception of himself—his self-concept. In Rogers' theory, then, human behavior is forever unintelligible without reference to the person's private world of experience. In direct opposition to B. F. Skinner and much of contemporary behaviorism, Rogers contends that we can never adequately understand human actions simply by examining objective, environmental conditions alone. Instead, we must *always look within the person* and attempt to see the world from his perspective in order to approach an understanding of his behavior.

As an illustration of this phenomenological position, consider a so-called objective situation where a group of people are involved—a college course in personality. The professor is the same, the students are the same, the room is the same, and the lectures are the same. What is *never* the same is the way that each person involved *subjectively experiences* and consequently responds to the entire course or any particular class meeting of it. For example, Student A, who usually finds the course positive and enriching, has an intense headache a particular day and experiences the lecture material as abstract, dull, and irrelevant. That he has been up virtually all night drinking and is functioning on two hours' sleep may have contributed to this experiential state. Thus, he finds himself dozing. Student B, who normally finds the course material irrelevant to her own concerns (she plans to be a hermit), the same day experiences it as quite relevant and relates to it well. Usually mute, she asks a lot of questions that day. For some reason, the professor has decided to discuss the topic of "basic insecurity," and student B finds this simply fascinating. For his part, the professor, who normally loves teaching his personality course, arrives that day with many conerns: he has not prepared any lecture at all, he's worried that the pittance which the university gives him in the guise of a salary will not meet his rising family expenses, he's concerned about gaining tenure at the university, and he is anxious about the results of his recent research project. So, on the spot, he decides to lecture on "basic insecurity" which, that day, he may really be more prepared to talk about than he thinks. Nonetheless, he delivers his lecture in an uncharacteristically nervous voice accompanied by other signs of tension not typically exhibited by him.

Without elaborating further, the point is that in Rogers' system the behavior of these three persons (or anyone else in the class—or in the world) cannot be explained by reference to objective external conditions alone. It can be adequately explained *only* in terms of each individual's private world of subjective experience—where he or she really *lives*. That's really "where it's at" in Rogers' view; more formally stated, subjectivity is the essence of the phenomenological position. Rogers' commitment to the subjectivity assumption could not be stronger.

6 Proactivity–Reactivity The Rogerian person is purposive, forward-moving, and oriented toward the future. As a being who internally generates his or her own behavior, this person is eminently proactive. The person's proactivity in Rogers' system becomes readily apparent when one examines where all human behavior originates, viz., the actualizing tendency. Because of this master motive inherent to all human life, humanity is forever moving forward, growing, and in brief, "proacting."

While Rogers recognizes that a certain amount of external stimulation is probably necessary for self-actualization to progress (Frick, 1971), outer stimuli appear to be things that the innate actualizing tendency feeds upon rather than reacts to. The person psychologically *devours* external stimuli rather than simply reacting to them. A classroom learning situation is a good example of this distinction. In Rogers' view, one does not learn simply as a direct function of being "taught" (i.e., reacting to external stimuli). But people can profit from classroom learning; they have an innate tendency to grow and expand their horizons (the actualizing tendency) and the right classroom stimulus situation can facilitate this growth by prompting them to move in directions that they otherwise would not have without this classroom exposure.

So, in Rogers' system, the person feeds upon external stimuli—they nourish his or her growth. But the sole moving force of human behavior is the actualizing tendency; one is not prodded into activity by external stimulation. This view reflects Rogers' strong commitment to the proactivity assumption.

7 Homeostasis–Heterostasis   Since this assumption deals with a motivational question, one need only turn again to Rogers' sole motivational construct to determine his position on it. Specifically, the actualizing tendency is a heterostatic concept.

As is very clear at this point, Rogers' actualizing tendency is always moving in the direction of growth, enhancement, and self-realization of the person. Drives that other theorists regard as homeostatic—e.g., hunger, sex, and competence—are subsumed by the heterostatic master motive in Rogers' system. And more—the actualizing tendency thrives on *tension increase, not tension reduction.* The Rogerian person naturally seeks stimulation, new challenges, and novel possibilities for personal growth. All this culminates in Rogers' view of the good life. Recall that it was described as a direction rather than a destination. Thus, Rogers' fully functioning person is always striving, always stretching, always seeking actualization of his or her potentialities. Rogers' commitment to the heterostatic assumption could not be stronger.

8 Knowability–Unknowability   Rogers' phenomenological position, when carried to its logical conclusion, necessarily implies that the human organism is unknowable in scientific terms. More specifically, as already noted, the subjectivity assumption is the philosophic essence of the phenomenological position. And subjectivity means that each individual lives in a private world of experience which he or she alone has the potential to comprehend. No one is fully able to understand anyone else and, hence, their nature. According to this view, neither can psychological science.

Rogers clearly addresses himself to this point in what is probably the most rigorous statement of his theory to date (Rogers, 1959). While he admits that there may be such a thing as "objective" truth or reality, the person is not going to arrive at it because each lives in a private world of subjective experience. As Rogers puts it: "Thus there is no such thing as Scientific Knowledge, there are only individual perceptions of what appears to each person to be such knowledge (Rogers, 1959, p. 192)." If there's no such thing as scientific knowledge, it's a sure bet that human nature is never going to be understood through it.

So, from Rogers' perspective, what are we doing in psychology? Perhaps the answer to this question is precisely why Rogers has been dubbed a "respected gadfly" of psychology by a scientific awards committee of the American Psychological Association and why he accepts this label so readily. For a professional lifetime, Carl Rogers has consistently argued against the traditional strongholds of scientific psychology (e.g., the structure and inhumane nature of graduate education in the field), pioneered scientific research in areas pertaining to subjective experience (e.g., psychotherapy research), and, in general, has done everything that he can to broaden the scope of scientific concepts and methodology to incorporate as much of human subjectivity as possible. Thus, by refocusing psychology on *human experience,* perhaps he hopes to catch a greater glimpse of what humanity is. While he has undoubtedly profited much from his scientific endeavors, however, one must conclude from reading Carl Rogers that he has learned far more about human nature from his many clients than he has from reading the literature of psychology or doing scientific research.

The following section reflects the research his theory has generated.

EMPIRICAL VALIDATION OF PHENOMENOLOGICAL THEORY CONCEPTS

Strictly speaking, Rogers' theory pertains not only to personality but also to psychotherapy and the process of change in human behavior. Practically all the empirical studies conducted by Rogers and his associates have been aimed at elucidating and understanding the nature of the therapeutic process, the conditions which facilitate personality growth, and the effectiveness of therapy to bring about permanent behavioral change. The emphasis on psychotherapy research has indirectly produced considerable data concerning the self-concept and its governance of the individual's psychological adjustment. This is understandable insofar as the concept of self is pivotal in Rogers' theory. It is to Rogers' credit that he has opened up psychotherapy and the nature of self as meaningful areas of research. Largely through his efforts, personologists are becoming more cognizant of the self as a useful explanatory construct in accounting for human behavior. More importantly, Rogers' formulation of a phenomenological theory has made the self an object of respectable empirical investigation. No one in contemporary psychology has been more influential than Carl Rogers in providing an intellectual climate in which research on the self structure can flourish.

In this section we will consider three illustrative studies bearing upon the scientific validity of Rogerian concepts. First, however, it is necessary that the reader become acquainted with Rogers' view of psychological science and research, the method by which he measures the self-concept, and the research strategy he employs to study the changes in self-concept during the course of therapy.

Rogers' View of Science and Research

Rogers is strongly committed to phenomenology as a basis for developing a science of persons and as a method of examining the empirical validity of theoretical concepts. It will be recalled that phenomenology refers to a disciplined effort to understand the essence of the person's subjective experience—specifically, how people come to know and understand their world and themselves. The focus of the phenomenological method emphasizes the data or phenomena of consciousness with the ultimate goal of comprehending the essence of things appearing in consciousness (Misiak and Sexton, 1973). Rogers states that such effort is justified because

> . . . it is satisfying to perceive the world as having order and because rewarding results often ensue when one understands the orderly relationships which appear to exist in nature. One of these rewarding results is that the ordering of one segment of experience in a theory immediately opens up new vistas of inquiry, research, and thought, thus leading one continually forward (1959, p. 188).

Relevant to the research enterprise, Rogers considers clinical observations, as obtained during psychotherapy, as a valid source of phenomenological data. These clinical observations, usually based on selected excerpts from tape-recorded interviews in client-centered therapy, are then systematically analyzed (by means of content analysis) in order that refined hypotheses may be formulated and subjected to scientific scrutiny. In short, it is Rogers' belief that self-referent attitudes and values as expressed during therapy constitute valid and reliable sources of information concerning the self-structure and its pervasive influence on behavior. At the same time, he admits that observational data must be restated in terms of experimental operations if a theory is to be confirmed.

> Science exists only in people. Each scientific project has its creative inception, its process, and its tentative conclusion in a person or persons. Knowledge—even scientific knowledge—is that which is subjectively acceptable (1955, p. 274).

Rogers applies similar logic to the utilization of science. He believes that since science itself is neutral, it will never depersonalize, manipulate, or control individuals. It is only people who can and will do that. Consequently, the way research findings in personology are utilized will depend on value choices made by human beings.

Rogers' notions of science are diametrically opposed to those espoused by B. F. Skinner (see Chapter 5). The respective views of these two eminent psychologists concerning the scientific control of human behavior were dramatized in a debate held before the 1956 convention of the American Psychological Association. In this debate, Rogers noted that he and Skinner are both committed to a science of human behavior. Moreover, both concurred that psychological science is making substantial progress in explaining behavior and developing the capacity to predict and control it. However, Rogers felt that Skinner has vastly underestimated the seriousness of the problems associated with behavioral control. Who will control whom? Who will control the controllers? By what means will behavioral control be exercised? And what forms of behavior will be deemed desirable in a Skinnerian-designed environment? The fact that values and subjective choice are implicitly involved in dealing with these kinds of questions is what makes Rogers hesitant to give unlimited power to the behavioral scientist. Ironically, Rogers has great faith in man in general, whereas he lacks Skinner's confidence in the scientist. Rogers proposes that science be used to create an open society (as opposed to Skinner's closed one) in which individuals are afforded the opportunity to develop the values of responsibility, happiness, security, productivity, and creativity. In short, Rogers believes personological research should ultimately be addressed to questions concerning the good life and how it may best be achieved.

Measuring the Self-Concept: The Q Sort

In the early 1950s William Stephenson (1953), then a colleague of Rogers at the University of Chicago, developed a general methodology, called the *Q technique*, for investigating an individual's self-concept. Rogers and his associates quickly recognized the potential value of Stephenson's work for their own empirical studies on changes in the perceived self during the course of psychotherapy. Accordingly, they adopted the *Q sort*, a specific rating procedure devised by Stephenson, as one of their basic research tools in gathering data about therapeutic improvement.

What is the Q sort? Essentially, it is a method of studying systematically an individual's views about himself and his relationships with others, although it has myriad possibilities. The procedure followed is quite simple. The subject is given a deck of cards, each containing a printed statement or adjective concerning some personality characteristic. The cards may contain such self-referent statements as "I am an aggressive person," "I like to be with other people," "I am emotionally mature." Or the items might be "methodical," "inventive," "sincere," "quick-witted." The subject's task is to sort the cards into a series of piles (usually seven in number), each corresponding to a point along a continuum ranging from those attributes which are *most* like to those which are *least* like him or her. The chief feature of the method is that the subject must sort the cards according to some prearranged or forced distribution. That is, he or she is required to place a specific number of cards in each of a specific number of piles. Although the number of piles varies from one study to another in accordance with the number of Q cards, the forced distribution is usually approximately normal. For example, in the Q-sort distribution illustrated in Figure 9-2, the subject is first required to select the two statements he believes are most characteristic of the person he or she is rating and place them in pile seven. Then he or she chooses four statements that are more characteristic than the remaining thirty-six (and less descriptive than those in pile seven) and place them in pile six. The subject continues in this manner until he or she

Figure 9-2 A forced Q-sort distribution for descriptive statements.

places the remaining two least descriptive statements in pile one. As the example indicates, the number of cards to be placed under each category fan out symmetrically from the center pile (number four), resulting in a forced normal distribution.

Two additional facts regarding the Q sort should be noted. First, statements or adjectives may arise from numerous sources—there is no fixed set of standardized Q-sort items. They may stem from a particular personality theory, from recorded therapeutic interviews, or from personality questionnaires. Second, the forced normal distribution allows for easy computation of statistical results since the mean and variance are held constant across subjects. The forced distribution also helps to control for response sets, since tendencies to give "average" or "extreme" ratings do exist. Conversely, the Q sort has been criticized for forcing subjects to sort statements in ways which may not accurately reflect their self-conceptions. For instance, a subject might feel that the majority of statements do not apply at all, yet he or she is forced by the directions to sort them into the prescribed categories. Another subject might feel that most of the statements are highly characteristic and do not belong in the middle category, yet he or she is also forced to abide by the instructions.

Research-oriented Rogerians generally have their subjects Q sort the statements twice: once for *self-description* and once for *ideal self-description.* For the *self-sort,* subjects are instructed to sort the cards to describe themselves as they see themselves at the present time. This self-sort operationalizes the subject's experience of herself as she is. Following completion of the self-sort, the subject then is instructed to use the same cards to describe the kind of person she would most like to be—her ideal person. This second sort is called the *ideal-sort.*

Q-sort data can be analyzed in several ways. However, the product-moment correlation coefficient is the most commonly used statistic for indicating the degree to which an individual's self-concept and ideal self-concept are congruent or divergent. Employing this method, each Q-sort statement is assigned two numbers, the first number representing the pile number for the self-sort and the second the pile number for the ideal-sort. It is these two numbers that are correlated. The magnitude of the correlation coefficient thus becomes an index of the degree of congruence or incongruence between the perceived self and the ideal self. A positive correlation reveals a state of congruence—whereas a negative correlation reveals a state of incongruence—of the perceived self and the ideal self. Correlation coefficients not significantly different from zero indicate that there is no relationship (similarity) between the way a person sees herself and the way she would like to be.

The research strategy employed by Rogers and his coworkers for investigating psychotherapeutic personality change is quite simple. Clients repeatedly perform self and ideal Q sorts during therapy, at the end of therapy, and in some instances during posttherapy intervals. Each time the correlation between the two sorts is calculated. It thus becomes possible to chart a progressive pattern of change in the relationship between the client's perceived self and ideal self over the course of psychotherapy by comparing the correlations between the two sorts. Rogers' studies also include a control group so as to ensure that any detectable changes found are due to therapy rather than the mere passage of time, familiarity with the Q sort, or other extraneous influences. Control subjects are matched with client subjects on such demographic variables as age, sex, education, and socioeconomic status. They complete self and ideal Q sorts at the same time intervals as does the client group. The only difference between the two groups is that the client group is subjected to the independent treatment variable, client-centered (Rogerian) therapy, while the control group is not. This procedure has enabled Rogers to validate many of his theoretical notions concerning personality growth and change and the therapeutic conditions that bring about these phenomena.

Self-Perception and Psychological Adjustment

As explained earlier, Rogers believes that psychological maladjustment results from incongruence between the self and experience. In other words, a psychologically disturbed person perceives himself and his relation to people and things in his environment in ways which fit some preconceived self-structure. He is therefore prone to deny or distort any experience which conflicts with his existing self-image because awareness of it would leave him vulnerable to anxiety, threat, and disorganization. In contrast to this, a psychologically healthy person is one who perceives himself and his interaction with others in a realistic manner (i.e., as outside observers would see them). Furthermore, the healthy person is open to experience (i.e., is nondefensive), accepts responsibility for his own behavior, and evaluates his experience in terms of the evidence coming from his own senses.

A prime example of how these theoretical notions have been operationally defined and put to empirical test is an early yet frequently cited study conducted by Chodorkoff (1954). This investigator tested three hypotheses regarding the functional relationships among self-perception, perceptual defense, and psychological adjustment:

    1 The greater the agreement between an individual's self-description and an objective description of him or her by others, the less perceptual defense he or she will exhibit.
    2 The greater the agreement between an individual's self-description and an objective appraisal of him or her by others, the more adequate will be his or her personal adjustment.
    3 The more adequate the personality adjustment of an individual, the less perceptual defense he or she will manifest.

    These theoretical predictions were tested by having thirty college students serve as subjects. The measure of self-description was obtained by having each subject Q sort 125 self-referent statements into thirteen piles from most characteristic to least characteristic. Another Q sort of the same items, made for each subject by four clinically trained judges, was employed as the "objective description" measure. The judges' Q sorting was based on clinical material about the subject gained from projective tests administered to each one, including Rorschach and TAT protocols, word association test data, and a biographical inventory.
    A measure of perceptual defense was secured in the following way. First, each subject responded to a word-association test consisting of 100 words, 50 emotional and 50 neutral. The subject's reaction time to each word was recorded by means of a voice-key type of reaction-time apparatus. Next, two groups of 10 words each were selected for each subject to be presented as the stimuli for a perceptual defense test. One group consisted of the emotional words that had the longest reaction times; the other group consisted of the neutral words with the shortest reaction times. This procedure made it possible to select for each subject personally relevant threatening and neutral stimuli. These 20 stimulus words were then randomly presented by means of a tachistoscope, a device which visually displays material for controlled durations of time (e.g., 1/500 second). The exposure time for each word was increased until it was correctly recognized, with this time being used as the recognition threshold score for that word. The measure of perceptual defense was operationally defined by Chodorkoff as the difference between the mean recognition threshold for threatening stimuli (emotional words such as "raped," "Kotex," "penis," "whore") and the mean recognition threshold for neutral stimuli (words such as "child," "apple," "stove," "tree"). The higher this difference, the greater the subject's perceptual defense tendencies were assumed to be.
    Personal adjustment, the third variable examined in Chodorkoff's study,

was derived from two measures: (1) Rorschach scores and (2) ratings made by the clinically experienced judges of eleven adjustment scales.

Each of the hypotheses was evaluated by computing the appropriate correlation coefficients. The first hypothesis stated that accuracy of self-description would be negatively correlated with perceptual defense. The correlation between these two variables was found to be highly significant ($r = -.53$). Thus, the more accurately the subject described himself, the less perceptual defense he or she showed. The second hypothesis compared the accuracy of self-description with the two measures of personal adjustment. A significant relationship was found between high scores on accuracy of self-description and judges' ratings of adjustment ($r = +.73$), but the relationship between accuracy of self-description and adjustment scores based on Rorschach scores failed to reach statistical significance ($r = +.34$). The third hypothesis was evaluated by comparing personal adjustment ratings with the measures of perceptual defense. A significant correlation was found between high scores on perceptual defense and low ratings of adjustment based on judges' ratings ($r = -.62$). However, the relationship between high perceptual defense scores and low adjustment scores based on Rorschach scores, while in the predicted direction, did not reach statistical significance ($r = -.29$).

General support for all three hypotheses led Chodorkoff to the following formulation:

> The better adjusted individual attempts to obtain mastery over threatening situations by getting to know, as quickly as possible, what it is that is threatening. He may be alerted to the possibility of threat and may be influenced by a set which leads him to try to differentiate and symbolize aspects of himself and his environment which are potentially threatening. The less adequately adjusted individual, in contrast, may be thought of as influenced by a set to keep threat inadequately differentiated and inadequately symbolized.
>
> . . . If an individual cannot differentiate and symbolize aspects of himself and his environment, his behavior in turn will not be adequate. He will also be unable to resolve threatening situations when they confront him, for if he does not recognize threat, how can he be expected to deal with it effectively? (1954, p. 510).

Self-Concept and Recall

According to Rogers, experiential materials inconsistent with the self-structure are denied accurate symbolization in awareness. For example, if a young woman's self-concept has been built exclusively around her "femininity," experiences that might imply that she has some masculine tendencies would threaten her severely. In all likelihood, she would erect defenses to avoid recognition of this disturbing thought. An attempt to validate this aspect of Rogerian theory was made by Suinn, Osborne, and Winfree (1962). These investigators hypothesized that memory material which is inconsistent with one's self-concept is more poorly remembered than memory material which is consistent with one's self-concept.

The procedure involved in testing this hypothesis consisted of having thirty college students in a classroom setting describe themselves on one hundred adjectives culled from the Gough Adjective Scale (Gough, 1955). Each subject rated each adjective on a scale ranging from 1 (most like me) to 6 (least like me). Directions were then given such that every subject believed that he or she had been rated on the same adjectives by two other students in the class. Five days later, each subject was presented a completed adjective rating scale said to represent the composite ratings made by the other students of him or her. This actually involved faked ratings designed to present each subject with a set of self-related items discrepant from his or her own self-concept. The faked adjective rating scale contained fifty adjective ratings that were zero degrees discrepant from the subject's own previous self-rating (group 0), twenty-five adjectives that were discrepant by one degree (group II), and twenty-five adjectives that were discrepant by two degrees (group II). Thus, group 0 adjective ratings were consistent with, while groups I and II ratings were to varying degrees inconsistent with, the subject's self-concept. The method of manipulating the discrepancy between self and other adjective ratings is best explained by illustration. If the subject described himself or herself on the adjective "considerate" with a rating of 6 (least like me), a zero discrepancy would be a composite rating also of 6, a one-degree discrepancy would be a rating of 5, and a two-degree discrepancy would be a rating of 4. The direction and magnitude of the self-other discrepancies were randomly chosen, as were the adjectives to form each group. Two days later, subjects again filled out the adjective rating scale, this time as they remembered the composite ratings to be.

Recall accuracy scores were computed for each subject for each of the three groups of adjectives in the following way. If the subject recalled the composite ratings correctly, he or she was given a score of 0 for that adjective; if he or she missed by one degree (e.g., by checking a rating of 3 where the composite rating was 2) a score of 1 was assigned, and so forth up to a maximum possible score of 3. High scores thus indicated low accuracy of recall. These scores were then summed across all subjects and divided by the sample size (thirty subjects) to provide a mean accuracy of recall score for each of the three groups of adjectives. As predicted, Suinn et al. found that accuracy of recall was best for adjectives used by others that were consistent with the self-concept and was poorest for adjectives used by others that were inconsistent with the self-concept. The mean accuracy scores for Groups 0, I, and II adjectives were 0.58, 0.68, and 1.09, respectively. All differences between means were statistically significant. These findings indicate that degree of accuracy of recall of self-related stimuli is a function of the degree to which the stimuli are consistent with the self-concept. More importantly, this study offers empirical support for a key aspect of Rogerian theory.

Self-Acceptance and Acceptance of Others

A final group of studies stemming from Rogers' theoretical position concerns the proposition that the more a person accepts himself the more likely he or she is to accept others. Such a theoretically proposed relationship between self-acceptance and acceptance of others is based on Rogers' observation that when clients enter therapy they typically have negative self-concepts; they are unable to accept themselves. However, once such clients become more accepting of themselves, they become more accepting of others. In other words, Rogers contends that if self-acceptance occurs (i.e., if the self-ideal discrepancy is small), then acceptance, respect, and value of others follows. Other theorists have also suggested that attitudes held toward the self are reflected in attitudes held toward others. Fromm (1956), for example, maintains that self-love and the love of others go hand in hand. He further notes that a failure to love the self is accompanied by a basic hostility toward others.

While numerous studies have supported the relationship between self-acceptance and acceptance of others, a majority of these have used as subjects college students or individuals receiving therapy (e.g., Berger, 1955; Phillips, 1951; Suinn, 1961). Specific to Rogerian theory, however, accumulating evidence indicates that self-acceptance and acceptance of others characterizes parent-child relationships. A study performed by Medinnus and Curtis (1963) is one example. These researchers tested the hypothesis that there is a significant positive relation between self-acceptance and child acceptance in a group of mothers of young children.

Subjects were fifty-six mothers of children enrolled in a cooperative nursery school. Two measures of maternal self-acceptance were obtained. The first consisted of mothers' responses to the Bills Index of Adjustment and Values, a self-report questionnaire yielding a measure of the degree to which self and ideal are different. A semantic differential scale of twenty bipolar adjectives in which the distance between the mothers' ratings of "Me (as I am)" and "Me (as I would most like to be)" was defined operationally as the second measure of maternal self-acceptance. The measure of child acceptance was derived from the same set of bipolar adjectives. Specifically, the distance between the mothers' ratings of "My child (as he is)" and "My child (as I would most like him to be)" was defined as the extent of the mother's acceptance of her child.

The intercorrelations between the two maternal self-acceptance scores and the child acceptance measure are shown in Table 9-1.

As can be seen, each of the three correlation coefficients is statistically significant in the predicted direction. These results support the Rogerian notion that mothers who are self-accepting (i.e., who possess positive self-regard) are far more likely to accept their children as they are than are non-self-accepting mothers. Additionally, such findings suggest that the extent to which a child

Table 9-1 Correlations between Maternal Self-Acceptance and Child-Acceptance Measures

Measures	Bills self-acceptance	Semantic differential child-acceptance
Semantic differential self-acceptance	−.57†	.33*
Bills self-acceptance		−.48†

Source: Adapted from Medinnus & Curtis, 1963, p. 543.
* <.05
† <.01
NOTE: The negative correlations are due to the method of scoring the tests. On the Bills self-acceptance measure, the higher scores indicate greater self-acceptance while the semantic differential self-acceptance and child-acceptance scores are discrepancy scores with the higher scores denoting less favorable attitudes.

develops a positive self-image depends crucially upon the extent to which his or her parents are able to accept themselves.

APPLICATION: CLIENT-CENTERED OR PERSON-TO-PERSON THERAPY

The variety of past and present types of psychotherapy offered to disturbed individuals is enough to boggle the imagination. Psychologists and psychiatrists have asked people to lie down on black leather couches and free-associate, tried to condition and countercondition them, had them enter "orgone boxes" to vibrate, encouraged them to go into empty rooms to let out primal screams, and told them to sit around nude in swimming pools and "encounter" one another. Yet, in spite of earlier evidence that various forms of traditional psychotherapy did not work (Eysenck, 1952, 1966), more recent and thorough evidence indicates that many types of therapy really are effective in helping people deal with their problems (Bergin, 1971; Meltzoff and Kornreich, 1970). Why? Or, phrased differently, how can so many diffuse therapeutic techniques really serve to help distressed people?

Rogers' essential answer to this question is that all true forms of psychotherapy have one element in common—a *relationship* between persons. Specifically, Rogers contends that the quality of the relationship between the therapist and the client is not only the single most important factor but also the only factor responsible for therapeutic personality change. Specific therapeutic techniques are secondary to the clinician-client relationship. This currently widespread approach to psychotherapy instituted by Carl Rogers is known as *client-centered therapy.*

Evolution of Rogerian Therapy: From Techniques to Relationships

Rogers' approach to psychotherapy has undergone considerable evolution over the years. While his basic assumptions have remained stable, his means of implementing them, like the Rogerian person that he depicts, have continually developed. Specifically, Rogers' approach was first known as *nondirective therapy* (some still refer to it that way today). This term reflected Rogers' main concern at the time with techniques by which behavioral change might be achieved. Because the client was assumed to have the capacity for self-directed personality change, Rogers pioneered techniques which enabled the therapist to be much less directive in the relationship than was the case with other forms of therapy. For example, nondirective therapists of old never gave advice, answered questions, or probed by asking their own questions. Instead, they systematically attempted to reflect back to the client what he or she had said and to clarify his or her feelings in the process (*reflection* and *clarification*). In effect, the therapist acted as a kind of mirror exactly the opposite of the type found in amusement parks. Amusement-park mirrors distort one's image in various ways. Conversely, in nondirective therapy it is the client's self-image that is distorted so that the therapist's essential task, as a "mirror," was to reflect back to the client more accurately what he or she was really saying and feeling. These techniques, while still employed today, are somewhat limiting if they constitute the only function that the therapist provides in the relationship. To illustrate, if a client innocently asks "What time is it?" it is probably more productive for the therapist to respond "It's 10:45" than to say warmly and empathically "You feel you want to know what time it is."

With the publication in 1951 of his book *Client-Centered Therapy*, Rogers' approach progressed further and came to be known primarily by this label, as it still is today. While still retaining his nondirective techniques, Rogers at this time was emphasizing the importance of the clients' perceptions, of therapeutically entering the clients' world of subjective experience and focusing upon the clients' perceptions of themselves, their lives, and their problems. Thus, the term "client-centered." Since that time, however, Rogers' approach has evolved to still another level. He has become much more overtly concerned with the issue of precisely what conditions must be met before the client can begin to resolve his or her problems. As stated earlier, he discovered that the relationship between therapist and client is the most important aspect underlying personality change; consequently, he funneled all his efforts on this in the late 1950s (Rogers, 1957b, 1958, 1959) and continues to do so today. Again, it should be stressed that Rogers' changes in thinking in this regard represent a progressive evolution to a more comprehensive and meaningful level rather than an abandonment of old, outmoded concepts. At present there is no appropriate "label" which precisely captures the essence of the newer developments, although Rogers has casually suggested (Frick, 1971) the term "person-to-person therapy" which, interestingly, he acquired from reading an article about himself in *Time* magazine. This label has not, to say the least, exactly captured the minds of professional psychologists, so that "client-centered" is still the most accepted term. Nonetheless, the newer term more accurately reflects the evolution of Rogers' thought from techniques to relationships.

The Therapeutic Relationship Itself: What's Happening

Rogers (1957b) has spelled out *six conditions* as both necessary and sufficient if therapeutic personality change is to occur. These conditions, when taken together, provide an excellent framework for describing what actually happens in client-centered therapy in theoretical terms.

1   *Two persons are in psychological contact.*   Really more of a precondition than a condition, Rogers' first assertion simply means that some relationship or psychological contact between two people must exist. A therapist, no matter how good he is, cannot aid a client if that client does not even know him. Perhaps, even more importantly, Rogers is postulating here that no significant positive personality change can occur outside of a relationship.

2   *The first, whom we shall term the client, is in a state of incongruence, being vulnerable or anxious.*   As described earlier, Rogers construes personality disorganization and psychopathology in terms of a significant discrepancy between the actual experience of the person and the person's self-concept insofar as it represents that experience. To illustrate this concept, Rogers (1957b) uses an example of a college student who, at a total or organismic level, experiences a fear of the university and of examinations given on the third floor of a certain building, since these demonstrate a fundamental inadequacy in himself. He is dreadfully afraid of this inadequacy and thus it is decidedly at odds with his self-conception. Consequently, he distorts the organismic experience in his awareness, consciously representing it instead as an unreasonable (phobic) fear of climbing stairs in this building (or any building) and an equally intense fear of crossing the open campus.

Thus, this student is out of touch with the wellsprings of his conscious experience, his total organismic experience; in this sense, he is a stranger within himself. Such an existential situation necessarily leaves him highly vulnerable since, at any unexpected moment, the world could thrust the truth upon him. Moreover, to the degree that he dimly perceives this deep incongruence within himself, he necessarily experiences tension or anxiety. His total position might be likened to the unfortunate existential condition of Chicken Little who, as the childhood tale would have it, was constantly going around waiting for and expecting the sky to fall. Given such an uncomfortable subjective state, it is easy to understand why the student seeks out the college counseling center for help. Undoubtedly, he will initially report to the psychologist that he intensely fears climbing stairs, walking across the campus, experiences anxiety, and does not know why.

3   *The second person, whom we shall term the therapist, is congruent or integrated in the relationship.*   When the student arrives at the counseling center, Rogers' third condition specifies that he should meet a person who is congruent, integrated, and, in a word, genuine in the relationship. That is, in the particular therapeutic relationship itself, the therapist "has it all together"; he is accurately representing his organismic experience in awareness and genuinely being himself without any knowing or unknowing facade. In brief, the therapist is whole and real (completely and fully himself), and the client should have the distinct and accurate feeling that he is baring his soul to a genuine person in that relationship.

Rogers does not feel that the therapist needs to be open to all experiences in his life. Outside the therapeutic relationship, for example, the therapist may occasionally experience anxiety, depression, hostility, or any other mood state that might suggest that he may not be fully integrated in all aspects of his life. But in that therapeutic relationship, for that one or two hours per week, it is imperative that he be congruent. This means that the therapist may occasionally experience feelings not traditionally considered ideal for psychotherapy; e.g., "Although I really like this client, I just don't feel like listening to him today—I'd rather be out golfing." Of course, since the focus of therapy is upon the client's feelings rather than the therapist's, the therapist need not verbalize this feeling as long as he is consciously aware of it within himself. Sometimes, however, the therapist's feelings become so intense that he may need to express them directly to the client or to his supervisor or colleague; e.g., "This client constantly expresses what I regard as racist attitudes, and I'm having great difficulty in accepting him because of this."

4 *The therapist experiences unconditional positive regard for the client.* The phrase "unconditional positive regard" essentially means that the therapist warmly *accepts* the client, prizes him as a person in the process of becoming, and passes no judgments on his feelings or experiences. In short, the therapist imposes no "conditions of worth" upon the client; he fully accepts him as he is without approval or disapproval. So when the student begins to describe his fear of climbing stairs and walking across campus, the therapist unconditionally accepts these feelings as part of the student's world of subjective experience. He does not make judgments on the student's feelings; e.g., "Look, son, I was in the marines and the only way you're going to become a man is to forget these stupid feelings and get out there right now and climb those stairs and walk head held high across that open campus."

Client-centered therapy thus proceeds in a nonthreatening atmosphere in which the client feels understood and accepted as a whole person. Such a therapeutic climate permits the client to get back in touch with his organismic level of experiencing, allowing him to represent that experience in conscious awareness without threat to his self-concept; e.g., "If this therapist, who is genuine and truly likes me, can unflinchingly accept these feelings as a legitimate part of who I am, why can't I?" Thus, the therapeutic situation allows the client to delve ever more deeply into himself, express his true feelings without fear of reproach, and ultimately integrate his feelings with a necessarily changed self-concept. Unconditional positive regard, to the degree that it can be achieved in any therapeutic relationship, enables the client to examine those experiences which have been inconsistent with his self-concept and of which he was previously unaware because they were anxiety provoking.

5 *The therapist experiences an empathic understanding of the client's internal frame of reference and endeavors to communicate this experience to the client.* The client-centered therapist has *empathy* for the client. As Rogers (1957b) describes it, empathy means that the therapist senses the client's private world of experience as if it were his own—but without ever losing that "as if" quality. In brief, the therapist *understands*. He is able to move about freely in the client's subjective world, perceiving as he perceives, feeling as he feels, experiencing as he experiences.

Accurately understanding the client's feelings, the therapist constantly tries to communicate this experience to the client; e.g., he knows how the student really feels about climbing stairs and walking across campus. Thus, the therapist is really with the client, enabling him to accept, understand, and clarify the often conflicting and confused feelings of the client. According to Rogers (1957b), the client often experiences the therapist's empathy as akin to a sudden burst of sunlight through a dense tangle of foliage in a forest. As the client struggles with his confused and distorted representations of experience, the therapist, precisely because he has entered fully into the client's subjective world, is able to make empathic statements that shed considerable light upon it. He accepts and understands the client and, together in the psychotherapeutic relationship, both are led to progressively greater heights of such acceptance and understanding.

6 *The communication to the client of the therapist's empathic understanding and unconditional positive regard is to a minimal degree achieved.* Careful consideration of this condition should erase the stereotype of the now defunct nondirective therapist who did nothing but sit around occasionally grunting warmly at the client and saying "Um-hum." Nor are the client-centered therapists of today limited to simple restatement and/or clarification of what the client says (e.g., "I've just cut myself and if you don't give me that band-aid, I'm going to bleed to death." "You feel you're bleeding to death.") which, when carried off improperly in the past, probably led many a client to want to ask the question "Polly want a cracker?"

While examination of taped interviews of today's client-centered therapists indicates that they still engage in the use of warm responding—saying "Um-hum" or "I see," reflecting and clarifying feelings—they are through and beyond this making every effort to *communicate* their empathy and positive regard to the client. In brief, it is worthless for the therapist to experience these attitudes unless the client knows it. So the therapist must communicate these attitudes through his every word and action, and the client must perceive these as reflecting the therapist's acceptance and understanding of him. To the degree that the client does, condition six is met and positive personality change can take place.

Psychotherapy and Gardening

To anyone schooled in Rogers' basic assumptions concerning man and subsequent personality theory, his approach to psychotherapy should make perfect sense. Believing that man innately will move toward growth, actualization, and health if the conditions are right, what Rogers is essentially doing in client-centered therapy is creating the "right conditions." The client's natural actualizing tendency can be relied upon to do the rest. In this sense, a Rogerian therapist sees himself much more as a "facilitator of growth" than a "curer of ills" (as in psychoanalysis) or "modifier of behavior" (as in behavior therapy). Moreover, client-centered therapy has probably led to more empirical research than any other specific therapeutic approach and, in the opinion of at least one leading writer in the counseling field (Patterson, 1973), it is *supported* by more research than any other therapeutic approach.

So Rogers' client-centered therapy (supported by empirical research) reflects his entire image of man in general and consequent more particular view of the role of the therapist in a helping relationship. Upon reflection, one is tempted to draw an analogy between a Rogerian therapist and a gardener, between client-centered therapy and gardening. When one recalls Rogers' earlier background in agriculture, the analogy becomes even more compelling. When one reads what Carl Rogers said in concluding his acceptance speech for the 1973 APA Distinguished Professional Contribution Award, the analogy becomes inescapable:

> And then I garden. Those mornings when I cannot find time to inspect my flowers, water the young shoots I am propagating, pull a few weeds, spray some destructive insects, and pour just the proper fertilizer on some budding plants, I feel cheated. My garden supplies the same intriguing question I have been trying to meet all my professional life: What are the effective conditions for growth? But in my garden, though the frustrations are just as immediate, the results, whether success or failure, are more quickly evident. And when, through patient, intelligent, and understanding care I have provided the conditions that result in the production of a rare or glorious bloom, I feel the same kind of satisfaction that I have felt in the facilitation of growth in a person or in a group of persons (Rogers, 1974, pp. 122–123).

SUMMARY

Reflecting his close affinity to humanistic psychology, Rogers holds that the innermost core of human nature is essentially good, purposive, and trustworthy. These basic attributes of human nature will surface if the proper conditions encourage the fulfillment of the individual's innate potential. In Rogers' system, all human motives are subsumed under a single master motive—the actualizing tendency—the innate tendency of the individual to actualize, maintain, and enhance himself or herself.

Within the broad context of the humanistic movement, Rogers' particular theoretical position is phenomenological. He holds that the only reality, from the person's perceptual vantage point, is subjective reality—the person's private world of experience. And central to that subjective world is the concept of self, Rogers' most important personological construct. In his system, elements important in self-concept development are the need for positive regard, conditions of worth, and unconditional positive regard.

Rogers argues that most ways of behaving that an individual adopts are consistent with her self-concept. Threat exists when a person senses an incongruity between her self-concept and total organismic experience; she then attempts to defend herself by means of perceptual distortion and denial. When the incongruence between self-concept and actual experience becomes too great, personality disorganization and psychopathology result. In sharp contrast, persons who are open to their experience, fully trust it, and are freely moving in the direction of actualizing themselves are termed "fully functioning" in Rogers' system.

Rogers' basic assumptions concerning human nature are generally strong, explicit, and reflective of the fundamental cleavage between phenomenology and behaviorism in American psychology. Rogers' phenomenological theory reflects (1) a strong commitment to the assumptions of freedom, rationality, holism, subjectivity, proactivity, heterostasis, and unknowability and (2) a moderate commitment to the constitutionalism assumption.

Rogers' phenomenological theory, particularly its psychotherapeutic aspects, has stimulated an enormous amount of research. In this chapter, a primary method of studying the self-concept, the Q sort, was discussed along with illustrative research bearing upon aspects of the self-concept. Brief attention was also given to Rogers' view of science.

In the concluding chapter section, Rogers' unique and widely employed approach to psychotherapy, client-centered therapy, was described as it has evolved over the years. Emphasizing the critical importance of the relationship between therapist and client, Rogers' six conditions necessary and sufficient for positive personality change were listed and discussed.

BIBLIOGRAPHY

American Psychologist, 1973, **28,** 71–74.

Berger, E. Relationships among acceptance of self, acceptance of others and MMPI scores. *Journal of Counseling Psychology,* 1955, **2,** 279–284.

Bergin, A. The evaluation of therapeutic outcomes. In A. Bergin & S. Garfield (Eds.), *Handbook of Psychotherapy and Behavior Change.* New York: Wiley, 1971, pp. 217–270.

Chodorkoff, B. Self-perception, perceptual defense, and adjustment. *Journal of Abnormal and Social Psychology,* 1954, **49,** 508–512.

Eysenck, H. The effects of psychotherapy: An evaluation. *Journal of Consulting Psychology,* 1952, **16,** 319–324.

Eysenck, H. *The effects of psychotherapy.* New York: International Science Press, 1966.

Frick, W. *Humanistic psychology: Interviews with Maslow, Murphy, and Rogers.* Columbus, Ohio: Merrill, 1971.

Fromm, E. *The art of loving.* New York: Harper & Row, 1956.

Gough, H. *Adjective check list.* University of California: Institute for Personality Assessment Research, 1955.

Medinnus, G., & Curtis, F. The relation between maternal self-acceptance and child acceptance. *Journal of Counseling Psychology,* 1963, **27,** 542–544.

Meltzoff, J., & Kornreich, M. *Research in psychotherapy.* Chicago: Aldine-Atherton, 1970.

Misiak, H., & Sexton, V. *Phenomenological, existential, and humanistic psychologies: A historical survey.* New York: Grune & Stratton, 1973.

Patterson, C. *Theories of counseling and psychotherapy* (2d ed.). New York: Harper & Row, 1973.

Phillips, E. Attitudes toward self and others: A brief questionnaire report. *Journal of Consulting Psychology,* 1951, **15,** 79–81.

Rogers, C. *The clinical treatment of the problem child.* Boston: Houghton Mifflin, 1939.

Rogers, C. *Counseling and psychotherapy: Newer concepts in practice.* Boston: Houghton Mifflin, 1942.

Rogers, C. *Client-centered therapy: Its current practice, implications, and theory.* Boston: Houghton Mifflin, 1951.

Rogers, C. Persons or science? A philosophical question. *American Psychologist,* 1955, **10,** 267–278.

Rogers, C. Some issues concerning the control of human behavior (symposium with B. F. Skinner). *Science,* 1956, **124,** 1057–1066.

Rogers, C. A note on the nature of man. *Journal of Counseling Psychology,* 1957a, **4,** 199–203.

Rogers, C. The necessary and sufficient conditions of therapeutic personality change. *Journal of Consulting Psychology,* 1957b, **21,** 95–103.

Rogers, C. The characteristics of a helping relationship. *Personnel and Guidance Journal,* 1958, **37,** 6–16.

Rogers, C. A theory of therapy, personality, and interpersonal relationships, as developed in the client-centered framework. In S. Koch (Ed.), *Psychology: A study of a science.* Vol. 3. New York: McGraw-Hill, 1959, pp. 184–256.

Rogers, C. *On becoming a person: A therapist's view of psychotherapy.* Boston: Houghton Mifflin, 1961.

Rogers, C. The actualizing tendency in relation to "motives"; and to consciousness. In M. Jones (Ed.), *Nebraska symposium on motivation.* Vol XI. Lincoln: University of Nebraska Press, 1963, pp. 1–24.

Rogers, C. Autobiography. In E. Boring & G. Lindzey (Eds.), *A history of psychology in autobiography.* Vol. 5. New York: Appleton-Century-Crofts, 1967, 341–384.

Rogers, C. *Freedom to learn: A view of what education might become.* Columbus, Ohio: Merrill, 1969.

Rogers, C. *Becoming partners: Marriage and its alternatives.* New York: Delacorte, 1972.

Rogers, C. My philosophy of interpersonal relationships and how it grew. *Journal of Humanistic Psychology,* 1973, **13,** 3–15.

Rogers, C. In retrospect: Forty-six years. *American Psychologist,* 1974, **29,** 115–123.

Rogers, C., & Dymond, R. (Eds.), *Psychotherapy and personality change.* Chicago: University of Chicago Press, 1954.

Stephenson, W. *The study of behavior: Q-technique and its methodology.* Chicago: University of Chicago Press, 1953.

Suinn, R. The relationship between self-acceptance and acceptance of others: A learning theory analysis. *Journal of Abnormal and Social Psychology,* 1961, **63,** 37–42.

Suinn, R., Osborne, D., & Winfree, P. The self-concept and accuracy of recall of inconsistent self-related information. *Journal of Clinical Psychology,* 1962, **18,** 473–474.

SUGGESTED READINGS

1 Butler, J. Self-concept change in psychotherapy. In S. Brown & D. Brenner (Eds.), *Science, psychology, and communication: Essays honoring William Stephenson.* New York: Teachers College Press, 1972, pp. 141–171.

2 Gendlin, E. Client-centered developments and work with schizophrenics. *Journal of Counseling Psychology,* 1962, **9,** 205–211.

3 Richards, F., & Richards, A. *Homonovus: The new man.* Boulder, Colo.: Shields Publishing, 1973.

4 Rogers, C., & Stevens, B. *Person to person: The problem of being human.* New York: Simon & Schuster Pocket Book, 1971.

5 Straus, E. *Phenomenological psychology.* New York: Basic Books, 1966.

6 Waterbor, R. Experiential bases of the sense of self. *Journal of Personality,* 1972, **40,** 162–179.

7 Wylie, R. The present status of self-theory. In E. Borgatta & W. Lambert (Eds.), *Handbook of personality theory and research.* Chicago: Rand McNally, 1968.

8 Wylie, R. *The self-concept* (rev. ed.). Vol. 1. Lincoln: University of Nebraska Press, 1974.

Chapter 10

The Future of Personality Theory and Research

Having reached the end of our journey through eight major types of personological theory, the reader will undoubtedly agree that the study of human personality is at once both the most exciting and the most baffling and frustrating area in psychology. The course along which we have traveled has revealed an incredible diversity of unique concepts and distinct formulations by which personologists attempt to explain the complexity of human behavior. Each theorist's position, while containing elements to admire or approve, has not overwhelmed the others. What remains to be done in this concluding chapter is to take stock of what we have studied and to attempt to identify some of the issues, trends, and problems likely to influence future developments in personality theory and research. In addition, we shall consider the degree to which the eight theoretical perspectives discussed in this text are likely to continue to exert an influence on present and future personologists.

Before proceeding, however, a few final words concerning the approach taken in this text to the study and comparison of personality theories seem appropriate. It is our conviction that the concept of basic assumptions concerning human nature offers both a compelling and useful framework for appreciating the broad range of viewpoints and theoretical orientations which exist in current personology.

BASIC ASSUMPTIONS IN PERSPECTIVE

The central, unifying theme of this text is that basic assumptions about the nature of the human organism constitute the bedrock from which theories of personality are formulated and ultimately tested. They also highlight the fundamental issues and problems about which personality theorists agree or disagree at the most basic philosophical level. In this concluding chapter, then, it is only fitting that we raise a few as yet unanswered questions and offer some final thoughts on the nature of these basic assumptions and their role in present and future theory building in personality psychology.

The first question to consider is the origin of the assumptions. They certainly do not descend on the theorist from out of the sky (at least, we assume that they do not). Instead, basic assumptions about human nature are part and parcel of the way that a theorist *is;* they reflect *his own personality structure.* Like other deeply held beliefs, values, and attitudes, a theorist's basic assumptions concerning man contribute to the complexity of what he is as a human being. Thus, these assumptions are acquired and evolve in the same way as the theorist's other basic beliefs about the nature of the world.

The implications of this argument are profound. Specifically, a personologist's conception of human behavior necessarily reflects to a large extent *what he basically thinks of himself* and those around him. For some theorists, the conclusion is inescapable—by studying their theories, we may be learning more about them than we are about the nature of their viewpoints on personality. Considered in this light, the biographical sketches presented at the beginning of each theory chapter should take on added significance.

A second question pertains to the role of basic assumptions in theory construction. Precisely what effects do they have upon a personologist in his initial stages of theory construction? Whether they are consciously considered or not, *a theorist's basic assumptions about human nature simultaneously broaden and narrow his perspective on personality.* Literally, the assumptions are mutually exclusive—belief in and acceptance of both poles on a continuum is impossible. As an illustration, consider the freedom-determinism assumption. Any theorist who assumes the free-will position will, by definition, examine and emphasize those aspects of human functioning suggesting that man is indeed free, e.g., man's highly developed thinking capacities which allow him to see alternatives and thus make choices. But this freedom assumption coupled with the sheer creativity of a personality theorist is apt to lead him farther afield—very probably in new directions and to undreamt-of-heights (in terms of previous personality theorizing)—as he searches for and finally manifests the freedom assumption in his ultimate theoretical account of personality.

Thus, his perspective on personality has been significantly broadened by his assumption of freedom. It has prompted him to explore explicit areas of human functioning in detail and to invent theoretical concepts to describe and explain them. Yet, simultaneously, his perspective has also been narrowed. He has not examined areas of human behavior more readily explicable in deterministic terms (at least as closely as a deterministically oriented theorist would), e.g., behaviors which appear to be physiologically determind or products of one's conditioning history. Insofar as these are also aspects of human behavior, the theorist has ignored some considerations or at least downplayed their importance. The freedom assumption, then, has guided the personologist down certain theoretical paths, opening his eyes to some aspects about human behavior that he otherwise might not have seen, while, at the same time, producing theoretical "blind spots" about other possible areas of man's psychological makeup.

Of course, this is also true of the theorist who begins by assuming a *deterministic* position. This assumption will take him down other theoretical pathways, emphasizing those aspects of behavior which appear to be deterministically based and ignoring or downplaying human actions that might reflect an underlying freedom. The freedom-determinism assumption is only one of eight discussed in this book. It is our contention that the other seven basic assumptions function in precisely the same way in theory construction. While each may be more or less potent in a given theorist's thinking (e.g., subjectivity–objectivity is very important in the theories of Rogers and Skinner and not so potent in the positions of Allport and Erikson), all eight assumptions have the potential to guide it.

Still a third issue is whether or not a personologist's basic assumptions about human nature are the sole influences upon his theory building. Bluntly said, *of course not.* Specifically, a personologist's basic assumptions constantly interact with a host of other influences as he goes about the process of constructing his theory. Factors other than basic assumptions which obviously can influence a theorist's thinking are the historical period in which he lives, his society, what is known in psychology and other disciplines at the time, what he knows about psychology and other disciplines at the time, his academic training and other exposure to the world of ideas, the thinking of his professors, the interaction with his colleagues (and, in some instances, his clients or patients), and, more generally, his total, individual life experiences. In brief, it cannot be forgotten that personality theorists are human beings engaged in the task of theorizing about human beings. Like the rest of us, their thinking is influenced by many forces.

As an illustration of this *interactive effect,* again consider the freedom-determinism assumption. Both Freud and Skinner are strict determinists; they agree completely that all human actions are utterly and totally determined, with no such possibility as free choice. But on the question of precisely what determines human behavior, these two theorists differ sharply. Why? Because the deterministic assumption is *interacting* with other sources of influence in each man's life. Freud, for example, was trained as a physician, was heavily influenced by European clinical medicine (discussed in Chapter 1), was living at a time and in a society repressive of sexual expression, and treated patients for a living. Thus, he was led to look *within* man for the behavioral determinants, to a biological kind of theoretical construct, to some locus of causality which his patients were unaware of in themselves, to that which was utterly bound up with the sexuality that his patients could not express in their daily lives and which troubled them so. The *id,* in all its biological, unconscious, and sexual power and glory, was the end result of Freud's search for the behavioral determinant.

In sharp contrast, B. F. Skinner, already showing a preference for "gadgets" during his younger days (look again at his biographical sketch), was academically weaned on the brass instrumentation, rigor, animal interests, preoccupation with the learning process, and wholehearted environmentalism of American behaviorism (also discussed in Chapter 1 as a historical source of influence upon personality theory). Skinner has earned his living as an academic psychologist in laboratories, working with animal and human subjects, inventing and building ingenious experimental devices, designing and carrying out experiments on the learning process, and, in general, manipulating environmental variables. Quite naturally, then, it is not surprising that Skinner would look *outside* the person for behavioral determinants. Obviously he has succeeded admirably in finding them in the environment in terms of his central and well-developed theoretical concept of *reinforcement.*

A similar case could be made for the positons of Maslow and Rogers on the freedom assumption. While both theorists basically agree that man is free, each presents a somewhat different picture of how that freedom manifests itself in human behavior (although the differences here are not nearly so dramatic as in the case of Freud and Skinner). Maslow viewed human freedom as an integral aspect of man's attempt to climb the motivational need ladder toward self-actualization; Rogers found it in a professional lifetime of therapy hours spent with his clients, observing and facilitating their ongoing struggle to grow as human beings. In sum, when one envisions the position of a given theorist on *all eight basic assumptions* continually interacting with his individual life experiences, one begins to grasp what really goes into the construction of a personality theory. This view in no way diminishes the important role of basic assumptions about human nature in theory building; it merely places these assumptions in proper perspective.

One final question remains: what will be the role of these basic assumptions in the personality psychology of the future? Our somewhat cautious answer is that because they deal with the fundamental issue of *what humanity is,* their role will remain unchanged. Basic assumptions concerning the nature of the human being will remain the foundation for all future theories of personality, regardless of their specific substantive content. What will change, though, are the theorists, the state of knowledge in psychology and other

Theorist		1890	1935	1940	1950	1960	1970	
Freud	(1856–1939)	(1890–1939)						Psychoanalytic theory
Erikson	(1902–)				(1950–1965)			Psychosocial theory
Murray	(1893–)			(1938–1959)				Need theory
Skinner	(1904–)			(1938–1960)				Behavioristic-learning theory
Allport	(1897–1967)		(1937–1961)					Trait theory
Kelly	(1905–1966)				(1955–1965)			Cognitive theory
Maslow	(1908–1970)				(1950–1965)			Humanistic theory
Rogers	(1902–)				(1951–1961)			Phenomenological theory

Figure 10-1 Historical period during which personality theory was constructed.

disciplines, and the world. New theorists will emerge, bringing their unique personalities and experiences to bear on these assumptions. Most certainly, they will glean new knowledge about man from psychology and other relevant disciplines. And, as Heraclitus noted centuries ago, the world can be expected to continue to change. What directions the changes will take and precisely how they will affect the personality psychology of the future cannot be predicted here. (Psychologists, much like meterologists, are infinitely better at explaining what already has happened rather than what actually will happen in the future.) It is a safe bet, however, that changed world conditions will have an impact on personality theory simply because they have operated so in the past. The effect of World War I on Freud's theorizing about aggression is but one example. In brief, then, basic assumptions concerning human nature will have new minds, new knowledge, and a new world with which to interface. They will, nonetheless, continue to be the bedrock of future personality psychology.

COMING OF AGE IN PERSONOLOGY

The development of personology as a bona fide scientific discipline belongs to the twentieth century. Consider Figure 10-1. With the exception of Freudian theory, which blossomed during the first third of this century, it is only within the last forty years that major personality theories have emerged. Also note that four of the theorists considered in this book are still actively writing and contributing to personality theory, and three of the remaining four died after 1965. It is obvious, then, that personology is a very young field of inquiry. But with age, it is hoped, comes wisdom. In the short span of four decades, personality psychology has "come of age" by establishing itself as a respectable and fruitful area of study. No doubt the flourishing activity in personology points toward the growing realization that humanity's most vital problems are *within;* they concern the person and his or her relationships to others. Indeed, understanding the nature of humanity and its works has become a precondition for the survival of our species. Gardner Murphy eloquently expressed the real significance of the study of personality for our lives when he wrote:

Lack of knowledge about human beings is not a trivial, but a major threat to life. Lack of knowledge about personality is perhaps the central core of the issue that is most relevant for us today: the issue of understanding what human beings can become under a new set of social arrangements (Norbeck, Price-Williams, and McCord, 1968, p. 38).

The Heart of the Matter

What, then, can be anticipated in the way of future developments in personality theory? What are the new and exciting frontiers for the personality theorist of tomorrow? Broadly speaking, whatever the formal shortcomings and deficiencies of the eight theories presented in this book may be, we staunchly believe that the ideas and insights embedded within them will have a decisive impact upon future conceptions of personality. Restated, *conceptual progress in the realm of personality theory will be based squarely on the contributions of past personologists.* This does not mean that future theories will be carbon copies of existing ones. On the contrary, as the short history of personology has disclosed, there is virtually no limit to the diversity of theoretical models of humanity that personologists can invent! There are as many possible conceptions of human nature as there are minds to conceive them. However, while personality theories, like fads, may come and go, the issues and problems with which our theorists have struggled will endure.

The question that one is apt to ask next is, what are the critical and persisting issues in personality theory? Basically they can be enumerated in terms of seven global questions: (1) how does the human personality *develop?* (2) what *motivates* human behavior? (3) how does the person come to *think* and *know* about himself and his environment? (4) what is the nature of human *social* life? (5) what makes each person *uniquely different* from any other person? (6) what are the principal determinants of personality *disturbance?* and (7) what are the major characteristics of the *healthy* adult? These are enormously broad and complex questions and the answers to them may never be known with complete certainty. Yet the necessity to know and understand more about each will be highly relevant to charting the future course of personality theorizing. This, then, returns us to our original premise—namely, that futuristic theory builders will be guided by the rich intellectual heritage of their predecessors. It is this belief that makes the study of Freud, Erikson, Murray, Skinner, Allport, Kelly, Maslow, and Rogers a worthwhile endeavor. Each in his own way has contributed something significant to the understanding of the mystery of the human personality.

THE PRESENT IN THE FUTURE

In this book we have presented illustrative studies bearing upon the empirical validity of various conceptions of personality. The objective in doing so was to convince the reader that in the final analysis a theory's most important scientific function is to stimulate or generate new research. To perform this vital function successfully, a theory must not only be capable of aiding us in the comprehension of existing knowledge but also be a fertile source of hypotheses that will lead to the discovery of new knowledge; in other words, a theory must have heuristic value to remain useful in the scientific community. Thus, if personality theories are to be something more than mere speculations about human behavior, we must be able to convert them into testable form and study them empirically. This is what constitutes the essence of science, differentiating it from the simple assertion of opinions or beliefs. It is also what will determine the *ultimate scientific significance* of current theories of personality.

This brings us to another point. Any theory of personality is merely a tentative statement constantly needing modification based on evidence gained from the testing of its offspring hypotheses. It must be so constructed that it can accommodate new empirical data. Accordingly, there may come a time in the life of any personality theory when the theory loses its elasticity and becomes obsolete. When a person's shoes no longer perform their function of allowing him to walk comfortably, he discards them for a new pair. Or if he gains weight, he buys a new belt. In the same way, a theory must be considered ultimately expendable, to be cast aside when it ceases to discharge its function of incorporating new discoveries about human behavior. In sum, personality theories must be self-corrective in the light of new evidence.

The validation of a theory, in principle, is a function of predictions and of the outcomes of empirical tests that are carefully constructed from the theory. On the basis of a good theory, for instance, the conditions of an experiment— the variables to be manipulated, monitored, or observed—would be clearly specifiable. Further to the point, validation of a personality construct is possible provided the investigator employs a measuring procedure which has been explicitly linked to the construct and its conceptual context. How have our eight theories fared in terms of this model of construct validation? First, while all the theories discussed in this text were found to have generated some research, in more than a few instances we were led to conclude that there is altogether too little empirical evidence at present on which to evaluate them. We also discovered that theories of personality differ markedly in terms of how fruitful they have been as stimulants to research. For example, Skinner's behavioristic-learning theory has produced an enormous quantity of research dealing with a broad range of topics and issues. A great deal of relevant research has also resulted from Freud's psychoanalytic theory, although certain of his basic concepts remain empirically untestable to this day. These two theorists have proved to be of considerable value in guiding new directions research ought to take and indicating ideas that should be explored.

Other theories were found to be less impressive in terms of their capacity to function as generators of new research. For instance, we noted that the bulk of studies accompanying the positions of Allport, Kelly, and Murray were not designed to test concrete predictions relevant to their respective viewpoints. What should not be overlooked, however, is the significant role these three theorists (notably Allport and Murray) have played in shaping current strategies of research in personality. Kelly's impact on the study of cognitive variables, while difficult to pinpoint, also cannot be denied. In fact, many believe his theory has considerably more potential to generate research than has as yet been realized by most personologists.

Our assessment of Erikson, Maslow, and Rogers was slightly more positive. Over the past two decades these three theorists have stimulated research activity in a variety of areas, a fair amount of which is directly pertinent to the validity of their own theoretical constructs. To be sure, the empirical adequacy of many of their concepts remains to be demonstrated. Yet the inspiration they have provided other personologists for studying the complex qualities of human nature suggests a promising and lasting influence for each in the future of personality theory and research.

Despite the obvious importance of understanding existing theories, one can hope that personality psychology will eventually develop a set of theoretical constructs more adequate than the present ones—constructs which are more amenable to empirical test. Personology has come a long way since Freud, but no one can claim that human behavior is knowable or that all new lines of thought and research have been exhausted. The following section outlines some tentative notions concerning the creative impetus for emerging theories of human behavior.

NEW FRONTIERS IN PERSONALITY RESEARCH

What sorts of problems and issues are likely to capture the attention of future personological investigators? Without appearing too prophetic, we suggest that the agenda of future work will demand a high priority of serious inquiry into five general problem areas. Each area, in our judgment, will require imaginative and critical study if our conceptions of personality are to be deepened and enriched.

1   *Study of especially productive, talented, and creative persons.*   For all practical purposes, the formal study of personality had its beginnings in Freud's concern with the causes and treatment of pathological behavior. The history of personological inquiry, therefore, reflects a strong emphasis on behavioral phenomena observed most readily in therapeutic situations. Even today the study of personality remains closely tied to the investigation of psychologically disturbed persons. But times are changing. And so do the concerns and interests of personologists. In recent years, there has been a growing awareness that personology should not be exclusively concerned with pathological or defensive aspects of human functioning. Consequently, the emphasis previously accorded to pathology-centered problems has given way

to the study of the characteristics of people who behave with unusual effectiveness. The "human potential movement" is clearly one source of liberating the study of healthy persons.

The best example of this approach is the work of Maslow (Chapter 8), who based his humanistic theory of personality on the study of particularly well-functioning individuals. His focus on "self-actualizers" is centrally important because it established a vision of what humanity is and can be. In turn, this has prompted an increasing volume of empirical work on creativity, competence motivation, empathy, positive affective states, self-esteem, self-realization, and a host of other psychological properties associated with exceptionally productive and integrative human activities (e.g., Helson and Crutchfield, 1970; MacKinnon, 1965). It seems reasonable to expect that the psychological study of unusually talented and gifted individuals will increase dramatically during the last decades of the twentieth century.

2 *Study of the physiological and neurological determinants/bases of personality.* In all likelihood, the contemporary scientific era will be recorded as the age of biology—and as a period in which advances in behavior genetics, biochemistry, psychopharmacology, and neurophysiology produced remarkable and decisive changes in the constructs and methods guiding inquiry in general psychology. Yet, with the exceptions of Freud and Murray (the only two theorists in this text who truly acknowledge and stress the biological bases of behavior), personologists have almost totally ignored the need to study the neurophysiological and biochemical components of human personality. Research-oriented personologists of the future can ill afford to neglect the tremendous upsurge of biological knowledge. It is those studies that focus on the reciprocal interaction of behavior with its biological base (made possible by powerful electrophysiological and other techniques) that will highlight future developments in the field of personality. In particular, studies concerned with how biochemical and neurophysiological processes are related to psychological functioning (cognition, imagery, affect, sensation) will merit major attention. Additionally, investigators will need to provide a coherent account of the meaning of psychobiological facts in terms of the development, behavior, and experience of the individual (Glass, 1968). Necessarily, such accounts will lead to new dimensions in personality theorizing. Progress in personality research will thus be made on two fronts: (*a*) empirical study of the biological underpinnings of behavior and (*b*) development of conceptual schemes which will more adequately explain the individual's biological heritage and how it affects many of the different forms of behavior commonly associated with the domain of personality.

3 *Study of personality change in middle and old age.* About one-quarter of our lives is spent growing up and three-quarters growing old. It is ironic, therefore, that psychologists have devoted so much of their efforts to the study of childhood and adolescence. Two major assumptions underlie and partially explain this one-sided emphasis on the study of child and adolescent develop-

ment: (*a*) selected adult behavior patterns are established at an early age and (*b*) parental treatment during the initial years of life is a significant determinant of personality formation. The historical impact of Freudian psychosexual theory is clearly evident in both these assumptions. It is also true that children and adolescents are more readily available and cooperative subjects for study than are older individuals; e.g., college sophomores are easier to round up and test than are your average thirty-five-year-olds. Nevertheless, several influential personologists, most notably Erikson, Allport, and Maslow, have convincingly argued that children and adolescents are "unfinished" personalities. Erikson deserves special credit for making us aware of the fact that the hurdles of personality development continue in some ways until death completes the life cycle. His formulation of a series of interlocking developmental crises encompassing the individual's entire life-span has forced psychologists to reexamine traditional beliefs concerning personality growth and change in adult life.

Despite such recognition by Erikson and others, our current knowledge about adult personality development remains at a primitive stage (Bischof, 1969). This situation will not continue. For one thing, life expectancy tables indicate that the life-span itself has increased markedly over the last two generations, so that there are literally more adults to study. Approximately one of every ten Americans today is over sixty-five, and the proportion is increasing every year. Society has also assumed a far more sensitive posture in relation to the care of its senior citizens (e.g., nursing homes, complexes for the elderly), making these people more accessible to the scientist. Finally, adults will command greater study for no other reason than to discover how the "story of human development ends." Thus, future basic research in personality will surely broaden its base of inquiry to include large-scale study of individuals between the ages of thirty and senescence (Birren, 1970). It would also seem reasonable to expect that the formulation of even more complex and comprehensive conceptions of human development (especially in relation to the middle and the late years of life) will be a consuming task for future theorists (Goulet and Baltes, 1970). This effort, in our view, will probably culminate in a dramatic broadening of the field presently labeled *life-span developmental psychology* (Baltes and Schaie, 1973).

4 *Study of the interaction of situational factors and personality variables and their relative contribution to behavior.* As the individual theory chapters made clear, it is customary for most personologists (Skinner excluded) to assume that personality variables or dispositions are responsible for and can adequately explain a person's behavior as it varies from one situation to another. Freud's psychodynamic theory and Allport's trait theory are by far the most thoroughgoing in their development of this point of view. These two theorists have explicitly assumed that personality is basically stable and continuous regardless of the situation—behavior is determined primarily by a person's trait structure. At the same time, it is obvious that at least some portion of human behavior is governed by the sociocultural context within which the person lives (e.g., living in a college environment versus living in an urban ghetto). Illustrative of this position is Murray's emphasis on sociocultural determinants as major sources of behavioral variability. Of course, Skinner's theory is exclusively environmental in emphasis, to the point of there being no organismic or intrapsychic variables with which situational factors can interact!

Nevertheless, most personologists have largely ignored the situational components of behavior (Mischel, 1973). Recent developments suggest a changing orientation. Inspired by work in anthropology and sociology, personologists are beginning to display greater awareness of and concern with the social determinants of personality structure and development and the contemporary social environment. Accordingly, a growing number of investigators are beginning to study how personality and situational factors interact in producing behavior (Bowers, 1973; Endler and Hunt, 1968). This trend could foster the development of a new system of theoretical constructs to characterize the person's total ecological situation so that it may be taken into account in the explanation and prediction of behavior (Insel and Moos, 1974). Recently, for instance, such new terminology as "role dispositions," "interpersonal reaction systems," and "social values" have crept into the personologist's vocabulary.

What we envision for the future, then, are experiments which consider the relative contribution of *both* situations and individual differences in behavior. For example, not only will Mary Jones be studied as wife and mother as she traditionally has been studied in the past, but also as a chairperson of a conference, consumer of goods, vacationer, marine biologist, and churchgoer. Rather than being merely one person with a variety of occupational and social roles, she will be studied at home, at the office, at the camping grounds, at the supermarket, and in church. To be sure, the question of how person variables and situational factors interact in evoking behavior is a complex one requiring new research strategies if answers are to be found. It is an urgent empirical question that will in all likelihood receive substantial attention in the years ahead.

5 *Study of problems relevant to the practical world of human affairs.* As we have repeatedly noted, the history of personological inquiry is intimately bound up with the study of psychopathology and personal adjustment. Efforts aimed at improving the human condition were defined largely in terms of what could be done to diagnose and treat neurotic individuals so that they could regain their mental health. This orientation especially characterizes the theories of Freud, Rogers, Kelly, and to some extent, Erikson.

However, change is an inevitable aspect of every field of intellectual and scientific endeavor. To be more specific, events within recent years have produced an accelerating demand for the psychological study of *pressing social problems* (Miller, 1969; Sherif, 1970). The explosion of knowledge and vast communication networks have combined to force our acceptance of a "neighbor" 10,000 miles away. War, medical advancements, ecological problems, generation gaps, assassinations, expanding birthrates in certain countries, exploitation and imprisonment of minority groups, explorations of unknown areas of land, sea, and space have caused us to reexamine our relationships to ourselves, each other, and our environment. Of necessity, then, growing numbers of psychological investigators have become gravely concerned about the social relevance of their work and the contributions they might ultimately make toward improving the quality of human life. This trend in developing a socially relevant psychology will undoubtedly have a profound effect upon the study of personality. Personality researchers of the future will need to broaden the scope of their activities considerably if they are to maintain a respectable and influential position in the behavioral sciences. Similarly, areas of application will need to become much more diverse.

Contemplating this projected picture in personality psychology against the background of what is presently ongoing in society as a whole, it seems safe to predict that prominent attention will be focused on the following problem areas: urban poverty, racial and sexual discrimination, population control, alienation, suicide, divorce, child abuse, drug addiction (including alcoholism), and crime. Clearly, the list could go on, and, equally obvious, the problems range across the length and breadth of human life itself.

One consequence of this trend toward closer involvement with the concrete world of human affairs may be that personality concepts and theories will become considerably more complex and comprehensive than those we know today. Another likely outcome is that personologists will become more intimately involved with the work of social psychologists, sociologists, anthropologists, and ethologists. It logically follows that the field of personality will adopt a more interdisciplinary approach in dealing with research problems. In turn, greater emphasis will be placed on naturalistic modes of inquiry, i.e., observation and study of persons in real-life situations. Field research is, in principle, an ideal setting for investigating human functioning in the personality area: we do wish to understand behavior outside the psychology building! That personology will eventually intrude into all sectors of humanity's social world seems undeniable.

The scientific study of personality is very much like fitting the pieces of a complex jigsaw puzzle together. The eight theories considered in this book have provided us many possible pieces for the puzzle. Some pieces will probably be discarded as not fitting the puzzle at all, whereas many others remain to be discovered. One thing seems certain, however: when the final picture emerges, many of the pieces offered by our eight theorists will be included.

SUMMARY

The central theme of this text is that basic assumptions about human nature constitute the bedrock from which personality theories are fashioned and tested. Concerning their origin, it was noted that a personologist's assumptions about human nature are acquired and developed in the same way as his other basic beliefs about the nature of the world. Hence, a personologist's conception of humanity reflects to a large extent what he thinks of himself and those around him.

Basic assumptions serve to both broaden and narrow a theorist's perspective on personality. For example, a theorist who adopts a free-will position will, by definition, attend to and emphasize those aspects of human functioning suggestive of the person's capacity to act as a free agent. At the same time, he will tend to ignore or downplay aspects of human behavior more readily explainable in deterministic terms.

Basic assumptions constantly interact with a host of other influences in shaping the personologist's theoretical account of behavior. Sources of influence other than basic assumptions which obviously can affect a theorist's thinking are the historical period in which he lives, his society, what is known in psychology and other disciplines at the time, his academic training and exposure to the world of ideas, and his composite life experiences.

The role of basic assumptions vis-à-vis the future of personology will not diminish in importance, since they deal with the issue of what humanity is. Thus, basic assumptions concerning human nature will remain the foundation for all future personality theories. What will change, though, are the theorists, the state of knowledge in psychology and related disciplines, and the world.

Personality psychology is a very young field of inquiry. With the exception of psychoanalytic theory, which blossomed during the first third of this century, it is only during the past four decades that personality theories have emerged. Yet personology has truly come of age by establishing itself as a viable area of study. The flourishing activity in personology is a function of the growing realization that people's most vital problems concern themselves and their relations to others.

Future theories will certainly not be carbon copies of existing ones. Yet, the ideas and insights embedded within the eight theories presented in this text will have a decisive impact upon future conceptions of personality. This is because our eight theorists have struggled to resolve critical and enduring issues and because they have each contributed something to the understanding of the mystery of human nature. Accordingly, future theorists will be guided by the rich intellectual heritage of their predecessors.

The ultimate scientific significance of current personality theories will depend upon the extent to which they generate new research. Furthermore, theories of personality must be self-corrective in the light of new empirical evidence if they are to remain useful within the scientific enterprise. While all the theories presented in this text have stimulated some research, in several instances we were led to conclude that there is altogether too little empirical evidence at present to evaluate them.

In the concluding section of this final chapter we suggest that new frontiers in personality research will be focused on five general problem areas: (1) study of productive, talented, and creative persons; (2) study of the physiological and neurological determinants/bases of personality; (3) study of personality change in middle and old age; (4) study of the interaction of situational factors and personality variables and their relative contribution to behavior; and (5) study of problems relevant to the practical world of human affairs. Imaginative and critical study of these areas promises to deepen and enrich our conceptions of personality.

BIBLIOGRAPHY

Baltes, P., & Schaie, K. (Eds.). *Life span developmental psychology: Personality and socialization.* New York: Academic Press, 1973.

Birren, J. Toward an experimental psychology of aging. *American Psychologist,* 1970, **25,** 124–135.

Bischof, L. *Adult psychology.* New York: Harper & Row, 1969.

Bowers, K. Situationism in psychology: An analysis and a critique. *Psychological Review,* 1973, **80,** 307–336.

Endler, N., & Hunt, J. McV. S-R inventories of hostility and comparisons of the proportions of variance from persons, responses, and situations for hostility and anxiousness. *Journal of Personality and Social Psychology,* 1968, **9,** 309–315.

Glass, D. (Ed.). *Biology and behavior: Genetics.* New York: Rockefeller University Press, 1968.

Goulet, L., & Baltes, P. (Eds.). *Life-span developmental psychology: Research and theory.* New York: Academic Press, 1970.

Helson, R., & Crutchfield, R. Creative types in mathematics. *Journal of Personality,* 1970, **38,** 177–197.

Insel, P., & Moos, R. Psychological environments: Expanding the scope of human ecology. *American Psychologist,* 1974, **29,** 179–188.

MacKinnon, D. Personality and the realization of creative potential. *American Psychologist,* 1965, **20,** 273–281.

Miller, G. Psychology as a means of promoting human welfare. *American Psychologist,* 1969, **24,** 1063–1075.

Mischel, W. Toward a cognitive social learning reconceptualization of personality. *Psychological Review,* 1973, **80,** 252–283.

Murphy, G. Psychological views of personality and contributions to its study. In E. Norbeck, D. Price-Williams, & W. McCord (Eds), *The study of personality: An interdisciplinary appraisal.* New York: Holt, Rinehart, and Winston, 1968, pp. 15–40.

Sherif, M. On the relevance of social psychology. *American Psychologist,* 1970 **25,** 144–156.

SUGGESTED READINGS

1 Carlson, R. Where is the person in personality research? *Psychological Bulletin,* 1971, **75,** 203–219.

2 Carson, R. *Interaction concepts of personality.* Chicago: Aldine, 1969.
3 Pribram, K. Toward a neurophysiological theory of the person. In K. Pribram (Ed.), *Brain and behavior: I. Mood, states, and mind.* Baltimore: Penguin Books, 1969.
4 Wenar, C. *Personality development.* Boston: Houghton Mifflin, 1971.
5 Wrightsman, L. *Assumptions about human nature.* Monterey, Calif.: Brooks/Cole, 1974.

INDEXES

NAME INDEX

SUBJECT INDEX